T0285283

Unknown Past

UNKNOWN PAST

Layla Murad, the Jewish-Muslim Star of Egypt

Hanan Hammad

STANFORD UNIVERSITY PRESS

Stanford, California

STANFORD, CALIFORNIA

© 2022 by Hanan Hammad. All rights reserved.

No part of this book may be reproduced or transmitted in any form or by any means, electronic or mechanical, including photocopying and recording, or in any information storage or retrieval system without the prior written permission of Stanford University Press.

Printed in the United States of America on acid-free, archival-quality paper

Library of Congress Control Number: 2022932360

Cataloging-in-Publication Data available from the Library of Congress.

ISBN: 9781503629424 (cloth)

ISBN: 9781503629776 (ppbk)

ISBN: 9781503629783 (epub)

Cover design: Rob Ehle

Cover photo: Layla Murad, from her film, *Ghazal al-Banat* (*Girls' Flirtation*, 1949), from cover of *al-Istodio (Studio)* magazine.

Typeset in 10.25/15 Adobe Caslon

To the memory of my mother Layla
To the future of my daughter Layla
With gratitude to Layla Murad and all the pleasure she has given to our lives

CONTENTS

ACKNOWLEDGMENTS

I can't remember the first time I heard or watched Layla Murad. Her voice was simply part of the soundscape of my childhood, and watching her black-and-white films on Thursdays and Fridays was our reward of the school week. The joy of listening to several of her songs every day after 6:00 p.m. on the Umm Kulthum radio station throughout summer breaks was shared by all my middle- and high-school girlfriends. My mom said she first noticed my unusual infatuation with Layla Murad when I would listen to the theme song of a radio series twice a day. I was too young to understand the lyrics, but the voice in the song was charmingly sad and pleasantly forgiving. I could not yet comprehend the pain and power in the song. My mom was right; the voice was Layla Murad's. My mom had also loved Layla Murad since childhood. Mama fondly reminisced about going as a little girl with her own mother to film theaters to watch Layla Murad's films. Most titles of those movies started with "Layla," also my mom's name. I envied my mom's and my grandma's generations because they frequented movie theaters. This pleasure exists no more for women in my town. While they watched all of Layla Murad's films in theaters, I could watch only what Egyptian television chose to broadcast. Before I learned to read, I learned from my mom about Layla Murad's films directed by Togo Mizrahi, which Egyptian television never broadcast. My mom's love for Layla Murad and all "the great oldies" left with me inextinguishable memories and a passion for Egyptian music and storytelling.

My love for Layla Murad grew with me. The mystery of her untimely retirement in her mid-thirties despite her popularity became one of my obsessions, and the way the Egyptian press discussed her legacy irritated me. I'm grateful to my professors Kamran Aghaie, Denise Spellberg, and Abraham Marcus, who encouraged me to transform those feelings into academic inquiry. They encouraged me to present my initial investigation on Layla Murad at the MESA conference in 2004 while still a clueless MA student. It took me more than a decade and a tenured professorship to write Layla Murad's life and career for this book. I'm grateful for all the financial and intellectual support I received from several institutions and their scholars. Woolf Institute hosted me as visiting fellow in Cambridge and generously funded a workshop I organized on minorities and popular culture in the Middle East at the University of London in summer 2015. That workshop inaugurated my intellectual companionship with two dear colleagues, Deborah Starr and Vivian Ibrahim. From the time of the workshop in London to a MESA panel exclusively on Layla Murad on her centennial birthday in 2018, Deborah and Vivian read different chapter drafts. Their feedback and comments were crucial in the evolution of this book. Later I learned that Deborah Starr and Beth Baron were the anonymous readers of the manuscript, and I deeply thank them for their meticulous review and for enormously helpful suggestions. The Department of History at Texas Christian University granted me the Pate Scholarship. TCU College of Liberal Arts supported me with a manuscript development grant. The Crown Center of Middle East Studies at Brandeis University offered me a senior sabbatical fellowship. I can't thank my friends Somy Kim and Anthony Melvin for adopting me into their family during an exceptionally challenging sabbatical year in Boston.

Acquiring material that academic archives and national libraries deem unworthy has been the biggest challenge for this research. I am fortunate to have generous collectors among my friends. Even before the research shaped up to be a book, Roberta (Robin) Dougherty generously gifted me some of her precious collections of celebrity periodicals. She made it possible for me and others to access this treasure when she donated her entire collec-tion to the University of Texas at Austin. Robin's gift and encouragement energized my commitment to the project. Lucie Ryzova gave me uncondi-tional access to her apartment in Cairo, where I found publications I would not have otherwise. The unmatchable kindness of my lifetime friend Ente-sar Saleh has always left me speechless. After returning from each research trip to Cairo, I would regret that I had missed collecting certain sources, and she would then graciously travel across greater Cairo to get me material I had failed to collect. Azza Ibrahim accompanied me on trips to libraries and archives and guided my attention to valuable sources. Among my Cairo friends, Sayed Mahmoud stands out for his invaluable connections and ideas. He generously continues to serve as my go-to person whenever I need con-tact information for individuals or sources anywhere in the Arab world. His brilliant ideas make him a crucial cultural hub even when Cairo is cruel and heartless. I would also like to thank the authors Ashraf Gharib and Samir Gharib (unrelated) for sharing their thoughts about Layla Murad and her legacy. My deepest gratitude goes to Ahmad Yassin Murad, the administrator of Layla Murad's Facebook group.[1] He has maintained one of the most lively and respectable platforms on an Egyptian star. He has patiently answered my questions and generously allowed me to use his collection of photos of Layla Murad. Shawki El-Zatmah kindly and generously surprised me with a precious package of part of his collection of periodicals. Liat Kozma scanned materials available only in the National Library in Jerusalem.

I'd also like to express my gratitude to the interlibrary loan staff at TCU library for their work. I'm in debt to many intellectual communities, friends, and colleagues whose thoughts and comments kept this project going. I'm thankful to Jim Ryan for hosting me at the Hagop Kevorkian Center for Near Eastern Studies at New York University, where Ada Petiwal and oth-ers read my draft and provided me with meticulous, constructive comments. I'm also thankful to Adam Mestyan and Frances Hasso for hosting me for a discussion with Duke University's Gender, Sexuality & Feminist Stud-ies seminar. Ted Swedenburg provided unwavering support to this project. He shared his unmatchable passion and knowledge about the popular cul-ture of the Arab world and the entire Middle East. Just hours before the shutdown imposed by the pandemic, Ted kindly hosted my public talk on Layla Murad at the University of Arkansas. I am also grateful to my friend Hesham Sallam for inviting me to share my thoughts about single motherhood and democracy from below in Egypt with the participants of the Political Contestation and New Social Forces in the Middle East and North Africa Conference at Stanford in 2018. This opportunity and my discussions with colleagues who participated in the Feminisms in the Middle East and North Africa Conference at Harvard in 2019 were crucial in developing the concluding chapter of this book. So many friends and colleagues gave me the most valuable resource: time. I'm grateful to my mentor Joel Beinin and to Joel Gordon for reading the entire manuscript and giving me insightful and constructive advice. I thank Naghmeh Sohrabi, David Siddhartha Patel, Gary Samore, Maryam Alemzadeh, and Daniel Neep for their comments on various chapters and the structure of the book.

Fort Worth would have been a social and intellectual desert without the unwavering support and love of friends Mona Narrian and Elva Orozco Mendoza. Sharing long hours of frustration, laughter, and intellectual exchange with them not only contributed to the completion of this project but also helped me keep my sanity in a time of deep loneliness and in moments of despair. Expanding our writing sessions with participants of the Annual AddRan Faculty Writing Boot Camp for one week every May multiplied the joy of writing. I'm grateful to Charlotte Hogg, aka the "Sarge" of the Writing Boot Camp, who ensured that the troops were engaged, productive, and well fed (before the pandemic). I'm also grateful to Guangyan (Gwen) Chen and Ariane Balizet, who, along with Elva and Mona, extended the writing group through the summers of 2017–2019. I also thank my former teaching assistant Ray Lucas for suggesting valuable scholarship on celebrity women in American history.

The challenge of writing in English as a second language became much easier with the constructive suggestions of my colleagues in the TCU Writing Center. I'm particularly grateful to Steve Sherwood, Cynthia Shearer, Lindsay Dunn, and Cheryl Slocumb. I'm also in debt to the kind support and mentorship of Peter Worthing, whose sincere support over the years instilled in me a sense of belonging and greatly helped me cope with the alienation I felt as a faculty member of color, a woman with a foreign accent, and the only historian of the Middle East at TCU. Finally, I thank my children, Ali and Layla, for tolerating Layla Murad's images all over the house and my talking about her all the time. I believe Ali and Layla when they say, "We also love her."

NOTE ON TRANSLITERATION
AND TRANSLATION

The text adopts a simplified form of the transliteration system for words in Modern Standard Arabic used by the *International Journal of Middle East Studies*. Diacritical marks have been omitted with the exception of the 'ayn, indicated by the symbol ', and the hamza, indicated by '. To reflect the social and cultural history of modern Egypt, the text preserves the colloquial Egyptian Arabic forms of many words, particularly titles of songs and films. For example, I write the letter *jim* (*j*) as *gim* (*g*). Proper names and places with well-known English spellings, such as Nasser or Cairo, have been maintained. Throughout the text, I make a reference to Layla Murad either by using her full name or only her first name. I call her Layla, rather than Murad, as an expression of my affection for her. The English titles of films are as given in IMDb whenever available; please keep in mind that "Laila" and "Leila" in these titles are different transliterations of the same Arabic "Layla." All translations from Arabic are mine unless otherwise noted.

Unknown Past

WHY LAYLA MURAD?

WHEN THE EGYPTIAN SINGER and movie star Layla Murad died in Cairo in November 1995, the headline in the Arabic celebrity magazine *al-Kawakib* read, "She lived as a Muslim, died as a Muslim, and was buried in the Muslim cemetery." The magazine meant to deny rumors that Murad (1918–1995) had returned to Judaism after converting to Islam in the 1940s. Questions about Murad's faith, loyalty to Egypt, connections with Israel, and sexual affairs with elite politicians haunted her life and her legacy decades after her death. Ironically, she achieved her success as a popular superstar long before her conversion to Islam. Being a Jew and a daughter of the famous Jewish singer Zaki Murad did not pose an obstacle to her popularity from the time she launched her career in 1932.

Until she released her last movie in 1955, Layla Murad starred in twenty-eight films, almost all of them considered classics in the Egyptian and Arab musical cinema. She was the highest-paid movie star, and her movies were among the highest grossing at the box office. Her fans and movie critics dubbed her the Cinderella of Egyptian cinema and the queen of Arab musicals. Then she stopped working in the cinema, or more accurately, was forced to stop, three years after the Free Officers successfully took power through a military coup, later known as the July Revolution of 1952. She was only thirty-seven years old when her career abruptly came to a stop in the mid-1950s. She struggled for a comeback for decades with no success. Yet despite Layla's life in the shadows, her popularity never faded away, and her fans have continued listening to her voice by means of records, radio broadcasts, and TV shows. Throughout her life and until the present day, Layla Murad has been one of the most popular and well-remembered female singers in the Arab world. Bootleg uploads of her films and songs on YouTube have garnered hundreds of thousands of views. Decades after her death, public interest in her life has continued, and generations of Egyptians have never ceased telling her story.

Layla Murad was born into a Jewish family in 1918, one year before the 1919 Revolution against the British occupation of Egypt that had begun in 1882. The nationalist revolution failed to force the British to evacuate the country but turned Egypt into a semi-independent monarchy. It ushered in what became known as the Liberal Era in modern Egypt (1923–1952). Far from democracy and still under British tutelage, Egypt was governed by a constitutional parliamentary system and enjoyed a thriving pluralistic and cosmopolitan public culture. Layla Murad grew up in her middle-class family in Cairo during a period of ethnoreligious diversity. Her father, Zaki Murad (ca. 1880–1946), was a well-known singer whose career thrived from the 1900s until the mid-1920s. His experience and connections in the music scene facilitated the launch of Layla's singing career while she was still a young teen in the early 1930s. Following her success as a vocalist, she starred in her first film, *Yahya al-Hub* (*Long Live Love*; Muhammad Karim, 1938), with superstar singer and musician Muhammad 'Abd al-Wahab (ca. 1902–1991).

In 1945, Layla Murad married actor Anwar Wagdi and with him formed the most memorable duo in Arab cinema. Layla and Anwar lived a successful professional but difficult domestic life. They divorced and remarried each other three times in seven years, and news about their domestic troubles filled celebrity-gossip columns. While married, Layla Murad documented her conversion to Islam in court records in 1947. She announced her conversion in 1948 in the wake of the first Arab-Israeli war in Palestine. Her success continued as she set a record as the highest-paid actress in 1950, and audiences voted her the best actress-singer in polls in 1951. Her popularity is evidenced by the fact that movie theaters showed two or three films featuring her in the same season almost every year between 1941 and 1952. Then, one month after the Egyptian Free Officers took power in July 1952, Syria

banned Layla Murad's films and songs because of rumors that she had secretly donated money to and visited Israel. The rumors were disproved by
Egyptian investigations conducted by the new military regime in Cairo, and
Layla Murad continued starring in new movies. She lent her voice to support
the Free Officers' regime through patriotic songs and by supporting army-
led initiatives in public life. Unexpectedly, she stopped working in cinema
after releasing the film *al-Habib al-Maghul* (*The Unknown Lover*; Hassan al-
Sayfi, 1955), despite many plans and attempts to resume her cinema career.
Radio and television regularly broadcast her songs and old films, keeping
her youthful image in the public memory as one of the most beloved divas
in Egypt and the Arab world. Audiences of all ages still listen to her short,
fast-rhythm songs and watch her musicals decades after her death. Contemporary singers perform her songs on albums and in live concerts dedicated to
celebrating the repertoire of Arab neoclassics. Critics and writers still publish
articles and books that continue to fuel mass interest in her.

Given the importance of singing within Egyptian culture and cinema,
Layla Murad is more than just a celebrity. She was a massive star and one
of Egypt's most beloved singers-actors, whose popularity remains intact decades after her death. On that basis alone, her life and career are worthy of
study. At the heart of this study, the central questions are why, after a hugely
successful start to her film career, did it stall in the mid-1950s? How did the
fact that she was born into a Jewish family and the Syrian ban against her
films affect her career? What effect did her relationship with one of the Free
Officers have? And what role did her sexuality, age, and changing body image
play? How is she remembered? More than a history of one famous woman
and her agency, Layla Murad's history chronicles that of Jewish wives, female
Muslim converts, and interfaith families in the history of modern Egypt.
I use her story as a prism through which to retell the history of Egyptian
culture and politics, while examining the role of female stars and the double
standards and social expectations they were subject to. Focusing on her decision to convert to Islam and the timing of its public revelation deepens our
understanding of the entanglement of socioreligious and gender politics.

Throughout the second half of the twentieth century, Layla Murad's life
became entangled with grand national and regional politics. Having taken
power in July 1952, the Free Officers called their military coup the Blessed

Movement. The popular support garnered by the Blessed Movement transformed the military coup into the 23 July Revolution. The Free Officers
exiled King Farouk (r. 1936–1952), abolished the monarchy, overthrew the
parliamentary regime, dissolved political parties, and declared the republic in
1953. From the beginning of their coup, the Free Officers underwent a brutal
internal struggle over power, through which Gamal Abdel Nasser emerged as
the leader of the military junta.[1] Having consolidated his rule as the second
president of the republic, Nasser (r. 1954–1970) launched ambitious economic
and human development programs. The foundational years of the republic were critical for the Egyptian Jews. In the early weeks after the 23 July
Revolution, the Free Officers confirmed their commitment to protecting the
Egyptian Jews. The formal leader of the Free Officers and first president,
General Muhammad Nagib (June 1953–November 1954), visited the main
synagogue in downtown Cairo on Yom Kippur of 1952. Nagib also visited
the Karaite synagogue in 'Abbasiyya, stating the regime's unequivocal commitment to the secular-liberal citizenship and rights: "There is no difference
between Jews, Muslims, or Christians. Religion is for God, and the nation is
for all."[2] However, Israeli espionage networks recruited individual local Jews
to carry out a series of acts of sabotage against Western interests in Cairo and
Alexandria in 1954, with the goal of embarrassing the new regime as incom-
petent and incapable of stabilizing Egypt. This campaign of sabotage, known
as the Lavon Affair and code-named Operation Susannah, followed by the
Tripartite Aggression, the Israeli-British-French invasion of Egypt (the Suez
War of 1956), made life increasingly difficult for Egyptian Jews. The regime
and its supporters were not careful about, and in some cases not interested in,
making a distinction between Jews and Zionists.

Layla Murad was caught up in the major political transitions of the
1950s—entanglements that cost her career. Despite her conversion to Islam
in the late 1940s, her experiences shed light on some of the pressures faced
by other Jews in Egypt in the 1950s. She was subject to vicious rumors that
she supported Israel, accusations of which the regime ultimately cleared her.
Investigating the scandal, this study reflects upon the popular press's role and
the impact of the Arab-Israeli conflict on the Jews of Egypt. In the wake
of the Free Officers' Revolution and while she was still struggling to clear
her name and regain the support of her Arab fans, Layla Murad became

romantically involved with one of the Free Officers, who disavowed her after she became pregnant.

A study of Murad's life and career allows us to examine the impact of regional and national politics on an individual's daily life. It fleshes out how individuals experienced and engaged with the grand politics of moving from a semicolonial monarchy to military rule, from the rise to the defeat of Arab nationalism and political Islam. How much did Layla Murad's position as a woman and a star of Jewish origin determine her personal and professional choices to take advantage of opportunities and avoid threats accompanying the transition from monarchy to Nasser's regime after 1954? Her enforced exit from the movie industry is the story of emotional and aspirational struggles many people experienced in postcolonial Egypt. In a single decade following the 1952 Revolution, Layla Murad, along with many other Egyptians, witnessed and experienced extreme emotional and professional swings owing to the Suez War, the departure of Jews from Egypt, and the transition from an open-market economy and what many called the pluralism of the Liberal Era to state capitalism and state control over media and the public sphere. During her lifetime, Egypt witnessed the days of turmoil of the Arab-Israeli wars (1948, 1956, 1967, and 1973) and the conclusion of Egypt and Israel's peace agreement (1979). She lived through the Egyptians' search for a definition of their national identity, from liberal pluralism, Arab nationalism, and the culture of peace to Islamism. All of these developments dramatically impacted her family and career, but she was neither powerful nor powerless. Reconstructing how Layla Murad went through these years requires more than a discussion and acknowledgment of an exceptional artist's agency in a complex society. It requires a search for the lived reality of intimate pains and hopes embodied in an individual's experience and its representation of many others' experiences.

Throughout the course of these rapid political and cultural changes, Layla Murad was sometimes exceptional and definitely in the minority. Nevertheless, her life often mirrored the gendered reality of the sociopolitical dynamics experienced by many women in twentieth-century Egypt. Like many women in modern Egypt, she was a working wife and a mother. Unlike many, however, she married and divorced famous and powerful men. She experienced personal and domestic troubles under the bright lights of

fame and the elusive fragility of minority women in the interfaith family
and social patriarchy. Under the public gaze, she became vulnerable while
searching for love and protection in a relationship with one of the young
Free Officers. Layla Murad's experiences should be situated within the legal
environment and lived experiences of an Egyptian state and society that still
wrestle with questions of gender, sexuality, single motherhood, and religious
minority. Examining the web of social concepts, relationships, institutions,
and individuals that formed her world renders her life illustrative of the lives
of many people, famous and ordinary alike. Biographical research can offer
rich insights into the dynamic interplay of individuals and history, inner and
outer worlds, self and others.[3] By blending the history of modern Egypt and
Layla Murad's biography, I strive to connect disparate social phenomena
and personal experiences. Although biography is still an unloved stepchild
of history, it provides more significant information than any other form of
historical narrative and illustrates how historical developments affected those
who shared her gender, ethnicity, class, and problems.[4] In other words, I capi-
talize on the popularity of Layla Murad's biography to break down the grand
metanarratives of Egyptian nationalism and recover what the nationalist narratives, intentionally or unintentionally, overlook, exclude, or silence.[5] As a
historian and an Egyptian, blending history with biography saves my critical
analysis from slipping into standard biographical and nationalist narratives
that either vilify or sanctify the subject.

   This book treats Layla Murad's trajectory as a prism through which to
examine and analyze historical transformations while focusing on her individual aspirations, triumphs, emotions, and pain. Her life and legacy
enable an accurate assessment of cinema's economic success and the place
of tolerance in Egyptian society before and after 1952. More important, her
experience personifies the politics of Arab nationalism and boycotting Israel in discourses and practices. A complete understanding of Egypt's history
following July 1952 cannot be attained without a grasp of the contradictory
emotions that individuals and groups experienced in their engagements
with the sociopolitical changes introduced by the regime. Layla Murad went
through her life as a daughter, sibling, co-worker, spouse, and lover within
close-knit and overlapping familial, social, institutional, and professional networks. Through her experience, this book interrogates the entertainment and

media industry and its relationships with national and regional politics, re-ligious minorities, and gender in critical moments of modern Egypt. Rather than making a case to celebrate the effectiveness of a successful celebrity woman's agency against patriarchal structures, Layla Murad's life illuminates the messy and contradictory realities wherein women embrace their agency, intentionally and otherwise, through manipulating and solidifying the pa-triarchy. Not every act of subverting patriarchal dominance reflects feminist resistance, nor does every deployment of a woman's agency for mercantile success or personal survival effectively avoid unintended outcomes. In her work and personal life, Layla Murad made choices that worked both for and against her, regardless of how feminist these choices might have been. In her successes as well as her failures, she was deliberate about her positionality and conscious of her agency and the limits of her options.

Commercial Entertainment

This book examines the role the entertainment industry has played in the social construction of gendered national identities, sexuality, and public morality in Egypt and the entire Arab world. Cinema has been "a tool for mass production of senses, an apparatus that sutures the subject in an il-lusory coherence and identity, and a system of stylistic strategies that weld pleasure and meaning to reproduce dominant social and sexual hierarchies."[6] This book's starting point is that commercial movies and celebrity publica-tions have been the most widely read "texts" across gender and classes in the twentieth-century Arab world. We need to be careful not to equate the commercial with vulgarity or contrast it with critically sophisticated produc-tions. All fictional films produced in Egypt and distributed across the Arab world during the mid-twentieth century were commercial, meaning they were produced as entertainment geared to audiences of all classes and levels of education. Movies varied in intellectual sophistication, realistic engage-ment with social issues, aesthetic values, and funding. Nevertheless, all aimed at being profitable by selling tickets and pleasing mass audiences.

Productions aimed primarily at achieving critical acclaim and awards led to a distinction between commercial and critically sophisticated filmmak-ing, which emerged in the mid-1950s. A historically comprehensive survey of popular Egyptian films that proved influential thanks to their box-office success and originality or that remained widely known has shown that popular films disseminated discourses on gender, class, and nationalism.[7] Movies produced in Egypt during the interwar period and the following decades constituted part of the historical formation of Egyptian modernity, a broad set of cultural, aesthetic, technological, economic, social, and political transformations.[8] Thus, Layla Murad's films are forms of discourse articulating and responding to modernity. Although interwar cinema attracted audiences from all social groups, it established the norms of the Egyptian middle class.[9] And although her movies were meant as escapist entertainment, they contributed to public discourse on gender, women's sexuality, and other social issues. Like all commercial films, they have great importance in helping to construct the cultural synthesis of the bourgeoisie.

I approach Layla Murad's films as multilayered texts of contending visions, comparing and contrasting the social discourses disseminated through them with the life actually led by this female star who gave these discourses a voice and an image. Contrasting Layla Murad's real life as a successful professional woman with her screen personas, I question how and why she so readily disseminated messages opposing women's work outside the home and advocated for curtailing women's sexuality. Her films were commercially successful and attracted audiences from all sectors of society. Like other successful performing artists, Layla Murad continually developed her skills and used her talents to achieve fame and wealth. She was aware that her success depended on her songs and movies reaching mass audiences and generating financial profits, and therefore, to achieve her goals, she had to selectively cooperate with individuals, groups, and institutions. She was neither manipulated nor wholly free; she actively engaged and cooperated with other agents to appear in the most successful pictures and earn as much money as she could.

The social history of a nation can be written through its film stars, as those stars, female stars in particular, reflect an image of the society to which the public adjusts its own image.[10] Less than a handful of Arab divas have attracted scholars' attention, while many others' personal and professional trajectories remain as unearthed sources for studying Arab sociocultural politics. Scholarship on Arab female performers has focused on their exceptional and successful agency in establishing themselves as national cultural icons.[11] Scholars have argued convincingly for the role of the Egyptian Umm Kulthum (ca. 1904–1975) and the Lebanese Fairuz (1934–) in nation-building and establishing themselves as national symbols in the twentieth century. The assumption that these divas were intentional in regard to their role overlooks how other social actors also contributed deliberately to the positionality of both women in Egyptian and Lebanese nationalism, respectively, and Arab culture. The role of women in national projects often burdened iconic stars with metaphoric roles in the nation-building process.[12] While the patriarchal socioculture stripped women of their sexuality, Fairuz had to exaggerate her motherhood and work extra hard to prove her appropriateness as a symbol for the nation.[13] Umm Kulthum, arguably the most important entertainer in the twentieth-century Arab world, helped to constitute Egyptian cultural and social life in such a way as to advance an ideology of Egyptianness and developed a personal idiom that is considered Muslim and authentically Egyptian and Arab.[14] But we must not overlook the narratives that groomed Arab divas to become national icons and used these talented women in formulating a nationalist metanarrative that is consistent and harmonious with itself. In other words, images and reality have blurred into each other and perhaps even defined each other.[15]

Throughout the twentieth century and until today—decades after her death—Layla Murad has remained a household name in Egyptian and Arab popular culture. Her personal and professional trajectories and how Egyptians have positioned her in their popular culture offer insights into the gendered religio-ethnic politics of the entertainment industry and the role of movie stars as both agents and tools in constructing class, gender, and sexual regimes. The construction and representation of Layla Murad's persona by the state and by middlebrow intellectuals from the political spectrum have shaped the memory of her life to serve their own needs. They have told their story, not hers, through the discursive processes of navigating ever-changing relationships between religion and Egyptian nationalism. While telling the story of Layla Murad's rise to the highest point of stardom, then her untimely and sudden disappearance from the cinema screen, Egyptians narrated their competing versions of the history of the modern Egyptian state and society and their attempts to understand the meaning of being Egyptian. I examine the narratives of the life and persona of Layla Murad in both the state-controlled and privately owned media as well as in extensive sharing on social media as public discourses on sexuality, ethnicity, and the place of Jews in modern Egyptian history and culture. As she and others have told it, her story explains the crucial role popular culture, commercial cinema, and celebrity publications played in constructing an exclusive Arab-Islamic Egyptian identity. Layla Murad's story illustrates how the Islamization of Egyptian society in the late twentieth century has roots in the secular media, particularly in celebrity and fan publications. As the media has secularized rituals of religious holidays, it has religionized movie stars. The story of the many lives of Layla Murad provides an opportunity to examine how popular culture was constantly informed and re-formed by Egyptians' interpretation of Egyptianness and inclusion in or exclusion from its boundaries. These interpretations demonstrate the manipulation of popular culture in the construction and expression of Egyptian identity in relation to Arabism, Islam, and proper womanhood.

This book shows how Layla Murad built a successful career and contributed to Arab and Egyptian popular culture, as well as how and why others made her into an object in discursive processes to construct contemporary Egyptian identity as inclusively Arab-Muslim. A national identity hinges upon a fluid and constantly changing relationship between self and others.[16] Layla Murad was a famous star and a Jew who converted to Islam in the gloom of the first Arab-Israeli war. Her impressive career blossomed under the monarchy and gave a singing voice to the new Free Officers during their rise to power after July 1952; it ended shortly after Nasser consolidated power in his hands, on the eve of the Suez War in 1956.

Gossip Publications and History

Layla Murad's rise to superstar in the interwar period is the story of the rise of sound film, national radio broadcast, and the popular press, all of which have played key roles in the making of modern mass-mediated popular and public cultures and made artists such as Layla Murad iconic figures. The interwar period witnessed an increase in the performing arts, thus increasing the need to cover celebrities and entertainment in the expanding mass media. Periodicals, particularly those not funded by political parties, had to rely on circulation and advertisements. Pictures of celebrity women wearing revealing clothing, with inviting gazes, and sensational stories about famous entertainers attracted mass readership. Celebrity coverage offered escapist entertainment, as did movies, and provided mass readers access to the world's stars, to whom most of them otherwise had none. Fan magazines and celebrity-gossip columns and entertainment sections in general periodicals not only guided readers to shows but also informed them about fashions and good taste and provided them with photos to be clipped and hung on the wall. Far from being objective, the playful tone of the gossip columns invited readers' judgmental engagement. Functionally, there were no clear-cut divisions among Egyptian periodicals. Rather than targeting a certain audience, for example, female-only readers, physical beauty and celebrity fashions captured the imaginations of all genders. Miscellaneous periodicals as *Ruz al-Yusuf* (launched in 1926) and *Akhbar al-Yum* (launched in 1944) included entertainment sections and gossip columns in addition to political content. *Al-Ahram*, the oldest daily periodical in Egypt, began publishing entertainment sections and crime news in the 1920s. Celebrity news, interviews with stars, and sensational crimes made cover stories for magazines such as *al-Musawar* and headlines for newspapers such as *Akhbar al-Yum*. For my purposes, celebrity and gossip publications include gossip columns and entertainment sections that appeared in almost all general periodicals, sections that were like mini–fan magazines and whose readership overlapped with but was not the same as readers of fan magazines such as *al-Kawakib* (*Stars*; first issue in March 1932) and *Ahl al-Fann* (*Artists*; first issue in April 1954).

Once showing no interest in studying mass-mediated popular culture and dismissing it as commercial, scholars have since examined both the cinematic depiction of the army and state-society relations and mass-mediated discourses on nationalism and gender.[17] Celebrity-gossip publications are a valuable source of sociocultural history, particularly for studying gender and sexuality[18] and historians have recently begun to use fan and celebrity publications to write the history of Egyptian cinema.[19] A leading anthropologist has argued for television as a key institution of national culture production in Egypt, which is also true for the importance of the popular press and celebrity publications.[20] Throughout the twentieth century, an obsession with celebrities grew, and the rise of the gossip periodicals confirmed and fueled popular culture's celebrity mania. Celebrity-gossip magazines have sold millions of copies, expanding popular culture as a site for cultural struggles. The popularity of these publications is not due to inauthentic messages imposed top-down by dominant groups upon mass audiences; the public plays an active role in receiving mass-mediated messages, ranging from refusal to selective acceptance of popular and mass culture.[21] Despite their reputation as trivial, fan and celebrity-gossip publications provide a site of engagement for their readers, who use these texts to generate conversation, manage relationships, and consider their ideas and values.[22]

Since their inception, Arabic pictorial periodicals have focused on celebrity news and reported on cinema and shows, turning artists into stars and icons in the mass national culture. These publications enjoyed wide readership and attracted audiences among both the educated and the semiliterate. Indeed, thanks to large photos and illustrations on most pages, even illiterate audiences could enjoy these publications; they consumed the pictures, heard others reading the texts, and imagined the captions and stories published with photos. Audiences for these publications did not necessarily need to buy them but often found them available in clubs, barbershops, dentist's offices, and lawyer's waiting rooms. Their sensational content would be easy to exchange during casual communications and useful for filling an awkward social moment or starting conversations with strangers while on trains or at parties.

In order to concentrate on middlebrow culture in the historical narrative, this study makes use of a wide range of celebrity and gossip publications in Egypt and Lebanon that no scholar has heretofore used for historical research. Cultural periodicals such as *al-Hilal*, *al-Muqtataf*, and *al-Risala* are readily available in the National Library in Cairo (Dar al-Kutub) and many university libraries in the United States and Europe. By contrast, neither Dar al-Kutub nor any US or European library can pride itself on having a sizable collection of the leading Arabic celebrity-gossip publications such as the Egyptian *al-Kawakib* or the Lebanese *al-Maw'id* and *al-Shabaka*. Nevertheless, these periodicals have been on the newsstand in Arab cities since the mid-twentieth century. The lack of substantial collections of these publications in national archives and libraries in Egypt and academic libraries in the United States and Europe bespeaks the systematic dismissal of these materials. Disregarding them is striking, given that dozens of magazines, most of them featuring bosomy women and celebrity gossip, enjoyed sizable markets in the 1930s and 1940s. Magazines such as *al-'Arusa, al-Ithnayn, al-Sabah,* and *al-Studio* continued on the newsstand for decades until the mid-1950s. Although researchers could not find this wealth of printed material in formal archives and libraries, individuals with financial means could purchase surviving copies from dealers in old books in Cairo and online. When I found these publications in secondhand bookstores or private collections, I often discovered several issues bound together with the original owner's name engraved on the hard cover. Obviously, some readers invested in these publications' longevity, seeing them as valuable and collectible, and proudly shelved them to decorate their homes and offices--evidence that not everyone viewed these publications as disposable entertainment for long train trips and so forth. Possibly even more than cultural periodicals they could be crucial in studying public culture and the making of sociocultural norms.

Excavating celebrity-gossip publications in Egypt and Lebanon, I discovered the first biography of Layla Murad, published in Beirut in 1956. In 1957 she published her first and only autobiography, serialized in the Egyptian magazine *al-Kawakib*. Both accounts appeared after false rumors of her connection with Israel (1952), her final divorce from her first husband, Anwar Wagdi (1953), Anwar Wagdi's death (1955), her relationship with one of the Free Officers (begun in late 1952), and her marriage to filmmaker Fatin 'Abd al-Wahab (1954). Since Anwar Wagdi had passed away, she and her first biographer, Egyptian movie critic al-Sayyid Shusha, conveniently presented her perspective, as she needed to rehabilitate her public image. She spoke about herself as a wife, mother, producer, and respected and beloved star. Neither account alluded to her relationship with Wagih Abaza, the Free Officer, or their having a child together in the summer of 1954. She sounded angry at Wagdi and desperate to cover up her relationship with Abaza. The mother of two children with different fathers, she was now into the third year of her marriage to Fatin 'Abd al-Wahab. In sum, she was bitter and struggling to survive political changes, together with rapid changes in the cinema industry and entertainment market.

From January 15 until February 26, 1957, the magazine *al-Kawakib* published seven weekly episodes of Layla Murad's autobiography, titled "Mudhakkarat Layla Murad" (Layla Murad's autobiography). From the memoir's journalistic style and her lack of self-reflection or deep thought, we might guess that Layla dictated the memoir to the magazine's editor rather than penning it herself. The few issues of the magazine held in the Egyptian National Library had undergone surgical procedures by which the episodes had been removed from the volume. While Layla Murad's picture appeared on the cover of the magazine's January 15, 1957, issue, with a headline announcing the publication of the first episode of the autobiography, all the pages of that episode had been removed; pages of the autobiography were also missing from the following six weekly issues preserved in one volume in the National Library.[23] The pervasive corruption and chaos of the state archives and libraries in Egypt make the questions of who damaged the targeted pages, as well as when and why, impossible to answer. I can assure readers that the pages were excised intentionally rather than randomly or out of misuse or lack of preservation. Scissors or something sharp and not hand-tearing removed those missing pages from the volume. Moreover, the archive of Dar al-Hilal, the publisher of al-Kawakib, is missing the entire year's issues altogether.

No author of a biography of Layla Murad or investigative report on her mentions her autobiographical memoir, which indicates a lack of awareness of that memoir's existence. None of those authors tried to use these issues of the periodical at the National Library or Dar al-Hilal. Ashraf Gharib, the author who went through the painstaking process of documenting press reporting on Layla during the early years of the 1950s, does not refer to her memoir. As a journalist working at the archive of Dar al-Hilal, the publisher of al-Kawakib, Gharib draws on the magazine's archives, to which he enjoyed full access and control, his failure to mention Layla's autobiographical series confirms that Dar al-Hilal's archive is missing the volumes altogether. When I visited Dar al-Hilal's archive, I could not locate these issues and had no reason to trust the archivists' transparency. I managed to acquire all the episodes by browsing secondhand bookstores in Cairo, the personal libraries of academic and nonacademic friends, and the shelves of a Moroccan collector who owns a large number of Arabic celebrity periodicals. The impoverished state archives and libraries versus the richness of private collections of individuals with and without academic interests sums up the predicament of historical researchers, particularly when they explore popular culture's past.

Because everything is autobiographical, I group the writings, interviews, and statements made by Layla Murad since she achieved stardom in the mid-1930s as autobiographical.[24] Beginning in the mid-1950s, she often gave her own perspective on her life, career, and domestic and regional politics, together with the entertainment industry. Whether Layla composed her memoir and statements herself or verbally communicated them to journalists who put them into writing, these accounts reveal what she intended or agreed to share with the public. While questioning the accuracy of her memory and intentions is fair, her memoir, autobiographical statements, and radio interview--truthful or not--express what Layla wished the public to know about herself and communicate her worldview.

Biographies of Layla Murad, written by generations of authors, are important for understanding Egyptians' self-image, and like biographies in other cultures, help construct collective symbols and cultural tropes and definitions of what it means to be Egyptian. Layla's autobiography and biographies fit into a textual tradition that creates and examines self-identity within family, society, gender, and nation. I have used published biographical writings on Layla Murad to show how Egyptians have more recently constructed their past self-image, one that is ultimately pluralistic and positive, and used this construction to lament the perceived "present declining."[25]

Chapter Overview

Layla Murad lived in interconnected and overlapping communities during a period of massive changes in the Egyptian state's policies, institutions, and public culture. Telling her stories provided Layla with an opportunity for self and social exploration, as well as self-promotion.[26] Biography and autobiography are pervasive throughout modern culture; gossip and celebrity magazines, podcasts, blogs, biopics, and social media posts serve as sites for biographical expression and experiment by both ordinary people and celebrities.[27] The frequency and uniformity of telling Layla's story have made knowing and telling the actual story more challenging and raised questions as to why and how her biographers tell her story in certain ways at certain times. By no means do I claim that my narrative recovers the most accurate and comprehensive account of Layla's lived experience; what it does is tell her story based on my understanding of the evidence I managed to collect.

Additionally, I examine her biographies and autobiography critically to investigate storytelling itself. This book researches the life and career of Layla
Murad in its intersection with the sociopolitical and cultural developments
of modern Egypt to determine how Egyptians have articulated their imagined past and identity. In chronological and thematic order, each chapter
intertwines Layla Murad's life with many key figures, institutions, and ideas
that shaped the history of Egyptian politics, the entertainment industry, cinema, and music in particular, and formed popular notions of gender, sexuality,
and national identity. The titles of the book and chapters draw from the titles
of her movies, which often capture the eventful years she and Egypt witnessed; I invite readers of this book to watch them.[28]

Chapter 1 tells Layla Murad's story from childhood until her first film
in 1938. Turning the schoolgirl into a famous singer and movie star coincided with the commercialization of mass entertainment and the building of
Egypt's profitable national cinema industry. The chapter interweaves Layla's
early career with the story of the microphone, sound film, and national radio
broadcasting in Egypt, technical novelties that all contributed to making
Layla Murad a household name, image, and voice from Alexandria to Aswan.
Layla was a member of the first generation of entertainers who became national celebrities during the formation of mass-mediated popular culture in
Egypt. The chapter pays close attention to the Egyptian musical's formation,
and well as to how the pioneering male filmmakers subjected Layla Murad
and all other women stars to their masculine and European aesthetic standards for the female body on-screen.

Layla Murad's cinema career intersected with those of the leading male
figures who developed the studio system in Egypt. With the commercialization of the cinema industry in the late 1930s and early 1940s, filmmaking
and cinema production in Egypt, as elsewhere, increasingly became a male
domain. Male cinema industrialists controlled the content from which movies profited by creating female stars. In the secular pluralist entertainment
industry, the virgin/whore dichotomy dominated the mass-mediated public
discourse and fed the anxiety over women's sexuality and urban modernism.
Chapter 2 addresses these issues through following Layla's cinema career up
to 1952, focusing mainly on her work with three men--Togo Mizrahi, Yusuf
Wahbi, and Anwar Wagdi--with whom she worked the most. I show how

each filmmaker framed her talents in highly marketable forms that combined artistic value with patriarchal discourse. Layla's films exemplify the paradox of the female superstar in a male-dominated industry. I argue that she successfully advanced her career within the framework of the existing social structure, thus becoming an agent herself in perpetuating conservative values pertaining to gender and female sexuality. The discourses that validated the patriarchal family and society contradicted her personal and professional choices and eventually worked against her interest. Through a feminist analysis of Layla's films, this chapter shows how cinema, as a modern mass medium, expressed and contributed to social anxiety over urban life while making virginity and sexual purity essential to modern gender ideals.

Like many married couples in twentieth-century Egypt, Layla Murad and her first husband, Anwar Wagdi, experienced the tensions between traditional gender work division and the modernizing structure wherein women could be professional and independent. Unlike most couples, however, their interfaith marriage and domestic disputes took place in the light of fame, where celebrity gossip sold movie tickets and magazines sold copies. Chapter 3 discusses the personal relationship between Layla and Anwar, focusing on the positionality of Jewish women and Muslim men in modern Egypt. As a Muslim husband, Anwar enjoyed all the privileges stipulated in Islamic Sharia law. As a Jewish wife, Layla's legal inferiority was twofold, while the Arab-Israeli conflict added complexity to her already precarious position. The chapter discusses how her domestic disputes and the regional conflicts necessarily made her conversion from Judaism to Islam a public issue. Because Layla and Anwar were invested in manipulating the interest of the public and employed the press as a tool in their domestic disputes, their relationship contributed to social debates about love and business, as well as the manufacturing of unrealistic images of the "new woman" and the "modern family."

Chapter 4 covers Egypt's dramatic transition from monarchy to Nasserism through the unpredictable changes in Layla Murad's personal and professional life. The chapter discusses the Syrian allegations that she visited and donated money to Israel and the impact of this crisis on her career. I argue that the Arab political elites used the Arab boycott against Israel, an unchallenged element in the politics of Arab elites for decades, for domestic consumption as a weapon in their internal battles. The chapter shows how

Arab populist politicians and bureaucrats, when making decisions to punish individuals for alleged collaboration, did not concern themselves with
proving the veracity of charges of cooperation with Israel. The treatment of
Layla Murad shows the recklessness of the Arab boycott's practices, notwithstanding the validity of its original goals: Arab regimes, politicians, and
bureaucrats weaponized the Arab boycott against individuals and groups
without systematic investigations to justify the boycott or demonstrate how
it was not anti-Semitic.

Based on careful examination of compelling evidence and an accurate
chronology of the eventful years of the 1950s and 1960s, Chapter 5 reveals that
Layla's affair with one of the Free Officers brought about the untimely end
of her cinema career. The romance between Layla and Free Officer Wagih
Abaza provides an excellent case in light of which to rethink the personally
based patronage networks of the state under President Nasser and of politics
among the Free Officers. We can achieve no complete understanding of the
Free Officers' politics and the Nasserist regime without analyzing masculine
gender and sexuality among those young men who took over the state in the
summer of 1952 and then engaged in power struggles among themselves.

Chapter 6 examines how Egyptians have positioned Layla Murad in their
popular culture since the launch of the peace process with Israel until now.
Since Anwar Sadat visited Jerusalem in 1977, both the regime and the opposition have constructed Layla's persona and employed her legacy to serve
competing agendas concerning relations with Israel, the state's role in the
economy, and the legacy of both the monarchy and Nasserism. The Egyptian regime returned Layla Murad to her long-denied central position in the
media and popular culture to facilitate the peace agreement with the Jewish
state, reverse Nasserist economic policies, and claim to be the guardian of
turath, that is, authentic cultural heritage. At the same time, those opposed
to the peace agreement evoked Layla's Jewish origins and her conversion to
Islam as a means of claiming a victory over Israel and of mobilizing the public against the normalization of relations with Israelis. Reconstructing Layla
Murad's persona as a sincere Muslim, who voluntarily abandoned Judaism,
condemned Israel, and stubbornly rejected Israeli overtures, provided Egyptians with the role model of an exclusively Muslim Egyptian identity while
using her Jewish origins as a token by means of which to lament an imagined

tolerant past. I use the telling of Layla Murad's story to depict Egyptian identity as a multilayered religious and gendered construct. The narrative shows how Egyptians' understanding of their identity changed over time, in part because of the prolonged Arab-Israeli conflict, Arab nationalism, and the Islamization of the Egyptian society against the backdrop of political regimes that fostered state security and neoliberal policies.

The book concludes with a gendered look at Egyptian history through the social taboo around single motherhood and changes in the social discourse about men refusing to acknowledge their parenthood of children born outside formal marriage. By no means do I suggest that progress has been linear, but the invisible changes around that taboo are striking and invite further research.

CHAPTER 1

THE SCHOOL GIRL
Making Layla Murad

Because of my inclination, it was natural to become a singer, but my father initially fought my desire. Like many fathers, he did not feel comfortable letting his child pursue the same profession he had. Despite his rejection, I made progress in my singing career, which led to my cinematic career.

Layla Murad, 1948

I did not wish to become a singer or actress; I wished to be a teacher or a housewife. I could not become a teacher because bad luck dogged my father despite an earlier time of affluence. My father used me as his last gamble to make a living for himself and my siblings. Earning a living was difficult for everyone; only singers and artists could earn plenty of money and live well.

Layla Murad, 1954

IN THE MID-1940S, superstar Layla Murad began formulating the public story of her life and career. She wished to control the narratives of how her father and family decided that she should become a professional entertainer. The contradictory accounts she gave, illustrated by the above quotes, communicate Layla's desire to make her trajectory conform to the expectations of the middle and upper classes. The narrative given by many entertainers in Egypt is that their parents opposed their career choice to become artists; similarly, in one account, Layla highlighted her own agency in choosing her career against her father's wishes; but in another, she highlighted her victimization as a child whose father had no other choice but to use her talent to support the family. Layla designed her narrative to accord with the ideals of the middle and upper classes while maintaining the public's empathy with her life and career choice. The story of Layla Murad's making illuminates the intersection of the star-making industry with the social and moral order and how the industry and social values influenced each other. Her early life is the story of making a massive star at the time of building a profitable Egyptian film industry and the construction of middle-class respectability in the interwar period. The new structures transformed entertainers into national icons and contributed to the debates on female entertainers' social respectability. New technologies such as the microphone, sound film, and national radio broadcast contributed to her transformation from a talented child whose family struggled to attain and hold on to middle-class status into an exceptional star. Telling the story of the beginnings of Layla's career requires close attention to the formation of Egyptian musical film and how male filmmakers established aesthetic values for the female body on-screen based on masculine perspectives.

The Struggle for Middle-Class Status

Layla Murad was born on February 12, 1918, but the documentation of her birth made February 17 her birthday. She was the third child and eldest daughter of nine children born to Zaki Murad Mordechai and Gamila Ibrahim Rushu. Only six children survived beyond childhood, and when the second-born died in infancy, Layla became the second-oldest child. Vocal talent ran in the family for generations. Solon Mordechai, Layla's paternal grandfather, was a Moroccan *hazzan*, or Jewish cantor; a pleasing voice was vital for *hazzans* to lead the congregation in prayer, serve as the readers of the Torah, and frequently perform during wedding rituals. The Mordechai family moved to Egypt in the second half of the nineteenth century. Little is known about the family's life in Morocco or the early years of their settlement in

Alexandria. Layla's father, Zaki Murad (ca. 1880–1946), launched his musical career in Cairo in the early 1900s and became a well-known singer. He belonged to the first group of Egyptian vocalists whose careers flourished with the professionalization of the music industry, owing his success to his commercial recordings, musical theater, and tours to entertain fans in the Arab world and diaspora. This allowed his family to enjoy a middle-class lifestyle in the al-Zahir and al-'Abbasiyya neighborhoods, which in the heyday of cosmopolitan Cairo comprised a diverse ethnic and religious, mostly middle-class population.

The sociocultural carnival of the daily life in these neighborhoods inspired Egyptian literature on the changing social landscape in the mid-1950s. For example, Ihsan 'Abd al-Quddus (1919–1990), who grew up in al-'Abbasiyya, situated his novel *Ana Hurra* (I am free), published in 1952, in the same area where Layla Murad spent her childhood.[1] In the novel, Jewish neighbors inspired the Muslim protagonist, Amina, to seek independence and autonomy through self-help and ignore the conservative and hypocritical society.[2]

Layla's memory of her childhood goes back to when she lived with her family in al-Nuzha Street, where her father managed his recording business in the same building.[3] In her father's workplace, Layla became familiar with musical instruments and recording machines, and witnessed singers and musicians recording their work and negotiating business. Layla sneaked in to listen to phonograph and gramophone records until she had memorized many songs, then sang them to her friends at school.

French language and education practices and an urban residential situation were critical factors in the rise of the Jewish community to the level of the bourgeoisie in Egyptian society.[4] Layla attended the Saint Anne School in al-Sakakini Street (in the al-Zahir neighborhood), then moved to L'École des Soeurs de Notre Dame des Apôtres in Ahmad Sa'id Street (in the al-'Abbasiyya neighborhood), both of them established by French Catholic missionaries in the late nineteenth century. The school compounds included a church and housing for the school's nuns, who taught in and administered the school. Gradually, Egyptian Catholic nuns took over the management of both schools while keeping French as the teaching language. Although Layla left school before completing her education, nuns played a role in shaping her childhood. As one might expect, the nuns enforced a strict disciplinary system, but they gave Layla a great deal of attention once they recognized the beauty of her voice. The school choir became Layla's first vocal training, church hymns became the first melodies she performed, and her classmates and the nuns were her first audiences. Remembering her childhood, Layla said, "I joined the school choir, and we went to the church attached to the school to perform hymns and morning chants. Whenever I performed solo, I felt my voice influenced the sisters."[5] However, Catholic schools did not focus on polishing girls' artistic talent to prepare them for professional careers or roles in public life. Middle- and upper-class families sent their daughters to the nuns' schools (*madaris al-rahibat*) to train them to become good housewives with refined taste, discipline, and etiquette. Graduation from these schools guaranteed that girls would attract husbands from well-off families; the ability to converse in French and play piano were considered desirable for future upper-middle-class wives. In Layla's case, the school's activities coincidently but unintentionally became professional preparation: "I felt I was an artist; I spent most of my time beside the phonograph listening to dozens of records that (my father) got for free from recording companies."[6]

At home, Layla amused her maternal grandfather, Ibrahim Rushu, by imitating famous male and female singers in dozens of songs she memorized.[7] The only family member who did not get the opportunity to hear her singing was her father: Layla feared that if her father heard her singing, he would become angry that she had wasted her time memorizing songs rather than studying. "I was very bad in math. . . . My father pulled me out of the boarding section at school to study math with me at home every day."[8] With the encouragement of teachers and peers, Layla performed songs of Umm Kulthum and 'Abd al-Wahab during a concert devoted to raising funds for the school.[9] The concert succeeded, and Layla became convinced of the beauty of her voice; thus she spent much of her time in her father's studio playing with his instruments. At that early age, Layla recognized her father's fame as a singer, a genuine artist, or *fannan asil*. She also knew that her father earned hundreds of pounds every month and spent all of his income on his lavish lifestyle, hosting friends and other artists for dinners and drinking parties in his office. This costly hospitality generated little financial gain; her father did not see the value of saving money. Whenever her father's business suffered, the entire family struggled to make ends meet; as his income fluctuated, Zaki's family's living conditions suffered dramatic ups and downs.

Although he was the father of several children and the only breadwinner for the entire family, Zaki Murad left for the Americas around 1927 and stayed abroad for about three years, performing, along with his brothers Nasim and Mayer, for Arab communities in the diaspora. His trip to the Americas represents an episode of the development of Arabism as a universal sense of identity among Arabic speakers and Arab descendants everywhere. Since the late nineteenth century, Arabs have lived in the Americas in large numbers and developed an understanding of relationship with each other and to the Arab land through a common language, a shared sense of taste, nostalgia, and cultural longing to enjoy certain types of entertainment and activities. Arab entertainers and performers touring *mahjar* (Arab diaspora) became cultural agents to connect Arabs in the diaspora with their homeland and old times. With fluctuating levels of success, Arab performers flocked to the Americas for performing tours. Performers sought money and fame, and diasporic Arabs sought to experience nostalgia and reaffirm their identity. Zaki Murad enjoyed success and recorded Sayyid Darwish's famous song "Zuruni Kulli Sana Marra" (Visit me once a year) for a New York–based company, thus assuring his popularity among the Arabs in North America.[10] He mingled and interacted with many Armenian, Syrian, Greek, Persian, and Sephardic Jewish artists who had moved into the ethnic neighborhoods and ghettos of New York in the first decades of the twentieth century.[11] Success tempted him to extend his tour; he made good money and sent enough to his family in Egypt for them to maintain a comfortable lifestyle. Then came the Great Depression. Not only was he unable to find a gig, he had bought stocks in companies that lost all their value during the economic collapse. As a result, he was unable to support his family in Cairo, and according to Layla, they lived in misery.

When Zaki stopped sending money to the family, Layla's mother, Gamila, was compelled to downsize the family's home several times. She moved the family to a smaller apartment and eliminated some of the children's education expenses. She sold most of the family's furniture to pay overdue bills, thinking that Zaki was making a fortune in America and would buy new furniture when he returned. But Zaki returned empty-handed except for a pile of worthless stock certificates.[12] Layla said that her father had only enough to pay for his return trip, while an earlier source suggested that he even had to borrow money to pay for his ticket.[13]

Zaki came home to find that the Depression had hit the Egyptian economy hard. Musical theaters faded away, and concerts suffered from a lack of audiences able to buy tickets. Performers struggled with unemployment. Even worse, the audience had forgotten about Zaki Murad during his absence, and the young, supertalented Muhammad 'Abd al-Wahab (ca. 1902–1991) now overshadowed him on the music scene. No evidence has surfaced to suggest that Zaki participated in concerts or any other singing activity in Egypt from the date of his return to his death in 1946. He went through a period of despair, and his eldest daughter knew it. Neither audiences nor concert organizers cared to hear his voice or invited him to sing. Layla joined a vocational school for girls that paid her a few piastres a day and prepared her to work as a dressmaker. Becoming a working girl signified the social decline of her family, who could no longer claim their middle-class status. When Zaki discovered Layla's talent for singing, he decided to train her for a music career. Ultimately successful in this new career, she never returned to school, and from that point forward she became responsible for supporting the entire family, assuming the responsibilities of an adult professional entertainer while still a child. She always lamented this, even when she became a superstar, though she acknowledged that only a singing career enabled her to earn a lot of money and her family to live well.[14]

Layla's voice became her father's capital, but turning her into a professional singer proved a difficult decision. Although Zaki Murad was an artist and accustomed to dealing with female entertainers, his values and expectations for the women in his household were conservative. He was reluctant to allow Layla to be seen in the public sphere, thereby letting society know that his daughter worked for a living. According to Shusha, Layla's first biographer, Zaki only made peace with the idea of his daughter becoming a professional entertainer when he realized that girls from good families became singers.[15]

Until the early 1900s, women working in entertainment came from the lower, working classes. They were viewed socially as a distinct group because they violated the norms of gender segregation and publicly interacted with

men. At the time of the advent of modern theater and music halls in the late
nineteenth century, no actresses appeared on the stage; boys and men were
cast in the female roles.[16] Most female stage entertainers were Syrian Christians and Jews.[17] Gradually, Egyptian Muslim women appeared on the stage
and gained celebrity status as their fame and popularity grew.

The wealthy and educated elites influenced commercial entertainment by
their respectable interests and tastes.[18] Singer Munira al-Mahdiyya (1884–
1965) was among the first generation of Muslim entertainers who gained
a respectable celebrity status and paved the road for women entertainers
hailing from a broader range of social classes, cutting across ethnoreligious
communities. Bahiga Hafiz Hanim (1908–1968) and Umm Kulthum (ca.
1904–1975) exemplify women combining social respectability and performance careers. The daughter of a pasha and niece of a prime minister, Bahiga
Hafiz studied music in Paris and became a professional musician, an actress,
and a pioneer filmmaker.[19] In recognition of Hafiz's social status, promotions
of her artistic production carried the upper-class honorific title *hanim*. Umm
Kulthum, who came from an economically humble, socioculturally conservative and religious family, became a legendary vocalist.

The entrance of respectable females into the world of art and entertainment resulted from ideological and technological changes. As Amira Michell
observes, the women's liberation discourses and movement that gained momentum in the 1920s impacted the existing traditions, both strengthening
and threatening women performers. The 1920s brought increased opportunities for women to perform for large, mixed, and interclass audiences.
Meanwhile, the conservatives blamed female performers for their perceived
promiscuity and the decline of morality. Women entertainers took advantage
of the new recording technology, launched in the first decade of the twentieth century, and the spread of radio sets, which enabled audiences to hear
women's voices without their physical presence, thus allowing them to perform yet keeping their image entirely chaste.[20] These developments brought
performers new audiences, especially since record players tended to be in
shared spaces, such as coffeehouses, and the sale of records substantially aug-
mented their incomes.[21]

Zaki concluded that Layla could make money as a professional vocalist without damaging his honor or reputation. Zaki's father-in-law, Ibrahim

Rushu, agreed, but some of Layla's uncles strongly opposed it. Zaki sought reassurance about his daughter's talent from fellow musicians and intellectual friends; Muhammad al-Qasabgi, a leading composer of the time, and the poet Ahmad Rami expressed confidence in Layla's talent and predicted great success. Layla cherished the memories of these days and decades later wrote: "As a child, I felt surrounded with genuine kindness, overwhelming care, and sincere wishes for me to become a respected singer."[22] Zaki initiated Layla's vocal training and taught her new and old *adwar*, a form of music developed by Shaikh Muhammad 'Abd al-Rahim al-Maslub in the nineteenth century. He commissioned the oud player in his band, Ahmad Subay', to teach Layla how to play that important instrument and then asked his friend Dawud Husni to complete her instruction. Dawud Husni (ca. 1870–1937) was not just a friend; he was a major composer with experience in both the new and traditional genres. He sharpened Layla's skills and grounded her in the repertoire of classical genres such as *adwar* and *muwashshah*. He taught her to perform all his great oldies and those of 'Abdu al-Hamuli and Muhammad 'Uthman, as well as the rest of the late nineteenth-century repertoire. Husni composed many of Layla's early hits, and she recorded one of his best and final melodies, *Hayrana Layah*.

Layla underwent training to strengthen her vocal skills rather than to enhance her ability to play instruments or compose music or lyrics. In the Arab musical traditions, singers did not necessarily write music or lyrics for their songs, but until the late nineteenth century many of them composed music and melodies for their own songs and for those of others. With the professionalization and commercialization of music performance in the early 1900s, few artists were able to both sing and compose music, although Muhammad 'Abd al-Wahab, Farid al-Atrash (1910–1974), and Muhammad Fawzi (1918–1966) stand as notable exceptions. Producing a song required a combination of three different talents: the lyricist, the music composer, and the vocalist; most singers bought lyrics and commissioned composers to write melodies and teach them to perform them.

Sources disagree about how Zaki Murad decided to introduce his daughter to public audiences and whether he launched her career with singing in private parties before giving public concerts. Layla gave her first solo concert in May 1932 and attracted enough attention to fill the theater in downtown

Cairo. Working in the entertainment business as an impresario, her maternal grandfather, Ibrahim Rushu, did not mind helping the girl launch her singing career; it was he and her father who successfully organized her first concert. They chose the Ramsis Theater for its modest size, which Layla could surely fill. Yusuf Wahbi, the famous actor and founder of the Ramsis Troupe, offered to rent his theater to others at a low rate during the troupe's breaks, and out of friendship with the old singer, Zaki Murad, he rented the theater to him on credit. The relatively small size of the Ramsis Theater also helped Layla's voice reach the entire audience without the aid of a microphone. To appear on the stage as a mature solo vocalist, fourteen-year-old Layla had to hide her immature body underneath a grown-up woman's clothing. Her ability to attract an audience large enough to fill a hall in order to hear her alone foretold her coming success and popularity.

Layla performed three pieces in her first public concert, only one of them new and her own. Choosing two famous old melodies composed by Muhammad 'Uthman and Abu al-'Ila Muhammad proved a sound decision: financially, the Murads did not have to buy lyrics or pay for music composers; artistically, and more important, the old melodies allowed Layla to exhibit her vocal skills and confidence by performing such well-known and intricate melodies. Riyad al-Sunbati, who became one of the most influential Arab composers in the twentieth century, crafted the music for Layla's first song. Al-Sunbati also played oud in Layla's *takht* (traditional Middle Eastern ensemble). She recorded that song, "Ah min al-gharam wa al-hub ah," two years later. Layla credited her success to al-Sunbati, saying, "He provided me with great support; whenever he did not accompany me to a party due to sickness or fatigue, I felt a big loss. He composed my melodies, played oud, and trained me. He was an empowering force for me."[23]

According to the contemporary press, the concert was a success.[24] Music historian Kamal al-Najmi notes that Zaki Murad mobilized all his connections in the Egyptian cultural scene to bring celebrities to his daughter's first public concert. Renowned poet Ahmad Shawqi attended the show and offered moral and financial support. Actress and journalist Ruz al-Yusuf, who had worked with Zaki in the musical play *al-'Ashra al-Tayyiba* in the early 1920s and had maintained her friendship with him, was also present at the concert; in her opinion, the attendance of Shawqi and several men with the honorific titles "Pasha" and "Bey" were promising signs of Layla's success-to-come among well-educated listeners.[25] A review of the concert in her magazine, *Ruz al-Yusuf,* said that Layla's beautiful appearance and moving voice had the audience cheering for many curtain calls,[26] and Layla gave a few additional concerts in Cairo that summer that were also successful. While her early performances reflected the stylistic influence of Umm Kulthum and 'Abd al-Wahab, she quickly developed her own style thanks to her vocal creativity and skill.[27]

Teenage Layla, now a professional singer, became the only source of income for the family. She gave public concerts and performed at private parties in Cairo and other major towns such as Tanta, Dusuq, and al-Mansura. Zaki collected her pay and gave Layla a daily allowance worth two pennies, or a half franc.[28] She employed deception to create the impression that she was a mature woman, for example, wearing high heels and lace stockings even though she was not used to wearing them. On occasion she faced difficult and embarrassing situations that triggered both laughter and sympathy from the audience. Layla said that once she actually fell asleep onstage; the audience laughed and clapped, and the kinder ones said that she could end the concert, as they were happy enough with her excellent performance.[29] On another occasion, she childishly left her skirt up when fixing her stockings onstage.[30] Layla's practice of dressing like an older woman contrasts markedly with that of Umm Kulthum, whose early appearance in a boy's outfit was intended to undermine, even deny, her femininity. This contrast might reflect the sociocultural differences between Layla's Carian urban middle-class family and Umm Kulthum's poor peasant family, and the social changes following the nationalist revolution of 1919. Upon coming from the countryside to reside in Cairo in the early 1920s, Umm Kulthum's father underlined his religious and conservative rural values through neutralizing his daughter's gender and undermining her sexual appeal. He continued to dress his daughter in a Bedouin boy's outfit for several years. This was not the case for Layla, who hailed from an urban middle-class family living in Cairo, with its vibrant entertainment industry and nightlife throughout the 1920s and 1930s.

For a while, Layla's family hung on to the illusion that Layla could work and continue her schooling, which meant the family could live up to modern middle-class educational ideals, but they soon realized that she could not do both. Working at night left her too tired to go to school in the morning, and reducing the number of her concerts did not improve the situation. Eventually she ceased going to school and tried homeschooling, particularly in order to master French, as did many middle-class women, especially those from Jewish families. When nuns visited her to express their admiration for her professional success, she was able to stop feeling embarrassed about her new career.[31]

Layla's movements were restricted, however, as her father had to accompany her to every gig. In keeping with his conservative beliefs and perhaps to assure himself of his position as head of the family, he refused to allow Layla to go to a show at Badi'a Masabni's nightclub, a landmark of nightlife in Cairo during the interwar period. According to Layla's account, her father even hit her for requesting that he do so.[32] Layla did not mean to label her father as abusive or restrictive: mentioning anecdotes of this type in her memoir underscored Layla's wish to be seen as an "ordinary" middle-class woman, that her work in entertainment did not exempt her from "good" traditional family values. She showed her love and appreciation for her father by acknowledging how hard he worked to establish her as a respected woman artist. In the last interview she gave to Egyptian radio in the late 1970s, Layla said that she could not overstate her father's contribution in developing her career.[33]

Indeed, Zaki thoroughly controlled his child's career, taking her to perform in small towns and villages far away from Cairo. His decision proved economically and professionally wise. A female singer coming from Cairo would attract large local audiences despite her youth and lack of experience, since those in the provinces did not often get a chance to listen to Cairene singers or to hear recently composed music and lyrics. Layla put her father's and Dawud Husni's training to work, performing songs by the great and famous composers of the late nineteenth and early twentieth centuries. The young singer thus had an opportunity to master her vocal skills and show off her talent while avoiding the heated competition of the Cairo market until she gained experience and maturity. Nevertheless, for a young girl who had no say in where she went or performed, these trips must have been physically and emotionally exhausting. Salih Mursi, one of her biographers, gives an account of her facing a sexual assault by a drunken prince during one of these provincial trips, though I could not find another source to verify the anecdote[34] and Layla herself did not mention it in her 1957 autobiography, although she included other challenging situations she had faced.

For one year Layla, still a young girl with a petite and still-growing body, toured Upper Egypt with her father. They ranged from Bani Swayf to Aswan and beyond, giving one or two concerts in every town and village with a train station. They would spend two to three days in one place, then move on to the next village. The audiences, far from being refined, often traveled to her shows on foot; seeing people in modest peasant clothing, wearing *balgha* (peasant slippers), and sitting on the floor next to their water jars during concerts touched and thrilled Layla. Well-off rural audiences expressed their admiration by sending gifts—some as odd as jars of cheese or ghee—to the hotels where Layla and her father stayed. Although at first her father rejected these gifts, he was compelled to accept them when the male givers used the *talaq* oath, that is, when the man swears he will divorce his wife if the recipient does not accept his offer or believe him.[35] It is doubtful that these gifts survived the trip back to Cairo, but they eloquently spoke to Layla's success and popularity.

There were a number of painful experiences that Layla viewed as "typical difficulties faced by great artists."[36] They did not have enough money to hire professional organizers and had to give up dealing with impresarios (*muta'ahid hafalat*) as well, following several bad experiences. Sometimes the impresario did not pay them or furnish their transportation home; sometimes the impresario collected the concert revenues and disappeared, leaving Layla and her father out in the open air without accommodations or transportation. Eventually, Zaki made use of his social connections to plan and organize the concerts instead.

Layla and Zaki were not alone in facing this type of situation, as impresarios notoriously did exploit performers. The standard arrangement was for the impresario to take responsibility for organizing and publicizing the concert, and for the rental and preparation of the performance venue; the entertainers and musicians received their pay after the concert based on ticket sales. Some impresarios made performers sign contracts, then embezzled the revenue and disappeared before the end of the show without paying the performers, musicians, or rent. Giving concerts in the Egyptian provinces could be even more difficult, since not all towns had hotels or other safe commercial accommodations for strangers. When an impresario absconded without arranging accommodations for the entertainers, the latter might not be able to find lodging or transportation to return home following the concert; the artists then might have to spend the night outdoors at the train station.

Muhammad 'Abd al-Wahab fell victim to this practice several times early in his career. After his success with private parties, clubs, and onstage, 'Abd al-Wahab decided to give public concerts. His fame and success promised handsome financial rewards, but his first impresario, a foreigner named Fitasyun (or Vitasione,) stole the revenue and disappeared, leaving 'Abd al-Wahab responsible for paying the musicians and theater rent. It was the poet Ahmad Shawqi who lent him the money to save the day. After this, 'Abd al-Wahab learned to obtain his payment before the beginning of his performance.[37]

These intensive provincial tours polished Layla's vocal skills and taught her how to achieve rapport with her audience. More important, because she had to sing without a microphone, this phase strengthened her voice. For decades afterward, she expressed her gratitude to her father for the experience but lamented how she suffered physically and emotionally during these trips, when she was still a child with a soft voice. Audiences expressed admiration for her voice, but some comments hurt her feelings, as when members of the audience complained that they could not hear her soft and low voice and shouted, "Raise your voice; we can't hear you!" Nevertheless, she eventually attracted many fans; people thronged at weddings to listen to her. Layla cherished these memories, saying, "Great artists have to climb the ladder [of success] step by step, not all in one jump, until one becomes a great artist achieving the desired success."[38]

Throughout the 1930s, Layla continued to perform at solo concerts (*wasalat*, sing. *wasla*, meaning one concert with intermission) that consisted of vocal and instrumental pieces together with improvisations that audiences viewed as classical and virtuosic.[39] In a concert in 1935, she performed a song in the *saba* mode that concluded with a song composed by Muhammad 'Uthman.[40] Performing the repertoire of great singers and composers of the late nineteenth and early twentieth centuries enhanced her popularity with those who disliked musical novelties. The press highlighted her young age and wrote, "Zaki Murad's child performs like the best mature vocalists."[41] But some others criticized her for not producing new tunes and urged her to open her wallet to buy original compositions.[42] Scholar and literary critic Zaki Mubarak (1892–1952) offered the sharpest critique in 1943, depicting her as parsimonious and simply unwilling to purchase new music and lyrics.[43] Gradually, Layla focused more on performing new melodies composed by al-Sunbati and Zakariya Ahmad, among others.[44] After her intensive immersion in the Cairo music scene, Zaki Murad introduced his daughter to Midhat 'Asim, the head of the oriental department of the national radio, run by the state, and the superstar Muhammad 'Abd al-Wahab, both of whom gave Layla access to the mass media and the broader audiences of nationally broadcast radio and cinema.

The Age of Mass Music and National Radio Broadcast

The technology worked to Layla's benefit throughout her career, starting with the introduction of microphone-amplifying sound systems to the performing arts. Microphones had a twofold effect on her generation of singers: those with powerful voices lost their advantage and in some cases even their careers when the microphone amplified flaws in their voices,[45] but those with soft voices, like Layla, gained from use of the microphone. Layla rose to stardom in the age of musical film and public radio broadcasting, both of which contributed to Egypt's emerging national popular culture. Film and radio conveyed the voices and images of performing artists, mostly based in Cairo, to Egypt's entire population; making some of them stars on the national level and beyond.

Radio broadcasting began in Egypt in the late 1920s in the form of private enterprise. A few famous singers were able to monopolize privately owned broadcast stations and turn them into platforms to slam their critics and fellow singers:[46] singer Mahmud Subh notoriously used coarse and hostile language in challenging Muhammad 'Abd al-Wahab on the air.[47] Various sorts of violations impelled authorities to ban all private broadcast stations on May 29, 1934; two days later, on May 31, 1934, the Egyptian government launched public radio broadcasting. Music and songs had been an integral part of the entertainment provided by the privately owned radio stations, and public radio continued and consolidated that tradition. The state kept a monopoly over radio broadcasts throughout the twentieth century.[48] The

daily program of public radio began with a Qu'ran recitation by Shaykh
Muhammad Rif'at (1882–1950); a briefing by the minister of transportation,
'Ali Pasha Ibrahim; and then piano music by Midhat 'Asim and songs by
Umm Kulthum, Muhammad 'Abd al-Wahab, Salih 'Abd al-Hayy, and Fa-
thiyya Ahmad.[49] One cannot exaggerate the importance of music and songs
to Egyptian radio and their role in building popularity for certain stars who
achieved dominance in the public sphere. Before radio and sound film, only
wealthy, elite audiences could experience public or private live performances
by famous singers, while the well-off and middle classes could afford gramo-
phones at home. Public radio broadcasting allowed the working classes to
listen to favorite vocalists using radio sets, which mushroomed in public
places like coffeehouses and at home.

As the head of Arabic programming for Egyptian public radio, Midhat
'Asim contracted Layla to sing live once a week, on Tuesdays. Mustafa Rida
Bey, founder of the Institute of Oriental Music, oversaw all radio music programming. An opponent of new music, Rida insisted that Layla sing only
the old genres, a stipulation to which Zaki Murad readily agreed. On July
6, 1934, five weeks after the launch of public radio broadcasting, the Egyptian public across the country listened for the first time to Layla Murad's
voice through the radio. Technical limitations did not allow the broadcast of
recordings, so artists had to perform live at the radio station in downtown
Cairo. Layla's father invariably accompanied her to the studio, where she met
and received encouragement from the great vocalists of the time, including
Umm Kulthum and Shaykh Muhammad Rif'at. The latter had arguably the
best voice for reciting the Qu'ran in the twentieth century, and listeners were
able to appreciate the exceptional beauty of his low voice thanks to the microphone technology. Not only did Layla receive encouragement from fellow
vocalists in the studio, but she immediately learned her listeners' reactions
once she left the studio; people gathered around her in the street, cheering
and offering her assurances of popularity and stardom. Recording companies
contracted with Layla to record and release performances of her traditional
genres of *adwar*, monologues, and *taqatiq*.

Once the Marconi recording systems became available, Egyptian radio recorded Layla's performance and broadcast the recorded version twice a week.
When radio broadcast her performance live, she performed only two songs

once a week; with recording technology, she recorded three songs that the radio broadcast twice a week. Eventually, the public radio authorities agreed to broadcast new music, and Layla performed her original songs for the radio for several years with great success. But in 1938, owing to a financial disagreement, Layla stopped performing on radio. Although she was still young, she had learned how to engage in tough negotiations, using her success, fame, and popularity to leverage her financial gain. Radio was paying her 7 Egyptian pounds for performing one song and 12 for a concert; she requested an increase to 20 pounds per performance, but the authorities would only increase the payment to 15. And so she quit, turning her focus to the cinema in the wake of the success of the first film in which she starred, *Yahya al-Hub* (*Long Live Love*), with 'Abd al-Wahab, and earned thousands of Egyptian pounds by making films.[50] Layla returned to radio ten years later, in 1948, but only to promote her film *Qalbi Dalili* (*My Heart Guides Me*) and introduce some of her songs from the film.[51] Ironically, the radio would again become the main venue for disseminating her songs after her last appearance in a film in 1955.

According to Layla, singing was not the fulfillment of her personal ambition but a means of making a living. She enjoyed singing at home and school but not giving public performances; doing so was not a matter of choice. Indeed, she felt embarrassment about the profession, which she viewed as incompatible with social respectability for a child raised by nuns among upper- and middle-class girls. At the peak of her success and stardom in 1946, Layla admitted that she became a singer only to stave off poverty, that she took pride in her profession only when 'Abd al-Wahab asked her to appear with him in a film and offered to produce her recordings.

> My father was a famous singer, but my mother's family condemned me for becoming a singer! My father traveled to America and stayed for four years, then came back to us penniless. I had to sing in concerts, weddings, and radio until I appeared in *Yahya al-Hub*.[52]

Sound Film Arrived in Egypt Singing

The exceptional position Layla Murad has enjoyed in the realm of Egyptian and Arab popular culture has stemmed from her cinematic career. One thinks of Umm Kulthum as the most prominent vocalist in modern

Egyptian and Arab history, but Layla Murad is the most important singing actress. Her achievements were underpinned by her remarkable talent, the ethos of film production, and the technical aspects of modes of entertainment; thus any discussion of Layla's cinematic career requires a brief history of sound and musical film in Egypt. Sound film arrived in Egypt in 1932, the same year Layla gave her first public concert. The young engineer Muhsin (Mohsen) Szabo, of Hungarian origin, succeeded in manufacturing an apparatus for recording sound and playing it back in Egypt and used it to film the inauguration of the Parliament of Egypt. Producer and actor Yusuf Wahbi (ca. 1898–1982) used Szabo's device to make the trailer for the first Egyptian sound film, *Awlad al-Dhawat* (*Sons of Aristocrats*; Muhammad Karim, 1932). The filmmaker, Muhammad Karim (ca. 1896–1972), shot the silent portion of the film in Wahbi's own Studio Ramsis in Cairo and the sound scenes (about 400 meters of film) in Paris. He spontaneously filmed French firefighters climbing ladders to put out a burning building and used the shot in the film to avoid having to shoot such a scene in the studio. [53]

One month after the release of *Awlad al-Dhawat*, the film *Unshudat al-Fu'ad* (*Song of the Heart*; Mario Volpe, 1932), featuring the female singer Nadra and directed by the Alexandrian-Italian filmmaker Mario Volpe, appeared in theaters. Both films were based on the murder in London of a wealthy Egyptian, Ali Kamil Fahmi Bey, by his French wife.[54] Authorities suspended showings of *Awlad al-Dhawat* following a complaint from foreigners in Egypt that the film defamed European women; then the director of public security in the Ministry of the Interior, Mr. Graves, watched the film and recommended showing it in theaters. Karim thought that distributors of foreign films in Egypt triggered the campaign in order to abort the local production of sound film before they had gained a share of the local market,[55] an assumption not too far from reality, as sound films allowed Egyptian cinema to dominate local and regional Arabic-speaking markets.[56] Egyptian talkies held a position of strength vis-à-vis foreign films among Arab audiences, particularly the illiterate, who could not read the subtitled translations and were more appreciative of their cultural traditions.[57] With the advent of sound, the number of film productions increased; according to one estimate, thirty-six production companies released nearly one hundred films during the 1930s.[58]

The release of *Unshudat al-Fu'ad* made evident the important role music and songs would play in the new sound films. The musical film built on and benefited from the vivid musical theater movement that had flourished since the late nineteenth century and attracted gifted Egyptian and Syrian artists.[59] The love for songs among musicals' audiences was far greater than their concern for the sophistication of the story line or the quality of the acting. Despite its being a weaker version of the same story as *Awlad al-Dhawat*, *Unshudat al-Fu'ad* enjoyed considerably more success across the Arab countries, thanks to Nadra's beautiful singing voice, Zakariya Ahmad's music, and Khalil Mutran's lyrics. Born in Beirut to an Egyptian father and a Lebanese mother, Nadra Amin (1907–1990) became the first singing star in Egyptian cinema. Her success convinced the superstar vocalist Muhammad 'Abd al-Wahab to star in the second Egyptian musical film, *al-Warda al-Bayda'* (*The White Rose*; Muhammad Karim, December 1932). *Al-Warda al-Bayda'* played in theaters for six weeks and grossed, by one estimate, a quarter of a million Egyptian pounds at the box office.[60] The musical film became a phenomenon among consumers nationwide as factories produced *al-Warda al-Bayda'* fabric and *al-Warda al-Bayda'* perfumes; groceries and hotels adopted the *al-Warda al-Bayda'* name.[61] Mini-statues of 'Abd al-Wahab and his female co-star, Samira Khulusi, became hot commodities.[62] And even before the films were released, recordings of the movies' songs were sold in local as well as international markets by record labels such as Cairophone and Baydaphone. The tremendous success that *al-Warda al-Bayda'* and *Unshudat al-Fu'ad* achieved both in and outside of Egypt laid the foundation for the overall popularity of Egyptian cinema abroad, particularly in the Arab world and in Arabic-speaking communities around the globe.[63]

Layla and 'Abd al-Wahab: *Long Live Love*

The success of musicals encouraged the actress, producer, director, and musician Bahiga Hafiz to re-release her film *al-Dahaya* (*The Victims*) after adding sound. Hafiz had produced and starred in the silent version of *al-Dahaya*, which was released in December 1932; in 1935, the sound version of the film marked the first appearance of Layla Murad on the silver screen. When Hafiz offered Layla a supporting role in addition to singing, Zaki and Layla were enthusiastic, hoping that Layla's appearance in the film would turn the

teenage singer into a star. Hafiz agreed that Zakariya Ahmad, one of Layla's
favorite composers and in her words "the undisputable leader and master of
his generation in composing authentic oriental melodies,"[64] would compose
the music for all of Layla's songs. But Hafiz disliked Ahmad's compositions
and expressed her critique in a way that Layla found "tasteless and hurtful to
Ahmad's feeling."[65] When Layla insisted on performing the melody the way
Ahmad had composed it, Hafiz threatened to give Layla's part to another
actress. As a compromise, Layla appeared in the film in only one party scene,
performing a single song,[66] "Yum al-Safa," which was her first cinematic
song and earned her a payment of 50 Egyptian pounds. Unfortunately, we
do not have Hafiz's side of the story, but Layla's account evinces the strong
wills of two female artists during the formative phase of Egyptian cinema.
Layla's account, assuming it's truthful, highlights her dignity and ability to
defend her artistic choices and her composer's work, even when her advocacy
meant losing her first opportunity to star in a film. Bahiga Hafiz, a musician
herself, was trained exclusively in the European classical genres and thus was
not surprised that her opinion weighed little as far as Zaki Murad, who supported his daughter, was concerned. Hafiz marketed the film as a *film ghina'i
natiq* (sound film with music).[67] Promotional posters used Layla's name,
voice, and image to attract audiences; her voice was advertised as angelic and
her performance as magical. The use of Layla's picture and name shows that
she had become popular enough to attract moviegoers, who indeed received
the film well; it stayed in theaters in Cairo and Alexandria for several weeks.

As Egyptian cinema came of age acoustically it became a critical plat-
form for singers, both male and female, who dominated movies throughout
the 1930s. The novelty of sound, music, and songs attracted audiences from
all classes; a collection of songs in a single film could appeal to audiences
with lyrics and music compositions from different genres: monologues in
colloquial Egyptian, a romantic poem in classical Arabic, and old folk *maw-
wal*. In this regard, musical film followed a tradition that went back to the
musical theater of Salama Higazi (1852–1917). Having achieved his popularity
as a composer and singer before starring in musical plays, Higazi composed
music to accompany lyrics and dialogue. To build his rapport with audiences,
he asked the songwriters to expand their lyrics and inserted *layali* to satisfy
his audiences, who attended the plays to enjoy his vocal performances rather

than the shows themselves. He often acceded to audiences' demands for him to perform or repeat solo songs and *layali* even when it interrupted the flow of the play.

Similarly, audiences of musical films cared more about the songs than the flow of the dialogue; the more songs the movie had, the more enchantment for audiences. The first sound films mostly consisted of collections of songs, taking up half the film's time, interrupted by dialogue, which took up the rest. Sound film brought famous singers before the eyes and ears of a mass working-class audience, who could afford a ticket to a movie theater but not to a concert hall. One could go to the movie theater in shabby clothing and even barefoot, whereas attending a concert required elegant, formal clothes. The popular press and celebrity magazines that mushroomed during this time sought to satisfy people's curiosity about the artists, printing pictorial accounts of stars' lives and contributing to their fame and popularity.

Musical film became an essential medium for poets to disseminate their verses among a broader audience. Influential writers of the time, including 'Abbas al-'Aqqad, composed the lyrics for musical films.[68] Ahmad Shawqi's prophecy that poetry would survive and take on new life through songs was realized by 'Abd al-Wahab, through whose melodies Shawqi's poems were made available to those of all classes and levels of education rather than being limited to print and thus accessible only for a small, literate audience. Mixing classical Arabic words with colloquial Egyptian in film songs enriched the vernacular with new words and made *Fusha* Arabic (Modern Standard Arabic) more accessible and more democratic. Musical films also impacted music composition, requiring shorter melodies.

Muhammad 'Abd al-Wahab spearheaded musical creativity on the silver screen, and musical films enabled his making revolutionary changes in the music scene. Championing modern music, he proposed that a modern melody of his be performed in a concert at the Royal Institute of Oriental Music hosted in 1927 in honor of the Afghani king, Amanullah. The institute, however, strongly opposed the idea and insisted on traditional songs for an audience consisting of politicians, statesmen, diplomats, and the upper-class elite. Three years later, the institute organized an international conference of Eastern music in which many Arab countries and Turkey participated, together with a concert attended by the Egyptian king Fu'ad and international guests. For the concert, 'Abd al-Wahab insisted on presenting his modern music and performed a colloquial lyric composed by Ahmad Shawqi, which offered an impressionist description of nature that was unusual for songs. In addition to the fresh content, 'Abd al-Wahab employed a blend of European and Middle Eastern instruments. The concert not only succeeded but the mixed instrumentation was taken up by bands throughout the country, changing the traditional *takht* forever. In his musical films, 'Abd al-Wahab also blended foreign and native tunes, melodies, and instruments for his songs, for example, combining the Latin American rhythm of rumba with Arabic music for the first time.[69]

Muhammad Karim laid the foundation for the visual structure of a cinematic song; his formula in *al-Warda al-Bayda'* became a model for following generations of filmmakers. 'Abd al-Wahab and Karim agreed that movies' songs had to be much shorter than live performances, which necessitated omitting lengthy musical introductions and long *lazma/fasil* that separated stanzas. The average length of a song became six minutes, short enough to fit in the movie yet long enough to produce a recording. Visually, the camera focused on the singer from a single angle until the singer finished a stanza, then moved to a natural scene, such as a flock of doves or the Nile, between stanzas. Karim's formula held sway among filmmakers until the 1960s; the only variations involved changing camera angles or distance, or moving the camera between the singer and their lover or between the singer and the audience in music halls during concerts—changes meant to prevent audience boredom. Musicals varied in how closely the lyrics were integrated with the story line; audiences watched musicals in large part to see and hear their favorite vocalists, regardless how well the songs fit into the movie's story line.

Starring in a film with 'Abd al-Wahab promised greater fame and prestige, and so Layla and her father worked hard to achieve that goal, which proved to be within reach after 'Abd al-Wahab announced that he would always co-star with a female singer. Layla was in an advantageous position, as she had already established herself as a successful singer capable of performing the older and neoclassics. Surprisingly, until 1937, when he was looking for a female vocalist to co-star in his third film, 'Abd al-Wahab had not yet met Layla. He accepted Zaki's invitation to meet his daughter for the first time; according to 'Abd al-Wahab, his old friend wanted him to consider his daughter, whose work would be a *gift* to 'Abd al-Wahab.[70] Initially, 'Abd al-Wahab thought Zaki was exaggerating his daughter's talent, but after listening to Layla, he agreed to hire her for *Yahya al-Hub*. According to Layla's account of that first meeting, she chose to perform "Yama Banit Qasr al-Amani," which 'Abd al-Wahab had performed in his film *Dumu' al-Hub* (*Tears of Love*; Muhammad Karim, 1935). It was a sophisticated piece that allowed Layla to show off her vocal talent, not to mention her courage in performing for 'Abd al-Wahab's. According to the latter's account, the most important quality that attracted him to Layla's voice was that "she never imitated anyone and her voice has what professionals call *'urab*, or special vibrations that made listeners recognize her voice immediately and never confuse it with any other voice."[71] 'Abd al-Wahab introduced her to filmmaker Muhammad Karim, insisting that he give her the leading female role in *Yahya al-Hub* (*Long Live Love*).

Shy Layla Murad and Macho Muhammad Karim

Muhammad Karim had heard Layla at a private party before 'Abd al-Wahab introduced her to him. He admitted that he liked her voice but had never thought of her as an actress, believing that she was too shy and unskilled in acting. But Muhammad 'Abd al-Wahab insisted that she be given the part because of her voice.[72] Karim had to accept that 'Abd al-Wahab could not afford to take any more time searching for a woman who could both sing and act, that he was too busy with his concerts; nor was he interested in directing another film at this time, as his company, Baydaphone, was still reaping the revenues from the recordings from his previous films. Meanwhile, Karim needed to begin making the film in order to get paid; he was the highest-paid director, but he chose to work on one project at a time, sometimes going without income for more than a year, and had committed himself to 'Abd al-Wahab's project. Preparing to direct a musical film was time-consuming for Karim; he had to find a story that suited 'Abd al-Wahab and develop a script that allowed for songs. When 'Abd al-Wahab was not ready to begin working on *Yahya al-Hub*, Karim, in desperation, announced that he would give up making musicals and be willing to work with stars other than 'Abd al-Wahab.[73] Finally, the playwright 'Abbas 'Allam provided Karim and 'Abd al-Wahab with a simple story line suitable for a musical film. Since 'Allam took weeks to write one line of dialogue,[74] 'Abd al-Wahab commissioned French-educated Muhammad Jamal al-Din Rifa'i and the highly cultured and punctual 'Abd al-Warith 'Asar to finish writing the script.[75] In addition to writing theater plays and movie scripts, 'Asar (ca. 1894–1982) was a brilliant actor whose performances in supporting roles was unforgettable. Poet Ahmad Rami, who was well known for composing songs for Umm Kulthum, started penning lyrics for the songs, and 'Abd al-Wahab began to compose the music, while Karim looked for the cast.

Her first experience in cinema educated Layla about many artistic and technical issues and exposed her to Karim's style of filmmaking. Karim, one of the most meticulous and exacting filmmakers in the history of Egyptian cinema, is highly placed in nationalistic accounts of Egyptian cinema's history. Many consider his *Zeinab* (1930) the first full-length feature film directed by a native Egyptian and his *Awlad al-Dhawat* (1932) the first Egyptian sound film,[76] even though pioneer cinema actress and producer Aziza Amir released the first full-length feature film in Egyptian cinema, *Laila*, in 1927. Historical sources do not confirm whether Amir or the Turkish director Wedad Orfi directed *Laila*.[77] The Alexandrian Jewish filmmaker Togo Mizrahi (1901–1986) released his first fiction film, *Kukayyin al-Hawiya* (*Cocaine, or Abyss*), in 1930. Nationalistic accounts of the history of Egyptian cinema may have declined to bestow the honor of directing the first full-length feature film on a woman or a Jew; Karim would have seemed more suitable for the honor. And even before Amir, Mizrahi, and Karim, Muhammad Bayumi (ca. 1894–1963) directed and produced the first Egyptian short film, *Barsum yabhath 'an wazifa* (*Barsum Is Looking for a Job*) in 1923.

Karim did not refrain from talking about what he considered Layla's "body defect that was uncorrectable, and she could not do anything to change it."[78] He did not identify the nature of this defect or in which part of her body, but he proudly talked about how hard he worked to disguise it during shooting. Karim's statement bespeaks the unrealistic aesthetic values he embraced. A slim and perfectly proportioned feminine body was his ideal, and he often insisted that his female actresses go on a diet to lose weight. For example, he liked Zuzu Madi's acting and agreed to give her a part in the film, provided she would lose weight. But although she starved herself for two months, he insisted that she was still "fat"; she cried until 'Abd al-Warith 'Asar intervened, saying she was fine, and Karim finally accepted her.[79] Karim imposed on all his actresses his opinions about female size and shape. Nagat 'Ali, star of his film *Dumu' al-Hub*, underwent the harshest treatment. According to 'Abd al-Wahab, Karim hated obesity and included in his contract with Nagat 'Ali a clause deducting 10 Egyptian pounds from her pay for every kilogram she gained while the film was being shot.[80] Putting Nagat on a severely restricted diet while in Paris, Karim allowed her to eat only one slice of grilled beef, one piece of toasted bread, and a green salad per day. Yet, mysteriously, Nagat gained weight. One morning everyone in the Parisian hotel where the film crew were staying was awakened by screaming and yelling. Karim was dragging Nagat Ali by the hand; he had caught her eating a piece of cake and could not control his anger. He then discovered that Nagat often sneaked to a bakery shop to eat all the desserts she liked to satisfy her hunger.[81]

While Karim subjected Layla to intensive training, he thought she was also suffering from emotional disturbances in her private life. Layla seemed to him to be depressed all the time and was physically so weak that she fainted whenever she had to perform some physical activity. Layla's younger sister, who always accompanied her to the studio, told Karim that Layla would go without eating for three days; upon learning this, he forced Layla to eat lunch in the studio every day until her health and energy were restored. Layla Murad was possibly the only actress whom Karim encouraged to eat, though his actions were not out of sympathy but to enable her to complete their project. Instead of worrying about this sad and weak girl, he complained that "actresses never appreciated their responsibilities and never appreciated the consequences of failure."[82] Eighteen years later Layla gave a different account of her poor health while shooting *Yahya al-Hub*. She revealed that Karim had asked her to go on a diet; owing to her eagerness to follow Karim's instructions and her fear of failure, Layla stopped eating for five days and lived only on fruit juice, a diet that brought her to the point of exhaustion. She fainted and was taken home until she restored her health.[83] Karim likely elected to make her eat lunch at the studio rather than losing more days of work.

Karim found Layla extremely shy, meek, and less than talented as an actress, and believed that her shyness was the cause of her poor acting. He said that she was too shy to laugh before the cameras, so to compensate, he would shoot her opening lips and record the voice of someone else laughing;[84] he taught her facial expression and body language. Layla was obedient but seemingly depressed and thought Karim was too harsh toward her—which was true: he believed that a woman's image on-screen must be perfect, despite the fact that aesthetic ideals and real life were not the same. According to him, "Every woman in this world has a defect in her body figure; ordinary women have to make an effort to hide any defect in real life, and actresses have to expend more effort because the camera amplifies defects in the eyes of millions of watchers."[85]

In his statements and his memoir, Karim emerges as supermacho and *Weststruken*, or *gharbzadeh*, to use the Iranian intellectual Jalal Al-e-Ahmad's term to refer to those who are excessively and uncritically fascinated by the West.[86] Karim praised everything Western and criticized everything Egyptian. In one notable case, he mocked the French actress in his *Awlad al-Dhawat*, Colette D'Arville, saying that she "lost her mind in the presence of oriental food, ate lots of kebabs, turkey, . . . etc., and gained weight." Then he admired her for going back to being her superior European self and following the rules set by her union; he liked that she was a Parisian and wanted to look pretty, and that she understood and followed his instructions. Karim criticized Egyptians for their lack of expertise, dirty workplaces, and lack of discipline. He frequently compared working conditions in Egypt with those in Europe and lamented his bad luck in having to work with Egyptians. He praised foreign technicians for their punctuality, cleanness, and discipline, and even compared the attitudes of ordinary Europeans to their Egyptian counterparts when they filmed on the streets. He lamented the pandemonium that broke out whenever a film crew shot in a public space and how individual Egyptians pushed one another aside to get their face in front of the camera; such activities hindered shooting, and Europeans were much more cooperative. Karim criticized Egypt's producers for their efforts to lower production costs, which resulted in their intervening in the filmmaker's artistic choices, as well as their investments in other businesses outside the movie industry. In turn, producers disliked Karim's perfectionism, leading them to favor other filmmakers.

Karim praised some Egyptian male actors, while expressing harsh and sexist critiques of Egyptian actresses. He credited his own work for exhibiting women's beauty but did not acknowledge the good work any actress contributed to the work's success. He pointed to their womanly defects, weight, lack of discipline, and failure to develop acting talent, together with the poor quality of their work, their lack of responsibility, their lack of professionalism, and their stupidity. He wrote about his work with Layla and others: "A filmmaker is like a daycare teacher. . . . He knows what is good for his little children, but they get upset when he scolds and stops them from looking through open windows lest they fall."[87] While he knew that cinema was a new profession for most actresses, Karim had no tolerance when they failed to understand how to perform the way he wished. Karim taught Layla a harsh lesson to teach her to obey him: when she stubbornly refused to hide a flaw in her figure, Karim shot and developed a scene showing the defect and forced her to view the scene; she begged him to redo the scene, a costly process. He was proud and pleased that his trick convinced Layla never again to disobey him;[88] it is no surprise that Layla, fearing Karim's wrath, starved herself for days to the point of fainting in the studio.[89]

Layla's first film was a challenging experience. In addition to Karim's harsh and sexist attitude, an intoxicated British soldier harassed and chased her around the pyramids one night during filming. She ran screaming for help, but there was no way to get rid of the riotous crowd.[90] The film crew had to stop working but did not press any criminal charges against the drunken soldier or even file a police report. Egypt was still subject to the Capitulations, which gave extraterritorial advantages to foreign subjects over Egyptians until their abolition in 1949, twelve years after the signing of the Montreux Convention of 1937 that followed the Anglo-Egyptian Treaty of 1936. Because the harasser belonged to the British occupation forces, a position that put him above the law, no one saw a point in reporting the incident. Layla also faced the dilemma of the on-screen kiss. According to the script of *Yahya al-Hub*, the female protagonist had to kiss her lover, Muhammad Fathi *afandi*, played by Muhammad 'Abd al-Wahab. Layla's father refused to allow her to do the scene even though Karim insisted. The work stopped for two days, and news about this disagreement leaked to the press.[91] Audiences, mostly fans of Muhammad 'Abd al-Wahab, sent angry messages to Layla, scolding her for rejecting a kiss from a man whom many girls of the Arab East longed for. But Layla stood her ground and did not allow any on-screen kisses for many years, until she acted with her first husband, Anwar

Wagdi. The debate over on-screen kissing had a history as long as the history of Egyptian films. The state's censor had the power to allow or to cut kisses in movie scripts. Even when the censor allowed a kissing scene, clergymen and other conservatives often criticized it: Shaykh Mahmud Abu al-ʿUyun criticized the kissing scene in Togo Mizrahi's *Awlad Misr* (*Children of Egypt*, 1930).[92] Layla Murad was not the first actress to refuse on-screen kisses; Umm Kulthum explicitly refused any on-screen kissing, beginning with her first film, *Widad* (*Wedad*; Fritz Kramp, 1936). The religious establishment maintained that the on-screen kiss was religiously unlawful; indeed, former minister of *awqaf* (religious endowment), Shaykh Ahmad Hassan al-Baquri (1907–1985), stated that a cinematic kiss even between married couples was sinful.[93]

Yahya al-Hub between Studio Misr and Paris

Between 1930 and 1936, various-sized studios in Cairo and Alexandria produced at least forty-four feature films. In 1936, Bank Misr's studio, Studio Misr, emerged as the leading Egyptian equivalent to Hollywood's major studios, a position the company retained for three decades.[94] Talʿat Harb Pasha, the founder and director of Banque Misr, tapped all his connections to bring cinema business to the studio. Muhammad ʿAbd al-Wahab agreed to film *Yahya al-Hub* at Studio Misr, provided the studio was well equipped and acquired a high-quality sound system,[95] and Harb Pasha affirmed that Studio Misr had purchased sound equipment similar to that available in French studios and had hired the German-trained Egyptian sound engineer Mustafa Wali. Wali had extensive experience, having worked in Berlin for twenty years before Harb brought him to Studio Misr; he had worked on *Widad* and *Nashid al-Amal* (*The Chant of Hope*; Ahmed Badrakhan, 1937) the first cinematic outings of Umm Kulthum and the first productions of Studio Misr. Umm Kulthum's films demonstrated that Wali was the most talented sound engineer in Egyptian musical film.

Nevertheless, the results of shooting *Yahya al-Hub* at Studio Misr were displeasing to both Karim and ʿAbd al-Wahab. Contrary to the nationalist propaganda that hailed the phenomenal success of Talʿat Harb and the efficiency of Bank Misr and its successful studio, the *Yahya al-Hub* experience revealed extensive bad management, defective equipment, dishonest crews,

and cunning administrators. According to one anecdote, Studio Misr's car-
penters submitted a bill for 40 Egyptian pounds to Karim for woodwork
when the real cost was no more than 4 Egyptian pounds; workers explained
that the manager of the studio, Ahmad Salim Bey, had instructed them to
multiply any bill for 'Abd al-Wahab's film by ten.[96] Actor, filmmaker, play
director, and writer Zaki Tulaymat (1894–1982) also observed Studio Misr's
mismanagement under Ahmad Salim, pointing out Salim's lack of the appropriate training, expertise, or skills to manage so vital an enterprise as Studio
Misr.[97] Having graduated from Cambridge University, fluent in English, and
hailing from an elite family, Salim (1910–1949) worked as an interpreter for
Tal'at Harb while Harb shopped for cinema equipment in Europe. Harb
appointed Salim as the first manager of the studio, despite his lack of experience or training. In Karim's assessment, Salim caused trouble at the studio
because he interfered in technical issues rather than confining himself to
administrative matters.[98]

Karim hired French cameraman Georges Benoit because he thought that
in 1937 there was no equivalent expert in Egypt. Benoit had worked with
Karim on *Dumu' al-Hub* (1935), whose credits proudly proclaimed in French:
"Prise de vues Studio Éclair Paris, enregistrement Tobis Klang Film" (Scenes
shot in Studio Éclair in Paris, recorded with Tobis Klang Film equipment).
The credits were meant to highlight the European component as proof of the
director's use of state-of-the-art techniques. Karim did not shy away from or
sugar-coat his preference for all things European: "I tried to make him [Ben-
oit] an example from which all Egyptian cameramen could benefit, and I
invited all of them to be present during the shooting, but none attended, they
were too proud. Only Wahid Farid, who worked hard and faithfully as an
assistant for Georges [Benoit], greatly learned from him."[99] Benoit liked Studio Misr's buildings and gardens, but he was not comfortable working there
because the equipment was too outdated for outdoor shooting. Karim also
hired a female French editor because he thought the montage work in Studio
Misr lacked precision. He found the montage room dirty; one could see a pan
full of eggs and pastrami frying on a small alcohol-fueled stove, which posed
the danger of exposing the highly flammable films to fire. Egyptian women
working in the montage department disliked the French editor and called
her "Mrs. Arrogant";[100] Karim would lock her in the montage room so that

she could work without disturbance. After work had been completed, every-one found the results appalling. The developed film was so dirty that Benoit's eyes filled with tears, and he kept screaming "Horrible!"[101] The unclean acids and unfiltered water that were available at Studio Misr for developing film caused white dots that moved on the screen like worms. Karim had to take the films to Paris to be redeveloped, although Ahmad Salim claimed that Studio Misr's lab was perfectly fine and that Karim merely wanted to go to Paris for recreation. Tal'at Harb's attempts to convince Karim not to go to Paris and continue working at Studio Misr failed.

The Parisian lab discovered many problems with the film and decided it could print only one copy. After extensive negotiation, the lab agreed to try its best to produce additional copies, even if they were only 70 percent clean. 'Abd al-Wahab arrived in Paris and reshot his song, "Ya Dunya Ya Gharami," employing twenty male and thirty female Parisian extras. Since Layla did not join them in France for reshooting, Karim took close-up shots only of 'Abd al-Wahab's face. After two months in Paris, Karim returned to Cairo with fifteen copies of *Yahya al-Hub*.[102] The total cost of the trip for four people, reshooting some scenes, hiring French extras, and redeveloping and print-ing the film came to less than the cost of developing the film in Egypt: one meter of film cost 5 piastres at Studio Misr and only 5 *milim*, or 10 percent of that, in Paris.

Theaters released *Yahya al-Hub* on January 24, 1938; the film was well received by audiences, and recordings of its songs sold out in a few weeks.[103] Layla plays Nadia, a cultured young woman with a powerful per-sonality who lives with her father, a pasha. She attends the conservatory, cherishes her father's kindness, and calls her loving and caring maternal uncle "mama." Nadia is funny and elegant, a character who inaugurated Lay-la's cinematic persona as a beloved diva. 'Abd al-Wahab plays Muhammad Fathi *afandi*, the son of a rural pasha who chooses to live off his monthly salary as a teller in the same bank where Nadia's maternal uncle has a mana-gerial position. Fathi *afandi* becomes Nadia's neighbor when he moves into a cheaper apartment next to her father's villa. Fathi and Nadia fall in love but face two obstacles to their marriage: Nadia believes Fathi was unfaith-ful, having mistakenly thought that his sister was his secret girlfriend, and then her father urges her to consider a marriage proposal from the son of his

wealthy friend. Both problems are easily solved once Nadia learns the identity of Fathi's sister and realizes that the son of her father's wealthy friend is
in fact Fathi *afandi*.

Promoting the film before its release, 'Abd al-Wahab spoke to the press
about the happy ending of the film, which was different from the sad ends
of his two previous films, *al-Warda al-Bayda'* and *Dumu' al-Hub* (both directed by Karim).[104] In the view of historians, *Yahya al-Hub* established many
traditions that other filmmakers replicated later, particularly in comedy and
musical films. Socially, the film reinforced class boundaries, asserting that
young men and women should fall in love and marry within their social class
and not cross class boundaries. The wealthy woman in the film falls in love
with a talented, hard-working, and honest poor man, but for them to marry,
he must turn out to be a wealthy man from the same class. The film also suggests, however, that love might be a powerful motive in encouraging the poor
to work harder to achieve success and encouraging wealthy lovers to overlook
class boundaries.[105] Likewise, it underscores the virtues of hard work, caring,
and self-making for wealthy men, in contrast to the depiction of the children
of wealthy families as carelessly free from responsibility and indifferent to respectability, relying on their families' wealth and power—a theme that would
likely have pleased working-class audiences. The film took those audiences
inside luxurious houses to experience the social lives of the upper classes,
scenes that working-class audiences craved and that fostered their eagerness
for understanding the wealthy.

Despite the new discourses of marriage based on love rather than material wealth and status, class distinctions permeate all of 'Abd al-Wahab's and
Karim's films. In all their films, the wealthy upper-class female protagonist
marries a man also from the upper class. The happy ending of *Yahya al-Hub* is
consistent with previous films in affirming that young couples should preserve class status regardless of the modern discourse favoring love as the basis
for marriage. In *Yahya al-Hub*, Nadia wants to marry her supposedly poor,
hard-working lover; her father, practicing friendly persuasion, hears her out
but then asks her to meet another, wealthy suitor, hoping she will find him
suitable. Happily, the hard-working and self-reliant young man who refuses
to live off his father's wealth and the wealthy suitor who hails from a com-
patible upper-class family are one and the same. Although Nadia is willing

to sacrifice wealth and class for the sake of love, she need not. The lovers
are happily married and are surrounded by their supportive families, mainly
because the loving couple come from the same social group and have similar
goals. This blend of social comedy and the quick-to-resolve social problem
became the standard story line in most of Layla Murad's films as well as
musical films in general. Mistaken identity, as happens with the young man's
sister and with his financial and social status, is easy to rectify, while at the
same time generating numerous amusing situations and holding the audience's attention with a calculated dose of suspense.

Both filmmaker Muhammad Karim and music superstar Muhammad
'Abd al-Wahab regarded *Yahya al-Hub* as an unforgettable landmark in their
professional journeys.[106] Audiences in Cairo and the provinces liked the film
because of its comedic content, as well as its being elegant and free of ob-
scenities. Well-written, beautiful songs and musical dialogue between Layla
and 'Abd al-Wahab added to the audience's delight. Critics praised 'Abd al-
Wahab for moving away from his previous emphasis on tragedy, exemplified
by his *Dumu' al-Hub*; comedic acting seemed closer to his nature, and it
appealed to the public. Karim and his stars participated actively in inducing
audiences to see the film. While Karim was in Paris, he picked up twenty
thousand perfumed cards that read "I'll be back" and had them distributed
among members of the audience as a promise to return to the theater and
watch *Yahya al-Hub* again. Distinguished guests attended the film's debut,
and 'Abd al-Wahab moved among the seats listening to their comments.
With people laughing and clapping, "tears of joy came to our eyes," Karim
wrote about himself and 'Abd al-Wahab.[107]

'Abd al-Wahab and Layla followed the tradition that stars attended the
release of their movies in Cairo and the provinces as an effective way of attracting larger audiences. The promotional strategy of movie stars traveling
outside Cairo to launch their films in Egyptian provinces and Arab cities
started in the silent film era; for example, Bahiga Hafiz traveled to Man-
sura on February 20, 1933, and to Port Said on April 5 of the same year to
attend the launch of her silent film *al-Dahaya*.[108] With the costlier production of sound films, making such trips became crucial for attracting larger
crowds and selling more tickets. Actress and producer Asya Daghir traveled
to al-Mansura on February 26, 1934, to attend a showing of her film *'Uyun*

Sahira (*Bewitching Eyes*; Ahmad Galal, 1934), then went from there to Alexandria on the same day to attend a showing at the American Cosmograph Theater.[109] Even Umm Kulthum did not exempt herself from the tradition, attending the opening of *Widad* in Port Said and *Nashid al-Amal* at the Cosmograph in Alexandria.[110] 'Abd al-Wahab attended the screening of *al-Warda al-Bayda'* at the Majestic Theater in Port Said on January 30, 1934, and at the Palace Theater in al-Mansura on February 5 of the same year,[111] as well as attending shows in Tanta and Alexandria that same year.[112]

Artists also traveled with their movies to different Arab countries. Lebanese star Asya Daghir went to Beirut to attend the launch of her film *Zawja bil-Niyaba* (*Wife in Waiting*; Ahmad Galal, 1936) in her home country, and the Lebanese government decorated her with a medal. 'Abd al-Wahab also traveled to Beirut and Damascus and sometimes performed songs live in theaters to promote *Yahya al-Hub*.[113] One day, during a screening of the film, the projector stopped, the lights were turned on, and the curtain opened to reveal 'Abd al-Wahab with his band on the stage to perform one of the movie's songs, "Ya wabur 'ul li," live. The song took six minutes in the film, but the live performance took one hour, and the matinée show ended at 11:00 p.m., two hours later than the scheduled time; he repeated the performance during the showing of the film for several nights. Whenever he gave a live performance, movie theaters added an extra 5 piastres to the ticket price. The practice of providing live shows in movie theaters as a way of attracting audiences had begun a few years earlier, in 1933, when some Alexandrian theaters included live belly dance shows in their movie programs.[114] However, 'Abd al-Wahab did not continue to do so for any of his films after *Yahya al-Hub*. There is no evidence that Layla Murad participated in any live concerts aimed at promoting the film.

Yahya al-Hub's liveliest critique came during a much later reshowing of the film in theaters in August 1942. Egyptian cinema lived off showing films in second-and third-tier theaters months and even years after their first release. Member of Parliament Muhammad Qurani Bey attacked the title of the film in Parliament, saying that films should call for "Long Live the Constitution!," "Long Live Egypt!," or "Long Live the Agreement!" (referring to the Anglo-Egyptian Treaty of 1936). He mocked street posters for the film: "Promotions for *Long Live Love* cover streets along with other such films like *When Women Love, Love Me Tonight, Give Me a Kiss.*" He also campaigned for a law prohibiting women from wearing swimsuits or any dresses that revealed their arms, legs, chests, or necks. And he protested against the government's fund for "promoting singing and acting," claiming that songs communicated shameless immorality and nonsense.[115] The Speaker of Parliament ridiculed Qurani's statement, pointing out that 'Abd al-Wahab had also starred in a film titled *Mamnu' al-Hub* (Love Is Forbidden, 1942). Owing to his ultraconservative social positions, Qurani's colleagues dubbed him "MP Shaykh Abu al-'Uyun," referring to a clergyman who had carried out similar campaigns in the press throughout the 1920s and 1930s. Contemporary press reports describe the mood during these parliamentary discussions as favoring and expediting laws against dance and alcohol consumption and prohibiting girls from watching romantic films, going to beaches, or attending cocktail parties. Claiming the need to police public morality, many members of Parliament called upon the government to police individuals in their daily activities and to weaponize laws against women's choices of how to spend leisure time.[116]

A Father's Fears

When *Yahya al-Hub* was first released, Zaki Murad disliked the film and feared it might have prematurely ended his daughter's career. Former singer Munira al-Mahdiyya had accused 'Abd al-Wahab of deliberately composing poor-quality melodies for her so that he might outshine her in the play *Cleopatra*. Zaki repeated the same accusation.[117] He was expressing a father's anxiety over his daughter's career, but his charge proved baseless. As a composer and producer, 'Abd al-Wahab cared about his film's artistic and financial success and promoted his new star. Layla performed three solos of 'Abd al-Wahab's composition and shared two duets with him; all five songs are among the best in the Egyptian repertoire as of today. Recordings of Layla's singles and duets with 'Abd al-Wahab sold out in few weeks, and their duet "Ya di al-na'im," in particular, enjoyed phenomenal success.[118] Fifteen years after releasing *Yahya al-Hub* and becoming a superstar, Layla Murad considered the film's premier the best day in her life: "I thought I was too shy to act, and my knowledge of acting was as poor as my knowledge of the hydrogen bomb. I thought the audience would receive me with a cold shrug and might even throw rocks at me. But when I saw myself on the screen, acting as if I were Sarah Bernhardt [the French play actress], I celebrated."[119]

Contrary to Zaki's fears, 'Abd al-Wahab bestowed almost instant financial success on his daughter when he had her give live concerts before releasing the film; he promoted her as a rising movie star and aroused the public's interest in their forthcoming picture. He chose Layla to sing with him at the wedding party of Makram 'Ubayd Pasha's brother; Makram 'Ubayd (1889–1961) was a former minister and one of the most influential leaders of the Wafd Party. In this way, 'Abd al-Wahab opened doors for Layla to become the star of the aristocrats' exclusive parties and the wealthy political elite.[120] His expression of confidence in Layla's talent and introduction to these elegant parties increased her popularity. Her association with elites also allowed her to charge more for her public concerts and private parties; the ticket price for Layla's concert in Upper Egypt rose to 1 Egyptian pound, an exorbitant price for a provincial concert on the stage of a local summer movie theater in Asyut. Although the venue could not promise more than a rough wooden seat in the open air on a hot summer evening, Layla's fame as the star of *Yahya al-Hub* was sufficient to justify the high price. It is worth noting that the title "Miss" preceded Layla's name—a sign of respectability.[121] The more audiences watched *Yahya al-Hub* in theaters, the more people bought the recordings of the movie's songs, both in Egypt and abroad.

Layla reaped the success of her first movie and translated it into money and control over her career. Layla's father managed her business and signed the contract for her first movie; according to Karim, all the talks were with Zaki, while "Layla was extremely shy but nice and polite."[122] Layla received 350 Egyptian pounds for starring in *Yahya al-Hub* and wished to sign an extended contract for two more films with Karim and 'Abd al-Wahab for the same amount, but Karim refused to take the risk. *Yahya al-Hub* grossed 26,500 Egyptian pounds, which came as no surprise, since 'Abd al-Wahab's *al-Warda al-Bayda'* grossed 28,000 Egyptian pounds.[123] Layla's success gave her the confidence to refuse to work with Karim and 'Abd al-Wahab in the next movie unless she received twice as much as for the first. She argued that her fee must compensate her for working full-time in the film, as her recent experience had taught her that she could not give performances during the shooting period, resulting in financial loss for her.[124] But Layla's argument failed to move Karim; the negotiations failed, and Raga' 'Abdu replaced her for 600 Egyptian pounds.[125] According to 'Abdu, appearing with 'Abd al-Wahab catapulted her into stardom and made hers a household name.[126]

Despite the fact that negotiations over doing a second film with 'Abd al-Wahab failed, Layla always expressed her gratitude for the opportunity to co-star with him in her first film.[127] "Like any young woman artist, I wished to work in cinema. [Working with 'Abd al-Wahab] was a great achievement even after the status I gained as a singer."[128] She had regretted leaving school and instead working to earn a living for the family, but performing with 'Abd al-Wahab restored her sense of respectability. Layla and 'Abd al-Wahab never co-starred in another film; after *Yahya al-Hub* 'Abd al-Wahab starred in only four more films. Nevertheless, he continued to play a role in Layla's career as a composer, as well as appearing and performing a song in her film *Ghazal al-Banat* (*The Flirtation of Girls*) in 1949, long after he stopped acting in movies. Despite recurring rumors that Layla and Muhammad Karim would work together again in a film, Karim disappeared from Layla's cinematic career. Instead, Layla's image and career on the silver screen were to shine through the brilliance of filmmakers Togo Mizrahi and Anwar Wagdi.

CHAPTER 2

THE COUNTRY GIRL

Branding Layla Murad

After *Layla* received great success, he [Togo Mizrahi] asked
me to play a blind girl in *Layla fi al-Zalam* [*Layla in the
Shadows*]. I screamed "Oh my God!" I learned to play a sick
woman, but how can I play a blind character? However, I
did it, and always thanks to him.[1]

Layla Murad, 1944

THE EXPERIENCED FILMMAKER Togo Mizrahi saw in Layla Murad
the talent that Muhammad Karim failed to appreciate. Leaving behind her
failed negotiations with 'Abd al-Wahab and Karim, Layla accepted an offer
to work with Togo Mizrahi on her second film, *Lailah Mumtira* (*Stormy
Night*), released in October 1939. She and Mizrahi followed the success of
Lailah Mumtira with four films: *Layla Bint al-Rif* (*Leila, the Girl from the
Country*; January 1941), *Layla Bint Madaris* (*Leila, the Schoolgirl*; October
1941), *Layla* (*Laila*; April 1942), and *Layla fi al-Zalam* (*Layla in the Shadows*; October 1944).[2] Mizrahi wrote, produced, and directed the films, and
more important, coached Layla to become the most successful actress-singer
in the Arab world. All five films were among the highest-grossing films in
Egyptian cinema during the interwar period. Mizrahi's choice to name the
female protagonist in four of the films "Layla" and place her first name in the

films' titles ensured that Layla became a household name. Before working with Layla Murad, Mizrahi had directed three comedies starring the Alexandrian Jewish actor Leon Angel (1900–1948), who developed the character "Chalom," which became Angel's on-screen name and persona. Yet the name Chalom appeared as part of a movie title only once, when Angel himself directed and starred in *Chalom al-turgaman* (*Chalom the Dragoman*; 1935).[3] The incorporation of her name in her movies' titles helped Layla become a unique cinematic persona, a trademark, and continued after she started working with other filmmakers, as she leveraged her fame in negotiating her fees with her producers, including Mizrahi himself.

Throughout her five films with Mizrahi, Layla polished her screen-performance skills and established the structure she followed for the remainder of her cinematic career. She performed five songs in each film, employing the best neoclassical musicians, including Muhammad al-Qasabgi, Riyad al-Sunbati, and Zakariya Ahmad, to compose the songs. With such modernizing composers, Layla broke away from the repertoire of the older generation, as well as honing the skills to show off her own voice's personality and rid herself of Umm Kulthum's influence.[4] Mizrahi's cast choices embellished Layla's stardom: in the first three films, he assigned the leading male role to the experienced Yusuf Wahbi (1898–1982), and then in two films to the rising star Husain Sidqi (1917–1976). Wahbi and Sidqi were from different generations and thus offered different sets of skills and experiences to share with Layla. Both of them continued to be part of her cinematic career, producing and directing films in which they co-starred with her. She continued her success with several other filmmakers after the end of her collaboration with Mizrahi. Perhaps more than any other filmmaker, Anwar Wagdi was responsible for reformulating her cinematic image after her work with Mizrahi. I shall discuss Layla's professional development via her interaction with the key male figures in her career and Egyptian cinematic history; Mizrahi, Wahbi, and Wagdi. Layla's history with male filmmakers illuminates how commercial cinema and the commercialization of stars increased the bargaining power of female stars to determine their fees; yet at the same time, female stars submitted to male producers and filmmakers, working in films that advocated for patriarchal social structures and disseminated male anxiety over women's sexuality. While articulating a critique of modernity through the modern medium of commercial cinema, Layla Murad's films promoted social patriarchy, offering it draped in colorful entertainment to men and women across classes and education levels.

Layla Murad and Togo Mizrahi

Layla Murad and Togo Mizrahi's collaborative works represent an important episode in the history of Egyptian and all of Arab cinema. Their films reveal intersections between the categories of cinema as a business, as entertainment, as art, and as social commentary. Layla began working with Mizrahi when she reached her maturity as a professional woman capable of managing her own talent and business. Until the launch of her cinematic career with *Yahya al-Hub*, Layla's father, Zaki Murad, had managed her business. The success of that film empowered Layla to renegotiate her wages; as recounted in the previous chapter, after Layla received 350 Egyptian pounds for *Yahya al-Hub*, she refused to sign with the producing company, Baydaphone, for less than 700 Egyptian pounds per film, which put an end to the possibility of her appearing with 'Abd al-Wahab in a second film directed by Muhammad Karim.[5] Mizrahi, who had already established himself as one of the leading figures in the film industry, offered Layla 1,200 Egyptian pounds for their first film together, *Lailah Mumtira*, and her father gladly signed the contract on her behalf. *Lailah Mumtira* proved to be a sound business decision, as the film cost only 6,000 Egyptian pounds to make and generated 9,000 Egyptian pounds in revenues for the first release.[6]

Following *Lailah Mumtira*, Layla Murad turned twenty-one, the legal age for an Egyptian citizen to have a fully independent legal and financial persona and responsibilities. She no longer needed her father as a legal guardian to represent her, and she had already exhausted her father's social networks, which had proved very useful in the early years of her career. When her mother passed away around that time, her father devoted more of his time to leisure, and so Layla now exercised full control over her financial and professional affairs. She proved herself a fierce negotiator and experienced professional. Encouraged by *Lailah Mumtira*'s success, Mizrahi prepared two scripts tailored for Layla, naming the protagonist in both films Layla and incorporating her name in their titles, demonstrating his intention to make Layla Murad a trademark that would bring audiences to theaters.

Layla rejected Mizrahi's offer of a slight raise from 1,200 Egyptian pounds to 1,250 per film and insisted on receiving 3,000 Egyptian pounds for each film. Confident about the films' financial success to come, Mizrahi accepted.[7] The title of their fourth film together, released in 1942, was one word, *Layla*, which signifies Layla Murad's having become a brand name. Her fee for *Layla* was more than double the fee she received for her previous film project with Mizrahi: 8,000 Egyptian pounds, an exorbitant fee at the time. Again, Mizrahi's business decision was sound: *Layla* set a box-office record.

Layla's financial negotiations with 'Abd al-Wahab and Karim and then with Mizrahi show that Layla was not a hopelessly romantic young woman isolated from reality but a confident adult with the courage to negotiate and the ability to maneuver. She appreciated her talent and intended to translate her skills into financial success. Following World War II the increase in movie production and demand for movie stars, particularly singing actresses, empowered Layla, and she understood the market well. She cherished her competent agency and became a tough negotiator with all her producers, including her future husband, Anwar Wagdi.

Aside from those featuring 'Abd al-Wahab and Umm Kulthum, films did not play in theaters in the 1930s and 1940s for longer than two weeks. The exceptional stardom of 'Abd al-Wahab and Umm Kulthum as vocalists, not actors, sold tickets to their fans who could not afford to attend live performances. Layla Murad's films with Mizrahi broke the rule; thanks to Mizrahi's brilliant direction together with Layla's beautiful voice and image, their five films together were among the highest-grossing films in their day. *Layla* broke all records and played in theaters for as long as fifteen to twenty-two weeks.[8] With Mizrahi, Layla became fully integrated into the studio system and submitted to the star-making industry, surrendering completely to Mizrahi's commercialization of their final product. He pulled out all the stops to generate profits from his films, including placing advertisements for consumer products in the film and using deceptive publicity. He deployed a frugal publicity campaign that did not exceed small weekly advertisements in the press but captured the attention of potential audiences through bizarre news and rumors.[9] For example, he created public sympathy for Layla by spreading the false news in the press that she had lost her down payment for *Lailah Mumtira* when she forgot the banknote in the pocket of her dress before she handed the dress over to be laundered.[10] He brought audiences to watch *Layla* by spreading rumors that Layla suffered from tuberculosis but was not aware of her condition, inducing sympathetic audiences to want to cheer up Layla, whom they believed to be dying.[11] Upon releasing another film, Layla fell sick and went to the hospital for an appendicitis operation; taking advantage of the situation for publicity, Mizrahi announced that Layla was undergoing sex-change operation. He circulated promotional material urging Layla's fans to "come to watch the movie that Layla played when she was still a woman."[12] According to Layla, her doctors allowed her to leave the hospital for the premiere; seeing the crowd coming to watch the film pleased her, but "there was a strange atmosphere, and in the way, people stared at me." Only later did Layla learn that Mizrahi had used her in this preposterous fashion to exploit people's curiosity about the newly developed sex-change operations.

Regardless of the morality of Mizrahi's publicity methods, his tactics bespeak his deep understanding of the commercialization of cinema; that is, that cinema is a product for mass consumption and caters to people across classes with differing levels of education and intellectual sophistication. Mizrahi and other pioneer producers realized that they needed to reach out to illiterate audiences, who did not read commercial ads in periodicals; nor did colorful billboard posters on central boulevards suffice to reach all potential viewers. In their quest to publicize their films among illiterate audiences in poor neighborhoods in Cairo and the provinces, producers and theater owners became creative and tricky. To get the word out and arouse people's curiosity, movie posters on huge wooden pyramids plied the streets on carriages dragged by donkeys and accompanied by brass bands; some parades handed out pictures of the film with images of the stars.[13] Some theaters offered soft drinks with a ticket; others provided tickets to students at reduced prices. Some theaters also offered live shows during intermission; others invited the audience to participate in raffles for monetary prizes up to 25 piastres for the winner.[14] Theaters honored coupons on cigarette packets and boxes of chocolates;[15] one company even gave audience members silk handkerchiefs bearing the movie stars' names and matchboxes with the stars' pictures.[16] Competition between theaters was limited, however, since there were not many of them; there were only one or two even in big towns such as

al-Mansura, al-Mahalla al-Kubra, Tanta, and al-Minya. Mizrahi understood
the market and worked to attract audiences through outrageous rumors and
emotional blackmail.

Mizrahi's Studio System and Egypt's Pluralism

We should appreciate Layla's impressive success in her five films with Mizrahi and in musical film in general in the context of Mizrahi's contribution
to the development of cinema as an art and an industry in the 1930s and
1940s.[17] Actor, producer, and filmmaker Togo Mizrahi was an Alexandrian
Jew with Italian nationality. He earned a degree in economics in France in
1923 and was fluent in several languages.[18] While working in a cotton export
company, he went back to Paris and received some training in Able Gance's
masterwork *Napoléon*, released in 1927. Mizrahi bought a 35mm camera and
used it to shoot landscapes in Paris, Rome, and Venice and succeeded in selling the films to a French company. He became the most prolific filmmaker
in Egypt, producing three films a season; in eight years, he directed twenty
films. The press admired and celebrated his achievement, calling him "*qadir*
[experienced and capable] and [having] rendered great service to the film
industry in Egypt."[19] Not all of Mizrahi's fellow filmmakers appreciated his
commercial and artistic success, instead looking down upon his frugal productions and modest studio in Alexandria. Muhammad Karim refused to
use Mizrahi's studio, describing it as a "garage where one could only produce
vulgar works."[20]

Mizrahi's first fiction film, al-*Kukayyin, al-Hawiya* (*Cocaine, the Abyss*;
1930), dealt with the social consequences of substance abuse among the
working classes. He promptly received a thank-you letter for combating
drugs from the Cairo chief of police, Sir Thomas Russell (Russell Pasha).
Encouraged by the film's financial success, Mizrahi bought a movie theater
in Alexandria and turned it into a studio in 1930.[21] He launched many successful projects in that studio before moving to Cairo eight years later. He
pioneered a studio system in Egypt wherein production studios made and
sold stars as brands with distinctive identities. As a producer, director, and
screenwriter, he formulated the main genres and successfully branded actors as stars with specific social identities; he branded the Carine actor 'Ali
al-Kassar as a Nubian, for example, and Shalom as a working-class Jew in a

series of successful films throughout the 1930s.[22] As in Hollywood, Mizrahi's pioneering commercial studio system considered the aesthetic and sociocultural aspects of feature filmmaking, making his movie productions a dynamic exchange between the film industry and its audience.[23] He sustained his success through genres, those popular narrative formulas including dramas, musicals, and historical films that all enjoyed popularity and dominated the screen in the first half of the twentieth century.

Mizrahi successfully reworked cinema production as a mix of art and industry, managing his productions as any other business geared toward making profit while also paying attention to each film's visual aesthetics and social message. As both an artist and an industrialist, he formulated the social comedy genre to disseminate commentaries about values and morality. His commercial cinema conveyed grand ideas about sex, gender, and pluralism. In five of Mizrahi's films between 1932 and 1937, Shalom (Leon Angel), a Jewish comedian with an unambiguously Jewish name, portrayed an ordinary working-class man living with his Muslim best friend. The publicity for the first of them, *05001*, advertised: "The first Egyptian story reveals the Egyptians' latent power." These successful films emphasized the harmonious relationships between Muslims and Jews and the full integration of Jews into Egyptian society; viewers could not miss the celebration of pluralism by way of the strong friendship between Shalom and 'Abdu, Jewish and Muslim working-class young men, in these films. The opening scene of *al-'Izz Bahdala* (*Mistreated by Affluence*; Togo Mizrahi, 1937), for example, shows Shalom and 'Abdu sharing a bed. Deborah Starr understands "in bed together" not as a metaphor of coexistence but as a key to unlocking Mizrahi's projection of sameness and difference, self and other, in 1930s Egypt.[24] Starr's reading of Shalom and 'Abdu's sameness underscores the performativity of coexistence through a discussion of what she calls the "Levantine idiom."[25] Produced when Egypt was experiencing a rise in Arab and Islamic nationalism that excluded the sizeable Jewish community, Mizrahi used cross-dressing, class-hopping, and hints of homosexuality to emphasize the performative and fluid nature of (Levantine) identity.[26] This Levantine aesthetic expresses a self-consciously repetitive performance: "The performance of identity is fluid and mutable, embracing vagueness and porousness of the boundaries of identity."[27] Viola Shafik suggests that Mizrahi's emphasis on the harmonious relationships among different religious communities reflects concerns about the loss of Egyptian pluralism as embodied in the 1919 Revolution rather than the assurance of its continuity.[28] However, having an explicitly Jewish protagonist played by a Jewish actor did not deter audiences from watching and enjoying the films. As indicated by their commercial success, the films' public perception provides evidence of the continuation of tolerance and coexistence; diverse communities can self-consciously value and construct plurality as part of their identities.[29] What may be important is not the "reality" of coexistence but rather its performance.

Mizrahi's Layla Brand

Mizrahi's contributions to Layla's success cannot be exaggerated. In five films, he reformulated her on-screen persona. She was radiant in his melodramas, even when the dialogue employed overdramatically theatrical language; no other filmmaker, aside from Anwar Wagdi, matched Mizrahi's achievement. Movie theaters inaugurated the season of October 1944 with the launch of Layla's first film with Kamal Salim, *Shuhada' al-Gharam* (*Victims of Love*; 1944) and her last film with Mizrahi, *Layla fi al-Zalam* (*Laila in the Shadows*; 1944). The great success of *Layla fi al-Zalam* as opposed to the limited popularity of *Shuhada' al-Gharam* shows how successful Mizrahi was in framing Layla's cinematic image and voice. Despite his more meager production budget, Mizrahi made canny choices that enhanced Layla's presentation: he made Layla's character central to every scene and chose not to cast other singer-actors with Layla in any of their five films together. Given that she performed five songs in each film, Layla dominated the screen for a third of each one.

Mizrahi chose Yusuf Wahbi, the most prominent figure in theatrical melodrama, to co-star with Layla in three films. Wahbi likewise boosted her career as a movie star gifted with a beautiful voice and acting talent. She gained valuable experience from Mizrahi and Wahbi as she performed in several different genres, from romantic comedy to melodrama. Mustafa Darwish and many other critics think that Togo Mizrahi swept Layla Murad up and made her into one of Egypt's top actresses of all time.[30] Layla glided smoothly from the colorfully velvet life of a pasha's daughter to that of an ailing, self-denying whore, from a rural-elite idealist to an urban fallen woman, from a funny and free-spirited woman to one who is depressed, blind, and terminally ill.

Layla's maturity as an actress is evident in her second film with Mizrahi and Wahbi, *Layla Bint al-Rif*, in which she plays two drastically different characters, a naïve rural woman and an arrogant urban-elite woman. In *Layla Bint Madaris*, her performance as a free-spirited, intelligent, and noble young woman reflects Layla's experience and talent, as she skillfully uses her voice, facial expressions, and body language to communicate the meaning. She performed her songs with soft facial expressions that enhance the lyrics, contrasting with Wahbi's overly dramatic acting. With *Layla* (1942) she became a phenomenal star. Playing a prostitute, Layla was so worried about people's perceptions that she did not attend the premiere, instead attending on the second day after receiving congratulations.[31] The protagonist is a fallen woman, but Layla's elegant performance turned the protagonist of the *Lady of the Camellias*, the same role played by Greta Garbo in the Hollywood production (*Camille*; George Cukor, 1936), into a fashion icon among Egyptian women. Her physical appeal disproved Karim's claims about her defective body; "Layla's waist" became a fashionable style of dress popular among women and a measure of how gifted a dressmaker was.

Layla's success in *Layla* invited critics to compare her favorably to Ruz al-Yusuf, who had played the same character on the stage decades earlier.[32] The songs from *Layla* were broadcast on the radio, which increased the impact of the promotions that appeared daily in the press. At that time, movie theaters lacked air-conditioning, so the first-tier movie theaters' first release of a film had to take place in the fall or winter; between May and September, open-air summer theaters and third-tier movie theaters showed the films from the previous seasons at discounted prices. Trying to take advantage of the last weeks of the winter season, Mizrahi released *Layla* in early April; remarkably, the film became such a sensation that it successfully continued playing until the end of July despite the summer heat. Wahbi had become too old to play a college student, and so Mizrahi chose Husain Sidqi (1917–1976) for the role of the male protagonist. Young, handsome, and educated in film acting, Sidqi was the perfect choice to play the romantic lover, whose emotions fluctuate between extreme love, jealousy, anger, and helpless sadness. Following their success in *Layla*, Mizrahi, Layla, and Sidqi worked together again in *Layla fi al-Zalam*.

Layla Murad and Husain Sidqi co-starred in five films between 1942 and 1955, the year of Layla's last film. In early spring 1944, Layla found her and Mizrahi's film *Layla fi al-Zalam* in direct competition with Muhammad 'Abd al-Wahab's *Rusasa fi al-Qalb* (*A Bullet in the Heart*; Muhammad Karim, 1944). Layla's film opened in theaters first, on February 24, and continued to play for several weeks after 'Abd al-Wahab and Karim released their *Rusasa fi al-Qalb* on March 17. Layla and Mizrahi won the hearts and minds of audiences and critics, while only 'Abd al-Wahab's popularity saved *Rusasa fi al-Qalb*. In the unavoidable comparison between Layla and Raqya Ibrahim, Karim's favorite actress, who starred in *Rusasa fi al-Qalb*, the press pointed out Raqya's weak acting and recognized Layla's superior performance; in particular, author and journalist Ahmad al-Sawi Muhammad, who later became editor-in-chief of *al-Ahram*, severely criticized *Rusasa fi al-Qalb* while praising *Layla fi al-Zalam*.[33] To add salt to the wound, al-Sawi accused 'Abd al-Wahab of being too cheap to pay Layla the high wage that she deserved and wrote that 'Abd al-Wahab did not hire Layla to co-star in his film because he was jealous of Layla, who had become "the greatest Egyptian singer and actress."[34] Muhammad Karim, who had underrated Layla's talent, had to admit that audiences watched his *Rusasa fi al-Qalb* to enjoy Muhammad 'Abd al-Wahab and his songs, but no one seemed to appreciate the director, the actors, or the author of the story.[35] Karim and Tawfiq al-Hakim, the author of *Rusasa fi al-Qalb*, accused al-Sawi of a lack of objectivity and holding personal grudges, while 'Abd al-Wahab refused to make any comment.[36] Not one of them countered the argument that *Layla fi al-Zalam* was a better film and that Layla's acting was superior to that of Raqya Ibrahim, or that Layla's songs were equal to 'Abd al-Wahab's. Not one of them denied that Layla had rejected an offer to work for 'Abd al-Wahab and Karim.

In *Layla fi al-Zalam*, which turned to be her last film with Mizrahi, Layla plays a blind young woman, a role so challenging that she had to undergo intensive preparation to prove herself as an actress. She said the character affected her so much that she kept behaving like a blind woman in her personal life.[37] She considered it one of her favorite parts and credited Togo Mizrahi as her teacher in cinema:

When I signed my [first] contract with Mr. Togo Mizrahi, I did not expect
I'd accomplish what I achieved today in acting. I made it clear that I'm only a
singer and can perform singing parts but have no acting abilities. He did his
best and took baby steps with me, then made me jump. I could not believe my
eyes when I saw myself in *Layla*. Is this me, Layla Murad, who acted happy,
gullible, sick, and dead? I believe he is a great teacher and filmmaker, and I'll
never forget his teachings and guidance.[38]

Stealing Scenes: Layla and Yusuf Wahbi

Yusuf Wahbi (1898–1982) played the leading male character in the first three
of Layla's films with Togo Mizrahi: *Lailah Mumtira*, *Layla Bint al-Rif*, and
Layla Bint Madaris. Hailing from a notable rural family in al-Fayyum province, Wahbi formally gained the honorific title *Bey*. He studied acting in
Italy, established the Ramsis Theater Troupe and Ramsis Cinema Studio, and
cofounded Nahhas Film for the Cinema Production company. He worked in
silent cinema and starred in the first Egyptian sound film, *Awlad al-Dhawat*
(*Sons of Aristocrats*; Muhammad Karim, 1932). In sum, when Yusuf Wahbi
Bey met Layla Murad for her first of Mizrahi's productions, he already had
a distinguished career as one of the most influential acting stars, producers,
and directors in cinema and theater. Yet despite Wahbi's stature and experience on the stage and screen, it was Layla's presence that dominated their
films, and her character, not his, that attracted the most attention. In all of
Mizrahi's films with Layla, he made the female protagonist the center of
focus and attention.

Layla had to both compete with and learn from the experienced Yusuf
Wahbi. He and Mizrahi taught her to take herself seriously as an actress in
order to focus the audience's attention on herself in every scene. She learned
to become what in Egyptian cinema vernacular is known as a "camera thief,"
that is, an actor who steals scenes. The term is a metaphor that designates
actors who are able to manipulate light and shadow, body and facial expressions, and the position of their bodies to capture the audience's attention so
that they ignore any other actors in the same scene. Being a camera thief
requires the professional skill to grab attention in a scene without changing
any words or stage directions. Yusuf Wahbi hoarded and honed these skills;
he also used his ultradramatic voice to hold the audience's attention. Some

anecdotes show that female stars, including Fatima Rushdi (1908–1996), refused to appear with Wahbi because of his ability to steal all of the audience's
attention.[39] With Mizrahi's help, Layla developed the same ability to capture
and hold viewers' attention in every scene in which she appeared.

By now, Layla had gained enough confidence to leave Mizrahi's studio
and work with other producers and filmmakers. Producers who had refused
to pay her 3,000 Egyptian pounds for a film a couple of years earlier now
agreed to pay her 12,000.[40] Wahbi was eager to repeat his successful appearance with Layla after Mizrahi replaced him with Husain Sidqi as the male
protagonist. He wrote a script titled *Gawhara* (*Jewel*) and convinced his partners in the Nahhas Film production company that he should co-star in it with
Layla. After Layla had signed the contract, Mizrahi persuaded her to reject
the film because she would have played a poor girl collecting cigarette ends in
the streets, which conflicted with the classy image that Mizrahi had framed
for her, as well as overturning the cinematic structure in which the focus of
the story line was on Layla's character. Since Wahbi wrote the script, partly
owned the producing company, and directed the film, he had full control over
the project: the male protagonist, played by himself, dominated the story and
appeared in almost every scene, leaving little space or time for the female
protagonist and other characters. Layla rejected the project, and the fine stipulated in her contract with the producer was paid on her behalf by Mizrahi,
who aimed to monopolize her talent and ensure that she appeared only in his
productions; he then signed a contract with her for his *Layla fi al-Zalam*.[41]

Responding to Layla's rejection, Wahbi recruited a rising Lebanese
singer named Alexandra Badran, whose stage name became Nur al-Huda
(1924–1998) and cast her in the film. *Gawhara* (1943) achieved considerable
success, which encouraged Wahbi to follow it up with another picture, *Berlanti* (1944), the following year. Many believed that Wahbi decided to bring
a singer-actress from Lebanon to compete with Layla in Egyptian cinema,
but in any case Wahbi's choice of Nur al-Huda proved economically astute:
Nur al-Huda accepted a mere 150 Egyptian pounds for the film, although
Wahbi also paid 2,500 Lebanese lira (about 285 pounds sterling) to a nightclub where Nur al-Huda worked in Beirut so she could go to Cairo.[42]

Between the release of *Layla* on April 2, 1942, and *Layla fi al-Zalam* on
October 19, 1944, movie theaters went for the longest time without a new film

by Layla Murad since Layla launched her cinematic career. Layla must have felt herself to be at a crossroads. Perhaps she regretted rejecting *Gawhara*, and its success may have made her rethink her choices. She had to reconsider the public mood, which had welcomed a poor collector of cigarette ends as a protagonist. She also likely considered the increasing competition from other singing stars, particularly those coming from Lebanon. Nur al-Huda became the most prolific singer-actress, starring in twenty-three films in the decade between 1943 and 1953 and working with the best singer-actors, including composers Muhammad 'Abd al-Wahab, Farid al-Atrash, and Muhammad Fawzi.

In addition to Nur al-Huda, the Lebanese Asmahan al-Atrash appeared with her brother Farid in their first film, *Intisar al-Shabab* (*Victory of Youth*; Ahmad Badrakhan, 1941), and Sabah appeared in Asya's production *al-Qalb luh Wahid* (*The Heart Has Its Reasons*; Henry Barakat, 1945). Although Layla rejected *Gawhara* because she did not wish to play a poor cigarette-end collector, she went on to play a poor radish-seller in *Shadiyat al-Wadi* (*The Singer in the Valley*; Yusuf Wahbi, 1947). She also appeared with Wahbi in Studio Misr's production *Darbat al-Qadar* (*The Blow of Fate*; Yusuf Wahbi, 1947). Wahbi wrote and directed both films, and the story line of *Darbat al-Qadar* was close to that of their first film together, *Lailah Mumtira*. Layla again played a naïve woman who gives birth to a child out of wedlock and pleads for societal forgiveness. This film accused deceptive young men of taking advantage of women who were poorly equipped and unprepared for the rapid changes of modernity. Warning about endangered women's virginity in unruly urban life proved to be Wahbi's favorite theme; his often-repeated phrase "A girl's honor is like a matchstick, it lights up only once" became part of Egyptian slang. The story line of *Shadiyat al-Wadi* was likewise close to another of his earlier films, *Gawhara*; both films depict a famous composer who turns a poor girl into a renowned professional singer. Neither *Darbat al-Qadar* nor *Shadiyat al-Wadi* met with notable success or failure. Layla and Wahbi continued their collaboration after Wahbi had to give up playing leading male roles, which went to younger stars such as Anwar Wagdi. Wahbi played himself, using his real name and persona, in Layla's and Wagdi's *Ghazal al-Banat* (*The Flirtation of Girls*; Anwar Wagdi, 1949). He also appeared with Layla and Wagdi in the supporting male role in *Habib al-Ruh* (*Eternal Love*; Anwar Wagdi, 1951).

Men Making Layla Murad's Cinema

Layla Murad's films with Mizrahi and Wahbi, along with other early Egyptian films, are significant for their role in constructing Egyptian social norms, specifically in normalizing particular notions of gender and sexuality. Art is rooted in socially constructed systems of taste, and lack of "good taste" is constructed through artistic expression.[43] Layla Murad's films were commercial, and commercial cinema provided commentary on contemporary social realities despite its function as escapist entertainment.[44] Her films in collaboration with male filmmakers and stars such as Mizrahi, Wahbi, Wagdi, and Sidqi expressed and publicized certain social ideologies concerning class, gender, and sexuality; after 1945, her marriage to Anwar Wagdi and conversion to Islam resulted in Islam's becoming an intrinsic aspect of her films.

Women played crucial roles in establishing the Egyptian film industry in its early years, the 1920s and 1930s. Delighting in the new medium, 'Aziza Amir, Fatma Rushdi, and Bahiga Hafiz, among others, directed, produced, and acted in films, employing their talent and personal financial resources to launch cinema as an art form rather than a business or profession. Layla Murad came to Egyptian cinema after it had become a male-dominated industry, aimed at providing entertainment to mass consumers and generating profit. Neither she nor the producers and filmmakers she worked with engaged in public discussions about abstract aesthetic notions or social reality. They assumed that films depicting the reality of the lives of workers and peasants would have only limited success, that most moviegoers had no desire to see the world in which they lived but wanted to spend time with the upper classes living in places of which they had no experience but only heard or read about in novels: places such as theaters, music halls, newspaper offices, grand hotels, stock markets, beach resorts, horse races, fashionable stores, sports clubs, and gambling clubs.[45] Most films at that time were dominated by themes of love and relationships between men and women. Love in films had to be simpler than in literature and theater plays: no psychoanalysis, no moral struggles.[46] Happy endings, that is, the marriage of the two lovers after overcoming any obstacles and the triumph of good over evil, provided uplift to audiences and gave them comfort. Not surprisingly, since male writers, producers, and filmmakers decided on the films' themes, Layla's films communicated an exclusively male perspective on women's bodies, sexuality, and position in the family and society: Yusuf Wahbi's concern with women's sexual honor, Husain Sidqi's emphasis on preserving patriarchal family values, and Anwar Wagdi's advocacy for love across classes infused Layla's films. These popular themes gave comfort rather than challenging mass audiences seeking entertainment that reinforced their convictions about women's position in the family and society. Thus, Layla's agency served to spread male-crafted social messages even when they clearly contradicted her real-life choices as a professional woman and wife.

Unruly Sexuality in Urban Life

Layla Murad's second film, *Lailah Mumtira* (written, produced, and directed by Togo Mizrahi), offers a blend of melodramatic speech, Egyptian belly dance, Sudanese dance, and Layla's beautiful voice singing five melodies. Consistent with Mizrahi's previous films, this one features panoramic views of Cairo, as Mizrahi situates the entire film in an urban setting. Saniya, played by Layla, has failed her baccalaureate exam twice on account of her lack of ability in math. Ali, a gangster, lures Saniya into a sexual encounter to force her father to accept their marriage, but then he flees the country to escape arrest for another crime, leaving Saniya pregnant and unmarried. To cover up Saniya's scandalous mistake, her nanny hires Ahmad Khaled (played by Yusuf Wahbi), an unemployed but highly educated engineer who urgently needs money to support his ailing mother, to marry her and provide her child with a legal father. Before falling into dire poverty in Cairo, Ahmad held a prestigious position as an engineer in Rome until the Italian fascist regime banned foreigners from working in industry and trade. (Since Wahbi himself had lived and studied in Rome, his ability to speak Italian lent realism to the film.) Following his superficial marriage to Saniya, Ahmad is mistreated by both Saniya and her father: Saniya's father looks upon him as a villain who took advantage of and impregnated his innocent daughter; Saniya views him as a bum who doesn't mind living off a woman's wealth. Saniya continues her reckless lifestyle, constantly partying with her upper-class friends. Ahmad eventually gets a job, though neither Saniya nor her father notices until his employer coincidentally attends a party at their villa and expresses his admiration for the hard-working, intelligent young man. Ahmad asks Saniya to give up her wild life, as she is his wife and thus obligated to protect his name and reputation, but she gives him the cold shoulder and insults him. He throws the money he received from her father in her face to let her know he doesn't need her money and show her that he is a man of dignity who refuses to allow his pseudowife to continue her wild lifestyle. He leaves for Sudan to pursue a project to generate hydraulic power from the Nile to illuminate Egyptian villages and operate factories. But living apart leads Saniya and Ahmad to realize they are in love with each other. Upon his unexpected return to Cairo, he eavesdrops on Saniya and her former boyfriend, who has also just returned to Egypt, and learns that Ali deceived Saniya, who was resisting his malevolent attempts to intervene in her life. Ahmad also learns that she has been respectful and loyal to him while he was gone. Ahmad hits Ali and drives him out of Saniya's life. The superficial marriage becomes a real marriage, based on mutual love and respect.

The film includes unbelievable coincidences, for example, Ahmad's return from Sudan and arrival at the house just when the gangster, Ali, is threatening and blackmailing Saniya. It is also implausible that Saniya suddenly fell in love with Ahmad when he threw the money in her face. Additionally, Saniya does not appear to be pregnant in any scene, nor does the audience get to see the baby; more important, it is not clear why Ahmad, who does not respect or trust Saniya, simply agrees to give his name to a child that isn't his. In the film Wahbi gave his usual melodramatic stage performance, which impacted Layla's performance, particularly when she knelt and kissed Ahmad's feet while asking for forgiveness in the final scene. This last scene sums up the film's message about sexuality and gender hierarchy: the good man stands tall with dignity, while the good woman shows her love, appreciation, and regret for a reckless moment by kneeling and kissing his feet. Women should avoid mingling with men lest they fall in love and fail to guard their sexual honor; a girl's virginity and a woman's sexual purity were essential to preserving her family status, no matter how modern or wealthy her family. Ahmad Khalid represents the modern Egyptian, or masculine *afandi*: educated, hard-working, caring about his mother, rejecting money from his wife, and full of dignity and pride. He combines modernism, Western education, and foreign languages with oriental authenticity. Discussions of the performativity of modernism combined with authenticity that define the masculinity of the middle-class bourgeoisie (*effendiyya*) differentiate Egyptian modernity from Western colonial models during the interwar years.[47] The masculine *afandi* embodies both modernism and authenticity, while his moral superiority and gender justify his patriarchal power over women, even when his wife is richer than he.

Lailah Mumtira was the first in a series of productions that were part of the "virginity industry," which continued in Egyptian cinema for decades to come. The film communicates a strong message about women's bodies and the importance of virginity and sexual purity. Story lines warning girls to stay away from bad boys resonate with the forces of traditionalist conservatism, stigmatizing women's sexual desire and branding their longing for love as inconsiderate inasmuch as they risked staining their family's honor. The gravest error such a woman could make was having premarital sex. But a repentant woman who gave up her free spirit and returned to the righteous path, that is, agreed to obey her husband, was worthy of forgiveness. The film endorses the patriarchal tradition, patronizing women as being weak, mindless, and easily falling victim to bad men and modern life, which offers them an excessive amount of freedom and leads them away from virtue.

According to *Lailah Mumtira*, women are not prepared for the sweeping changes of modern urban life; Saniya's failure to attain academic success leaves her no path other than being a wife and mother. According to the film, a woman's ideal position in society is to become a responsible wife willing to kneel and kiss her protecting husband's feet. Messages sent by the film are contradictory, expressing male anxiety over women's sexuality in the age of women's liberation. On the one hand, women's sexuality is dangerous, and women are unable to preserve their and their families' sexual honor. On the other hand, women are victims of the modern life that men lure them into without familial preparation or supervision. Echoing the romanticism that dominated the literary scene in the early twentieth century, *Lailah Mumtira* suggests that fallen women deserve a second chance provided they surrender to male authority. As early as 1910, the writer Mustafa Lutfi al-Manfaluti (1876–1924) encouraged men to marry sex workers and provide them with the compassion and love that would make them give up their trade:[48] a good, caring man is capable of teaching a woman self-respect and bringing her back to the righteous path. The male protagonist in *Lailah Mumtira* transforms

Saniya from a madcap, party-loving woman into a respectful and respectable wife, owing to his personal characteristics that combine the functional aspects of modern life: a modern education that includes traditional values and ethics, a desire to work hard, and a willingness to sacrifice in order to uphold his mother's and his wife's respectability.

The film represents the construction of the new masculinity, as manifested in Ahmad's engineering degree, work experience in Italy, and willingness to move to Sudan to execute his impressive construction project. Driven by nationalism, he designs a project to strengthen his nation and modernize its economy. He never compromises his authentic morality and refuses to live off his father-in-law's wealth as a hired husband. Ahmad initially accepts the money in order to cover the medical costs of his ailing mother; he also accepts the deal out of pity for Saniya's respectable family, whose reputation will be damaged unless he covers up her illicit pregnancy. After marrying Saniya, he rejects the easy life she offers him in return for turning a blind eye to her imprudent lifestyle. He does not allow her to emasculate him in return for money; instead, he accepts the responsibility of a man to work hard and earn his living, as well as protecting Saniya from her former lover, the gangster who tries to blackmail her.

Lailah Mumtira sets up an apparent dichotomy between "good" and "bad" modern urban life. The noble male protagonist, Ahmad, rose to the emotional and moral challenges he faced when moving to Europe for education and embraced "good nationalist masculinity," which continues as he moves between Egypt and Sudan to engineer a project that will contribute to Egypt's modernization. The gangster who deceived Saniya, Ali, epitomizes vulgarity, greed, and all the urban vices; he mocks education and manages an underworld business in a nightclub. *Lailah Mumtira* established the Egyptian cinematic tradition of representing nightclubs as vile places. An exclusively urban hangout, the nightclub is an unruly space populated by drunken gangsters, hustlers, drug dealers, and villains who use women's sexual honor as a means of blackmailing honorable families. The film also warns against men and women intermingling at parties where the urban wealthy spend their leisure time with no respect for traditional moral values, parties that became an emblem of corrupt modern life. Defaming nightclubs and those who patronize them gratified audiences who could not afford to spend their leisure time there.

Mizrahi and Wahbi's films with Layla are typical of Egyptian melodrama in the interwar period, when rape and seduction narratives dominated the silver screen. According to one estimate, more than 50 percent of Egyptian films during the 1942/43 season presented the seduction or rape of women.[49] This proliferation of such narratives should be read in the context of the "strong national sentiments" in the years before the 1952 Free Officer's coup.[50] As Beth Baron has documented extensively, the nationalist Egyptian press, dating back at least as far as 1919, commonly depicted Egypt as a woman and British occupation as the "rape of the nation."[51]

Eight years after the release of *Lailah Mumtira*, Yusuf Wahbi and Layla Murad co-starred again in *Darbat al-Qadar*, whose story line was not very different from *Lailah Mumtira*. Based on a story by Émile Zola, *Madeleine Férat* (1868), the film was directed by Wahbi. After her illegitimate infant dies, the female protagonist of *Darbat al-Qadar* returns to the righteous path, obeying gender and sexual mores and becoming a faithful wife and caring stepmother. She helps her respectable husband overcome the pain caused by his former wife, who abandoned him and their child for urban nightlife. The couple's new life comes under threat when the husband's brother returns from Europe, and Layla realizes that the brother is her former boyfriend who had impregnated and abandoned her. Once more, the villains—the ex-wife and the brother—embody modern urban life's moral and material corruption, trading sexual honor and family values for the destructive pleasures of nightlife. The film also advocates for the rehabilitation of women and their being welcomed back to the premises of a respectable life.

Consumerism Is Good in the Corrupt, Seductive City

In their second film, *Layla Bint al-Rif* (*Layla the Girl from the Country*; Togo Mizrahi, 1941), Mizrahi, Wahbi, and Layla repeated their warnings against the uncontrollable sexuality and corrupt urban life unleashed by modernity. and lament the loss of authentic rural purity and beauty. In the film, Yusuf's mother is the matriarch of a wealthy rural family who forces her son (played by Wahbi) to marry her niece, Layla, who is already in love with her urbanite

cousin, Yusuf. (Marriage between cousins was, and still is, not unusual in
Egypt, particularly among landowning families. Islamic law sanctions marriage between cousins, which landowning families encourage in order to keep
their land undivided.) Yusuf agrees to marry his cousin so that his mother
won't disown him; he needs his mother's wealth in order to avoid working
and to fund his luxurious life in Cairo, where he devotes his time to the
pleasures of nightlife. He considers his cousin Layla a crude peasant girl who
would be unable to adapt to his "modern city life." Moving with her to Cairo
after marriage, he isolates her in an apartment in their house and continues
to enjoy drinking and dancing parties with his friends. Samira, an old girlfriend of Layla's from the French boarding school that Layla had attended,
meets her and learns about her situation. Samira reminds Layla that their
French education has equipped her well to adapt to Yusuf's lifestyle and suggests she teach him a lesson.

Samira helps Layla change her appearance to show off her elegant beauty
and urbanity, surpassing all the other women in Yusuf's circle. Although
Layla's beauty stuns her wayward husband, she rejects his initial attempts
to reconcile with her in order to teach him a lesson about dignity and self-
respect. One of Yusuf's friends tries to manipulate Layla's alienation in order
to gain access to her wealth. Yusuf mistakenly thinks that Layla rejected him
because she had an affair with that friend; he divorces her. But Layla's rejection and return to her home village lead Yusuf to see how meaningless,
empty, and immoral his city life is. He realizes the importance of putting
his medical education to work and devotes himself to treating patients from
all classes and advancing his career. Then, by coincidence, the friend who
failed to seduce Layla is severely injured in a car accident and brought to
Yusuf for an operation. The dying friend confesses that his attempt to destroy
Yusuf and Layla's marriage failed because Layla was faithful to Yusuf. The
film ends with Yusuf rushing to the village and begging Layla for forgiveness,
which she happily grants. Thus, *Layla Bint al-Rif* presents a harsh contrast
between the "innocence" of the Egyptian countryside and "immoral" urban
modernism. Modern life is wasteful, allowing wealthy modern men to squander money and time dancing, drinking, and courting loose women, and those
with good Western educations to squander their valuable educations rather
than put their skills to good use in serving society.

From the very first scene, the film romanticizes the countryside, with Layla Murad performing her song "al-Hub" (Love). Knowing her cousin Yusuf is on his way back to the village, Layla gathers flowers and arranges them in vases. But roaming the fields, singing in the open air, and picking flowers while dressed in traditional female peasant garb had nothing to do with the actual rural life of that time. Wealthy rural women did not dress as peasants, and they lived segregated indoors; they had no opportunity to enjoy free-spirited singing and picking flowers. The scene depicting Egyptian villages as places of purity and happiness contradicted reality: the decline of public health, rampant poverty, and unemployment among Egyptian peasants has been well documented by contemporary scholarship.[52] By contrast, the ultraclean and romantic rural milieu depicted in the film enjoy modern communication technologies such as the telegraph; the rural mother orders men in her household to send a telegram recalling her son from the city, and a reel of images shows how the mother's oral order becomes a typed telegram, wired and then delivered by a bicycle-riding postman. These images celebrate transportation and communications technology as tools to facilitate human mobility and connectedness, not to transform values or challenge traditions. In that idealized milieu, women are powerful and in control of the family's wealth: Yusuf's mother chooses his future wife against his will and lectures him on peasant women's virtue. So powerful a rural mother doesn't need feminism; she already controls the men in her household. Being more than escapist entertainment, *Layla Bint al-Rif* idealizes the Egyptian countryside as a repository of authentic values that embrace both social respectability and modern technology, thereby positioning the village as the virtuous opposite of the corrupt city.

Department Stores in the Age of Mass Consumption

Mizrahi embedded commercials overtly throughout *Layla Bin al-Rif*, advertising department stores, jewelry and furniture stores, brands of soap, and other products.[53] Department stores gained high visibility in public life through intensive advertising in the early twentieth century's expanding print media.[54] During the interwar period, many stars appeared in commercial advertisements published in the print press: Umm Kulthum, for instance, was the advertising star for the Nabulsi Faruq brand of soap in the late 1930s and throughout the 1940s, while Layla Murad was featured in advertisements for cigarettes and motorcycles. Occasionally, film credits included the names of furniture stores that provided items for shootings, such as furniture and curtains. Department stores were also used as the settings for films, short stories, cartoons, and advertisements beginning in the early twentieth century;[55] popular films such as *Salama fi Kheir* (*Salama Is Safe*; Niyazi Mustafa, 1937) and *Lu'bat al-Sitt* (*The Lady's Puppet*; Wali al-Din Samih, 1946) used fictional department stores as settings for many of their key scenes. Mizrahi made use of commercial advertisement as a source of funding, although we are unsure whether he was the first director to do so because many films produced during the early decades of Egyptian cinema are missing. Prior to *Layla Bint al-Rif*, Mizrahi included an advertisement for Philips radio and products from the large retailer Shorbaji in his film *al-Sa'a Saba'a* (*Seven O'Clock*; 1936), and his film *al-'Izz bahdala* (*Mistreated by Affluence*; 1939) promoted Mizrahi's studio productions by showing a building in the background displaying posters for his other films.[56]

Layla Bint al-Rif urged viewers to buy and consume urban modern commodities, a message that contradicts the film's critique of the seductions of modern life. The camera takes viewers on a scenic tour showing upbeat Cairo life, slowing down to focus on the façades of some establishments or billboards on the road and allowing audiences to read the names of products and stores. The brand names on shopping bags, printed in Arabic and European languages, are highly visible, while the film's dialogue incorporates brand names promoting various products, aimed particularly at illiterate audiences. These overtly commercial advertisements, which add nothing to the story, targeted audiences as consumers from all classes, upper, middle, and lower. Mizrahi's reel of urban commodities and stores shrewdly entertained viewers while at the same time generating more revenue from the paid advertisements. The contradiction between encouraging and benefiting from consumerism, on the one hand, and story lines condemning a westernized urban lifestyle, on the other, reveals a selectivity in dealing with modernism and westernization.

In rationalizing a selectivity toward westernization, *Lailah Mumtira* and *Layla Bint al-Rif* espoused learning European languages and receiving a European education in institutions such as Cambridge University and the

Pensionnat de la Mère de Dieu in Egypt. The films communicate that modern education is valuable when put to use to help people and when men and women combine it with authentic traditional values. The character Layla in *Layla Bint al-Rif* is portrayed as an exemplary Egyptian woman, refashioning herself to adapt to modern urban life in order to please her husband, yet at the same time still embracing sexual honor and family values. Her husband, on the contrary, exemplifies the downside of modern values, neglecting his European medical education and blindly infatuated by the superficial offerings of modern life, such as dancing and drinking parties. In the film, it is women who preserve the authentic moral values of Egypt: while Yusuf's wife refashions herself to achieve a modern look, she preserves her chastity, and she pushes him to discover the value and importance of hard work and use his modern education for serving the nation. In both films, Mizrahi struck a gender balance in debating authenticity versus westernization and urban recklessness versus authenticity in the countryside. Cinema, a modern mass communication medium, promulgated regressive ideas about women's bodies and sexuality. Mizrahi's and Wahbi's films, including films featuring Layla Murad, contributed to underlining women's virginity in modern social morality and deemed women's sexuality as a damaging force that needed to be contained. Their films featuring Layla Murad also supported the division of labor according to the patriarchal gender regime in which the man employs his education to serve the nation, while the woman employs her education to better perform her domestic duties as a modern wife.

Mizrahi based his film *Layla* (1942) on Alexandre Dumas's *The Lady of the Camellias*, setting the story in 1892 Cairo. Despite some slight influence of the American film from 1937, Mizrahi succeeded in Egyptianizing the story while staying faithful to the original French novel. The social norms of the elite classes in the late nineteenth century are shown, such as the segregation between men and women at parties and the anxiety of conservative parents about the moral virtue of their sons. The son is allowed by his family to live away from home in the capital city for education but is assigned a male servant to watch over him, and once he has graduated, his parents expect him to marry a woman from a suitable family. But the son falls in love with a prostitute, Layla, who provides her services to elite men capable of supporting her lavish lifestyle. When she in turn falls in love with the student, she happily devotes herself to him despite the fact that she cannot afford her medical expenses. Her noble nature leads her to accede to the plea of the father of her lover to stay away from his son in order to protect his future and the status of their family, thereby sacrificing both love and life. Layla dies of tuberculosis , leaving her lover to think that she has gone back to her clients; from his father he learns of her noble sacrifice.

The film epitomizes the romantic approach that had dominated Arabic literature since the early 1900s, as embodied in Mustafa al-Manfaluti's translation of the novel and his plea for forgiving fallen women and providing them with salvation through marriage. *Layla* combines the dichotomy of the whore and the self-sacrificing woman. In most of her other films with Mizrahi and Wahbi, Layla portrays a fallen woman returning to the righteous path of sacrifice and love. In *Layla Bint Madaris* (*Layla, the Schoolgirl*; Togo Mizrahi, 1941), Layla sacrifices herself to save her beloved from knowing that his fiancée cheated on him with another man. In her last film directed by Mizrahi, *Layla fi al-Zalam* (*Layla in the Shadows*; 1944), Layla loses her sight and sacrifices her love, in order to save her beloved from a miserable life with her.

The call to restrict women to their domestic duty of obeying and serving their husbands comes across loud and clear in Layla's films *Habib al-Ruh* (*Eternal Love*; Anwar Wagdi, 1951) and *Adam wa Hawwa'* (*Adam and Eve*; Husain Sidqi, 1951). Actor, producer, and filmmaker Husain Sidqi, in particular, was open about his commitment to producing films that communicated his conservative values and religiosity as a devout Muslim. Sidqi built a mosque adjacent to his own home in the al-Ma'adi neighborhood of southern Cairo. Muslim Brotherhood sources claim that he was one of their followers, or at least a sympathizer.[57] (The same sources have made similar claims about many other stars, including Anwar Wagdi, which I shall refute in the following chapter.) Whether or not Sidqi had a connection to the Brotherhood, the conservative patriarchal discourse of his films was in no way different from those of Wahbi or Anwar Wagdi.

Layla in Post-Mizrahi Cinema

In 1944, movie theaters showed two films starring Layla Murad: *Layla fi al-Zalam* in February, her last film with Togo Mizrahi, and *Shuhada' al-Gharam* (*Victims of Love*) in October, directed by Kamal Salim (1913–1945), with Anwar

Wagdi playing opposite her in both films. *Layla fi al-Zalam* bolstered Layla's self-confidence and readiness to work with filmmakers other than Mizrahi; she also needed to refashion herself in the face of increased competition from Lebanese singer-actresses. Layla worked with the pioneering social realist filmmaker Kamal Salim, whose films charted the way for realism in Egyptian cinema. Before *Shuhada' al-Gharam*, he had directed six films, four of them musicals; singing stars Umm Kulthum and Farid al-Atrash worked with him. Salim was fond of musicals, the most appealing genre to audiences and most successful at the box office throughout the 1930s and 1940s.

Making *Shuhada' al-Gharam* with Salim was a new experience for Layla in several ways: for the first time, she appeared in historical clothing and in historical locations. Based on Shakespeare's *Romeo and Juliet*, *Shuhada al-Gharam*'s story line itself was nothing new; Egyptian audiences had seen an adaptation of the same story by the end of the nineteenth century on the stage of Iskandar Farah theater and on the movie screen in 1942 in Muhammad Karim's *Mamnu' al-Hub*. Salim refashioned the story by situating his film in the Mamluk period (1250–1517) and blending the romantic story with the life of the popular classes in contemporary Cairo. He shot parts of the film in the Citadel of Saladin and included actual scenes of the Baktashiyya Sufi band and its lodge, scenes that exposed the unpleasing run-down conditions of the lodge and its band members, thereby provoking their leader, Baba Siri, to complain to the Royal Palace about the film. The complaint led to a debate in the press, but the Royal Palace ignored it.[58] Neglecting the complaint reflected the weak position of Sufi bands in Egyptian public life and politics rather than the power of cinema or a tendency to embrace freedom of expression. Explicit sexual scenes and obscene dialogue were (and still are) the most frequent reason for censoring films throughout the history of Egyptian cinema since the silent film *Ma'sat al-Haya* (*Life Is Misery*; Wedad Orfi, 1929). Authorities also suspended showings of films or banned them altogether based on complaints or fear of widespread protests. For example, the Royal Palace banned *Lashin* (Fritz Kramp, 1938) until the filmmakers changed the original script that called for a popular revolution against a corrupt monarch. A few months after the release of *Shuhada' al-Gharam*, the government banned the film *al-Suq al-Sawda'* (*Black Market*; Kamil al-Tilmisani, 1945) on account of its critical socioeconomic content.

Layla's films directed and produced by Mizrahi successfully played in theaters for nineteen weeks, and Layla used that success to increase her fees. Producer Gabriel Talhami agreed to pay her 12,000 Egyptian pounds for *Shuhada' al-Gharam*.[59] Hoping to cover the extravagant cost and earn a profit, Talhami launched a heavy promotional campaign before releasing the film.[60] The Kursaal Theater turned its façade into the famous balcony of the Shakespearian *Romeo and Juliet*, with images of Layla Murad and her co-star, singer Ibrahim Hamuda. The façade attracted public attention, but audience enthusiasm didn't last and *Shuhada' al-Gharam* was not as successful as Layla's previous films. Illustrator and author Salah Tantawi criticized Salim's script, which turned the romantic tragedy into a thriller overloaded with tribal wars, chases, and sword fights, and said that Layla's character appeared depressed and that all her songs sounded like tearful weeping. Tantawi described the songs composed by Riyad al-Sunbati and Muhammad al-Qasabgi as "bad music and prosaic lyrics."[61] Layla suffered under massive wigs and accessories as well as heavy historical clothing; her facial and body movements were inexpressive. Film critic and scriptwriter Rafiq al-Sabban attributes the film's failure to Ibrahim Hamuda's performance and his inability to convince the audience that he was Romeo, in addition to Salim's inability to manage Layla's talent.[62]

Learning from his experience in *Shuhada al-Gharam*, Salim modified a new script he had written for Anwar Wagdi to produce and co-star in with Layla Murad, *Layla Bint al-Fuqara'* (*Layla, Daughter of the Poor*; Anwar Wagdi, 1945). As Mizrahi had done before him, Salim framed Layla's persona as the central character and adopted her name and brand. Wagdi started promoting the film long before shooting began, and in the interim Salim died of a heart attack. Layla supported the replacement of Salim by Wagdi. We are not sure who suggested that Wagdi should direct the film even though he had no previous experience in filmmaking, but in her autobiography, serialized in 1957, Layla takes credit for suggesting that Wagdi become the new director and describes Wagdi's reaction: "After an interval of silence, Anwar exclaimed: Could it be possible? Would you be fine with me directing a film in which I star? I said: I agree; I'm sure you'll succeed. Then everyone agreed that Anwar would direct the film in addition to playing the leading role. During shooting, Anwar entered my life."[63] Thus, Wagdi directed the film and came to an agreement with Salim's widow to credit himself for the scriptwriting. Layla and Wagdi were married in the summer of 1945 before they finished shooting, ushering in the most memorable duo in Arab cinema.

Anwar Wagdi's Grand Show

Encouraged by the popular demand for entertainment after World War II, in 1945 Anwar Wagdi, in partnership with others, established a production company. The public wanted and needed a good time, and cinema proved to be the most popular form of entertainment. Many new production companies emerged to invest wartime profits in the entertainment industry, which increased overall production and profits and decreased costs; the number of production companies grew from 42 before the war to 141 after. Companies that sought to make a profit through low-budget, low-quality production, however, shut down after one or two films, decreasing the number of companies to 69 over ten years. The number of films released multiplied in the postwar period: while theaters showed 125 films between 1935 and 1945, with an average of 16 films per season, theaters showed 28 films in the 1944/5 season alone. Between 1945 and 1952, average annual production reached 51 films, and the 1951/52 season witnessed the largest number, 60 new films.[64] The enthusiasm for films that attracted wartime profiteers led to a wave of criticism disparaging low quality of most of the productions despite their financial success. Meanwhile, some stars ventured into movie production as a means of reinvesting their savings and talent; one of the most successful such enterprises, both artistically and commercially, was Anwar Wagdi's company. Although all his productions belonged to the commercial genre, they were of high quality and lavish. Between the establishment of al-Aflam al-Mutahida: Anwar Wagdi & Co., or United Film Co. (Anwar Wagdi & Co.), in 1945 and Wagdi's death in 1955, the company produced twenty-one films, many of which are considered classics.

The establishment of this production company was a significant turning point in Wagdi's career. During the last ten years of his life, Wagdi became a superstar, a successful filmmaker, a scriptwriter, and a producer, and he married Layla Murad, who was among the highest-paid stars during that period. Appreciating his success, he shared with the public his story of rising from the bottom of the film industry to become inconceivably rich and successful.

Wagdi did not star in all his company's productions, but he starred in all of those that featured Layla Murad, and he wrote, directed, and produced all of those except one, *al-Hawa wa al-Shabab* (*Love and Youth*; Niyazi Mustafa, 1948). Al-Mutahida produced films in all genres: musicals, comedies, action films, and romantic social dramas. The company produced some of the most successful comedies starring Isma'il Yasin and many musicals, which featured singers such as Shadya, Nur al-Huda, Munir Murad (Layla's brother), and 'Abd al-'Aziz Mahmud, as well as Layla Murad. Wagdi took a calculated risk and produced a series of musicals starring the exceptional child Fayruz, who, dubbed as the Shirley Temple of the East, became a huge success, attracting audiences who delighted in her acting, singing, and dancing.

Before Anwar Wagdi, some filmmakers, such as Kamal Salim, produced, wrote, and directed but did not act; only Togo Mizrahi and Yusuf Wahbi, like Wagdi, did all four. Mizrahi acted under his screen name, Ahmad al-Mashriqi, in his early films but after 1935 gave up acting and devoted himself to producing and directing; Wahbi continued to combine work in both cinema and theater throughout his career and, via his Ramsis Troupe, gave Wagdi his first acting job. Praising Anwar in 1949, Wahbi said that he considered Wagdi a younger version of himself and reminisced that he stood out among the extras in the troupe because of his hard work and distinguished physical appearance, that is, his light complexion and black hair.[65] In his efforts to attract attention, young Wagdi never refused a work order, even for manual work that had no relation to his main job as an actor, agreeing to move and carry furniture and accessories just as Wahbi had done while studying and working in Italy. Wahbi also extolled his talent, firmness, determination, and publicity skills. Indeed, Wagdi exceeded Wahbi's skill in management: while Wahbi went bankrupt more than once, Wagdi steadily grew his wealth and attracted superstar musician Muhammad 'Abd al-Wahab to join as a partner in order to attain financial security. For similar reasons, other artists in the 1940s invested the profits from their performances in various businesses, ranging from cinema and music production to real estate.

The Egyptian film industry relied on imported reels of film stock, and in the late 1940s, film producers faced an acute shortage of imported reels. Nevertheless, Anwar Wagdi's company produced five films in 1949 alone.[66] In recognition of the success of his production *al-Batal* (*The Champion*; Hilmi

Raflah, 1950), Wagdi generously sent actress and dancer Tahiyya Carioca, who starred in the film, the gift of a Buick. Despite dire predictions of a decline facing Egyptian cinema and the fear of losing local and Arab audiences to European and American productions in the late 1940s and early 1950s, Anwar Wagdi ensured that the Egyptian film industry flourished, and his financial success reflected the popularity of his excellent films. He mocked various societies and organizations whose business was to discuss ways of promoting Egyptian cinema, saying: "Societies, committees, and conferences are established to rescue the failures."[67] He successfully distributed his lavish films to movie theaters in Egypt and across Arab world and asserted: "Audiences are intelligent and appreciate artistry. They can distinguish between what is good and what is bad. They would not support bad films even if the Committee to Elevate Cinema, the Chamber of Cinema Industry, cinema unions, and cinema conferences recommended such films. . . . Survival of the fittest."[68] His experience working in many genres with different filmmakers with various styles enabled him to successfully combine acting, scriptwriting, filmmaking, and producing. He was also the most prolific individual working in the film industry, working on others' productions as well as his own. Between 1930, before the arrival of the sound film, until his premature death in 1955, he appeared in seventy-two films, wrote sixteen, and directed thirteen. Many are still among the finest and most popular films in Egyptian cinematic history; perhaps most notably, he starred in the most important production of that time, *Amir al-Intiqam* (*The Avenging Prince / The Count of Monte Cristo*; Henry Barakat, 1950), based on Alexandre Dumas's *Count of Monte Cristo* and produced by Assia Dagher.

The Poor Rich Girls and Their *Afandi* Savior

Wagdi's first job of producing and directing, *Layla Bint al-Fuqara'*, reflected Kamal Salim's cinematographic style, particularly in staging grand musical showpieces in a traditional working-class urban milieu. Theaters showed the film on May 11, less than six weeks after Salim's death on April 2, 1945. Salim must have already designed scenes and chosen and prepared shooting locations and clothing, although we do not know whether Salim shot parts of the film or how much of his work appeared onscreen. Nevertheless, Salim's realist style is evident in the first scene of the film, in which Layla appears as a lower-middle-class woman rather than her usual glamourous persona. The film begins with a Sufi parade and Layla chanting for the *mawlid* (birthday) of Saint Sayyida Zeinab (the Prophet Muhammad's granddaughter). It ends with the Hasaballah brass band dressed in military uniform and playing for the wedding in the traditional Sayyida Zeinab neighborhood.[69]

The *mawlid* setting and sound echo Salim's style in highlighting and celebrating ordinary life in the alleys and traditional neighborhoods of Cairo. Despite his short life, Kamal Salim enjoyed a unique position during the interwar period for his depiction of everyday life among the popular classes. Critics and historians have widely considered his film *al-'Azima* (*The Will*; 1939), which moved the camera out of the lavish residences of the elite to places where most of the population lived, a masterpiece of Egyptian realism. Opening *Layla Bint al-Fuqara'* with the *mawlid* of al-Sayyida Zeinab, a scene that highlights the popular Sufi culture in Egypt, bears Salim's touch. The scene depicts the famous shrine of Sayyida Zeinab, with chanting, Sufi dervishes, and marching in this populous neighborhood of traditional Cairo. Layla's chanting her love to al-Sayyida Zeinab while on the balcony of her home surrounded by family and friends embodies Salim's vision of celebrating working-class traditions of love, spirituality, and solidarity. Remarkably, the scene and the song underscored Layla's character as an ordinary Egyptian Muslim, even though Layla Murad was still Jewish at the time.[70] The scene incorporated a large number of extras, blending documentary and staged shots of the *mawlid* and weaving together the music and the voices of Zakariya Ahmad, Muhammad al-Bakkar, Layla, and the choir in a tremendous harmonious chant. *Akhbar al-Yum*'s editor, Mustafa Amin, praised the film as "one of the most beautiful musicals I have seen, and even its faults increased its beauty."[71] Amin praised Layla's acting and singing, along with Wagdi and all the supporting comedic actors. However, he did not care for Layla's wearing a head veil while chanting Sayyida Zeinab's song, failing to appreciate the value of her sacrificing her usual elegant appearance, even in few scenes, to look like an ordinary woman. But Layla had learned her lesson after refusing to play a poor woman in *Gawhara*, as discussed earlier, and began cautiously to refashion herself in *Layla Bint al-Fuqara'*.

Beginning with *Layla Bint al-Fuqara'* and before becoming Layla's husband, Wagdi occupied a position equivalent to Mizrahi's in Layla's professional trajectory. Layla returned as a leading female star whose fashionable style of clothing Egyptian women imitated, in particular adopting a style known as *Jabonis* (Japanese).[72] As the film was an adaptation of the Cinderella story, the prince became an Egyptian army officer. The male protagonist in *Layla Bint al-Fuqara'* is in military uniform and is not a reckless, partying young man. His wealthy father is a pasha and former officer who is having difficulty valuing the honor and nobility of the poor over wealth and social status. But in the film's decisive moment, he joins his son in acknowledging the noble hearts and souls of the poor and considering the poor, rather than money or status, essential to national glory. *Layla Bint al-Fuqara'* marks an early appearance of the military uniform on the cinema screen, a decade before it became an overwhelming trend following the Revolution of 1952. The military identity of the lover is prominent throughout the film: he drives a military jeep and is wed in a military tux with the stars showing his rank on his shoulders. The film struck a balance that satisfied both the poor and the rich; the poor were still the national stock of nobility, authenticity, and honor, while the rich were servants of the nation, hard-working and kind.

Following *Layla Bint al-Fuqara'*, the public dubbed Layla Murad "Cinderella," the first Egyptian star to have that nickname.[73] The film inaugurated Wagdi and Layla's cinematic discourses on love's power over class difference. In five of the eight films in which they co-starred and that Wagdi produced or directed, the loving protagonists belong to different social classes. In their first film, *Layla Bint al-Fuqara'*, and their last, *Bint al-Akabir* (*Daughter of the Nobility*, Anwar Wagdi, 1953), the wide gap in wealth and social status between the lovers is the main problem. Both films were loaded with bombastic discourse about human equality regardless of wealth and power—love, not wealth, is the foundation of a happy life—but they never delved into the causes of poverty and the unjust socioeconomic structures widening the gap between classes. This gave comfort to the poor while at the same time not offending the rich, even though poverty and social injustice were rampant and wealth was concentrated in a few hands.

The rest of Layla and Anwar's films hailed the middle-class *afandi* as the savior of wealthy women longing for love and in need of protection. The *afandi*, or modern educated and professional man, had to help these women break free of the shackles of archaic traditions. In *Layla Bint al-Aghnya'* (*Layla the Rich Girl*; Anwar Wagdi, 1946), journalist Wahid *afandi* saves the wealthy runaway bride, Layla, whose abusive stepmother wants to marry her off to her nephew. In *Qalbi Dalili* (*My Heart Guides Me*; Anwar Wagdi, 1947), policeman Wahid *afandi* saves Layla from dangerous gangsters after the police and the gang mistake her for a female gang member. In *Ghazal al-Banat* (*The Flirtation of Girls*; Anwar Wagdi, 1949), pilot Wahid *afandi* saves Layla from a hustler from whom her poor teacher has failed to protect her. These discourses reflect the fact that most moviegoers were from the working and middle classes, whereas the upper classes represented a tiny segment of the population; commercial films were intended to appeal to the largest possible audience rather than serve as a call for social justice and close the gap between the haves and have-nots.

Films also contributed to the construction of the New Man, the *afandi* whose social status and social capital came from his modern education and modern profession, combined with traditional moral and physical strength. In the films of that time, the employment of masculine physical power was essential to winning the high moral ground over other classes, particularly the corrupt wealthy and marginalized criminals. Layla allegorically represents Egypt as a woman, and Wahid *afandi* contributes to normalizing *afandi* masculinity, or the "afandication" of the social virtues.

Starting with the first film he directed, *Layla Bint al-Fuqara'*, Wagdi proved himself to be an exceptional director of musicals, who transformed singing movies from melodious pictures to grand musical shows on the screen. Layla Murad's song for the *mawlid* of Sayyida Zeinab represents a drastic change in the construction of the cinematic song. Wagdi's style of making musicals and reframing Layla's cinematic persona became clearer in their second film, *Layla Bint al-Aghnya'*, in which he changed the landscape of the film song from focusing on one singer exchanging looks with a lover or gazing at a view of nature to situating the singer in the midst of a grand show and thus becoming part of a large dynamic crowd of dancers, musicians, and other actors.

Along with Layla's vocal performances, audiences were treated to dance, comedy sketches, and more. Wagdi moved the grand musical shows of music halls, theaters, and night clubs to the screen and immersed moviegoers in the atmospheres of spaces they aspired to experience but could not afford. In that sense, he democratized theatrical musicals and gave audiences who might have heard about Theatre Printania or Badi'a Masabni Hall but could not afford to go there a chance to savor it.

In his following films featuring Layla Murad or the child star Fayruz, Wagdi provided the audience with a fabulous bouquet of grand shows in which dozens of dancers in extravagant clothing appeared against beautifully designed scenic backdrops accompanied by melodious sounds. He moved the lavish musical show from the theater, which only well-off Carian audiences were able to afford, to the silver screen, making them available to large cross-class audiences in most towns in Egypt and the rest of the Arab world. These musicals were popular with listeners seeking great vocalists and *tarab* (a traditional form of music associated with emotional ecstasy and enchantment) and viewers seeking action, comedy, and dance. In *Layla Bint al-Aghnya'*, a traditional *zar* party (ritual ceremony for healing from ailments caused by spirits haunting human bodies) in a rural house turns into a giant dance show, with the participation of dozens of belly dancers in glamorous outfits along with Layla's voice.[74] The scene was not realistic nor did it make sense, but it was pleasurable to watch. Grand shows in *'Anbar* (*Anbar*; Anwar Wagdi, 1948) mixed comedy with the musical, blending in belly dancers, Middle Eastern drummers, and Layla's voice performing some of the finest songs from the nineteenth-century repertoire. These exquisite films that Wagdi made with Layla, musicals in the full sense of the word and not just movies incorporating a collection of songs, brought a welcome combination of joy and smart entertainment to the movies.

Although Anwar's productions were lavish, their plots were fairly simple and easy to follow, and their scripts contained dialogue loaded with both jokes and romantic exchanges, all of which appealed to popular audiences. Decades later, Egyptian critics and experts chose his *Ghazal al-Banat* as one of the best films in the history of Egyptian cinema and Wagdi as one of its most prominent filmmakers post–World War II.[75] They noted that Wagdi produced quality and financially lucrative musicals that gave audiences an intense dose of emotional and visual entertainment.[76] Following in Mizrahi's footsteps, Wagdi made films that combined comedy, the musical, the thriller, and melodrama while taking on critical social themes, particularly family stability, parenting, and childcare and -rearing. Layla reached the zenith of her career with Anwar Wagdi, while her domestic life with him as her husband went from one crisis to another.

CHAPTER 3

ADAM AND EVE

Interfaith Family, Fame, and Gossip

> I'll never forget when my wife Layla Murad slapped me in
> the face in the film *Layla Bint al-Rif.* . . . May God forgive
> the filmmaker for making my beloved wife, who works day
> and night for my comfort, slap me.
>
> *Anwar Wagdi, interview with*
> *al-Kawakib magazine,*
> *September 1950*

ANWAR WAGDI'S STATEMENT exemplifies the kind of half-truthful information about his and Layla Murad's domestic and public life that generated widespread interest in the couple over the years. The slap scene in fact
took place but long before Layla and Anwar were married and indeed before
anyone expected them to become a couple. Fans of these superstars continually sought glimpses into their domestic spaces and private times, and Layla
and Anwar readily welcomed sharing their personal lives with audiences. In
the pre-Nasser free-market era, the famous couple made use of celebrity reports and gossip columns to feed public interest and recruit consumers for
their entertainment products, while the press used Layla and Anwar's private life to sell copies and attract more advertisers. With the rate of literacy
among men and women increasing, celebrity and gossip publications enjoyed

a sizeable market, providing audiences across classes and of different education levels, including the semiliterate, with human interest stories that they
could employ in their daily conversations and sociable exchanges.[1]

Journalists, celebrities, and the public competed in shaping these stories,
creating a high-stakes drama that was seemingly as endless as it was unpredictable and suspenseful.[2] The public performance of intimate love and hate
and of domestic and professional cohabitation contributed to the construction of gender roles, of the ideal modern man and woman, and of the roles of
work and family in men's and women's lives. Gossip publications circulating
sensational anecdotes and commentaries played a far more critical role in
shaping the social construction of gender than other genres. Because their
reports are easy to share across classes, levels of education, and social status,
celebrity-gossip periodicals were effective in disseminating notions concerning gender, sexuality, domesticity, and morality.

Western fan and celebrity-gossip periodicals generally target female readership and entertainment content. In the Egyptian context, the distinction
between highbrow and middlebrow culture was never clear-cut, nor was there
a clear division between different genres of periodicals and their primary
readership and columnists. Intellectuals such as Taha Husain and 'Abbas al-
'Aqqad wrote for gossip and celebrity periodicals, and men formed a greater
percentage of the readership owing to their higher rate of literacy, financial
control, and ability to frequent public spaces where reading and hearing news
were available even without buying copies. The physical beauty and fashions
of female celebrities attracted both male and female readers; men who loved
beauty and women who sought and wished to acquire it were faithful readers
of such celebrity periodicals as *al-Kawakib* and *al-Fann*. Almost all daily and
weekly periodicals featured sections for entertainment, which in addition to
critiques, reviews, and reports about new movies and shows, provided gossip
and covered sensational scandals. A conservative daily such as *al-Ahram* did
not differ in that respect from weekly pictorials such as *al-Musawar*; sensational reports and interviews with celebrities made front-page headlines even
for political newspapers such as *Akhbar al-Yum*. Therefore, I shall use the
terms "celebrity" and "gossip press" somewhat loosely rather than exclusively
for fan and celebrity magazines; despite the political focus of the conservative
daily *al-Ahram* and the liberal weekly *Ruz al-Yusuf*, both published sensational

material. Terms such as "rag publications" and "yellow press," by which gossip
and celebrity publications are labeled in the West, were not used in Egypt
until the late twentieth century, when the term "scandalous press" (*sahafat al-
fada'ih*) appeared.[3] More neutral terms such as "social" and "art publications"
(*sahafa ijtima'iyya* and *faniyya*) were more common; even when elitist intellectuals dismissed readers and writers of celebrity periodicals, they labeled them
as the half-cultured (*ansaf muthaqqafin*). Blurring boundaries between cultural
high- and middlebrows, these gossip and celebrity publications enjoyed a wide
readership among both educated and uneducated men and women and by
means of such human interest and gossip stories facilitated the dissemination
of social ideas across classes and other social divisions.

Like many married couples in twentieth-century Egypt, Layla and
Anwar, her first husband, experienced the tensions between the traditional
gendered division of labor and the modern structure wherein women could
be independent and professional. Unlike most couples, however, they lived
through interfaith marriage and domestic disputes in the light of fame,
where human interest and gossip sold movie tickets and copies of celebrity
magazines. Layla and Anwar divorced and remarried each other three times
in seven years. They were married in May 1945, divorced, and then remarried
again by the end of 1949. A few months later, they were divorced again, in
March 1950, then remarried a few weeks later in early May. Their third divorce, after which Islamic law forbade them to remarry each other again, took
place in July 1952—even though they resumed their relationship until their
final separation in March 1953. Their marriage illuminates the positionality
of Jewish women married to Muslim men in modern Egypt. As a Muslim
husband, Anwar enjoyed all the privileges stipulated in Islamic Sharia law;
as a Jewish wife, Layla's legal inferiority was twofold, while the Arab-Israeli
conflict added complexity to her already weak position. Domestic disputes
and regional conflicts both dictated her public conversion from Judaism to
Islam. Layla and Anwar invested in manipulating public interest, making use
of the press in their disputes. Their relationship contributed to social debates
about love and business and the manufacturing of unrealistic images of the
"new woman" and the "modern family."

Layla and Anwar together used the press to empower themselves as
a couple, while each of them separately used the press to disempower the

other whenever their relationship declined. The couple invested in building their stardom and maintaining a high public profile in order to sell more movie tickets, while the press published celebrity gossip to sell more copies. Layla and Anwar's relationship was transformed from an individual case of a troubled marriage to public discourse about gender relations in modern social life; an individual tale of troubled domestic life made public by the popular press became a shared experience among both literate and illiterate Egyptians from all classes.[4] Celebrity-gossip periodicals tend to be mostly pictorial; pictures of performers and movie posters were used to attract audiences even among those who could not read and turned actors and singers into icons of mass national culture. Sensational stories about Layla and Anwar's domestic life mass-communicated both the ideals and the realities of marriage, family, and working women, reinforcing certain notions about the intersection of gender, religion, domestic life, and work in modern Egypt.

Love, romance, and domestic disagreements were, and still are, powerfully attractive to consumers of commercial cinema and commercial publications alike. Layla readily shared with the public stories about her first childhood crush, her first love, and her failed marriage plans. She made use of fan and celebrity magazines to construct her public persona as a modern woman whose aspirations were denied, who was compelled as a child to support her family and became a smart professional. Layla's story about her first childhood crush took place when she was attending the *rahibat* school. Her father saw Layla walking arm in arm with the teenage son of a neighboring family while the boy smoked a cigarette, pretending to be a grownup. Her father spontaneously struck both of them, which was the end of the story.[5] Whether the story was true or not, Layla never meant to represent her father as an abusive parent; perhaps she thought it was an amusing anecdote that illustrated her family's concern with normative middle-class morality (*adab*).

Layla likewise talked publicly about her first true love, giving two rather different accounts of why the love story did not end up in marriage. In one account, she rejected a marriage proposal from a rich man hailing from a notable family because he wanted her to give up her career while she was a rising star, a decision she said that she never regretted, though it was not an easy one.[6] The suitor appeared in Layla's life when she had already achieved success in her singing career and aspired to become a movie star. However, her dream seemed increasingly farther away when World War II interrupted the import of materials and led to the closure of outside distribution markets; the number of movies produced decreased, and some production companies shut down, leaving many artists out of work and some facing poverty. The choice between an uncertain career and a promising marriage "was hard and made me unable to sleep."[7] Although Layla's family accepted the wealthy suitor, she decided to reject his offer of marriage. Luckily, she met filmmaker Togo Mizrahi and signed the contract for her second film, *Lailah Mumtira*, with Yusuf Wahbi, which inaugurated the series of films dubbed as *al-Layali* that transformed her into a luminous movie star and raised her wages to thousands of Egyptian pounds. She concluded: "If I had chosen the rich suitor under my family's pressure, I would not have become more than a wife in a rich man's house."[8]

Two months before publishing this account, however, Layla said in her serialized autobiography that she fell in love for the first time with a millionaire who was rejected by her father when he asked Layla to give up her career and live with him in Argentina; she wasn't clear whether he was Argentinian or not. According to this account, she truly loved this man, who was ten years older than she was, but had no choice but to accept her parents' decision.[9] We cannot verify either of Layla's accounts, nor can we confirm whether the wealthy suitor in one account and the Argentina lover in the other were the same person; Layla called the man in both accounts her first love and her first suitor. Both anecdotes resonate with a story her biographer, Salih Mursi, published in *al-Kawakib* in the mid-1970s.[10] According to this narrative, Layla fell in love with a wealthy diplomat when she was spending summer vacation with her family in Alexandria during World War II. Since she was shooting *Layla* with Togo Mizrahi during the summer of 1941, it is unlikely that Layla and her family spent that summer in Alexandria, given the war and Italy's threats to invade Alexandria. According to Mursi's account, Layla fell in love with an attractive, middle-aged diplomat and went out with him for three years. Their excursions in his automobile throughout Cairo led to their love story becoming known, and he introduced her to his aristocratic family. After the death of Layla's mother, the lover proposed to Layla, and his aristocratic family accepted their marriage plan, provided Layla gave up her career.

Layla was at the peak of her success as one of the most famous stars in the Arab world, yet she, according to Mursi's account, sacrificed her love and chose not to marry her lover because of her commitment to take care of her siblings. Layla's own sacrifice parallels the sacrifice she portrays in the film *Layla*, which she was shooting when her love story with the diplomat began, in which a woman sacrifices her love for the sake of her lover's family. Layla had control over all three versions of the story, two in 1957 and one penned by Mursi in the 1970s. The first two were given when she was professionally active with the purpose of demonstrating her intelligence, reason, and ability to make tough but sound choices, while at the same time showing that she lived up to middle-class notions of respectability by submitting to her parents' wishes despite her professional success. Her interview with Mursi took place in early 1970; he published it a few years later when Layla was no longer part of the music scene. Mursi may have written precisely what Layla told him, or perhaps she approved a version modified by him to bring her biography into alignment with her onscreen persona as a romantic woman who sacrifices herself for others' well-being.

It is possible that Layla had three lovers: the wealthy suitor who proposed to her before her first film with Mizrahi, the aristocratic diplomat whom she met her after becoming a well-established star, and the millionaire who wanted her to live with him in Argentina. It is also possible that the three suitors are fictional or are one man portrayed differently in the various accounts. We cannot be sure that these accounts appeared in the press exactly as she narrated them. Since the 1940s, celebrity-gossip journalists have composed and published stories about stars' personal lives and then credited the stars themselves with authorship; stars have accepted these narratives because they felt unable to challenge the press or because these narratives added to their stardom.[11] Whatever the case, the binaries of love versus work, family versus career, and stardom versus domestic commitments came into play in Layla's life after she and Anwar were married in the summer of 1945.

Layla and Anwar: From Colleagues to Married Couple

Before Anwar Wagdi asked Layla Murad to star in his first production, *Layla Bint al-Fuqara'*, in 1945, he and Layla had appeared together in two of Togo Mizrahi's films in 1944, *Layla Bint al-Rif* and *Layla fi al-Zalam*, as well as working together in Kamal Salim's *Shuhada' al-Gharam*. Layla starred in all three films, while Anwar played supporting roles; he also starred in several films but was unable to convince Salim to assign him the leading role in *Shuhada' al-Gharam*. Working together in this way enabled close interaction between Anwar and Layla during the long hours of work, enough to know each other fairly well. Getting married during the shooting of *Layla Bint al-Fuqara'*, they formed the most famous duo in the history of the Arab entertainment industry.

Unlike Layla, who grew up in a musical household and launched her cinematic career in a leading role, Anwar grew up in a family with no connection to the performing arts; indeed, according to him, his family opposed his decision to quit a stable day job and devote himself to a precarious acting career.[12] Many attributed Anwar's exceptional career as a producer, filmmaker, and actor to his hard work.[13] Enhancing his public persona as a self-made man at the peak of his success in 1950, he shared with the public that he had experienced poverty and starvation at the beginning of his career.[14] By the mid-1940s, Anwar was a divorcé with a playboy image; many thought he was a womanizer who used his handsome appearance to have many romantic affairs. After marrying and then divorcing Ilham Husain, a rising star who appeared with Muhammad 'Abd al-Wahab in the film *Yum Sa'id* (*A Happy Day*; Muhammad Karim, 1940), Anwar proposed to actress Layla Fawzi (1918–2005), but her father refused. His infatuation with Layla Fawzi resurfaced shortly after his final separation from Layla Murad in the early 1950s. But despite the fact that he had already been married twice, with each marriage lasting only a few months, the womanizer-playboy image does not seem realistic in view of his intensive work schedule: between 1940 and 1945, Anwar worked on five films a year.

Before her marriage, Layla Murad maintained her public image as a modest young woman who went to business meetings and shooting locations accompanied by her father or one of her siblings. In 1945, she was twenty-seven years old, the highest-paid actress in Egyptian cinema, and single. The love between Layla and Anwar may have developed quickly after their intensive work together in 1944 and 1945. When Anwar proposed to her, it seemed like a good idea: Anwar was handsome, driven, hard-working, and had already accumulated enough wealth to launch a production company.

Despite his playboy image, his previous experiences with marriage confirmed his inclination toward family life and his preference to have a wife working in cinema. Unlike the previous proposals she did or could have received, Layla did not have to choose between work and marriage. While working in *Layla Bint al-Fuqara'*, Anwar expressed his feelings for Layla through his gazes and by bringing her flowers regularly, volunteering to give her rides after work, and appearing anxious whenever someone flirted with her. When rumors of their love and expected marriage broke out in the celebrity-gossip magazines, cautious Layla published a denial, urging journalists to be careful and truthful before publicizing sensitive personal information.[15] But after two months of denial, the couple went alone to the court at noon on July 15, 1945, to register their marriage before Muhammad Salih al-Nawawi, the head of the Ma'adhun department in Cairo's Sharia court. They did not announce their marriage, and speculation that the couple might tie the knot after releasing the film continued. That summer, the weekly magazine *Musamarat al-Gib* explained that the conflicting reports reflected the infatuation of thousands of fans and lovers of Layla and Anwar.[16] Eventually, Anwar invited reporters to the studio and asked the entire cast to be present while the wedding scene was shot. With Layla still in her wedding gown and Anwar in a tuxedo, the couple announced that they had already been married; that scene documented their wedding both in the film and in real life. Released on November 5, 1945, *Layla Bint al-Fuqara'* was a great success at the box office, with 70,000 Egyptian pounds in revenue according to one estimate.[17] One has to wonder how much the conflicting reports about the couple's love and marriage, together with the staged wedding in the studio, stoked fans' interest and brought larger audiences to theaters. Layla and Anwar's story is one of love, marriage, domestic disputes, and divorces taking place under the public gaze, and the couple used it to serve business and increase revenues.

Interfaith Marriage

Layla and Anwar signed their marriage contract at the Islamic Sharia court on a special form for interfaith marriage. Interreligious marriage was so extremely rare among Egyptians that interfaith marriages and religious conversions for the sake of love among stars garnered the interest of gossip publications.[18] Islamic Sharia law prohibits marriage between Muslim

women and non-Muslim men, but the same religious difference does not pose
a legal obstacle when a Muslim man marries a Christian or Jew and when
both spouses keep their faith after marriage. Nevertheless, sociocultures in
most communities deem interfaith marriage a threat to communal coherency.
Historically, people have tended to marry within their religious, ethnic, or
professional communities. Class, more than ethnicity, was the insurmountable
barrier in Ottoman Egypt.[19] Despite the modernization of the institution of
marriage, interfaith marriage continued to pose a dilemma: either one embraces modern ideas, including the right to marry whomever one loves, or
one commits to the survival of one's culture and religion by marrying within
the same faith. Notions of equality, religious tolerance, and nondiscrimination
collided with the need to preserve religious norms, and the majority of people
took marrying inside the same religious group for granted.

Attempting to discourage marriage outside the community, the Jewish
court in Egypt published lists of children born to families who did not follow the Jewish law in marriage.[20] Yet despite public objections and concerns
voiced by Jewish clergymen in the press and the court, more Jewish women
married Muslims and Christians in the interwar period,[21] one reason being
the inability of families to offer a monetary gift to grooms (*dota* [*nedunyah*]),
or dowry.[22] The bride's family was obligated to provide the groom with a
dowry, and a Jewish father would save money from the day his daughter
was born until her wedding to make that customary payment. That tradition, however, did not exist in the Muslim community, in which men must
offer *mahr* or *sadaq* (a dowry) to women. The *dota* problem became so acute
that Jewish philanthropists formed associations to help poor girls from both
Karaite and Rabbinate Jewish sects to pay *dota* to be married. The Jewish
press, such as the newspaper *al-Kalim*, blamed young men for being so igno-
rant and silly that they insulted Jewish women and cared only about women's
wealth and their ability to offer them a large dowry. And so Jewish fathers
of girls struggled to save money, and poor Jewish girls did not get married.[23]

Interfaith marriage among Jews became so common that it raised concerns in the Jewish community. The Jewish press criticized young Jewish
men and women for marrying non-Jews or foreigners. Some Jewish men
and women marrying Muslims or Christians changed their religion. In addition to the *dota* problem, there were likely other reasons for the increase

in the number of marriages outside the Jewish community. Some Jews considered Western culture to be superior and married Westerners to enjoy the Capitulations' extra privileges. Marriage to Muslims was similarly alarming, raising concerns within both the Jewish and Christian communities. In 1950, representatives of non-Muslim communities asked the prime minister for a change in the law to allow non-Muslim husbands whose wives converted to Islam to continue being married if they chose not to convert as well; this was meant to give such husbands the same rights as husbands who converted to Islam while their wives did not. But the rector of al-Azhar and the Committee of Fatwa refused the request, holding that all Muslim schools of law agreed that a marriage must be dissolved once a woman embraced Islam and her husband did not.[24]

Contracting Marriage

While Layla may have been able to limit the power of men in her household over her personal and professional choices before marriage, once she signed the marriage contract her gender became a factor, arguably the most important one, in determining her options. By virtue of marrying a Muslim man, Layla's personal status fell outside the jurisdiction of the Jewish court that handled marital and family affairs among Egyptian and non-Egyptian Jews. But her marriage placed her under the jurisdiction of the Muslim Sharia court. According to Islamic Sharia, the marriage was legally valid and thus needed no authentication or recognition from the Jewish court. Some non-Muslim couples, that is, Jewish or Christian couples, chose to register their marriage in Islamic courts seeking rights such as dowries, alimony, divorce, and polygamy that were not afforded them by their religious courts.[25] Jewish law forbade presenting private matters such as marriage and divorce to gentile authorities, but Jews voluntarily appealed to the authority of Muslim courts in the sixteenth and seventeenth centuries.[26] Amnon Cohen concludes that Jews viewed the Muslim court as an essential part of the fiber of personal and community life, and not that they considered Jewish courts ineffectual or inferior. The Jewish community had every reason to trust the Muslim courts, because "greater weight was often attributed to the testimony of Jews."[27]

Placing Layla's marriage under the jurisdiction of the Islamic Sharia court was different from the historical pattern in which non-Muslim couples of the same faith chose to register their marriage in the Islamic court. Like all non-Muslim women marrying Muslim men, Layla Murad had no choice but to marry in the Islamic court and accept that her own religious courts would not adjudicate her marriage or any resulting conflicts. Canonical Islamic Sharia rules gave husbands more authority in terms of polygamy, divorce, child custody, and inheritance, but since Islamic marriage is a contract, both parties can stipulate certain conditions. In premodern contracts, couples could specify conditions in individually handwritten agreements. Wives included specific clauses to protect their interests, such as barring her husband's extended absence from the home or allowing the wife an automatic divorce should the husband take another wife; husbands pledged to provide a specific clothing allowance and a certain standard of living.[28] In the twentieth century, marriage contracts gradually became printed forms that often included just the bare necessities.

Interfaith contracts departed from conventional marriage contracts between two Muslims, explicitly stipulating the conditions of an Islamic marriage, including the rights and duties of the Muslim man and his non-Muslim wife concerning polygamy, divorce, dowry and maintenance, child custody, and inheritance. Interfaith contracts addressed these matters selectively. At Layla and Anwar's wedding ceremony, the *ma'dhun* (public officer authorized to solemnize marriage) would seem to have accepted the couple's information as they uttered it then and there rather than verifying official documents. Their estimated ages in the marriage contract were lower than their actual ages: Anwar Wagdi was estimated to be approximately thirty-two years old, although he had already turned forty, and Layla to be approximately twenty-four years old, three years younger than her actual age.

Layla's marriage document also explicitly identified her as Israelite (meaning Jewish), a virgin, and born in Cairo. It stipulated six rules taken from the most conservative patriarchal interpretation of Islamic law. She signed, confirming that the *ma'dhun* had explained to her the following:

1. Despite any objection the wife might have, the Muslim husband has the right to marry two, three, or four wives simultaneously.

2. The husband has the right to divorce his wife at any time he pleases with or without the wife's consent. He also has the right to prevent her from

leaving his house without his permission and to compel her to live in his *shar'i* house (a house with provisions stipulated in the Sharia law). He may forcibly compel her to obey him.

3. If the husband divorces his wife *raj'yan* (recoverable divorce), he has the right to take her back without her consent during her *'idda* (the period of three menstrual cycles after the divorce or three lunar months if the wife is past menopause). If the divorce was *ba'in* (irrecoverable), the husband may only take her back with her consent and a new contract and new dowry. If they divorce a third time or the divorce is a "triple divorce," that is, the husband has repudiated his wife by divorcing her three times, he can only take her back after she performs *nikah* (gets married) with another husband and then is divorced or widowed.

4. If the husband divorces his wife before the marriage is consummated, she deserves only half of her appointed dowry. The wife deserves the complete dowry if the divorce takes place after the marriage's consummation. In the case of divorce after the marriage's consummation, she deserves maintenance expenses during her *'idda* period.

5. If children are born to the couple, they must follow the *madhhab* (school of Islamic law) of the Muslim husband. If he divorces his wife, she receives payment for nursing the children and has custody and payment based on the judge's estimate or by agreement between the couple. Custody is seven years for boys and nine for girls unless the judge decides differently.

6. The difference of religion prevents the surviving husband or wife from inheriting from one another should one of them die.

None of these conditions and rules appeared in standard marriage contracts between Muslim men and women. Officials in the Egyptian Ministry of Justice imposed their own understanding of the Islamic identity of an interfaith union in creating discrepancies between non-Muslim–Muslim and standard Muslim-Muslim marriage contracts.[29] The official printed form designated for documenting interfaith marriage emphasized the rights of a Muslim husband, ignored the rights of a non-Muslim wife, and confirmed the Islamic identity of their future children. They ensured that interfaith marriage would remain strictly Islamic and left no room for doubt regarding

Egyptian Muslim husbands' legal rights versus those of their non-Muslim wives.[30] Interfaith contracts deprived non-Muslim wives of the rights granted to Muslim women, intentionally making unavailable to non-Muslim wives the Muslim wife's right to stipulate conditions in her contract. For example, in the interfaith marriage contract polygamy was solely and unconditionally the husband's right. Yet alternatively, the contract might have stipulated that the husband could not take a second wife, and that in the event he did so, the wife could obtain an automatic divorce.[31] This would have been in accordance with the Hanafi school of Islamic law, the basis for the Egyptian family code; numerous wives in Ottoman Egypt took advantage of that right. On the interfaith marriage form, polygamy was the first condition to be listed, though it was an exceedingly uncommon practice in Egypt. Census records reveal that polygamy was on the decline: in 1927, only 4.8 percent of marriages were polygamous, and the rate had decreased to 3.4 percent by 1937.

Layla's interfaith contract did not reflect any of the changes to Egyptian law made in 1929 regarding the husband's right to divorce. Hanafi jurisprudence tended to adapt doctrines of other more flexible legal schools on divorce to provide women with more options and protections. The changes made in 1929 continued the Hanafi tradition of drawing on the more liberal Maliki and Shafi'i schools of law in an effort to restrict the husband's unilateral right to divorce.[32] Four articles of Law No. 25 of 1929 legalized the following conditions under which a husband's repudiation of divorce would be invalid; Hanan Kholousy has condensed those articles as follows:

> (1) the oath was uttered by a man who was drunk or under duress; (2) the oath forced a woman or another party into a particular action; (3) regardless of the number of oaths uttered, only one oath was allowed at any one time; and (4) a divorce oath must be explicitly stated.[33]

Layla's interfaith contract did not mention any of these conditions, as evidenced by the provision that her Muslim husband could divorce her whenever he pleased. It detailed the obligations of dowry and support to a non-Muslim wife if her husband divorced her, but it ignored her right to a judicial divorce under the conditions mentioned in Laws No. 25 of 1920 and No. 25 of 1929, including the husband's contraction of a chronic or contagious disease, his failure to provide maintenance, his desertion, and his maltreatment.[34]

As for any Islamic marriage contract, two males were required as witnesses to Layla and Anwar's contract. Rather than arranging for two relatives or close friends, who would have considered being witnesses an honor and a compliment, to go with them, the couple would appear to have made do with two random strangers, a Sharia lawyer and a clerk, both of whom worked at the court. This may indicate that the couple rushed to the court without due social arrangements or planning, although we cannot be sure whether anyone from Layla's family accompanied her or whether the *ma'dhun* disallowed the possibility of having Jewish witnesses. Sunni jurists are unanimous that the presence of witnesses is essential and that they must be either two men or a man and two women, adult, sane, and free. If both parties of the marriage are Muslim, the witnesses must be Muslim. But Hanafi jurists accept *kitabi* (literally, members of the people of scripture, i.e., Christian or Jewish) witnesses if the wife to be is a *kitabi*.[35] On September 5, 1923, Dar al-Ifta' in Egypt authorized a fatwa accepting *kitabi* witnesses when the wife was a *kitabi*.[36]

Contrary to the social norm of having a male guardian represent a woman getting married for the first time, Layla represented herself before the *ma'dhun* in Cairo's Sharia court; being over twenty-one years old, Layla enjoyed full legal responsibility and curatorship, and thus was entitled to represent herself. Social norms among ordinary Egyptian families require a male to represent the bride, particularly if she weds for the first time; that male could be the bride's father, grandfather, uncle, brother, or an elder from her community. Violating that tradition may indicate that the woman's family does not welcome the marriage or that the bride has a particular social status, for example, highly independent or highly marginalized. Layla's father was still alive, and she had three mature brothers, one of them older than she. Layla's self-representation was an expression of her independence as well as some impatience to conclude the marriage.

We have no evidence that Layla's and Anwar's families resented their union because of their different religions. Layla and Anwar were independent adults and professionals whose families relied on them for material support; it is possible that the powerful positions that Layla and Anwar enjoyed in their respective family households protected their decision from strong opposition, if there was any opposition at all. We can conclude that Anwar's and Layla's families did not oppose the marriage or were not in a position to translate their opposition into action. Anwar's sociable personality appealed to Layla's siblings, particularly Muris (later Munir) and Ibrahim; both brothers later worked for his production company, which suggests mutual professional and personal bonding. Any concerns that Layla's father or other family members might have had about the interfaith marriage, of course, could have been appeased by Layla's keeping to her Jewish faith. Zaki was strongly committed to his Jewishness until the end of his life: he maintained his registration in the Jewish community records and was buried in the Jewish cemetery. There had been no previous case of interfaith marriage in Zaki's family, despite his professional and personal association with individuals from all faiths, particularly with Muslims. But following Layla's marriage to Anwar, interfaith marriage became more common among the Murad family: the youngest sister, Samiha Murad, married a Muslim filmmaker, 'Ali Rida; and following his divorce from his Jewish wife, Muris/Munir Murad married the Muslim actress Suhair al-Babli in the late 1950s.

Seemingly, Layla's love for Anwar came suddenly and overwhelmingly. Until shooting *Layla Bint al-Fuqara'* in May 1945, Layla and Anwar's relationship was strictly a business relationship. When negotiating her contract for *Layla Bint al-Fuqara'*, she did not reduce her fee, unlike other stars who often agreed to reduce their payment as a friendly gesture toward fellow actors starting production companies. Layla signed with Anwar's startup company and charged her high standard wage, either because she did not have a close friendship with Anwar or because she privileged her business interests over any personal ones. Yet she did agree to take the risk with Anwar in his first outing as a filmmaker, then fell in love with him and accepted his proposal of marriage after only a few weeks of shooting. Signing the marriage contract at the court without friends or family and the surprising staged wedding in the studio kept fans in suspense, but it was not the only option nor necessarily the best one for Layla. Had she not rushed into marriage, she could have taken the time to consult legal experts and learned that Islamic law considered marriage a civil contractual agreement rather than a religious sacrament; the couple could have negotiated the terms of the contract before the marriage took place, and Layla in particular could have negotiated for many of the privileges awarded the husband in the standard interfaith marriage contract.

Layla would seem to have entered into her marriage with Anwar equipped with all the qualifications and experience that would betoken an equal partnership. In reality, she had to face and struggle against the restrictions imposed on her by the institution of marriage. At home, she found herself in a gender- and religious-based hierarchy whereby her legal inferiority was twofold: she became a minority wife in a patriarchal and Muslim-majority society, the Jewish wife of a Muslim man subject to family laws based on a conservative patriarchal interpretation of Islamic Sharia. The rest of her life would be governed by the fragile positionality of her gender- and religious-minority status. Layla's marriage exemplifies the structural vulnerability that followed from her female gender and her religious minority status. These social categories are not neatly separable in daily life; thus, how they intersected with one another, creating very particular effects, will need to be explored.[37] By no means do I mean to suggest that Layla's lived experience was a series of choices decided by her being a Jew or a woman; but her being a Jewish woman and wife to a Muslim man in a majority-Muslim society functioned as master categories, that is, social divisions that emerge as more critical in specific historical situations and related to particular people.[38]

Following his first production in 1945 and until his premature death in 1955, Anwar became a tycoon in the film industry as well as a controversial public figure, mainly owing to his relationship with Layla. The success of *Layla Bint al-Fuqara'* encouraged Anwar to dissolve his partnership with others in al-Film al-Misri: Anwar Wagdi & Co. in order to establish a new production company, al-Aflam al-Mutahida: Anwar Wagdi & Co., which he owned exclusively. His new company bought the proprietary copyright to *Bint al-Fuqara'*, and Anwar began charting a new phase of his career. In addition to acting, directing, and managing his own productions, Anwar never stopped acting in films produced and directed by others; he was able to become selective and play only leading roles, as well as raising his acting fee from 1,000 to 3,000 Egyptian pounds per film.[39]

Forming a duo with Layla Murad on-screen, as well as in real life, was central to Anwar's production company. Layla Murad, who was the highest-paid actor or actress in Egypt, became Anwar's most significant financial and artistic asset. His attempts to monopolize her talent and her insistence on guarding her independence caused continuing tensions and triggered frequent domestic disputes that invariably leaked to the press. Between disputes and reconciliations, Layla certified her conversion from Judaism to Islam in 1947. She and Anwar publicized her conversion against the backdrop of the first Arab-Israeli war, in the summer of 1948. All her siblings except two, Murad and Malak, converted to Islam in the late 1940s. As all but one of them bore names common to people from a variety of faiths, only her youngest brother had to change his non-Muslim name, from Muris to Muhammad Munir. Like her interfaith marriage, Layla's religious conversion was not unprecedented among artists: aside from the Murad family, Najma Ibrahim converted from Judaism, and Omar al-Sharif, Mary Munib, Aziz' Eid, and George and Dawlat Abyad all converted from Christianity.[40]

Layla's Conversion: Her Version of the Story

Layla submitted a formal request to the Cairo Governorate on December 8, 1947, to document her conversion to Islam. The governorate transferred the matter to the Islamic Sharia court, where she had to appear before the chief of documentation and declarations, 'Abd al-Raziq al-Buhayri, and the court's president, His Excellency Judge Shaykh Hassan Ma'mun, on December 27, 1947. Layla performed the conversion rituals, mostly reciting the *shahada* (the Muslim creed—"There is no God but God, and Muhammad is God's messenger") and testifying that she gave up any other religion but Islam. She chose not to change her name and kept the name Layla Zaki Murad as her Muslim name. Mahmud Afandi Ahmad, the secretary of *Dar al-Ifta'*, and Ahmad Hassan, a reporter at the *al-Balagh* newspaper, testified at the court as witnesses to her conversion. Several months later, Layla announced her conversion to Islam and publicly released pictures of herself wearing the Islamic veil (*hijab*), praying, and receiving religious lessons from Shcikh Mahmud Abu al-'Uyun.[41] Layla attempted to dissociate her conversion from political developments, telling the press that she had converted two years earlier but kept her conversion private because her father was still alive and she was concerned about his feelings while he struggled with health problems in his last days. Layla's statement means that she privately embraced Islam in 1946, registered it in state records in 1947, and announced it publicly in 1948. Each step had a different meaning, goal, and consequences.

Why Layla converted is a question more complicated than the simplistic nationalistic construction of tolerance in the Egyptian liberal era (1923–1952) or the Zionist commonplace that Jews always face persecution. Religious conversion may be a personal and private matter; one may convert privately as a response to changes in personal beliefs and worldview. Documenting the changes in religious belief and embracing a new faith in state records could be an endeavor to change one's legal status and the way the one is treated by the state. Publicizing conversion might be a plea to join a community of faith, a plea for different social treatment. In Egypt, at the time of Layla's conversion to Islam, it offered an opportunity to negotiate personal status and establish new relations that would allow at least partial empowerment within the patriarchal system, although female converts found themselves in a position of liminality as the state guaranteed their new rights while seizing some of their female subjectivity, as they became subject to particular interpretations of the Sharia law that favored men.[42] Becoming a Muslim did not mean that Layla was cut off from her Jewish roots or abandoned her Jewish family members; embracing Islam did not mean she did not care about Jews or stripped herself of her Jewishness. Following her conversion, she visited the synagogue in the Jewish Quarter in Cairo; she asked for prayers to comfort her father's soul, a step that appeased individual Jews who were not happy with her conversion.[43] We do not know how often she and her family observed Jewish rituals, but evidence shows that the family cared about belonging to the Jewish community. Layla's father performed in synagogues and recorded Jewish *taratil* (hymns); in one of Zaki's recordings in Hebrew, we can hear a female child's voice chanting—that child was probably Layla.[44] Zaki visited Jerusalem in 1921 on tour, as did many other artists, including Egyptian Umm Kulthum and Syrian Asmahan, who toured Palestine and the Levant. While in Jerusalem, Zaki spent time with fellow musicians from all religions, but he stayed in the homes of Jewish friends and family members who came from Aleppo and were probably from his wife's side of the family.[45] Sending children to a Christian missionary school, training his daughter in Islamic chanting, and respecting Islam should not cast doubt on Zaki's and his children's Jewishness. It is because Layla knew how vital the Jewish faith was to her father that she kept her conversion secret until after his death, an indication that she did not convert simply on account of the situation in Palestine, in order to protect herself from any backlash against Egyptian Jews or from the suspicion that she sympathized with Zionism. Nevertheless, some amount of political motivation for the timing of her decision to convert to Islam and to publicize her conversion cannot be ruled out: she filed her petition to convert in early December 1947, only a few days after the UN approved the plan for the partition of Palestine on November 29.

Why Layla converted is a question she alone could answer. According to her account, she converted of her own free will, even though Anwar either didn't care or didn't want her to convert.[46] She said that conversion seemed unexceptional to her because she had grown up respecting Islam and many members of her family were Muslim.[47] She confirmed that her main reason for converting was her marriage to a Muslim husband, a personal matter. In 1957, Layla discussed her conversion to Islam in detail. Examining that account helps us understand her agency as a female professional, a celebrity, and a minority woman in an interfaith marriage. In her autobiography she wrote:

> When I got married to Anwar, I genuinely believed that religious difference is not the norm between married couples. I urged him to announce my conversion to Islam. I did not miss a chance to beg him to share my wish to embrace Islam. One day, Anwar surprised me by saying I must convert to Islam immediately because our marriage could not continue with our religious differences.[48] I enthusiastically welcomed that [suggestion] and asked to expedite [doing] it. He [Anwar] invited the late Shaykh Mahmud Abu al-'Uyun, and I embraced Islam in his presence, then went to the official authorities to document it.[49]

Laws and practices of citizenship in Egypt privileged men over women and Muslims over non-Muslims.[50] Layla's account speaks to an issue rarely discussed openly in modern Egypt: the citizenship of minority women. The fragility of the position of minority wives before the law is twofold, combining the weak legal positions of women and of religious minorities. In her account, Layla hints that her conversion took place much earlier than Anwar's acknowledgment, as he resisted her wish to announce her conversion. She also affirms that it was Anwar who decided when to announce her conversion and who arranged the staged pictures with Shaykh Abu al-'Uyun to be used for publicity in 1948.[51] Notwithstanding Anwar's intention to publicize the conversion in July 1948 during the first Arab-Zionist war in Palestine, Layla had taken the necessary action to document her legal conversion in 1947. Anwar did not sign her conversion document as a witness; in fact, we do not know whether he accompanied her to the court or even knew about her conversion. At the crucial intersection of gender and religion, Layla's conversion provided at least partial empowerment against the patriarchal system that favored Muslim men, even though it also reconfirmed the system of social differences based on religion and gender.[52] Documenting her conversion ensured that the state guaranteed her new rights as a Muslim citizen and a Muslim wife, that she gained the legal privileges as well as responsibilities of a Muslim woman as stipulated in the state's laws. Her documented conversion altered her legal position in the institution of marriage.

We do not know whether Layla meant to hide her conversion when she chose to register her conversion to Islam without announcing it in the press. High-ranking legal officials handled the court's legal procedures, and she herself selected a reporter and an employee in the religious institution of Dar al-Ifta' to be her witnesses, witnesses who might have contributed to publicizing Layla's conversion or at least decided not to keep it secret. One would suppose that she asked the reporter who served as a witness not to publish the news until she had prepared her family for the new reality. In any case, her conversion became public on July 26, 1948, with the publication of pictures of her wearing the hijab and reading the Qur'an on the cover of *al-Ithnayn wa al-Dunya* magazine.[53] She and Anwar orchestrated the celebratory coverage, including interviews with both of them, and staged pictures in their private home months later. They made her conversion public against the backdrop of the war in Palestine in 1948. We cannot dismiss the influence of the anti-Jewish sentiment that was gaining ground among different sectors of Egyptians on the timing of the announcement; the war in Palestine was clearly behind Anwar's sudden insistence on her converting in order to continue their marriage. Anti-Jewish sentiment culminated in June 1948 when someone threw a grenade into Cairo's Jewish Quarter, resulting in twenty-two deaths and forty-one injuries.

Publicizing her conversion ten weeks after the first Arab-Israeli war broke out in May 1948 altered Layla's social position to that of a Muslim

Egyptian and thus may have provided her some protection from the negative sentiments against Jews triggered by the war; if she had no need of such
protection, she would not have needed to publicize the private matter of
her religious conversion. The choice of Shaykh Mahmud Abu al-'Uyun to
stage her publicized conversion images bestowed a great deal of credibility
on the publicity campaign. Shaykh Abu al-'Uyun was among the signatories
of the fatwa of al-Azhar 'Ulma denouncing the UN partition resolution in
1947 and urging jihad on the part of Muslims in Palestine. He had enjoyed a
high profile in Egyptian public life since his nationalist activism in the 1919
Revolution and religious efforts to abolish licensed prostitution in the 1920s.
More important, when he appeared with Layla publicizing her conversion,
he held a religious position of great authority as general secretary of al-Azhar
Mosque and its associated religious educational institutions.

When and how Layla and Anwar publicized her conversion challenges
the common notion about the supposed high levels of tolerance in what is
known in Egyptian historiography as the Liberal Era (1923–1952). Contemporary Egyptian sources often cite Layla Murad's popularity and success
together with that of many other entertainers from religious-minority communities as evidence of tolerance and pluralism in pre-1952 Egyptian society.
However, celebrities do not necessarily constitute the best evidence for such
tolerance and pluralism. Entertainment was not a well-respected profession;
becoming a public performer challenged the notion of respectability held by
bourgeois Muslim and Coptic communities; indeed, until the early twentieth century, many public performers came from non-Egyptian and minority
communities. The respectable status of Muslim musicians Salama Higazi
and Sayyid Darwish, Christian actors George and Dawlat Abyad, and Jewish musicians Dawud Husni and Zaki Murad testifies to changes in social
respectability of performers as well as the role of mass media in making
entertainers stars in public life. By definition, public performance contradicted the Egyptian virtue of *satr*, which literally means becoming covered
or invisible and idiomatically refers to sexual, moral, and socioeconomic respectability.[54] Pioneer Egyptian Muslim women performers faced an uphill
struggle to achieve social respectability: Fatima Rushdi began her acting career playing male roles; Umm Kulthum began her singing career dressed like
an Arab boy; and Bahiga Hafiz's family shunned her.

This societal change came with the rise of mass-mediated entertainment, which turned performers into national household names who played leading roles in formulating national popular culture. Thanks to these sociocultural changes, Layla was the first and possibly the only minority entertainer to attain a level of respectability comparable to that of the exceptional Muslim vocalist Umm Kulthum. Even among Layla's generation, the female singer Raga' 'Abdu (1919–1999) concealed her Christian faith by adopting a neutral stage name instead of her overtly Coptic name, Raga' 'Abd al-Masih. Stars with obviously Jewish names, such as Sirina Ibrahim and Salha Qasin, faded away, while many Jewish actresses adopted neutral names: Nanit became Nagwa Salim, and Rachel became Raqya Ibrahim. European fascism and anti-Semitism had only a limited presence among small numbers of Egyptian intellectuals and activists in the interwar period,[55] while Egyptian support for the Palestinian struggle against Zionists and the British fostered some anti-Jewish sentiment among some political groups such as the Muslim Brotherhood and Young Egypt. The culture of tolerance had its limits, and Layla was subject to some of the anti-Jewish stereotyping that manifested in Egyptian society in the face of Zionist activities in Palestine. In the early 1940s author Zaki Mubarak described Layla's voice as having an "Israeli [Hebrew] accent that makes her the singer of the Jews;"[56] in 1943 a critic wrote about her: "That Jew would be more successful if she stretches her hand and becomes generous in [funding] melody."[57]

In July of 1949, on account of her domestic troubles with Anwar, Layla requested and acquired a copy of the legal document of her conversion (on which I base this analysis). Her shaky marriage prompted her to document her conversion in the state's records and to acquire an official copy for her own records. This documentation would provide her with some legal protection during the seemingly endless financial disputes with her Muslim husband, disputes that were a prominent feature of her shaky marriage.[58]

Domestic Troubles

In 1949, the domestic disagreements between the couple became too serious to keep secret. After a brief separation, the couple reconciled and issued a public statement in December 1949, sharing with fans that they were committed to each other and that their love was as strong as ever. Nonetheless, news about their disputes continued to appear in the press as frequently as news about their films; the press labeled their continual fights and arguments as "the everyday story." Reports confirmed that Layla frequently fled the marital house; she would come back subsequent to the mediation of friends, and then the same cycle would be repeated. The problematic relationship between the celebrity couple culminated in "a personal tragedy:"[59] reports confirmed rumors that Anwar physically abused Layla and that she felt unsafe as a result. According to some accounts, Layla spoke to journalists about Anwar's abuse and then asked them not to publish, lest Anwar violently punish her. Eventually, journalists stopped taking what she shared with them seriously; according to one account, an editor made her sign an agreement before publishing an interview about Anwar's domestic abuse.[60] Her frequent escapes from their marital apartment in downtown Cairo following every disagreement might have reflected her fear, or might have been attempts to pressure him into accepting her demands. In any case, the press urged Layla to stop running away even if she had the right to leave and had legitimate reasons to do so,[61] typical traditional advice that prioritizes the continuation of family life over women's safety. Both social pressure and the hope of saving her marriage led Layla to promise her fans that she would not leave the house and say jokingly that she would make Anwar leave if the situation reached an unbearable point.[62]

Since no police or hospital records provide any domestic violence documentation, we cannot verify or accurately assess the level of abuse, nor can we cannot any abuse that might have taken place in private. But a contemporary journalist gave an eyewitness account of Anwar's callous attitude toward Layla in public. Shortly after Anwar's death, journalist Muhammad Shusha wrote that Anwar was so cruel to Layla that he hit her and gave by way of an example something that took place during the shooting of their masterpiece, *Ghazal al-Banat*, in 1949. When Layla tripped and fell on a pile of wood in the studio, she screamed in pain; everyone rushed to check on her except Anwar who, according to Shusha, pretended he was busy looking through the camera. Shusha urged him to pay attention to Layla and comfort her, but Anwar gave him the cold shoulder, telling him, "She just tripped, and it is not a big deal, but if I went to her, she would cry more and make a scene and won't work today, so it is better to ignore her."[63] Layla's only public comment about Anwar's abuse came in her interview with Egyptian Public Radio in 1979. She expressed her regret that she had not known about Anwar's deteriorating health conditions and said that his kidney disease caused his fiery temper. While expressing deep affection for him, she said, "I did not know that his pain and disease caused him to be constantly furious. . . . I wish I had known, but I was too young to understand."[64] She spoke again about the special love she had for Anwar in a televised interview with composer Baligh Hamdi which aired on Abu Dhabi television in 1978.[65]

While the couple reached the peak of their success together in *Ghazal al-Banat*, released in September 1949, their marriage faltered. After a short period of separation, they got back together and thanked their fans whose "phone calls, telegraphs, and letters played the dove of peace."[66] In a humorous and joyful statement dated December 1, 1949, signed by the couple in their apartment in the famous Immobilia building, Layla and Anwar promised to live happily together and never give up on each other.[67] But peace lasted no longer than three months; and again their colleagues served as mediators, encouraging the couple to return to their marital home. With help from the press, Layla and Anwar had already made their fans a third party in their relationship, using it to generate sympathy. Neither of them tried to protect or advocate for their right to privacy; on the contrary, the couple asked journalists from their apartment in Immobilia to ensure the continuation of their marriage. But on Sunday, March 26, 1950, they signed their second divorce decree in the office of lawyer 'Abbas al-Gamal.[68] They allowed journalists to photograph and publish pictures of them signing the divorce decree. The manager of Anwar's company, Mahmud al-Shafi'i, and the Sharia lawyer Sulayman al-Ibyari signed the divorce document as witnesses. In the same session, the couple's representatives discussed and finalized the financial settlements; former state minister Mustafa Mar'i represented Layla, and lawyer Zuhayr Garana represented Anwar. Finalizing the divorce and financial settlements in a law office in the presence of legal and financial representatives emphasized their insistence on a final separation, as well as indicating how financial and legal disagreements dominated their relationship. Despite their love for each other, Layla and Anwar turned to legal experts and politicians to negotiate the financial details of their shaky marriage and multiple divorces, and they employed their connections with journalists to communicate about their private life to the public on their be-half. It is important to note that Layla was not a naïve, heartbroken woman unaware of or indifferent to her financial and legal rights; as a professional and a businesswoman, she turned to experts and powerful men to represent her and make sure she got her due. The settlement, unsurprisingly, did not satisfy Anwar or Layla, but it was a professional business settlement, not marred by emotional or passionate outbursts.

Many people believed that the couple were still deeply in love, regard-less of the anger and hatred they expressed toward each other. The celebrity magazine *al-Kawakib* shrewdly procured and published pictures of each of them attending two different concerts held at the same time on the first Thursday of the month: Anwar attended a concert given by Nagat al-Saghira in Alexandria and Layla a concert by Umm Kulthum in Cairo. During the concerts, in which Nagat and Umm Kulthum performed the same song, "Sahran Liwahdi" (Awake alone), they were surrounded by friends. Both of them were elegantly dressed, but their faces betrayed sorrow and despair; Anwar, in particular, seemed lost and deeply depressed. The public divorce and public suffering invited discourse about modern family life and love ver-sus money and business; the editor of *al-Studio* wrote, "It is a harsh lesson about the life of artists. Everyone envies them for fame, glory, and money, but their private life is hell."[69] Friends and fans sent hundreds of messages to the press, urging the celebrity couple to reverse their decision. Reports predicted that their pain and suffering would bring them together again, and indeed the prediction came true: the couple remarried each other again in the fol-lowing months. And then, again, the couple went through another divorce in early July 1952, with a final separation in early 1953.[70]

A few months after reconciliation and working together to contain the damage caused by a crisis of false rumors that Layla had donated money to Israel, rumors about their imminent separation broke out in early 1953. They tried to disprove the false rumors about her donating money to Israel by appearing in public together. They jointly attended a forum discussing cen-sorship in the publishing house of *al-Fann* magazine, on January 12, 1953; their arrival together was intended as a statement that, though divorced, they were still a couple.[71] The advertisements for their last film together, *Bint al-Akabir*, appeared alongside the news of their divorce in the same periodicals.[72]

Promoting his image as a supporter of the Free Officers' regime at the same time as the film, Anwar employed bombastic language in praise of the new regime. Publicity materials included such statements as "A new film for a new era," "Best film to achieve the present regime's goal of destroying the class system and achieving equality for all before the constitution," "Everyone is equal, and the good citizen is one who works for their nation," and "The story that destroyed the shackles of injustice and abolished the class system."[73]

All accounts agree that Layla and Anwar's marital troubles were rooted in their business and financial disagreements. Initially, the couple offered similar narratives but from different perspectives on their disputes. After Anwar's death in 1955, Layla's perspective prevailed—Anwar's heirs were too busy with their financial disagreements over the division of his estate to care about defending his legacy or challenging Layla's narratives. In the course of time, Layla gave conflicting accounts, reflecting how her feelings and perspective on her past changed over time. Between divorces and following the final separation, Layla complained that Anwar tried to monopolize her even though she needed to work for other producers in order to cover her expenses. She addressed the possibility of jealousy in her first account of their final separation, while Anwar was still alive, saying that she never let jealousy affect their marriage: "Whenever he worked with women he had had affairs with before marriage, I hurt but never talked or objected." In a straightforward answer about the real reason for their disagreements and divorce, she said: "Work! He did not want me to work for any other company except his. I have financial responsibilities, and if I had a fortune as Qut al-Qulub has, I would have agreed."[74] Layla's statement suggested a relationship between Anwar and Qut al-Qulub, a Lebanese actress and singer who launched her career in nightclubs in the Levant and then came to Cairo to make use of her wealth in producing and starring in films.[75] Qut al-Qulub never worked with Anwar or appeared in any of his productions, even though she was thirty years his junior.

Layla and Anwar accused each other of greed, among other things. Anwar complained that Layla's work with competing producers hurt his business and decreased his company's revenues. He also complained that Layla's intense work schedule undermined her domestic commitment as a wife; he wanted her to devote herself to giving him a child, but her work, wealth, and fame made her feel sufficiently independent to disregard his wishes. Layla in turn blamed Anwar for rendering her unable to meet her financial duties and responsibilities, in particular her ongoing commitment to supporting her siblings, which was no secret. After Anwar's death, claims that he had forced her to work for him for free and never paid for her work in his productions surfaced. Layla's first biography, penned by the Egyptian journalist Muhammad al-Sayyid Shusha and published in 1956 in Beirut, one year after Anwar's death, concluded that financial disputes had turned their private life into hell and chased love out of their home. Shusha claimed that "she received 10,000 EGP a film, but never received her wage whenever she worked in his [Anwar's] productions. She had to work for other producers, which always upset him to the extent that he ejected a famous actor from their house so she would not appear with that star in a movie."[76] Layla gave the same account when she told her side of the story in 1957 but claimed that she did not mean to stain the memory of the deceased Anwar Wagdi, who "remained even after divorce a dear colleague."[77] She talked about their professional and financial disagreements:

> Our disagreements increased when he said he would not let me work with other producers while I worked for him for free. When he realized that I accepted offers from other companies, our situation descended into one violent crisis after another. Our life together continued that way; every day, a new disagreement [broke out], and friends intervened for reconciliation. Our dispute became familiar, continually repeating itself, and always left me with unbearable pain. My life became unstable, and I lacked hope. Our marital life started cracking, and everyone knew our life together was dangerously unstable. We overcame a disagreement only to confront a new one. It could have been possible to bear with these disagreements with some tolerance and patience, except that Anwar was infatuated with colossal propaganda. He leaked news about our disagreements to the public and the press, considering this successful publicity.[78]

Layla wrote that Anwar told producers that "he would not allow me to work in their productions and wished to monopolize my talent. Every time we quarreled over that, he apologized and explained he did so because he felt jealous out of love for me." According to Layla, after Muhammad 'Abd al-Wahab set up a partnership with him, Anwar rejected 'Abd al-Wahab's plan to produce the film *'Ashiq Walhan* (*Madly in Love*) starring Layla,[79] as well as terminating her film project *Nur Ba'd al-Zalam*, which 'Abd al-Wahab planned to produce for her in 1952.[80] Layla accused Anwar of being vehemently opposed to her working with Abd al-Wahab, the most influential Egyptian musician of the twentieth century. That Layla was fond of 'Abd al-Wahab, who in 1938 gave her her first opportunity to become a movie star, was no secret. Anwar partnered with 'Abd al-Wahab, and their company produced films starring Anwar and Layla; Layla claimed that Anwar harshly criticized all the melodies 'Abd al-Wahab composed for her in these productions.

Based on Layla's one-sided account, actor Kamal al-Shinnawi, who had witnessed disagreements between the couple and mediated between them before the second divorce, produced and starred in a fictional film, *Tariq al-Dumu'* (*The Way of Tears*; Hilmi Halim, 1961), vilifying Anwar. Business competition and professional jealousy tarnished the relationship between Anwar and the younger, handsome star al-Shinnawi. At the conclusion of the film, when Anwar is very ill and approaching death, he feels guilty and tries to make it up to Layla by offering her a large sum of money, which she refuses.[81] Al-Shinnawi's unflattering account of Anwar's character resonates with that of filmmaker Muhammad Karim, who provided a disturbing narrative about Anwar early in his career during his marriage to Ilham Husain. Karim chose Ilham for the leading role in *Yum Sa'id* (*A Happy Day*; Muhammad Karim, 1940) in 1940, appreciating her beauty and dedication. Because Ilham was still a minor—only seventeen years old—her husband became her legal guardian; in that capacity, Anwar signed Ilham's work contract and work permit and collected her fees. According to Karim, Ilham had to walk to work for miles because Anwar refused to give her money for transportation.[82]

The various accounts concerning Anwar's and Layla's troubled relationship are in agreement on two issues: financial disagreements and Layla's victimization resulting from Anwar's harsh business conduct and his attempts to monopolize her work. Narratives emphasizing Layla's victimization, however, overlook her formidable financial and business skills, underestimate the benefits she received from working in Anwar's productions, and ignore her high productivity during the time she was married to Anwar. Layla's business skills manifested in her cinematic career early when she doubled her fee for her second film with Togo Mizrahi. Once she reached the age of twenty-one, she removed her father from her business management, and her skills made her Egypt's highest-paid actress. Those who worked with her experienced her prowess in negotiating business deals. She rejected a second film project with Karim and 'Abd al-Wahab, despite her great respect for the latter, because she wanted more money. Many years later, 'Abd al-Wahab said about Layla's financial management, "She carefully bargains over a bundle of parsley as she bargains over an astrakhan fur coat."[83]

One anecdote supporting 'Abd al-Wahab's observation took place during the shooting of *Khatim Sulayman* (*Solomon's Ring*; Hassan Ramzi, 1947). Layla arrived at Studio Galal in a cab; as she was exiting the vehicle, she slammed the door, shattering the window glass. The cab driver insisted on charging Layla 1.2 Egyptian pounds, but Layla refused to pay him, insisting that she was not responsible for the damage. The producing manager paid the driver the fare and the fee for the broken window, which he added to the production cost.[84] Layla received 12,000 Egyptian pounds for that film but refused to pay .01 percent of that amount to a working-class man because she didn't have to—which shows (among other things) that she was determined not to be taken advantage of.

The open challenge to accounts of Layla as victim and Anwar as villain came decades later. Filmmaker Hassan al-Sayfi, who worked in Anwar's production company and assisted him in directing many films, including five films starring Layla, denied that Anwar made Layla work for free in his productions. Al-Sayfi said that he was responsible for paying Layla and getting her to sign the receipts, and that Layla was professional and formal in conducting business with her husband's company, coming down from her and Anwar's private apartment to Anwar's company offices, both in the same Immobilia building, to collect her money and sign receipts and contracts.[85] Layla's eldest son, Ashraf Abaza, said that his mother loved Anwar and never claimed that he did not pay her fees.[86] These accounts by Layla's contemporaries provide anecdotal evidence countering the claims that Anwar took advantage of Layla, offering a counternarrative to Layla's depiction as a naïve woman exploited by her greedy husband.

Layla's productivity while married to Anwar increased almost twofold
compared to that before their marriage. Anwar's company produced only
one-third of her films. Between launching her cinematic career in 1938 until
her marriage to Anwar in 1945, Layla appeared in nine films, which means
she starred in 1.125 films a year. During her eight years of marriage to Anwar,
Layla starred in seventeen films: 2.125 films a year. Anwar produced only six
of these seventeen films (35%) in addition to *Bint al-Fuqara'*, which I count
as a pre-marriage production. In 1947, she released four films in one year,
only one of them with Anwar, which demonstrates her power and ability to
stand up for herself and act independently from him. Her productivity after
her marriage was remarkable, especially considering that she had become a
wife, with additional domestic and family responsibilities. After their first
divorce, she likely sought financial security in her work, not in her marriage.
In some cases, she signed work contracts despite Anwar's opposition; in others, he readily supported her, realizing the necessity or importance of her
work—perhaps he appreciated that her work released him from any financial responsibility toward her, as well as the increase in their mutual income.
Whether or not Anwar wanted to monopolize her and extract the greatest
amount of profit from her work, she continued to be professionally independent and worked with other producers more than she worked for Anwar.

Layla also gained significantly from Anwar's high-quality and generously
funded productions, which surely contributed to her negotiating power with
other producers. Anwar's production company paid for writers of lyrics and
composers of music for the songs Layla performed in her films. These songs
became hers, and she performed them for payment in private concerts and
radio broadcasts. His company also covered the cost of the elegant dresses
she wore in films. The French fashion house Chanel Haute Couture designed
the double cloche dress she wore while singing "Habib a-Ruh" (1951) in the
film by that title; the dress had crystal and silver stripes and a wing-like back
that made Layla look like an angel. The dress cost a fortune, and Layla wore
it in her public concerts after her final separation with Anwar in 1953. Anwar
generously supported her cinematic look and their extravagant lifestyle. Her
biographer, Salih Mursi, points to what he considers the contradictions of
Anwar's personality and his financial behavior toward Layla: "Anwar was like
a tornado in his business conduct. He was not stingy but was a businessman.

When he tried to reduce how much he paid her, they quarreled, but these situations were bearable. Whenever they traveled to Europe, Anwar bought Layla clothing worth thousands of Egyptian pounds, but he turned life into hell whenever she considered an offer from another producer."[87]

When they were married in 1945, Anwar and Layla agreed that she would continue working for him as well as other producers. When working for him, she would be paid in full, and she would keep her bank account separate; Anwar was aware of and respected her need to support her family and siblings, and therefore to control her own finances. He could also have arranged his finances another way, reducing the amount he paid Layla as an indirect way of making her contribute to the expenses of their lavish lifestyle instead of covering them all by himself. In her view, he was responsible for paying for their living expenses as well as expensive gifts for her and vacations; thus, in his view, it would seem only fair for her to work on his productions for less pay.

Their financial and domestic expectations continued to clash. Anwar found himself in an increasingly difficult position. Layla's films produced by others competed with his productions, yet he could only praise her work lest he undermine the biggest star working for his company. As a wealthy husband, he set store by his male privilege, but to his disappointment Layla did not need his money or his protection. Her fame and popularity were equal to, if not greater than, his. They were in love, but they were also professionals, equally tough negotiators in financial and business matters. They were a married couple, but also stars competing for popularity and fans' love and loyalty. Their intensive work schedules left little time to spend together as a loving couple. And, of course, Layla and Anwar were never entirely alone, as the gaze of fans and the press was omnipresent.

Publicity and the press had been essential tools in Layla and Anwar's domestic and professional life. From the beginning of their marriage, they used their domestic life, in good times and bad, to promote their films and their fame, to build their public image as a superstar duo, as a married couple, and as individual public figures. Both with and without their consent, the boundaries between their domestic and public life became blurred and their domestic and public affairs became indistinguishable. They had never shied away from exposing their personal lives to the public gaze: factual and fake news, half-truths and lies, benign and hurtful rumors, favorable and offensive information, all publicized their work and personas, and contributed to their stardom. They pursued public attention, converted it into profits, and used the mixture of private, artistic, and business news and gossip to sell movie tickets.

Layla and Anwar each adopted different strategies to promote their public image during their marriage and after their final separation. What each of them chose to disclose to or hide from the public gaze reflects the social expectations and gender disparity involved in the morality and sexuality of their time. While they were married, Anwar dominated the public narrative of their private life, thanks to his company's propaganda machine and his status as a tycoon in the film industry. For better or worse, Anwar invited audiences to share his longing for Layla as well as his pain. He aroused and fanned public curiosity, talking about both his happiness and his misery living with Layla. Shortly after rumors about their separation began circulating in 1946, Anwar extolled his marriage to Layla as the luckiest thing in his life, employing a gambling metaphor (the "derby horse race") for picking a spouse. He said that he'd picked a loser in his first marriage, but when he married Layla, "I won the primo. Layla Murad is not only a famous actress and singer but also a great wife." He also told the press some seemingly fabricated stories, such as that a crazy fan of Layla's once stormed their house at midnight to ask Layla to divorce Anwar and marry him; Layla hit him with a broomstick.[88]

When the Italian star Assia Noris (1912–1998) visited Cairo in 1949, Anwar and Layla hosted her. In *al-Kawakib*'s coverage of the visit, Layla was represented as Anwar's silent, supportive wife. According to the newspaper, Noris stared at Layla for a while and then told Anwar: "Your wife is nice and beautiful. She gives me a good idea about the Egyptian cinema and its expected amazing future."[89] Layla was not always quiet; in another situation, she publicly mocked Anwar and made a joke about his gaining weight, a sensitive issue for Anwar, since it threatened his ability to be cast in leading male roles. In fact, younger male stars openly asked Anwar to give up performing the young-lover parts in view of his advanced age and weight.

Sensational press coverage in interwar Egypt reached beyond the barrier of illiteracy, and both Layla and Anwar manipulated it in order to construct

their public personas. Following *Layla Bint al-Fuqara'*, their first movie as
a couple, Layla moved out to stay with her family and Anwar frequently
appeared in public alone; his company personnel let journalists think that divorce might be imminent.[90] Later, after their final separation, Layla clarified
that she had returned to her family in order to care for a sick family member, not because of any domestic problem with Anwar; she adverted to this
incident to illustrate Anwar's insatiable and tasteless appetite for publicity.[91]
Journalist Husain 'Uthman called the incident "American divorce," or fake
news.[92] Considering the couple's continuing troubles, however, despite what
Layla said later, it is possible that she moved back with her family because
of a fight with Anwar and that he publicized it in order to promote his first
production. The couple were still relatively newly wed, so stories and speculation about their disagreements as well as a possible separation and divorce,
would be rather sensational. Indeed, in this case the news did the trick and
increased public interest in the couple and in *Layla Bint al-Fuqara'*.[93] Not
everyone deplored Anwar's thirst for publicity: Yusuf Wahbi praised him
for his ability to attract attention in order to sell tickets, while the editor of
al-Kawakib viewed the fabrication of stories involving stars as imaginative
public relations.[94]

Gossip and celebrity periodicals laid the foundation for Layla's image
as being fragile and victimized, which became the typical construction of
her persona throughout the following decades. Salih Gawdat, editor of *al-
Kawakib*, treated Layla as if her personal attributes were the same as those
of the characters she played in films: "Layla in [real] life is Layla that you
see on-screen. [She is] that delicate, dreaming, and unfairly treated woman
who wins in the end. [She is] that emotional and loving woman."[95] Gawdat
also introduced the gendered narrative contrasting Layla's and Anwar's characters: Layla was the lyre (*qithara*), whose melody is soft and meek, while
Anwar was a jazz band, loud and noisy. Gawdat explained that "Layla and
Anwar are [as different as] day and night, East and West. They coexist but
never mix." He said that Layla had told him that for her, singing was as sa-
cred as praying and should only be performed by the heart in solitude while
one looks at heaven and that it was because her father forced her that she
began to perform in public: "I sang while I hated doing so. Once the stage's
curtain was down, I withdrew to my room, closed the door, and drowned

in tears."[96] Gawdat quoted her in reference to her shy personality, which "kept her away from people and caused tension with Anwar." Suggesting that Anwar did not appreciate Layla or her talent, Gawdat quoted his response to a question about his opinion of Layla's singing: "I don't know, she does not sing at home . . . she only screams and yells."[97] Gawdat's construction of Layla's persona as a shy woman became commonplace, even though it is belied by recordings of informal get-togethers among friends in which Layla talks, sings, and jokes with and mocks journalists and artists. Some of these recordings come from personal collections and are available on YouTube. Listeners can hear for themselves how much of a free spirit Layla was.[98]

Layla and Anwar, and Audiences in Between

How Layla Murad and Anwar Wagdi managed their public images following their final split provides a clear illustration of the performativity of constructed gender and sexuality, on display in the space provided by the press. Layla represented herself as a strong woman who made the tough decision for final separation and laid down sound professional and financial plans; Anwar, on the other hand, represented himself as a romantic lover suffering from devastating loneliness. In sharing their intimate feelings and domestic life with the public through the press, they did not care about their own and one another's privacy. After admitting that she had initially accepted the option of a temporary marriage (*muhallal*) in order to remarry Anwar, Layla announced that Anwar had exited her life for good, and she began to make post-divorce professional and financial investments.[99] She started building an apartment block and established a cinema production company, al-Kawakib Film: Layla Murad & Co. While Layla was becoming a producer and a woman of property, Anwar presented himself as a heartbroken man and a playboy, trying to fathom his pain and telling journalists that his problem with Layla was the same as that of Adam with Eve: "I cannot live with her, I cannot live without her."[100] He urged scientists, philosophers, and fans to find him a solution and embellished his public persona as a despairing lover seeking redemption and solace by charming other women and appearing with them in public dancing at boisterous parties. He did not object to the press publishing a picture of him intimately and passionately hugging another woman in a public place.[101] The press did not regard his behavior as normal and commented on his health, as he seemed to be in poor condition and out of shape.[102] Reporters described his flirting with beautiful women as "attempts to attract attention and raise curiosity."[103] In July 1953, Anwar traveled to France, then to Lebanon, on a previously scheduled work trip, planning to spend at least two weeks abroad before returning to Cairo to start directing a new film.[104] According to Salim al-Lawzi, *al-Kawakib*'s correspondent in Beirut, Anwar traveled continually throughout the Middle East and Europe after the divorce, seeking to heal his broken heart;[105] he described Anwar as "*Majnun Layla*" (driven mad by love for Layla) wandering the earth in his madness.[106] In Beirut, as in France, Anwar appeared frequently in public with beautiful women but denied any serious relationship with a Brazilian woman he met in Paris who had accompanied him to Beirut, maintaining that he was still in love with Layla.

In her autobiography, Layla mentioned Anwar's having affairs but was not specific. Following their final separation, Muhammad Badi' Sirbiya, the editor of the Lebanese *al-Maw'id*, interviewed Layla and Anwar separately in Cairo. Layla revealed to Sirbiya that Anwar had dismissed her feelings as those of a wife who was jealous of his female fans, while she cared about his feelings. She mentioned one specific incident in which Anwar brought a beautiful Frenchwoman from Paris and rented her an apartment in Cairo. Anwar denied that he was having an affair with the woman, saying that he had invited her to Cairo to appear in some of his pictures. He made her leave Egypt when Layla confronted him demanding divorce. The couple reconciled and resumed their life together until the third divorce took place.[107] In sum, the incident with the Frenchwoman did not lead to the third and final divorce. However, two decades later, when Salih Mursi published Layla's serialized biography in the mid-1970s, he dramatized the incident, claiming that Layla caught Anwar cheating on her with the Frenchwoman and that this incident was decisive in their final separation.[108] Mursi invented an implausible account that Layla disguised herself as a *baladi* (urban lower- or working-class) woman in order to catch Anwar with his alleged French mistress.

Anwar had been open about his desire to have a child, and after their final separation, he spoke of the depression, boredom, loneliness, and despair that made his life seem like a grave. But he denied rumors that he was looking for a wife who would conceive children for him; he "could not find a woman who could replace Layla Murad. . . . My love for Layla while we are apart is more beautiful and more pleasurable."[109] Upon returning to Cairo, Anwar garnered public attention by talking about his failure to remarry because he was still madly in love with Layla. In his search for another partner who could replace Layla in his heart, Anwar said he planned to marry a woman who was not Egyptian, whom he described, to use his own words, as "beauty and modernism [sic],"[110] but he abandoned the plan when his friends advised him that a foreign wife would not understand him. His plans to marry other women, Egyptian or non-Egyptian, repeatedly failed, he said, because the proposed woman would be hurt when she realized how much he was still in love with Layla. According to him, whenever he appeared with a woman in public, people told him that he would never find another woman who would equal Layla, and his friends warned him that his fans would never accept his taking another wife. Anwar garnered public interest by asking audiences to find a solution for him, because "as a young man (shabb), I could not go on in life alone."[111] He was almost fifty years old at the time.

Anwar offered a substantial monetary prize, 100 Egyptian pounds, to the reader who would mail him the best advice on how to resolve his emotional crisis with Layla and help him deal with his need to live with a loving partner.[112] This sufficed to keep the public interested in Anwar's broken heart and attract them to theaters to watch the last film starring Layla and Anwar together. While waiting for readers' advice about his desperate love for Layla, Anwar launched an investment project of building a new apartment block in downtown Cairo.[113] His publicity campaign openly bashed Layla and portrayed himself as a victim. To refute the whispers (and shouts) that he was an exploitative, abusive husband, Anwar promoted the image of himself as an abandoned lover and lonely divorced man, playing the gender card by exploiting every misogynistic streak in the public culture. He expressed pain whenever the public cast him in the shadow of Layla's fame and popularity: "My name is mentioned only in combination with Layla's; people have no mercy."[114] Displaying photographs showing President Muhammad Nagib's profile on his wall, Anwar continued talking about Layla's heartless negotiations, which were "far from emotional and empty of any romantic feelings. She gave me strange conditions as if we were negotiating a commercial transaction, not exchanging faithful love. My hope collapsed, and I refused to continue negotiations. Layla has changed and wasted my true gratitude for her help in achieving my success once she dictated her conditions to resume our marriage life."[115]

To cement his construction of Layla as a materialistic and business-oriented woman who fell far short of the social expectations of a good wife, Anwar played on his yearning to become a father. He claimed that Layla deliberately avoided pregnancy so that she could continue to work as a performer and earn more money to support her siblings, even though Layla had expressed her wish to become a mother in the early 1950s.[116] After their third divorce, Anwar continued to denigrate Layla, referring to social values that looked down upon women who did not want to or could not conceive while sympathizing with the male desire to reproduce children, especially male. Anwar claimed that Layla was barren and that he wanted to remarry in order to have a son. He told the press:

> I need a son. I am, thank God, well off. My fame could not grow further; my art business goes as well as I could wish. I have nothing to long for in my life except having a son carry my name and inherit my wealth. When I was married to Mrs. Layla Murad, doctors assured me that there was no medical treatment to help Layla conceive. She will never be able to give me what I long for.[117]

Anwar made two false and contradictory claims to generate public sympathy for himself while vilifying Layla. He claimed that she refused to have a child with him lest she become unemployed during pregnancy and while caring for the baby. But he also claimed that she was barren, and thus that he had no choice but to find another wife to give him a child. Anwar was right about one thing: Layla never got pregnant while they were married; but she was not barren. While married to Anwar, Layla had physical examinations having to do with her ability to conceive, though she never shared the results with the public. Anwar said that a doctor had told him that no medication could help her conceive, a statement that Anwar interpreted as meaning she was barren. But the same statement can be interpreted differently: that there appeared to be nothing preventing her from conceiving and that therefore no medication could help. At that time, Anwar was struggling with a serious disease that caused his premature death in 1955. The second interpretation proved to be correct, as Layla became pregnant during her short-lived relationship with Wagih Abaza; she also became pregnant with her second child shortly after she married Fatin 'Abd al-Wahab. It would appear that Layla was quite fertile and that there was no physical impediment to her conceiving a child with Anwar. However, it should not be inferred that Anwar was deliberately lying about Layla's ability to bear children with him. It is likely that he himself never underwent a medical examination to determine his fertility and reproductive health. Until the mid-1950s, such a medical examination was unthinkable; any delay or failure of conception was blamed on the wife. Modern couples might consider visiting a male gynecologist or obstetrician rather than a midwife, but many men would equate an examination to determine a male's fertility with questioning his virility and consider it an assault on his masculinity.

Anwar accentuated his public persona as a man obsessed with having a son. He published an implausible story about a Lebanese beggar whom he met in Beirut. According to the anecdote, the man used to be very wealthy, but when he lost any hope of having a son to inherit his wealth, he lost his drive for work and success. The man dissolved his business and devoted his life to pleasure, thinking that his wealth would support him until his death, even if he lived to be eighty years old. When the man reached eighty, he was penniless and too old to work; he had to beg people for food.[118] In response, Layla publicly refused to resume life with Anwar and shut the door on any possibility of resuming their marriage. She was already involved with Wagih Abaza when she vilified Anwar, telling the press: "It [what he said] is his usual standard words that have become a memorized text. He is a great perfectionist actor, he's perfect in playing the victim part, but I did not victimize him. I will not engage in any discussion with him, he shouted SOS to readers, but I made up my mind, and I insist on keeping silent and keeping myself away from him. I don't want to hear from or about him."[119]

In these public exchanges, Layla and Anwar used the press, namely celebrity and gossip publications, to promote their disagreements and beliefs on gender. Celebrity publications needed their scandalous gossip and uncivil exchanges to attract readership.[120] Anwar and Layla needed celebrity publications to build attractive public images as much as the press needed them to trash each other in public. In doing so, stars and the press advocated certain values inregard to gender relations, women's position in society, and domestic life. Women are victims, and men are conquerors. Their public argumentation solidified public discourses that reduced women's social role to wives and reproductive bodies, while men were elevated to the role of wealth makers and the sole gender that should cherish professional success and preserve patriarchy.

Publicity stills for the film *al-Dahaya* (1935) featuring Layla Murad's image (bottom right) and describing her singing as "angelic."

Yahya al-Hub (*Long Live Love*; Muhammad Karim, 1938), the first movie co-starring Layla Murad and the superstar Muhammad 'Abd al-Wahab. The movie's success was phenomenal, and it set a record at the box office.

In five films under the direction of experienced filmmaker Togo Mizrahi, Layla Murad became a sensational singer-actress whose films were blockbusters throughout the Middle East. The image shows the publicity still for *Layla* (Togo Mizrahi, 1942) from the Tehran theater in Iran; the Persian title of the film was *Lady Camellia*, the title of the novel on which the movie was based.

Poster for the film *Adam wa Hawwa'* (*Adam and Eve*; 1951) co-starring and directed by Husain Sidqi. The film is the best example of normalizing patriarchal values and male dominance in Layla Murad's movies.

Poster for the film *Habib al-Ruh* (*Eternal Love*; Anwar Wagdi, 1951). The film encourages women to abandon their talents and careers to pursue love in a patriarchal marriage.

Advertisement for the last movie co-starring Layla Murad and Anwar Wagdi, *Bint al-Akabir* (*Daughter of the Nobility*; Anwar Wagdi, 1953). The ad highlights Layla's song for the Muslim pilgrimage to Mecca. The publicity campaign for this film claimed that the film strives to destroy the class system and build social justice.

Layla Murad and Anwar Wagdi, in military uniform in *Layla Bint al-Fuqara'* (*Layla, Daughter of the Poor*; Anwar Wagdi, 1945) (top) and in police uniform in *Qalbi Dalili* (*My Heart Guides Me*; Anwar Wagdi, 1947) (bottom). Both films promoted the modern middle-class masculine *afandi* as the savior of women from all classes.

The contemporary press reported extensively on the marital disputes between Layla Murad and her first husband, Anwar Wagdi, while the celebrity couple equally courted such publicity. The couple are kissing in a picture they sent to the press after one of their breakups (top). The couple circulated another to publicize a third honeymoon, marking their reconciliation after their second divorce (bottom).

As a celebrity couple, Layla Murad and Anwar Wagdi used their fame and success to promote different commodities. This image of them publicizes Wasp cigarettes.

Layla Murad publicizing her conversion to Islam on the cover of al-Ithnayn wa al-Dunya magazine on July 26, 1948. Source: *al-Ithnayn*, July 26, 1948

Three staged pictures of Layla Murad publicizing her conversion and learning about Islam from Sheikh Abu al-'Uyun. These images appeared in the press in 1948, and Egyptian traditional and social media have widely circulated them in the last few years. Source: *al-Ithnayn*, July 26, 1948

Layla Murad dressed like a Palestinian woman while performing "Operetta Palestine" in *Shadi-yat al-Wadi* (*The Singer in the Valley*), released in 1947 on the eve of the 1948 war in Palestine. The image is courtesy of Mr. Ahmad Yasin Murad, Laila Mourad Facebook page group.

Following the July 1952 Revolution, Layla Murad became the voice of the Free Officers' regime, and the regime supported her in refuting the false rumors that she had donated money to Israel. Layla practices for the liberation anthem of the Free Officers' regime (left); army officers receive her during her participation in the Free Officers' national fundraising known as the Mercy Train (right). Source: *al-Kawakib*, August 4, 1953

في ضيافة قائد الجناح وجيه اباظه

The only picture of Layla Murad and her soon-to-be, secret husband, Free Officer Wagih Abaza, in the latter's house in al-Sharqiyya province. *Al-Fann* magazine ran the picture only once during its coverage of Layla's trip with the Mercy Train in January 1953; back then, no other publication dared to publish any image or explicit news about Layla's relationship with Abaza. From left to right: Layla Murad, actor Sa'id Abu Bakr, Free Officer Wagih Abaza. Source: *al-Fann*, January 1953

إن الفقيد الرئيس جمال عبد الناصر، والى يمينه الصاغ كمال الدين حسين ، والصاغ صلاح سالم ، وعلى يساره
القائد عبد اللطيف البغدادي والى يساره السيدوى للخصم ، وعلى اليمين فرغام لخمية أقسمه عبد الجلال ..

الفن يحتفل بليلة الجلاء

كانت ليلة حاسمة في تاريخنا ، ليلة مجيدة انتظرناها اثنين وسبعين عاما .. ليلة غرب عن أفق مصر شبح
الاحتلال فكان أن خرجت جموع الشعب الحر الى ساحة التحرير نشترك مع أبطال ثورتها وجلائها فى مهرجان
اهل الفن

President Nasser and his Free Officer colleagues attending the evacuation festivals in October 1954, at which Layla tearfully performed "Ask about Me." From left to right: Salah Salim; Kamal al-Din Hussein and his child; Gamal Abd al-Nasser; and 'Abd al-Latif al-Baghdadi. Layla's secret husband and publicity official Free Officer Wagih Abaza did not attend, marking a crisis in his relationship with Layla Murad. Source: *al-Kawakib*, October 26, 1954

Layla Murad and other women artists attended Nasser's funeral at Omar Makram Mosque, in downtown Cairo, in September 1970. From left to right: Fayda Kamil, Karima Mukhtar, 'Aqila Ratib, and Layla Murad. Twenty-five years later, in November 1995, artists attended Layla Murad's funeral in the same mosque.

Layla Murad's obituary as it appeared in the daily newspaper *al-Ahram* on November 23, 1995. After quoting from the Qu'ran, the obituary reports that Layla Murad's burial took place the previous day and that the funeral reception would take place on November 23, 1995, in the Omar Makram Mosque. The obituary uses her full formal name, Layla Zaki Murad, and describes her as a great artist. It mentions her sons, living and deceased siblings, one niece, and names of the families she was related to by marriage. The obituary made no mention of the Abaza family, not even in the name of Ashraf, Layla's son with Wagih Abaza.

بسم الله الرحمن الرحيم
«ياايتها النفس المطمئنة ارجعى الى ربك راضية مرضية فادخلى فى عبادى وادخلى جنتى صدق الله العظيم»
شيعت امس جنازة
الفنانة الكبيرة

ليلى زكى مراد

والـــدة
اشرف المدير بفندق شيراتون الجزيرة
وزكى المخــرج الســينمــائى
وشقيقة كل من
المرحوم مراد وإبراهيم ومنير مراد والسيدة
سميحه بامريكا والمرحومة السيدة ملك
وخـــالة
الانسة زينب شطا بشـركـسة ريفو
والمرحومة نسيبة وقريبة كل من
عائلات القطرى والاهلى بالشرقية وبيرم
وعبدالعزيز وشطا وعـبدالناصر
وعبدالوهاب حسن والجزرى وسامى موسى
وسـتـقــام ليلة الـعـزاء بدار
المناسبيات بجامع عمر مكرم
اليــوم الخــمــيس الموافق
١٩٩٥/١١/٢٣
تلغرافيا : ليلى مراد جاردن سيتى
ولا عزاء للسيدات

ALKWAKEB
2114-5-12-1995

The Egyptian press commemorates Layla Murad's death. The main headlines of *al-Kawakib* magazine's cover on December 5, 1995, reads:

> She lived Muslim, died Muslim, and was buried in the Muslim cemetery
>
> What did she say in her last will?
>
> The truth of her relationship with Jews and King Faruk
>
> The evidence of her innocence ordered by Nasser

Al-Kawakib chose Layla's image as the cover in celebration of the landmark 2000th issue on November 28, 1989. The magazine published that picture for the first time on March 6, 1956.

Many state institutions celebrate Layla Murad's legacy. Left: an image of the "Lived Here" plaque installed outside Layla Murad's house at 1 al-Fasqiyya Street, Garden City, Cairo. Right: an image of the 1999 postage stamp honoring her.

Singers Angham Mustafa and Ahmad Hassan perform Layla Murad's repertoire in a concert celebrating Layla's centennial birthday in December 2018. The female hijabi singer, Angham Mustafa, is a good example of the performative religious conservative in contemporary Egypt. Source: Rawafeed, http://www.rawafeed.net/news/5233.html.

A cartoon appropriating Layla Murad on her centennial birthday to serve the current regime's propaganda. The cartoon shows Layla with the lyrics of her song in support of the Egyptian army fighting to liberate the Sinai Peninsula. Layla performed that song after the 1967 defeat, but this cartoon appropriates the song to frame it as support for the Egyptian military campaign against Islamists in Sinai. The Egyptian press distorted the lyrics, changing one phrase from "return Palestine Arab" to "fight against terrorists." Source: *al-Akhbar*, February 21, 2018

CHAPTER 4

THE BLOW OF FATE

The Politics of Boycotting Israel

Our colleagues in Syria and Lebanon have published
many stories with lots of information about Layla Murad's
donation of fifty thousand pounds to Israel and her
donation of three thousand pounds to restore the Jewish
synagogue which a zealous young man bombed in Cairo.

Al-Sabah, October 10, 1952

Layla Murad never had a political color or national
inclination except she is a whole-hearted Arab Muslim; she
is beloved by all Arabs, and she loves them back.

Anwar Wagdi, October 20, 1952

Mrs. Layla Murad did not travel to Israel, and all that has been
published about her donation to Israel is completely false.

Officer Wagih Abaza, October 27, 1952

BETWEEN 1952 AND 1954, Egypt underwent the Free Officers military
coup that overthrew the king, demolished the monarchy, and inaugurated the
first president. During the same short period, Layla Murad divorced her first
husband, lent her voice to support the new regime, and had a child with one
of the Free Officers. The image of the beloved diva vacillated between false

rumors that labeled her as a Zionist agent of Israel and official efforts to make her the voice of Egyptian nationalism. The many fast-paced developments made Layla's life and career after 1952 dramatically different that it had been. The story of her life after the 1952 Revolution typifies the interruptions and ruptures among the Arab and Egyptian political elites and their systems of power, control, and discourse. Layla made personal and professional choices in the light of Egyptian and Arab politics and struggled to navigate the unsettled and unclear new Arab and Egyptian order. Now is the time to discuss the rumor of her alleged contact with Israel and its impact on her life and career. Arab political elites used the Arab boycott against Israel, an unchallenged piece of the politics of Arab elites for decades, for domestic consumption as a weapon in their internal competitions. The Syrian ban against Layla Murad is an excellent example of how Arab populist politicians and bureaucrats did not concern themselves with providing evidence while making decisions to punish individuals for alleged collaboration. The Arab boycott, depicted as serving the Palestinian cause, was instead used as a weapon to tarnish the reputation of Arab individuals. The Syrian treatment of Layla Murad provides a case in point of the reckless practices of the Arab boycott, notwithstanding the validity of its original goals. Arab regimes, politicians, and bureaucrats weaponized the Arab ban against individuals and groups without launching systematic investigations to identify and provide evidence to justify their decision to boycott. Nor did they try to convince the outside world of the justness of the boycott's meaning, goals, or benefits for the Palestinian cause, or attempt to demonstrate how the boycott was not anti-Semitic.

Reeling Crises, from Domestic to Political

Following the divorce in July 1952, Anwar traveled to France to receive medical treatment, while Layla got busy shooting *Sayyidat al-Qitar* (*Lady of the Train*; Yousuf Shahin, 1952). When Layla heard about Anwar's critical medical condition in mid-July, she flew to Paris, where she received the news about the Free Officers' Revolution, or the Blessed Movement, on July 23, 1952.[1]

Layla returned to Cairo at the beginning of August and spent one week working around the clock to finish shooting *Sayyidat al-Qitar*.[2] Producer 'Abd al-Halim Nasr insisted on releasing the film on the 'Eid holiday, the prime time for new releases. Upon finishing her work, Layla returned to Paris on August 8 to accompany Anwar; despite their divorce, the couple were still seemingly in love, and Layla was deeply concerned about Anwar's health. The couple extended their stay in Europe to escape Cairo's hot summer. On August 28, 1952, movie theaters in Cairo and across Egypt showed *Sayyidat al-Qitar* as planned, accompanied by an intensive publicity campaign. Yet, despite its high quality, the film did not make its way to theaters in Syria and faced substantial financial losses.[3] The reason for the film's failure was purely political: the Syrian government blacklisted Layla Murad. As the Egyptian daily *al-Ahram* reported on September 12, 1952, the Syrian government banned the broadcasting and showing of all Layla Murad's songs and films in Syria because she had visited Israel and made a donation of 50,000 Egyptian pounds.

The Syrian government considered the alleged visit and donation a violation of the Arab boycott resolutions. The Arab League Council had declared on December 2, 1945, that all Zionist products and manufactured goods were to be boycotted. It encouraged all Arab institutions, organizations, merchants, commission agents, and individuals to refuse to deal in, distribute, or consume Zionist goods. Following the establishment of Israel in 1948, the Arab boycott protocols prohibited companies from doing business with that country. Firms that traded with other companies that did business with Israel were blacklisted and all direct trade between Israel and the Arab nations was prohibited.

On September 13, 1952, *al-Ahram* published a report from the Associated Press in which Layla denied having made the donation and said that she had never had such a large amount of money. She believed that "some of those who work in cinema are behind this false news, and the Egyptian people and the Egyptian government know me well and will never believe these false claims."[4] She said that professional jealousy of her artistic excellence had targeted her throughout her career with vicious rumors.

Rumors about Layla's alleged contact with Israel initially found fertile ground. The Egyptian gossip and celebrity magazine *al-Sabah* ran a report confirming the Syrian allegations.[5] Not only repeating the false claim about the donation to Israel, *al-Sabah* propagated rumors that Layla remained Jewish and worked for the interests of and supported Zionists. Quoting an obscure Lebanese periodical called *al-Ahad* (*Sunday*), *al-Sabah* claimed that Anwar Wagdi was furious about the donation until Muhammad 'Abd al-Wahab mediated between him and Layla. The report also claimed that the couple fought while shooting their film *Bint al-Akabir* because Layla refused to work on Saturdays, observing the Jewish Shabbat, and forced Anwar to appoint her Jewish brother Ibrahim as a director in his company. According to *al-Sabah*, Anwar initially resisted "because it was inappropriate to have a Jewish director in an Arab company working in Arab Egypt and distributing its films in Arab countries. Nevertheless, Layla won, and her brother became the director. Since then, her brother has filled the company with Jews, and all the company's employees came from the Chosen People."[6] That the report was false was evident: Layla's brothers had worked in Anwar's company both before and after they converted to Islam in 1948. There was no evidence to indicate that Anwar's company hired more Jews than any other production company; moreover, Anwar's savvy management practices did not prioritize personal connections over the business, even when he hired Layla's brothers.

Al-Sabah put Layla Murad's life at risk by associating her with a transnational Zionist conspiracy. The magazine claimed that Layla had received a Jewish person in her apartment in the Immobilia building and given him a 3,000-pound donation for Israel before that unnamed person left Egypt for France. *Al-Sabah* also claimed that Jewish merchants from Cyprus, who often came to Cairo to buy films to show on their island, bought Layla Murad's movies in order to send them to Israel and used the revenue to help newcomer Jews in the Promised Land. *Al-Sabah* provided no evidence for these claims but hinted that Anwar was their source of information, asking him to state the truth as he knew it, "since the Syrian and Lebanese colleagues were adamant that they got their information from truthful sources."[7] *Al-Sabah* represents an extreme case among Egyptian periodicals in its stand against Layla Murad and Egyptian Jews; during my research, I did not come across any other reports suggesting that Layla was still Jewish. Here *al-Sabah* equates being Jewish with supporting Israel, a notion that did not become commonplace in Egypt until what is known as the Tripartite Aggression or Suez War in 1956. Nevertheless, *al-Sabah*'s discourse manifests the full force of the allegations against Layla and the problematic position in which she involuntarily found herself.

The director of Syrian radio Ahmad 'Ali came to Cairo in mid-September 1952 to participate in the Arab League's regular meetings, which took place in September and March every year. Answering the press, the Syrian official said that he decided to blacklist Layla based on evidence from the Syrian security authorities. He added that Layla Murad was responsible for refuting the evidence, not merely denying having made the donation. He did not specify what that evidence was or share it, nor did he reveal the evidence when he visited Egyptian radio officials to offer materials that "represent the revolutionary spirit of the Syrian army."[8] Surprisingly, Egyptian radio banned Layla's songs until mid-October 1952, when the Egyptian consulate in Damascus reported that the Syrian government had no evidence to prove that the alleged donation took place or that any connection existed between Layla Murad and Israel.[9] Before he left Cairo, Ahmad 'Ali met with the manager of Anwar Wagdi's production company, Mahmud al-Shafi'i. 'Ali suggested that Anwar Wagdi make a statement saying that he had not divorced Layla on account of any suspicions about her loyalty and Arab identity. He also asked that Layla provide bank statements showing that there had been no recent large withdrawals from her accounts or transactions together with a statement from the French security forces that she had not left France since her arrival there.[10] The Egyptian consulate in Paris scrutinized Layla's passport and issued an official statement on September 17 confirming that Layla arrived in Paris from Cairo on August 8 and had not left French soil since then.[11] On September 20, while still in Paris, Anwar issued a statement, handwritten and signed on his company's letterhead, declaring that his divorce with Layla took place because of domestic disagreements similar to those that occur in many families. He insisted that the divorce had nothing to do with any religious or political disagreements. "Layla Murad has been a true Muslim for seven years . . . never had a special political color or national inclination except she is full-heartedly an Arab Muslim. She is beloved by all Arabs, and she loves them back."[12] As Ahmad 'Ali had requested, Mahmud al-Shafi'i went to Damascus with bank statements showing that Layla had 36,149 Egyptian pounds in the Ottoman Bank and 3,071 in the Arab Bank. Both banks confirmed that Layla had never had 50,000 Egyptian pounds in her accounts and that she had not made any significant money transfers to or from her accounts during the last three months. Additionally, al-Shafi'i presented letters from all the other banks operating in Egypt, testifying that Layla did not have any accounts with them.

Layla and Anwar delayed their return from Paris until October 22, 1952. During that period, contradictory rumors broke out, including that Egyptian authorities had confiscated Layla's properties, barred her from entering the country, and sent police to arrest her once her ship arrived at the Egyptian seaport.[13] Producers and distributors of Layla's movies grew wary, since Egyptian films, including those of Layla Murad, generated 55 percent of their revenues from the Arab states, 20 percent from the Syrian and Lebanese markets alone.[14] 'Abd al-Halim Nasr, the producer who had released Layla's film *Sayyidat al-Qitar* days before Syria blacklisted her, had already initiated a legal procedure against her so he would not have to pay the installments of her fees. Nasr also asked Layla to return her first payment on the pretext that she was responsible for the film's being banned in Arab and local markets and thus responsible for his losing his investments in the film.

Layla became the topic of a public meeting hosted by Dar al-Hilal, the publisher of many influential periodicals. Many stars and producers attended the meeting with the Revolutionary Command Council (RCC) representative. Headed by General Muhammad Nagib, the RCC was de facto the ruling body of the country. In that meeting, the representative of the leadership was Officer Wagih Abaza, head of the Department of Public Affairs of the Armed Forces who served as the RCC liaison with artists and the media. Singer, composer, actor, and producer Muhammad Fawzi expressed the anxiety shared among cinema industrialists that the Syrian ban could cause substantial financial losses. Since Fawzi had produced two films for Layla, he expected to lose 30,000 Egyptian pounds and said: "We need to know the truth. . . . If Layla truly donated to Israel, I'm the first to ask for banning her movies in Syria, Egypt, and all Arab countries."[15] Based on the meeting's press coverage, we can conclude that the artists and producers cared mainly about business, their relationship with the state, and performing their patriotism; no one expressed concerns about Layla's well-being or a desire to help her out, know how she felt, or advise her to distance herself from Israel.

The RCC representative confirmed that the Egyptian foreign ministry had contacted the Egyptian ambassador in France and the Egyptian consulate in Syria, neither of which confirmed nor denied the rumors. The

authorities also announced that further investigations conducted by the
Secret Intelligence Department (*qalam al-mukhabarat al-sirriyya*) had confirmed that the rumor was a total lie and falsehood.[16] Producer Hassan
Ramzi and others suggested that the regime issue a public statement to announce that the Syrian report was fallacious, but the representative of the
regime replied, "It is not an issue that the leadership ought to make a statement about."[17] As a compromise, journalist Anwar Ahmad suggested that,
in order to kill the rumor, the cinema syndicate formally ask the leadership
about the matter and publish their response, which the group agreed upon
immediately. Actor Sirag Munir was already convinced that what Syrian
journalists had publicized was fallacious. In his capacity as president of the
Union of the Artist Syndicates, which included musicians' and actors' syndicates, Munir sent an inquiry to the Department of Public Affairs on October
24, 1952: "If the rumors prove truthful, the Union of Artists' Syndicates has
to make a speedy and decisive decision about her."[18] Wagih Abaza issued
the now-famous statement in the form of a telegram sent to the Chamber
of Cinema Industry on October 27, 1952. Abaza's telegram confirmed that
concerned government departments had conducted investigations and that
"Mrs. Layla Murad did not travel to Israel and all that has been published
about her donation to Israel is completely false."

One may assume that authorities had conducted these investigations
even before receiving inquiries from the chamber and the syndicates. The
meeting revealed the heavy hand of the new military regime and its keen-
ness to control the public sphere. Aside from the issue of Layla Murad, that
meeting marked how the new regime appreciated cinema's power as a medium and industry, and thus the need to control it. Artists expressed anxiety
about their livelihood and freedom. Layla did not return to Egypt until she
received assurances that the authorities had nothing against her and that the
Free Officers' regime supported her. Her return in itself testified strongly
to her innocence: when Layla and Anwar returned to Egypt with no security obstacles upon entering the country, everyone realized that the state had
nothing against the couple. Layla and Anwar spent their last weeks in Paris
working tirelessly to collect evidence and documents that refuted any claim
that Layla had any connection to Israel.

Who Triggered the False Rumor?

Unofficial investigations confirmed that the Syrian press circulated the rumors about Layla one month after they first appeared in a Lebanese magazine. Messages from angry fans flooded Syrian radio asking that Layla's songs be banned, and Syrian radio gave in. Eventually, the Egyptian consulate in Damascus asked the Syrian authorities to investigate and provide the Egyptian government with any evidence. The consulate reported to Cairo that the Syrians had no evidence, leading to the conclusion that the Syrians had based their decision on lies and false rumors. The Egyptian regime gave the green light to clear Layla and launched systematic efforts to contain the rumors. The Egyptian periodical *al-Fann* ran a comprehensive investigative report accusing a Lebanese celebrity magazine and its editor, whom *al-Fann* did not name, of fabricating the fake news about Layla Murad: "It [that magazine] had fabricated news about the death of an Egyptian singer who was still alive."[19] It accused the Lebanese editor of spreading the fabricated news and hurtful rumors owing to a personal grudge against Anwar Wagdi. *Al-Fann* could have been right, but it is noteworthy that Lebanese grudges were neither personal nor against Layla Murad and Anwar Wagdi only. Maltreatment of Lebanese stars, who faced all sorts of trouble in conducting their business in Egypt, aroused anger and frustration among Lebanese performers and their media liaisons.

Egyptian officials investigated whether Layla had visited and donated money to Israel but made no effort to trace the origins of this false information, nor did they attempt to hold those who triggered the hurtful rumors accountable. Since neither the Egyptian nor the Syrian side investigated who spread the false information, we do not know who did it or with what intentions. No one claimed responsibility; when a producer found himself accused of triggering the rumors, he considered the accusation offensive enough to launch a lawsuit. Two months after the Egyptian regime exonerated Layla, producer Anton Khuri threatened to sue *Dunya al-Kawakib* magazine for claiming that he was the source of the hurtful rumors. Khuri, who had visited Syria earlier that summer, insisted that he had nothing to do with the rumors, that he had in fact returned quickly to Cairo without meeting any Syrian journalists or producers because he had had an accident one day after his arrival.[20]

Eighteen months after the rumors surfaced, the Egyptian *al-Kawakib* magazine published a report from its correspondent in Beirut accusing the Lebanese press of living off the publications of attention-getting false reports to attract readership, giving several examples of reckless headlines: (Egyptian dancer-actress) Samya Gamal committing suicide, (musician) Muhammad 'Abd al-Wahab getting shot, Anwar Wagdi being killed in a car accident, Tahiyya Carioca running away from a prison in Cairo and showing up in Budapest, and Layla Murad visiting Tel Aviv.[21] According to the report, a Lebanese journalist heard a person saying that Layla Murad toured in Palestine in 1944, and that she gave a concert in a music hall in Jaffa and donated some of the revenue for charity. Nothing about that tour was unusual: Egyptian performers, including Umm Kulthum and Muhammad 'Abd al-Wahab, gave tours in Palestine before the establishment of Israel in 1948. The Lebanese journalist distorted the account by dropping the tour's actual date, as if Layla had visited and donated money to the state of Israel. Before this report, another Lebanese journalist had run a headline reading "Layla Murad Is Killed," after he misheard the distributor of her film *Sayyidat al-Qitar* talking about the storyline of the film, in which Layla plays a famous singer who goes missing after a train accident. Only a telegram from Layla Murad herself stating that she was still alive scotched the rumor.

Layla Murad implicitly accused Anwar Wagdi of launching the false rumors following their final separation in early 1953 and made her accusation explicit two years after Anwar's death. Layla's accusation of Anwar resonated with speculation on the part of *al-Sabah* magazine, which in October 1952 asked Anwar to speak up and verify the Syrian reports. In her serialized autobiography, published in *al-Kawakib* in early 1957, Layla wrote: "Anwar pretended to accept my conditions [to return to him after the third divorce]. Then, he surprised me by launching false rumors. The rumor aimed at damaging my reputation as a respectable woman and an Egyptian who loves her homeland and is willing to sacrifice her life for Egypt. All that I cared about then was to prove that the rumors were false. These rumors were extremely hurtful and damaging for me. . . . RIP, he was not reluctant to hurt the woman he knew, more than anyone else, how dignified she was and how much she enthusiastically loved her homeland Egypt. I became a victim of many rumors made up by Anwar."[22]

Layla provided no evidence that Anwar was the source of the rumors, nor did she explain why she thought that he sought to hurt her while at the same time he was willing to negotiate a reconciliation. Layla's narrative confuses the chronology of events by claiming that she stopped negotiating for the reconciliation in response to his launching the hurtful rumors. Might Layla have heard about the rumors when they appeared in the Lebanese periodical and rushed to Paris to ask Anwar whether he was behind them rather than to be with him in his health crisis? Did Layla choose to publicly perform her role as Anwar's partner watching over him beside his sickbed only in order to negate the rumors? Such a scenario is unlikely. Layla expressed shock when Arab and international media outlets published news of the Syrian ban in mid-September 1952. If she had known or cared about the initial Lebanese report in early July and seriously thought Anwar was behind it, surely she would have tried to disgrace him immediately. Her later claim against Anwar also came in retaliation for his rejecting her conditions for resuming their marriage. Her explicit charge against him after his death, with no substantiating evidence, and her dismissal of all his efforts to contain the hurtful rumors show that Layla seized the opportunity to lash out against the deceased man: she retaliated for her pain over their failed marriage, for what she considered her financial losses during their work together, and for his marriage to Layla Fawzi, who became his primary beneficiary. Layla may have based her conclusion on Anwar's anger, but we can reject that conclusion because Anwar was savvy enough to realize that any damage to Layla's public image, reputation, or popularity would make audiences give up on the films in which he starred with her. The Arab boycott of Layla Murad meant banning Anwar Wagdi's productions, and he would be the most significant financial loser. It is also possible, however, that Anwar said something hurtful during a moment of anger without considering the consequences, and that the Lebanese and Syrian press rushed to believe his statement--if Anwar ever made it--and reported it as if it were true. The Syrian government acted against Layla without conducting any investigation; their actions manifest their extreme suspicion toward Arab Jews, assuming them to be Israeli agents by default.

By all accounts, Anwar worked tirelessly to defeat the rumors. While he and Layla were in Paris and upon their return to Cairo, they swiftly acted together to contain the damage. They resumed their life as a couple and as professional partners and launched a successful public relations campaign in the fall of 1952. In December, the Department of Censorship canceled all formerly granted permits for movie scripts issued before July 23, 1952, which allowed Anwar to secure a new permit for *Bint al-Akabir*.[23] The film's promotional materials highlighted Layla's song for Muslim pilgrims, in which she chanted her love and longing to visit the Prophet Muhammad and perform pilgrimage rituals in Mecca.

In a series of interviews, Anwar promised to produce a film starring Layla with the title *al-Zulm Haram (Injustice Is a Sin)*, telling her story during the crisis.[24] Layla expressed her own wish to make a film titled *Muslim Layla*, telling her story of embracing Islam. Neither project ever materialized; interestingly, Anwar used *al-Zulm Haram* as the title for a film he wrote and released in 1954. Layla and Anwar visited Fu'ad University (now Cairo University) together in December 1952. They attended an open forum, where they appeared to a full house of students and faculty from the Liberal Arts, Law, and Science Colleges. Prestigious professors, including journalism professor Ibrahim 'Abdu and sociologist 'Abd al-'Aziz 'Izzat, led the discussions between the celebrity couple and the students. The couple spent three hours with the students singing, laughing, signing autographs, taking pictures, and answering questions. The professors expressed their happiness that Layla Murad had managed to prove her innocence in the face of reckless accusations triggered by malicious envy.[25]

Until early 1953, Layla and Anwar appeared together in public more frequently, attended public and private events, and gave press interviews as a couple. Anwar publicized future production projects featuring Layla, reflecting his complete confidence in her and their continuing popularity and success. They received Habib al-Malak, one of the most important film distributors in Iraq, during his visit to Cairo in November.[26] Anwar also signed contracts with two Syrian distributers, Tahsin al-Kud and Khalil Salih, to distribute his films in Syria.[27] In February 1953, Anwar Wagdi visited Syria and Lebanon to ensure the distribution of his films there, including his latest production featuring Layla Murad, *Bint al-Akabir*; according to some reports, he sold the film along with other productions to the Syrian distributor Ibrahim al-Mudallal. Anwar also contacted top officials in Damascus and shared with them, one more time, documents averring that Layla never contacted or cooperated with Israel. Upon returning to Cairo, Anwar published a column in *al-Musawar* magazine praising the Syrian people and the Syrian leader Adib al-Shishikli.[28] He used somewhat hyperbolic language in describing the progress and unity of the "the hardworking, honest, and nationalist Syrians."[29] According to the Egyptian press, Syrian officials agreed that Layla was innocent; thus, "we expect an official decision this week, and her voice [Layla's voice] will be back to the Syrians."[30] Al-Shishikli's regime had more significant concerns than problems with Layla Murad: not long after Anwar's visit, the regime faced its downfall owing to popular protests and a military coup in February 1954. He was spending time in Damascus's cafes, Anwar said, when Syrian state employees asked him for a monetary bribe to lift the ban. When Syrian officials learned what he had said, they stubbornly continued the ban, or as Layla said, using the Egyptian proverb: "He (Anwar) blinded the eye when he tried to beautify it."[31] Unsurprisingly, the optimistic expectations about lifting the boycott of Layla's works proved to be false, as we will see below.

Consensual Affairs between Layla and the Army

The new Free Officers' regime became instrumental in restoring Layla's image, embracing her as a patriotic Egyptian. In November 1952, the army allowed her, along with a group of other stars, to visit army units in their barracks and spend several hours entertaining men in uniform. According to press reports, soldiers dubbed Layla their most beloved singer, choosing her as their favorite rather than Anwar Wagdi, Yusuf Wahbi, the singer Shadya, or the comedians Isma'il Yasin, Shukuku, or Mary Munib. The soldiers, who invited the stars to revisit them, depicted Layla as "a tender heart" and described Anwar Wagdi as "a chivalrous gentleman."[32] The visit and publicity around it demonstrated the mutual support and interdependence between the new military elite and artists. More important, allowing her to visit soldiers in their barracks made an explicit statement about the regime's full trust and embrace of Layla, countering any rumors against her. The visit ushered in the incorporation of stars, including Layla, into the new regime's scheme of militarizing the public sphere. Military personnel staffed the government cabinet and occupied the principal civilian offices as well as parliament.

Militarization colored all aspects of public life in the country, from male clothing fashions to movies and charity work. Accordingly, Layla became a force in refashioning public life and society, and the regime welcomed her contributions and cooperation; they lent each other mutual support and legitimacy, the regime in its early, uncertain phase and Layla facing vicious rumors threatening her career and even her life. The regime's co-opting of the star and the star's embracing of those in military power became an increasingly clear part of Layla's artistic production and participation in public life.

By the end of 1952, the entertainment industry in Cairo wore patriotic and military uniforms, and performers enlisted themselves in backing the new military elite. Actresses appeared on the covers of celebrity magazines wrapped in the Egyptian flag and chanted the slogan of the new revolutionary regime: "al-Ithad wa al-Nizam wa al-'Amal" (Unity, discipline, and work).[33] Armed Forces sponsored concerts attended by the country's new leaders, including President Muhammad Nagib, Gamal 'Abd al-Nasser, and the rest of the RCC (Revolutionary Command Council). These concerts attracted large audiences who celebrated the success of and backed the Free Officers' Blessed Movement: on January 26, 1953, for example, 3,500 people attended a concert in al-Tahrir Theater in downtown Cairo.[34]

Layla Murad became the voice of the new regime in terms of celebrating and performing patriotism. In response to the Free Officers' endorsement, she visited General Muhammad Nagib's office before the end of the year and handed his secretary, Officer Magdi Hasanayn, a check for 1,000 pounds as a donation to the Egyptian army; the military leaders welcomed the donation and praised Layla as a role model of patriotism among artists.[35] She called President Muhammad Nagib "my father" and publicized a photo of her holding a framed picture of Nagib and looking at it with admiration. She became the "official" singing voice of the Free Officers when she performed the liberation anthem ("Nashid al-Tahrir") widely known as "'Ala Allah al-Qawiy al-I'timad" (Upon almighty God we depend). The former head of Egyptian radio, Midhat 'Asim, had composed the anthem's melody and lyrics to greet Nagib and the Free Officers during the launch of *Mustafa Kamil* (Ahmad Badrkhan, 1952), a biopic about the Egyptian nationalist leader Mustafa Kamil (1874–1908)[36] that had been banned by the authorities during the monarchy because it strongly denounced the British occupation and was released by the Free Officers once they came to power. To promote its highly patriotic content, Nagib had intended to attend the debut of the film in December 1952, but Officer Anwar Sadat, a member of the RCC, represented him instead. 'Asim made clear the intensive engagement of the new regime, represented by Officer Wagih Abaza, in formulating the *nashid*. Abaza visited 'Asim at his home to discuss the program for the film launch and to review his work-in-progress. 'Asim readily accepted Abaza's suggestion to use the musical format of the military march for the anthem "to attract attention and activate senses to listen."[37] He also adopted Abaza's other suggestion, to add sentences about Sudan to the anthem. More important, Abaza supported Layla Murad's request to perform the anthem, which 'Asim welcomed enthusiastically.[38] 'Asim's account proves that making Layla the voice of the new regime as a result of her close association with Abaza was intentional.

Studio Misr used the anthem in a short film along with Muhammad 'Abd al-Wahab's "Nashid al-Wadi" "to energize the high values of the liberation movement."[39] The radio broadcast Layla's "Nashid al-Tahrir" anthem extensively upon its recording in December 1952. Published radio program schedules from that period reveal that Layla's songs, including the anthem, were frequently broadcast: between December 23 and 26, 1952, the anthem was broadcast twice a day, along with Layla's songs from the film *Ghazal al-Banat*.[40] When Nasser ousted Nagib and put him under house arrest in 1954, the Nasser regime banned the anthem crafted to glorify Nagib.[41] Ironically, the anthem that celebrated lifting the ban on a film from the monarchy became the first piece of music produced under and then banned by the republic.

Layla Murad, along with many other performers, participated in the trips known as the Mercy Train (*Qitar al-Rahma*). The regime launched the Mercy Train in December 1952 as an army-sponsored effort combining charity work and support for the people of Gaza, who came under Egyptian administration in the wake of the 1948 war.[42] Contemporary press coverage credited Nagib's secretary, Officer Magdi Hasanayn, for the idea of trains carrying artists to encourage the public to make donations, and President Nagib for supporting it with enthusiasm.[43] Upon ousting Nagib in 1954, the Nasserist regime amplified Wagih Abaza's participation and credited him with the idea and organization of the trips. Volunteering artists enthusiastically followed the regime's instructions to give concerts and comedy shows in the provinces along with patriotic speeches to encourage public support for the military's Blessed Movement and its goals.[44] The new regime's primary goal was to harness popular support, not to collect money; it was aware of its precarious position in the eyes of the public and decided to build on the provincial trips that Nagib and other Free Officers had made in the summer following July 1952. These trips were intended to introduce the Free Officers to the provincial populations that had not yet grown used to having a military regime. The regime had also become aware of the importance of using the soft power of performing artists in keeping themselves in power, after they had tried using their guns during the labor strike in Kafr al-Dawwar in August 1952.

On Wednesday, December 31, 1952, Muhammad Nagib arrived at Cairo Station to greet artists boarding a train for Aswan.[45] The following day two trains left Cairo, one heading west to Alexandria and one heading east to Damietta. Officer Magdi Hasanayn made a farewell speech to the participants at the station with high-flown rhetoric about patriotism and anticolonialism. Anwar boarded the train going west, while Layla boarded the train going east. Top stars from all performance genres—comic and tragic actors, acrobats, belly dancers, and so on—participated in the three trips, all of them employing their talents to arouse patriotic sentiments in their audiences. Yusuf Wahbi gave dramatic speeches, Anwar Wagdi read fiery statements, and Isma'il Yasin and Mary Munib cracked patriotic jokes. With Layla on the train were the actors and singers Layla Fawzi, Su'ad Makkawi, Shukuku, Mary Munib, Amina Rizq, Hassan Fayik, Kamal al-Shinnawi, Huda Shams al-Din, Karim Mahmud, Galal Harb, and Zahrat al-'Ula, and the filmmaker Gamal Madkur. The press coverage highlighted how immersed Layla was in nationalism and loyalty to Egypt and the regime; news reports even mentioned that she got so emotional that she had tears in her eyes when she heard the officers' patriotic speeches.[46]

As the biggest superstar on the trip, Layla garnered most of the attention when she starred in concerts held under the new regime's motto, "al-Ithad wa al-nizam wa al-'amal," and when she ended a concert with her anthem (unity, discipline, and work), audiences made more generous donations. As the train stopped to collect donations in every town along the way, in towns such as

Shirbin and al-Mansura, Layla gave enthusiastic speeches on the importance of Arab unity to restoring Arab glory.[47] Uniformed men representing the RCC greeted the Mercy Train in each town and kept track of donations. In Damietta alone, Layla's train raised 4,000 Egyptian pounds in cash, in addition to commodities worth 6,000 Egyptian pounds.

The sight of army personnel in their military uniforms riding on the trains and collecting donations during concerts made people feel coerced or pressured to donate, to cover the cost of concerts, and to offer local accommodations to the stars. According to the press coverage, donations were overwhelming in amount and of many kinds. Photographs showed participants--artists, media personnel, and officials--all collecting cash and donations of commodities from unorganized crowds. This chaotic method of collecting donations must have made registering and keeping track of them a challenging process for bureaucrats and officers. In the euphoria of enthusiastic patriotism and rallying around the army, doubts about the transparency of collecting and delivering the donations were hushed up. But in his memoir, published years after Nasser's death, Muhammad Nagib accused the Free Officers of embezzling the donations.[48] The difficulty of assessing the financial revenues generated by the initiative would reasonably lead to such doubts. However, the trips contributed immensely to the popularity of the Free Officers and their military regime in the Egyptian provinces. Performing in public concerts and giving and collecting donations on behalf of the military regime opened the door for stars to enjoy closer relationships and mutual dependency with the new regime's personnel. Muhammad Nagib himself participated in this type of public relations and donation collection. He attended concerts such as the one organized by Jam'iyyat Abna' al-'Uruba (Children of Arabism Society) in September 1953 to collect donations for his Liberation Rally, the first organ of the Free Officers' regime. Arab diplomats attended the concert, which included an auction and Arab dress fashions.[49] All of the participating performers explicitly celebrated Muhammad Nagib's leadership and made his image the poster for the initiative--which is why Nasser's regime pushed the entire Mercy Train initiative out of the public memory once Nagib was ousted. Nasser's regime in turn launched Ma'unat al-Shita' (Winter Help), an initiative to collect donations for the Egyptian poor. It continued into the late 1970s and grew into a government bureaucracy that imposed selling stamps to the entire population, including poor school students, workers, and state employees. Launched in the 1950s, these Mercy Train, then Winter Help and other similar initiatives, embodied military control over civil society, including charity work.[50]

Layla's participation in army-sponsored concerts cemented her integration into the new regime and confirmed that the regime completely exonerated her from any alleged link with Israel. She starred in the army-sponsored festivals celebrating the first anniversary of the Free Officers Blessed Movement in Cairo and Alexandria on July 22–26, 1953, and donated her fees to the army.[51] Only dancer Samya Gamal and Lebanese singer Nagah Sallam followed suit, while all other performers collected their fees before leaving the concert.[52] Layla's gesture demonstrated strikingly her willingness to sacrifice material gain in the name of patriotism, that is, her loyalty to the new military regime. She rode in convertible cars and toured downtown Cairo, lip-synching patriotic songs already broadcast by way of microphones installed in accompanying cars and in major squares, such as al-Tahrir.[53] More than a quarter of a century later, Layla reminisced about these street tours as the best parts and fondest recollections of her career.[54]

The Egyptian press advocated for Layla's innocence and commitment to the Arabs and Islam. On January 27, 1953, to boost her popularity and show confidence in her innocence, al-Kawakib magazine distributed a postcard with Layla's picture as a gift with each copy;[55] in November 1956, they likewise distributed a poster of Layla with each copy of Al-Kawakib,[56] which doubtless embellished the walls of more than a few fans' homes and workplaces. The press continued urging Layla to return to work and published news about her possible return to singing and acting in a celebratory tone.[57] Considering the new military elite's tendency to control the public sphere and freedom of expression throughout the first two years, we can assume that the Egyptian press had the regime's green light to back her. Even after the Nasserist state became an all-out dictatorship following the internal struggle over power known as the Crisis of Democracy in 1954, the press still supported her.

In these circumstances, the Syrian ban against Layla and the discourse around it appear as a historical development that bespeaks a broader atmosphere of suspicion toward Jews in the Arab lands. Accusations associating

Jews with Zionism that displaced Palestinians were applied unevenly. In 1946, under the editorship of two Jewish journalists, *al-Misbah* magazine falsely accused Jewish filmmaker and producer Togo Mizrahi of Zionism. Against the backdrop of Zionist activities in Palestine, the Jewish community in Egypt were compelled to prove their dissociation by means of self-reporting and the exposure of Zionist sympathies or collaboration.[58] At the same time, until her final departure from Egypt in the mid-1950s, no one targeted Zionist actress Raqya Ibrahim despite her suspicious activities. In the aftermath of July 1952, for a period of several years, she spent time both in and out of the country, with apologetic discourses from her colleagues and the press providing her with cover, intentionally or not. Even when she left the country for good, no one questioned her intentions; the public dutifully accepted her false claims that she would study filmmaking abroad. Muhammad Karim had bitter memories of their last time working together, writing about her lack of courtesy and decency, arrogance, and unprofessionalism, but he did not raise suspicions about her Zionism or contact with Israel. Whether dictated by personal or national grudges, targeting Layla Murad and covering up Raqya Ibrahim fitted in with the Egyptian discourse on embedding Islam at the heart of Egyptianness and later met Egypt's needs to claim a victory over Israel. Even in the late twentieth century, nobody paid attention to Raqya's case because Egypt had lost her to Israel; she was one of Egypt's defeats, by the same measure as Layla was considered a victory.

The Egyptian press celebrated Layla's exoneration as ultimately proved by the armed forces' statement and urged the Syrians to lift the ban. *Al-Fann* magazine elevated the matter to an issue of national concern and pleaded with Adib al-Shishikly, the Syrian leader, to devote some of his time to resolving the case "that concerned all Egyptians until the truth emerged. The General Leadership confirmed Layla's innocence. . . . Since the Egyptian government exonerated Layla, there is no reason for the boycott unless it [the boycott] is against Egypt."[59] The press was also receptive to Layla's self-defense and ran her somewhat bombastic accounts of her patriotism and support for the new military elite and their Blessed Movement. Displaying her enthusiasm, Layla shared her feelings with the press when she heard about the army's movement on July 23 while she was in Europe with her husband. She gave an unbelievable account saying that she used to hide her

Egyptian identity during her previous visits to Europe owing to the king's scandalous corruption. "Thanks to the army's leap [the term widely used at the time to describe the military takeover in July 1952], Europeans tipped their hats to Egyptians and shouted long live Nagib! . . . When I saw Nagib's picture in newspapers for the first time, I felt he was my father who would nurture me and my homeland. I offer my modest effort to serve the Blessed Movement."[60] Layla's public image and association with the new regime reached a peak in the months following the crisis, with the press publishing reports affirming Layla's popularity around the Arab world. One report claimed that Layla was the most popular singer-actress in Saudi Arabia and that 'Abd al-Wahab was the male equivalent--despite the fact that Saudi Arabia did not allow movie theaters;[61] the report explained that Saudis read Egyptian celebrity publications and listened to Egyptian radio broadcasts.

The League of Arab Discourse with No Action

The Egyptian regime missed a chance to reverse the Syrian decision in the summer of 1953 when Cairo hosted the First Arab Radio Conference, with delegates from many Arab states including Syria. The event turned into a series of speeches with no action. President Muhammad Nagib gave a speech at the conference's inauguration wishing that all Arab radio stations would become "one station speaking in the Arab voice."[62] There is no evidence to indicate that the Egyptians discussed the Syrian ban on Layla's songs with the Syrian delegate. Published reports recounted "empty" talks about cooperation. *Al-Kawakib* rightly wrote, "The conference ended as usual with meetings in which delegates exchanged speeches and toasts, then delegates met for tea and dinner and formed subcommittees and used bombastic words to announce decisions that had no way of ever materializing."[63]

Layla's problems with the Syrian government and media together with Arab resentment toward Egyptian cinema provide a different narrative on Arab solidarity and Arab nationalism in the colonial and postcolonial Arab popular culture industry. The false rumors about Layla's alleged connections with Israel broke out when the Syrians and Lebanese became angry about Egyptian treatment of their artists. The second half of the 1940s witnessed heated debates over the issue. Egyptian artists and producers desired to incorporate Arab performers in their productions in order to promote their films in the Arab markets. Egypt possessed the infrastructure for cinematic musical productions and the media apparatus necessary for the Arab stardom industry. It is no surprise that appearing in Egyptian films and giving concerts in Cairo constituted a critical step for artists in building a broad Arab career and boosting their fame and fees in their home countries and beyond.

On the other hand, Arab stars charged less even as they contributed to the success of Egyptian movies in Arab markets. Incorporating Arab performers into Egyptian productions assured a warmer welcome at the Arab box office, hence greater profits. Arab performers also accepted parts that Egyptian stars rejected as well as working for less pay. For example, as we have seen, after Layla Murad had rejected the part, Nur al-Huda agreed to appear as a beggar in the film *Jawhara* and received 150 Egyptian pounds, whereas Layla would have been paid several thousand pounds. Moreover, Arab performers were in a weaker position in the event that a legal dispute broke out with Egyptian producers.

In sum, Arab performers were a good deal for Egyptian producers, but the Egyptian syndicates placed obstacles in their way. The syndicate of actors and the syndicate of musicians in Egypt spearheaded the imposition of discriminatory policies against Arab artists. Under the leadership of Umm Kulthum, the Egyptian syndicate of musicians worked closely with various government departments to bar Arab artists from performing in Egypt, to subject them to heavy taxation, and to refuse to grant them entry visas or work permits. The highly regarded composer, singer, and actor Farid al-Atrash, who was from Jabal Druze, Syria, and built his career in Cairo, championed the cause of Lebanese and Arab performers, challenging Umm Kulthum. Yet the issue lingered as Arab performers continued to suffer bureaucratic and financial hostility from Egypt's bureaucrats and artists' syndicates; complaints by Arab artists of discrimination against them in Egypt lingered throughout the 1940s and into the 1950s.

Some Egyptian artists expressed their concern over the discrimination against Arab artists in Cairo and contrasted these practices with the hospitable way Arab countries and people treated Egyptian performers, facilitating their entry into their countries and allowing them to work, as well as allowing them to make handsome profits and leave with large amounts of cash. According to Egyptian producers Hassan Ramzi and Anton Khuri,

the Customs Department of the Ministry of Interior Affairs tried its best to
hinder Arab artists' entry into Egypt.[64] Sirag Munir, who was new to his position as president of the actors' syndicate, said that taxes levied from Arabs
on behalf of the Egyptian syndicate were inappropriate. The syndicate board
decided to abolish them in its first meeting in April 1954 and pursue non-
discriminatory approaches to treating Arabs and Egyptians alike. Replacing
Umm Kulthum as the head of the musicians' syndicate, Muhammad ʻAbd
al-Wahab promised to adopt policies supporting Arab artists.

The Egyptian Customs Department used the vice squad police to scru-
tinize Arab artists in Cairo before granting them a residency permit, a
humiliating procedure for Arab artists.[65] Arab artists could be denied an
entry visa without a plausible reason. For example, producer Anton Khuri
shared with journalists and members of the RCC that authorities denied
the famous Iraqi singer ʻAfifa Iskandar an entry because she frequently visited London.[66] Lebanese singers Suʻad Muhammad and Nur al-Huda fell
victim to these practices and stopped working in Egypt altogether. In an
extreme incident of harassing artists from Arab countries, Egyptian authorities arrested Suʻad Muhammad, charging her with smuggling gold out of the
country in 1952, shortly before the rumors about Layla Murad broke out in
Lebanon and Syria. Egyptian authorities did not allow Suʻad Muhammad
to leave Egypt for seven months, until the court acquitted her.[67] She spent
these months without clothing supplies or financial support, a situation that
Officer Anwar Sadat, member of the RCC and later president of Egypt, described as an embarrassment.[68] Upon her return home, Suʻad Muhammad
described Egypt as "a large prison."[69]

One week before the Syrian boycott against Layla Murad, Egyptian authorities denied the Lebanese actress and singer Nur al-Huda an entry visa
to Egypt, although she had secured a work permit from the Egyptian con-
sul in Beirut; she had to reboard the same airplane that brought her from
Beirut to Cairo and fly back to Lebanon.[70] One year earlier, authorities had
refused to grant her a visa to attend the debut of her film *Shibbak Habibi*
(*My Lover's Window*; ʻAbbas Kamil, 1951). Layla expressed concern about Nur
al-Huda's absence, saying that cinema was an art with no borders and that
no one should hinder artists from coming to Egypt from other countries. "It
should be the opposite, and we should attract them so that we benefit from

their talent and ensure that our films will prosper in their countries. Banning artists from other countries from working here encourages their countries to reject our films."[71]

Layla's fears were not unfounded. By the early 1950s, Syrian and Lebanese movie theaters had begun refusing to show Egyptian films, leading to a depression in the Egyptian film industry. Critics of Egyptian cinema pointed to the low quality of Egyptian films as compared to Italian and American productions, and said that Egyptian films were less creative. Arab audiences grew bored with the silly plotlines of Egyptian movies, and the overloading of these films with songs and belly dancing had come to be seen as tasteless to the increasingly better-educated and more sophisticated Arab viewers. Occasionally, the Arab press subjected Egyptian stars to vicious rumors denigrating their morality and political stands. For example, the Lebanese media accused Yusuf Wahbi of attempting to take sexual advantage of young Lebanese singers and actresses; one particular star-in-the-making was said to have declined Wahbi's unwanted advances to the extent that she gave up her career in Cairo and went back to Lebanon. Claiming that Layla Murad had donated money to Israel was probably the most vicious rumor against an Egyptian star. Arab gossip publications and officials working in cinema enabled the spread of such fake news by offering no proof or counterevidence in regard to their charges.

Conflicting views about Arab artists in Egyptian cinema reflected conflicting economic and financial interests and galvanized competing ideologies. Rhetoric about "Egyptian hospitality," "Hollywood of the Arab East," and "Arab brethren and solidarity" proved meaningless and empty whenever it came into conflict with individual or group interests. A less talked-about but more animating force was the business and economy of cinema and music production. Since the late 1940s, Syrian and Lebanese distributors and movie theaters increasingly refused to show Egyptian films, labeling them as low quality. Egyptian cinema industrialists admitted there was a problem but claimed that Egyptian cinema had continued to make progress and was equal in quality to international cinema productions.[72] Arab countries aspired to protect their emerging local film industries, as for example in Lebanon and Iraq.[73] Arab governments also refused to transfer revenues generated by showing Egyptian films in their theaters in hard currency; sources indicate that until June 1949, Arab countries owed Egyptian producers frozen revenues worth 190,000 Egyptian pounds.[74] Eventually, Arab regimes shut down Egyptian distributors' offices in their capital cities and decided to levy a charge of up to 40 percent of the revenues to allow Egyptian films in their markets.[75] These developments hit Egyptian cinema very hard: producers grossed half of the revenues earned by exporting their productions, mainly to Syria, Lebanon, Iraq, Iran, and North Africa.[76] In the context of the continuing agitations against the Egyptian film industry and frustrations among Arab artists owing to continuing official and nonofficial harassments, it is understandable that the Syrian and Lebanese press, officials, and audiences embraced the baseless rumors about Layla Murad. The sweeping and drastic Syrian decision against Murad was not because of doubts about her loyalty to Egypt but because she was Egyptian. The rumors, regardless of their source, provided a pretext to retaliate against an Egyptian star.

Syria was the seat of the newly established Arab League Bureau for Boycotting Israel. Hosting the bureau contributed to Syrian regional hegemonic status via the bureau's leadership of the opposition against any regional normalization with Israel. Established in 1951, the central Bureau for Boycotting Israel operated in Damascus to prepare biannual reports on individuals and companies who violated the Arab League's decisions about banning any Arab cooperation with Israel. Many Arab countries, including Egypt, also established regional branches to assist the central bureau in Damascus. The ministries of defense in Egypt and Syria oversaw the regional bureaus in Cairo and Damascus; in contrast, the ministries of economy, treasury, or commerce oversaw the regional bureaus in other countries, such as Libya and Iraq.[77] In the rapidly changing political landscape of the Arab world, the bureau paid close attention to Arab and foreign artists and public figures. Decisions about celebrities attracted public attention, and thus their cases helped galvanize the concept of the boycott and highlighted the bureau's activities in the Arab press and other mass media. At the same time, Arab periodicals supported calls to boycott famous and popular Arab and foreign performers in order to increase their circulation. For example, the Lebanese celebrity magazine *al-Shabaka* called for the Bureau of Arab Boycott against Israel in Damascus to blacklist Egyptian-born Francophone singer Dalida because she had allegedly performed Arabic songs praising

Israel in Morocco.[78] The magazine could not confirm the allegation, which did not sound reasonable: Dalida would not have gone out of her way to sing in Arabic rather than French in an Arab-Francophone country to glorify Israel. The attack on Dalida was not the first. The editor of the Egyptian daily *al-Jumhuriyya*, Nasser al-Din al-Nashashibi, launched campaigns in the early 1960s calling on Arab states to blacklist Dalida and other stars, including Elizabeth Taylor and Danny Kaye, because of their support for Israel and Zionism. Al-Nashashibi called for a ban on such films as *Judgment at Nuremberg* and for the government to refuse to grant permits to shoot the film *Cleopatra* in Egypt.[79]

On the other hand, some prominent Egyptian intellectuals called for reasonable, dispassionate discussions around how to deal with performers sympathizing with Israel and Zionism rather than blacklisting and boycotting them. Novelist Yusuf Idris published two articles in February 1962 criticizing the frequent boycott campaigns against international performers: "Every time we do not allow a star into our countries because they express sympathy or support of Israel, we serve Israel because we provoke international public opinion to disrespect and ridicule us."[80] Idris suggested inviting those stars to learn about "our culture, arts, and literature and to engage them in discussions and provide knowledge about our causes. We would help our cause rather than keep screaming: 'catch a Zionist, catch Israeli propaganda.'"[81]

The blacklisting process was erratic: it was unclear whether boycott officials collected any evidence before placing an individual or company on the list. No two countries had identical lists, and some countries did not enforce the secondary boycott. Arab politicians and bureaucrats continued to use the blacklisting of Arab performers for ideological reasons. For example, the Syrians imposed a boycott on the Lebanese singer Nagah Sallam and then lifted the ban in 1966.[82] Sawt al-'Arab (Voice of the Arabs radio station), under the infamous Ahmad Sa'id, who fed Arab listeners bombastic lies about fake Egyptian victories during the defeat in the Six-Day War in 1967, banned Farid al-Atrash's songs despite his overwhelming popularity across the Arab world because al-Atrash said publicly that as a Levantine he did not receive fair treatment in Egypt.[83] Sa'id had to reverse this decision as the result of a campaign protesting al-Atrash's blacklisting, particularly by journalists

Nasser al-Din al-Nashashibi and Musa Sabri. Farid himself had to compromise and withdraw his complaints against particular Egyptian programs
such as the radio show 'Ala al-Nasiya, which received criticism from Arab
singers such as Sabah, Fayza Ahmad, and al-Atrash for ignoring their songs.

Layla's case provides an excellent example of how easy it was to make the
accusation of violating the Arab boycott against Israel, without producing
any evidence. More important, her case shows how Arab political elites and
interest groups made allegations in order to manipulate the public rather than
establish the truth. The Syrians neither explicitly withdrew the allegation nor
did they attempt to convince other Arab regimes or the Arab League to join
them. They also failed to provide concrete evidence to convince the Egyptian
regime of its truth. The baseless allegation could not stand up to scrutiny and
appeared to be another instance of dirty business. The Egyptian office of the
boycott never commented on the Layla Murad issue.

Interestingly enough, Lebanese radio did not follow the Syrian decision
to boycott Layla Murad, considering the ban contingent on the provision
of evidence.[84] It is noteworthy that the first biography of Layla Murad,
penned by an Egyptian author, came from a Lebanese publishing house in
Beirut, al-Mughamira al-Hasna', in 1956, indicating that Lebanon did not
follow the Syrian boycott. Although the Lebanese press was the first site to
launch the rumors, the Lebanese state did not take them seriously. Meanwhile, penalizing Layla fit into the Syrian scheme of elevating its regional
hegemony through championing the Arab boycott; thus, only Syria acted
on the basis of rumors as if they were facts. In May 1955, reports confirmed
that the Egyptian embassy in Damascus requested that the Syrian Military
Intelligence Agency open Syria's doors to Layla Murad, since the agency had
become confident that Layla was innocent and that the allegations against
her were untrue.[85] But only the unification of Syria and Egypt in February
1958 de facto ended the Syrian boycott against Layla, with no party both-
ering to produce evidence or counterevidence to support their arguments.
It is noteworthy that Mahmud Riyad, a former military intelligence officer,
served as Egypt's ambassador in Damascus between 1955 and 1958. Riyad was
a member of the Egyptian delegation at the signing the unification treaty in
1958 and became Nasser's political advisor until 1962. Having military intelligence personnel in Damascus's posts during these crucial years was another

indication that the Syrian regime had no concrete evidence against Layla that they could have shared with the Egyptian personnel in Damascus or that the latter could have learned about. While the Egyptian regime did not doubt her innocence, however, it did not put sufficient pressure on the Syrian side to formally lift the ban before 1958.

Blacklisting Layla or any other performer for alleged contact with Israel or sympathy with Zionism served to make Syria the perennial leader of the opposition to the political normalization of Israel. Whenever allegations were proved wrong, lifting the boycott or taking any corrective action was impeded by Syria's dysfunctional bureaucracy and political instability throughout the 1950s. Between 1946 and 1956, Syria had twenty different cabinets and drafted four separate constitutions. Syria's so-called democratic years of the 1950s were the country's longest experience with a populist authoritarian government and the locus of the fiercest and most prolonged contest for regional hegemony.[86] Unstable regimes used the media as a vehicle to popularize and normalize authoritarian solutions to the problems confronting the country and its neighbors.[87] Energetic rhetoric about the boycott of Israel and high-profile decisions to blacklist performers strengthened the regional position of the domestically unstable regimes in Syria.

In a recent book, Egyptian journalist Ashraf Gharib falsely claims that Syria reversed its decision about blacklisting Layla once the rumors were proven to be false and that Syrian radio broadcast Layla's songs and Syrian movie theaters showed Layla's films.[88] In fact, Syrians kept the ban intact, and until the unification between Egypt and Syria, producers were reluctant to contract with her for new films while the Syrians still banned them.[89] Following the unification, which formed the United Arab Republic in February 1958, the Syrian and Egyptian Ministries of Interior Affairs merged into one, with a communication bureau in Damascus. Eight Egyptian officers from drug, fraud, and customs police departments staffed the bureau under the leadership of Egyptian colonel Muhammad Sayf al-Yazal Khalifa. Theoretically, the bureau was intended to provide technical help to the Syrian police; in this way, the police forces in the northern and southern regions, that is, in Egypt and Syria, could follow the same routines and regulations. However, Egyptian police officers transferred some information to Cairo, which made their Syrian counterparts believe that they were spying on them.

Disagreements broke out between the Syrian police and the Egyptian officers,[90] over whether the Egyptians should maintain access to and control over confidential information of the Syrian police forces. The fact that the issue of Layla Murad never came to the fore again and that the Syrians made no effort to maintain the boycott, which dissolved spontaneously, confirms that the Syrians had no evidence against her. The Egyptians did not bother to get the Syrians to admit so publicly, letting the boycott against Layla dissolve on its own without any statement from them. Perhaps they preferred not to make a public show of support for Layla, which would have embarrassed their Syrian allies, or perhaps Layla simply lacked the means to pressure or remind the Egyptian officials in Syria to do so.

Layla celebrated the euphoric moment of the Egyptian-Syrian unification that lifted the Syrian boycott against her. She recorded a song for the radio titled "Bism allah wa bism al-wihda" (In the name of God and the name of unity). She announced her return to her acting career in February 1958, in the week following the unification. She also publicized her plans to star in two films and bought lyrics for five new songs to record for Egyptian radio.[91] Letters from Syria asking about Layla Murad's news and her resumption of work started to trickle in and appear in sections of publications devoted to readers' messages.[92] Also, on the eve of political unification, a Syrian businessman bought the rights to distribute the entire production of Itihad al-Sinima'iyyn (Union of Cinema Industry) for 175,000 Egyptian pounds, the largest deal in the history of Egyptian cinema at the time.[93] That deal was especially significant in view of the cold shoulder that Syrian and Lebanese distributers had given to Egyptian producers throughout the 1950s, preferring American and European films. And yet, although the Syrian ban was no longer a barrier for Layla, none of her planned film projects materialized. Any realistic explanation of her disappearance from the scene must find reasons other than, or in addition to, the Syrian ban. Nonetheless, Layla's case clearly illustrates how some Arab regimes used the Palestinian cause for inter-Arab struggles rather than pressuring Israel and empowering Palestinians.

Surviving the Crisis

Layla's public presence and performance during the first few years following the crisis indicated that she could continue her career. She enjoyed the

Egyptian regime's endorsement. Along with other performers who shifted their loyalty from Nagib to Nasser, Layla celebrated Nasser's triumph in the internal struggle against Nagib and sang for him when he signed the Treaty of Evacuation with the British in 1954. She participated in the army-sponsored festivals for Evacuation Day, October 20, 1954, where Nasser and the RCC members were present, a strong signal of Nasser's endorsement of Layla after ousting Nagib.

Layla firmly stood up for herself and successfully sued producer 'Abd al-Halim Nasr for her full payment for the film *Sayyidat al-Qitar* as stipulated in the contract. Along with her brothers, she established a production company, al-Kawakib Film: Layla Murad & Co., which released its first production in March 1953. The company produced one film starring Layla the following year. Did she have to produce this film, *al-Haya al-Hub* (*Life Is Love*; Sayf al-Din Shawkat, 1954), because producers were avoiding the risk of working with her while the Syrian market banned her work? That she had established the production company al-Kawakib Film in early 1952 shows that her plans to produce the film predated the rumors. The company gave Layla's brother Munir his first opportunity to become a star in *Ana wa Habiby* (*My Lover and I*; Kamil al-Tilmisani, 1953). Layla supported her brother, attending the film's launch and proudly hugging him before press cameras. She probably established the company as part of her professional plans for the aftermath of the divorce and to provide for her brothers, as she stated later. Anwar was still interested in producing and co-starring in films with her. He publicized his production plans, including one film featuring Layla Murad, and continued negotiations via his assistant director, Hassan al-Sayfi, for her to star in his *Khataf Mirati* (*He Stole My Wife*; Hassan al-Sayfi, 1954), although his relationship with his future wife, Layla Fawzi, who also played a part in the film, meant replacing Layla Murad with Sabah. More important, Wahid Farid, film producer with Misr al-Jadida Film, demonstrated that producers were still willing to work with her by giving Layla the leading part in *al-Habib al-Maghul* (*The Unknown Lover*; Hassan al-Sayfi, 1955), which turned out to be her last film.

Parenting two children, born in 1954 and 1955, slowed her down, but she performed many new songs aired on Egyptian radio. She contributed to the careers of a new generation of composers, including Kamal al-Tawil, Ra'uf

Dhuhni, Muhammad al-Mugi, Hilmi Bakr, Baligh Hamdi, and her brother Munir Murad. Layla received 400 Egyptian pounds for each song, and thus the radio became a crucial venue for carrying her voice to listeners and securing a good income. Egyptian radio included Layla in a small group of performers who enjoyed a special agreement that paid them a large sum of money for recording a song, which covered the fees of the songwriter, composer, and band members, with additional royalties for each time a radio station broadcast the song. Along with Layla, Umm Kulthum was paid the highest recording fee and largest amount of royalties, followed by 'Abd al-Wahab and Farid al-Atrash; the rest of the vocalists were divided into first, second, and third tiers.[94] 'Abd al-Halim Hafiz, the primary voice of the Nasser regime, had to bargain in 1958 to join this group who enjoyed the special agreement, as their payments exceeded his even when he was among the first-tier singers.

Layla optimistically announced that she would star in two films, though neither materialized. The first, to be produced by Ramsis Nagib and based on a story by Ihsan 'Abd al-Quddus, was titled "Da'ni li-waladi" (Leave me for my son); the second was titled "Laylat al-Wada'" (Farewell night).[95] News about her film projects highlighted "her return after her two-year disappearance."[96] Layla attributed her "absence" during the previous two years to health issues after giving birth to her second son, Zaki, by cesarean section, explaining that she had to go on a diet to lose the twenty pounds she had gained once she recovered. During her absence, rumors arose that she had suffered a breakdown and had to be hospitalized, that she had lost her voice, and that composers refused to provide her with new melodies. She blamed the press for spreading rumors about her health and even death following Zaki's birth, yet reports that she had suffered a breakdown and had to be hospitalized in 1957 were true. As she admitted in *al-Musawar* magazine in 1958, her family's love and support helped her recover.

The extensive publicity about the movie contracts she signed and new songs she recorded shows that the Syrian boycott did not end her career. Under full control of the Nasserist state, Egyptian radio continued backing Layla, carried her voice to listeners, and ensured that income flowed to her through her royalties. The Egyptian press continuously encouraged and welcomed her public appearances and checked on her during her periods of silence or absences from the public eye. Celebrity publications were filled

with readers' requests for broadcasting Layla's songs, questions about her latest work, and demands that she make new films with particular male stars.
In several letters to *al-Kawakib*, signed by Ms. Zahra from Aleppo, a fan
expressed how much she and the people of Syria "loved Layla to death" and
asked the magazine to run Layla's picture on its cover;[97] the editor answered
that Layla would start shooting her new film in two months.[98] In 1958, nothing indicated that *al-Habib al-Maghul* (*The Unknown Lover*, Hassan al-Sayfi,
1955) would be Layla's last picture.

How Much Did the Israel Rumor Cost Layla Murad?

Layla's career survived the crisis of the Israel rumor, but it negatively impacted her productivity and caused her to lose some work opportunities. The
Syrian ban on Layla's films caused each of her producers to lose 3,000 Egyptian pounds, the price of showing her films there. All the companies tried
to have the ban lifted, and those that had signed with her rescinded their
contracts, waiting for the ban to be lifted.[99] Producer 'Abd al-Halim Nasr
refused to pay her for the remainder of her contract for *Sayyidat al-Qitar*
(3,000 Egyptian pounds) because of the financial losses he suffered owing
to the Syrian ban. Layla sued him and won the case, as the contract stipulated that he had to pay her 3,000 Egyptian pounds upon releasing the film,
and nothing in the contract made payment contingent on the film's success.
Before 1956, Egyptian journalists tried to discuss lifting the ban with Syrian
diplomats in Cairo, the Syrian embassy's chargé d'affaires, Sami Khuri, told
journalists that the Syrian government had not changed its decision.[100]

The rumors cost Layla an opportunity to make a film with Farid al-
Atrash, arguably the most popular star in the Levant and across the rest of
the Arab world. The press ran a report that al-Atrash had asked Layla to star
in two films with him.[101] Layla's brother Munir represented her in negotiations over some of Layla's conditions, including her wages, but the project
never materialized, as al-Atrash, along with many other producers, feared
that the film would suffer financial losses in the Arab market.

In the early phase of Layla's disappearance after *al-Habib al-Maghul*,
the press, most notably *al-Kawakib* magazine, paid Layla a great deal of
attention, encouraging her to come back and keeping her in the eyes and
memory of the audience. In addition to publishing her serialized memoir,

the magazine issued calls to give Layla work, reminding readers what a great singer and actress she was. Some of what they wrote reveals, implicitly or explicitly, that Layla was going through troubled times. Late in 1957, *al-Kawakib* blamed her for her mysterious disappearance, charging her with refusing to communicate with the press or engage in public activities.[102] The magazine lamented that Layla was deliberately making herself a mystery and living behind masks. When a journalist asked to meet her for an interview, she made excuses to avoid doing so. When granting an interview, she asked to hear the questions in advance over the phone, an unusual practice, and if the journalist declined, she refused to receive the journalist, and pretended that she was not at home despite the prearranged appointment. In one incident, Layla denied the journalist access to her three times. Eventually that journalist talked to Fatin 'Abd al-Wahab (her husband at the time), who said that Layla wanted the journalist to interview a specific producer. The journalist refused this unprecedented condition and canceled the interview, and Layla continued veiling her life in mystery.[103]

Three months earlier, poet and editor Salih Gawdat had affectionately asked, "Where is Layla Murad?"[104] He wrote that he was receiving letters from Layla's fans wondering whether she was still in Egypt or had emigrated; he thought the question valid because Layla had disappeared from public view: it had been years since the people of Egypt had heard her on the radio, listened to her in a concert, or watched her in a new film. He reminded everyone that "Layla was the first to sing for the [July 1952] Revolution and performed "Upon Almighty God We Depend," and now the Revolution celebrates its fifth anniversary, while people do not hear Layla's voice."[105] Gawdat made a strong argument for Layla's patriotism and loyalty to the new regime, an argument that could have suggested that the regime or some powerful individual(s) had banned Layla's songs from radio and hindered Layla's participation in movies and concerts. Gawdat rebutted any false rumors about Layla's having emigrated. The crisis clearly had a negative impact on Layla's career, but it did not end it. Answering why she did not appear in films after 1955 directs our attention to her relationship with Free Officer Wagih Abaza and the patronage networks of the Nasserist state, to be discussed in the next chapter.

CHAPTER 5

THE UNKNOWN LOVER
Layla Murad and the Free Officer

Ask about me
Mercy for my tearful eyes
Because I love you, it's too hard
to think your love was not for me.

Layla Murad, summer 1954

I wish to be back, wish to be Layla Murad again.

Layla Murad, 1978

ON A SATURDAY MORNING, Layla boarded the Mercy Train on its trip from Cairo station to Damietta, and Anwar Wagdi passionately kissed her cheek before the train began to move. This public display of affection confirmed that the couple were still together and on good terms: Anwar had accepted many of Layla's conditions and demands, and both were considering a *muhallal* so that they could legally resume their marriage. A huge crowd bid farewell to the artists, who waved and smiled through the train's windows. Free Officer Gamal Salim boarded the train in his military uniform, representing the RCC (the military regime's leadership). He allowed journalists to take pictures of himself with Layla Murad in the train compartment; the press coverage of the journey, notably Salim's pictures with Layla Murad, highlighted that she was the biggest star on that trip. A few weeks after the trip, Layla unilaterally announced her final separation from Anwar Wagdi, which shut down forever any further speculations about the resumption of their living and working together. This dramatic turnabout may be explained by what happened during and shortly after the trip, which may also account for the premature collapse of Layla's career three years later. We can make sense of the unpredictable changes in her personal and professional life through the dramatic transition from the monarchy to Nasserism, in turn shedding light on this transition by means of Layla's trajectory. The romance between Layla and Free Officer Wagih Abaza provides an excellent opportunity to rethink politics among the Free Officers and the Nasserist state in terms of gender and masculinity. No complete understanding of the Free Officers' politics and the Nasserist regime is possible without analyzing masculinity, gender, and sexuality among the young men who took over the state in the summer of 1952 and then engaged in power struggles among themselves. Some Free Officers employed their newfound power to take advantage of female celebrities wishing to adapt to the political changes and expunge their records of supporting ousted King Farouk and his family. The mixture of men's coercion and women's desire for protection triggered and shaped love affairs and marriages. Some courted female celebrities for a casual fling; those whose relationships became permanent often made their wives give up their careers and become housewives. Internal conflicts among those powerful young men allowed sexual rumors to leak to the public, but no one could openly discuss the credibility of such rumors until decades later, owing to censorship and the lack of an active civil society. The outcome of affairs and marriages between political power and commercial beauty varied: some women became more vulnerable, while others gained power.

The Free Officers' regime in Egypt exonerated Layla from Syrian allegations of having visited and made donations to Israel. The regime elevated her to becoming the voice of their Blessed Movement. But, though Layla seemingly survived the crisis, she disappeared from the movie screen despite her continuing popularity. We should read Layla's vulnerability through the lens of gender and sex at the intersection of ethnic-religious positionality. Before seizing upon her Jewish origins to explain the difficulties she experienced under the rise of Nasser's Arab nationalism, we should pay attention to the interplay of her gender, sexuality, and political choices with her Jewish origins and stardom. Just as we can read America's history through Billie Holiday's or Nina Simone's trajectories, we can read contemporary Egypt's history through Layla Murad's. In the course of her life, competing nationalisms, policies toward minorities, civil rights, women's rights, fame, and the popular culture industry all intersected to personify conflicts and struggles. Abstract notions of nationalism, pluralism, otherness, and tolerance became oppressive discourses, with the ability to shape and to crush an individual's personal and professional life.

The Mercy Trip

The Mercy Train arrived at Damietta at 4 p.m. and was met with brass bands playing patriotic melodies as if the stars were "victorious conquerors." Artists offered shows in Damietta, then in al-Mansura and in many small towns along the way to al-Zaqaziq, the capital of al-Sharqiyya Governorate. Free Officer Wagih Abaza and local notables, including the governor of al-Sharqiyya, met the train at the station. Abaza made clear that he was receiving the artists not in his official capacity as a representative of the RCC but as one of the local notables in al-Sharqiyya Province. He showed off his power, familial position, and wealth in a way that no other Free Officer had done before. During a concert held in the town's movie theater, the local church's bishop donated a gold necklace consisting of rings shaped like crescents and crosses; the donor's position and the depiction of interfaith harmony, the legacy of the 1919 Revolution, added significant value to the piece. Artists auctioned the necklace, and Abaza won the bid for the extraordinarily high price of 120 Egyptian pounds; another member of the Abaza family donated 500 Egyptian pounds to the train. Wagih Abaza invited all the artists who participated in the trip for lunch at his house in a display of the Abazas' consummate hospitality. He already had a personal connection with Layla, as he had worked with her and Anwar Wagdi to rebut the Syrian allegations a few months earlier. He paid particular attention to her, and they spent some time together away from the noisy group, accompanied only by comedian Sa'id Abu Bakr, who had been a close friend of Layla and Anwar's and worked as a liaison to bring them back together. The photojournalist of *al-Fann* magazine was alert enough to snap a picture of that private moment, an image that appeared only once: neither *al-Fann* nor any other periodical dared to it again for the obvious reason reason that Abaza did not want his close relationship with Layla to go public.

Who Was Wagih Abaza?

Hailing from a notable family in al-Sharqiyya Province, Wagih Abaza (1917–1994) entered the military academy in 1937; he said that his father was fluent in French and worked as a journalist. Abaza graduated from the military academy and the aviation school in April and May of 1939, respectively. As an Egyptian Air Force officer, he became the editor of *Silah al-Tayaran* (*Air Force*) magazine, which allowed him to develop contacts with authors and journalists. He joined the Free Officers and participated in anticolonial resistance in the Suez Canal Zone. He held the rank of captain in 1952, when the military coup turned into a revolution and spawned an authoritarian populist regime. Under Gamal Abdel Nasser (r. 1954–1970), Abaza held prestigious public offices, including Cairo's governorship. Thanks to the influential positions held by him and many members of his family, the Abazas survived the Nasserist policies of limiting land ownership: until his retirement, he retained possession of forty acres in his name.[1]

In the wake of the July 1952 coup, Abaza became the first director of public relations of the new regime, known as the Department of Public Affairs of the Armed Forces. The Free Officers trusted the Department of Public Affairs to introduce them to the public. Except for General Muhammad Nagib, those officers were young, unknown to the public, and lacked political experience. The Department of Public Affairs operated in the early days following the coup, known in those days as the Blessed Movement and then as the July Revolution, as a propaganda organ for the Free Officers. Abaza and his comrades established new periodicals to serve as RCC mouthpieces, and he commissioned cinema productions and sponsored public festivals and rallies for the same purpose. While still wearing the military uniform, Abaza became a member of the Journalism Syndicate, the professional journalists' trade union. Although he was not a member of the RCC, he represented it in communicating with performing artists and journalists. In that capacity, he participated in the editorship of the new regime's publications, such as *al-Tahrir* (*Liberation*) magazine, and contributed to the establishment of Sawt al-'Arab (Voice of the Arabs) radio station. He also founded and directed two companies, the Nile Cinema Production Company and Nile Advertising Company. Since the Department of Public Affairs of the Armed Forces employed performers to invite the public to rally with them around the new elite, Abaza met intensively with both journalists and artists to communicate the new regime's dictates concerning their work.

During the internal power struggle between President Muhammad Nagib and his prime minister, Gamal 'Abd al-Nasser, in March 1954, Abaza backed Nasser and played a role in his triumph, which preserved army control over the civilian government. During the conspiracy to oust Nagib, who advocated for the return of civilian politics, Abaza ordered his fellows in the Air Force to fly their military aircraft at a low level above the barracks of the cavalry, who supported Nagib.[2] Throughout Nasser's reign, Abaza occupied positions of power. He left the Department of Public Affairs in 1955 to become secretary of the Liberation Rally, the organ established by the military junta as the sole political party, replacing the previous, outlawed parties and the demolished multiparty system, in his home governorate of al-Sharqiyya, and then became secretary of the National Union, the political organization that replaced the Liberation Rally in 1957 there. In the first parliamentary elections, Abaza won a seat representing his home province, which came as no surprise, since Nasser's regime ensured that no one else competed with the military candidates, guaranteeing that the officers would prevail. Abaza became governor of the governorates of al-Buhayra in 1960, of al-Gharbiyya in 1968, and Greater Cairo in 1970. In Sadat's successful purge against Nasser loyalists in May 1971, Sadat removed Abaza and sent him to jail for a few years. Shortly after his pardon for health reasons in 1975, Abaza benefited from Sadat's free-market policy (*infitah*), establishing himself as an auto-dealership tycoon and representing French Peugeot in Egypt. His family joined the ruling National Democratic Party, and many members of the family, including Wagih's uncle and children, occupied ministerial positions and parliamentary seats under Sadat and his successors.

The Free Officer and the Vulnerable Star

Layla Murad's relationship with Wagih Abaza began at the time of the rumor crisis in the fall of 1952. As director of public affairs of the Armed

Forces and the military regime's liaison with artists and media professionals, Abaza publicized the outcome of the state's investigations concerning
the alleged connection between Layla and Israel in autumn 1952, signing the
official statement that cleared her reputation and put an end to any doubts
about her commitment to Egypt and Arabs. Nevertheless, the crisis underscored Layla's vulnerability as a star and a Jewish woman who had converted
to Islam who now needed to adjust quickly to changes in the movie industry,
Egyptian society, and regional politics. Layla's search for personal and professional assurances carried her Abaza's way, as he had emerged as a powerful
patron for those in the art and media industry who needed to connect and
network with the new regime. Layla's intimate relationship with the Free Officer helped her become the voice of the regime and then prevented her from
continuing her career in cinema.

Layla Murad and Wagih Abaza's relationship seems to have begun when
he arranged for her and other performers to visit military barracks in Cairo
and participate in the Mercy Train. Sources are not clear as to when this
limited, professional relationship developed into a romantic intimacy, because Layla wished to appear in public as Anwar Wagdi's partner during the
months following the rumor crisis. Shortly after her return from the Mercy
Train trip in January 1953, in March 1953, Layla unilaterally announced her
final separation from Anwar and disparaged him in a press interview. Surprised and angry, he was unable to respond; her burgeoning relationship with
Abaza intimidated him, so much so that he withdrew a statement he had
sent for publication in response to Layla's interview.[3]

However, the account that the former director of Egyptian radio, Midhat
'Asim, gave in mid-1953 about the composing of the regime's liberation
anthem in late 1952 hints that the relationship between Layla and Abaza
morphed into romance and strengthened during and shortly after the Mercy
Train trip. 'Asim wrote that Layla coincidentally visited him at home during the course of a work session between him and Free Officer Abaza, and
'Asim asked her to perform the new piece, a request that everyone supported
enthusiastically.[4] There is no doubt about Layla's having a professional relationship with 'Asim from the time he contracted her to sing for public radio
in 1935. Nevertheless, his statement that Layla had visited him coincidentally
when Abaza was having a work session at his house and that the accidental

meeting made her the singer of the regime's anthem does not sound realistic; it is more likely that 'Asim, Abaza, and Layla prearranged their work session while the relationship between Layla and Abaza was already underway. 'Asim's account thus raises questions about the intentionality of making Layla the voice of the new regime, especially in view of her close association with Abaza, whose Department of Public Affairs chose her to star in a concert marking the Blessed Movement's first anniversary. Layla donated her fees to the army, and along with other Egyptian performers and artists coming from other Arab countries, happily attended the reception held by Abaza in honor of participating artists.[5]

The relationship between Layla and Abaza became an ill-kept-secret marriage, although they never publicly came out as a married couple; everyone around them knew about their relationship, but no one could speak about it openly in public. The short-lived relationship came to an end before the birth of their son, Ashraf, in July 1954, but whether they broke up gradually or suddenly cannot be known. Layla's unplanned pregnancy put the couple and their relationship in a critical situation. The romance had developed mostly in private and parallel to Abaza's public and formal family life. The young officer who rose with his comrades to the zenith of political power overnight was a married man; his oldest son was almost ten years old. There were no indications that Abaza meant to elevate his relationship with Layla to the position of a formal public marriage or publicly recognize Layla as a second wife and have her in a second household. Layla saw in him a source of protection, as he was one of the military elites who evaluated the patriotic standings of individuals and decided whom to purge. He and his comrades were still figuring out the meaning and limits of the power in their hands, and each was navigating their internal struggles to maintain power. This does not mean that Layla had not fallen in love with Abaza or had undertaken the relationship solely on the basis of a business calculation. They were the same age; Layla was elegant, beautiful, and charismatic, Abaza young, handsome, and powerful. She was divorced, hurt, and vulnerable. It might have been love, business, or a blend of both: since neither of them ever talked publicly or left a statement about their relationship, it's virtually impossible to know how they felt about one another, the limits of love and business in their relationship, whether they considered their relationship casual or a serious commitment, and how each of them felt after their breakup.

When Wagih Abaza courted Layla Murad in 1953, she was vulnerable professionally, socially, and emotionally owing to the rumors of her connection with Israel, the Syrian ban on her work, and the rapid changes in political and public life since July 1952. The repeated disputes and divorces with Anwar Wagdi must have damaged her love for and confidence in him, not to mention that he faced, like all performers, uncertainty in his career because of the political situation. Abaza, on the other hand, provided protection and power that helped her survive her personal crises and the political changes in Egypt. Under the influence of what Abaza could offer her, Layla abruptly halted all negotiations to resume her marriage to Anwar, who accepted all her conditions, including returning her jewelry and transferring to her the ownership of their marital apartment. He was shooting in Asyut but came back to Cairo to meet with her in the house of their mutual friend, actor Saʿid Abu Bakr, and give her a check, but Layla did not show up and shut down any communications.[6]

Layla's relationship with Abaza was seemingly going well, encouraging her to produce a film glorifying the Egyptian army in the 1948 war, *al-Haya al-Hub* (*Life Is Love*; Sayf al-Din Shawkat, 1954), which resonated with Abaza's propaganda work for the Egyptian military and confirmed Layla's commitment to the Arab side. Layla played the role of a nurse falling in love with an officer fighting for Palestine, although her character was unrealistic and lacked any depth. As Salah Tantawi rightly observed, the film expressed political propaganda whose slogans had little to do with real people.[7] Tantawi, who had been a big fan of Layla, wondered, "Where is such a young woman who completely devotes her life and efforts to patients only because she embraces her duty and believes in the Palestinian cause?"[8] The film was obviously a love letter from Layla to the Egyptian Army and to Wagih Abaza, whose influence on the film was apparent: the beloved was a young officer, and his image in uniform dominated the screen. The film was the first in a wave of Egyptian films featuring similar male protagonists.[9] Layla claimed that *al-Haya al-Hub* was a great success, but she never again produced her own films. Whether it achieved financial success or not, her primary aim was to prove her sincere patriotism and commitment to the

Palestinian cause, which she had done before in her film *Shadiyat al-Wadi* (*The Singer in the Valley*; Wahbi, 1947). In *Shadiyat al-Wadi* Layla performed an operetta centered on the Palestinian cause, but unfortunately that film got lost and thus the operetta slipped out of public memory; we only know of the existence of the operetta from the film's pamphlet.[10] Yet by releasing *al-Haya al-Hub* in April 1954, Layla found herself in deep trouble with the same man she expected to provide her with protection in a fast-changing world.

The press coverage on Layla while Abaza courted her was altogether positive, with no disruptive information or news. She appeared on Alexandria's beaches with family, friends, and colleagues for a summer vacation[11] and invited the press to cover her there, while sharing no private business with the public. On a lighter note, singer and composer Muhammad Fawzi reported that Layla lived extravagantly, "lived for the day, and her dining table stretched almost to the beach and was full of great food."[12] Reports highlighted her character as so kind and generous that she responded to fans' letters by attending their weddings.[13] The press did not discuss her love life and affairs explicitly, which appeared only as snippets of gossip that made no mention of her name. A critical reading of what these headlines implicitly reveals some attempts to silence the news or gossip about Layla's romantic life. The press had already come under censorship imposed by the new regime in which Abaza enjoyed a dominant position; no censor would have allowed news about any of the Free Officers' romantic relationships to be published.

Reports about a possible engagement between a star and an official whose position was relevant to her work appeared in the press in the summer of 1953,[14] although this brief and anonymous report carried no information and had no news value. While news mentioning the names of the couple explicitly never appeared, anonymous gossip became an alternative way to evade the censors and publicize information without running the risk of an open confrontation with the regime's powerful men. Those who knew about the developing relations between Layla and Wagih could easily make an informed guess; others could make a good guess considering that the news section of that same edition of *al-Kawakib* ran Layla Murad's name explicitly three times.[15]

When Layla and Wagih were courting, she moved to another apartment and minimized her public appearances. Rumors that she had given up work

proved false, as she produced her film *al-Haya al-Hub*, but she had to disappear from the public gaze to hide her pregnancy. Her pregnancy deemed it
necessary to make the relationship official and public, although that could have
negative social and political consequences for Wagih, for whom the relationship was becoming a burden. Why did he refuse to acknowledge his romance
with Layla and take her as a second wife, a privilege that the state and Islamic
Sharia laws granted men? Although polygamy was legal and religiously sanctioned, it was increasingly frowned upon as modern Egyptian society came
to equate modernism with the nuclear family and monogamy. Polygamy had
become tasteless and socially offensive, imposing a stigma on middle-class husbands and their wives. Women would use their agency to stop their husbands
from taking second wives; the more powerful the wife, the more successful she
was likely to be in framing polygamy as hurtful and offensive.

I'timad 'Abd al-Rahman Bey Abaza, Wagih's wife, came from his wealthy
and close-knit Abaza family, which prided itself on its "pure" Arab roots and
did not allow its member to marry outside the family. This tradition kept the
family's wealth undivided and perpetuated the myth of "Arab blood purity."
I'timad's branch of the Abaza family wielded considerable power and wealth,
as her father, 'Abd al-Rahman Abaza, carried the honorific elitist title "Bey,"
and her brother Muhammad Abaza was a judge. Wagih could not afford to
divorce I'timad or to upset her by taking a second wife; for him to break the
marriage bond was unimaginable: they had several children together, and
their marriage cemented the Abaza family's tradition of in-family marriage.
Moreover, Wagih may have felt a strong affection for I'timad; pictures in the
family album show young Wagih and I'timad behaving like a modern loving
couple, strolling the urban streets hand in hand in modern, Western-style
clothing. They were the embodiment of the modern nuclear family, with no
place for polygamy. The comment Abaza wrote on the back of the picture
communicated their strong bond: "Nothing is greater and sweeter than going
together through life's struggles hand in hand and heart with heart. . . . All
my life is represented in this picture."[16] The moment was authentic: the couple gazed at the camera for the sake of their family album, not for the public.
Wagih and the other Free Officers, including President Nasser, kept their
wives, wearing the most up-to-date fashions and no headscarves, away from
politics and out of the public gaze.

Whether Wagih was in love with his wife or with Layla, having Layla as a second wife in public would have been too costly socially and politically for him. Wagih treated his involvement with her as a fleeting moment; he and other Free Officers rejoiced in their newfound power through relationships with women who were celebrities or formerly of royal status. Although married, the Free Officers were still young, and many individuals from the highest echelons of society sought their help and protection; Layla Murad was not exceptional in that regard. Several Free Officers mixed business and pleasure, becoming involved in romantic affairs with royal women seeking to escape from Egypt and smuggle some of their wealth out of the country. Occasionally, promises of love in return for protection and security turned into secretive 'urfi (unofficial) marriages out of a fear of God and the potential scandal should an affair become known. Because Islamic Sharia considered a marriage viable as long as there were two male or one male and two female witnesses and did not require couples to document the marriage in a court or state records, 'urfi marriages, though unrecorded by the state and kept secret except for witnesses, enabled couples to avoid the guilt and criminalization of zina (adultery). The arrest of the leftist officer Mustafa Kamal Sidqi in 1953 revealed his secret marriage to the belly dancer and actress Tahiyya Carioca (1919–1999). Carioca quickly divorced the officer, who faced being purged in the early years of the Free Officers' regime. Field Marshal and second man after Nasser, 'Abd al-Hakim 'Amir (1919–1967), secretly took the actress Berlanti 'Abd al-Hamid (1935–2010) as a second wife; she had a child with 'Amir and lived in the shadows until--according to the regime's account--'Amir committed suicide after the defeat of Egypt in 1967. Rumors also associated 'Amir with the Algerian singer Warda (1939–2012), who was a rising star at that time.[17] Singer-actress Maha Sabri (1932–1989) married Officer 'Ali Shafiq, secretary to 'Amir. Although Sabri rejected 'urfi marriage and insisted on making the marriage official and public, her trajectory was not very different from Berlanti's: her husband lost his political power and faced a trial and imprisonment following the 1967 defeat. Sabri struggled for years to return to work to make a living for herself and her son; she finally managed to resume her career only after Nasser died and President Anwar Sadat succeeded him in 1970.

Egyptian social culture never normalized polygamy, despite its being sanctioned by Islamic law, and modern discourses disapproved of it. Having semi-secret relationships with women could boost a man's image, as being attractive and virile, but taking more than one wife could tarnish his image, as being backward. Affairs and *'urfi* marriages with celebrities and elite women were always a mixed blessing for those involved, particularly when the Free Officers employed sexual gossip to undermine each other in their competition for higher positions. Despite the control exercised over the public sphere and censorship, news and rumors about some of the officers' affairs leaked to the public, fostering gossip about the hypersexual officers and their abuse of power to establish romantic relationships.

Available sources, many of which appeared decades after Nasser's death, provide conflicting accounts of how, when, and why Nasser interfered to end some of these relationships. There are reports that he feared that leaks about hypersexual and hypermasculine officers might turn the public image of the Free Officers into one of licentious and lustful, reckless men rather than committed and disciplined leaders capable of liberating their nation. Other accounts assert that Nasser used these relationships in his never-ending struggles against his comrades, to consolidate power in his own hands. He removed his colleague in the RCC, Officer Salah Salim, from his position as minister of national guidance (communications)--according to journalist Musa Sabri, as punishment for his relationship with Princess Fayza and the resulting gossip that Salim helped her smuggle some of her wealth outside the country illegally. Nasser exiled the princess without consulting Salim; journalist Nasser al-Din al-Nashashibi suggests that Muhammad Hasanayn Haykal, the journalist closest to Nasser, played a role in worsening the relations between Nasser and Salim. By all accounts, Nasser's inclination toward totalitarianism led him to marginalize his more powerful comrades; the sexual and romantic affairs of the young Free Officers provided him and others with the needed pretexts.

Analyzing affairs and informal marriages allows us to study politics under the Free Officers through the lens of masculine gender. The free Officers used each other's love affairs in competition for more influential positions in the small circle of decision-makers. Wagih had witnessed Nasser's anger over Gamal Salim and Princess Fayza's relationship, which led to the princess's expulsion; now, having a child with Layla threatened to expose their relationship to the public. He would have looked like a reckless womanizer in the eyes of the people, put his relationship with Nasser in jeopardy, and fomented domestic troubles with his formal wife. When Layla became pregnant, the young military elite gossiped and mocked Wagih, making irritating jokes that his child with Layla would be Jewish or would have Jewish maternal aunts and uncles. Anwar Sadat, later president of Egypt, competed with Wagih over managing the Department of Public Affairs of the Armed Forces.[18] Arguably less dynamic than Wagih, Sadat enjoyed a stronger position as an RCC member. Aspiring to full control of the Free Officers' media, Sadat made use of the gossip about Layla and Wagih's relationship, as well as Wagih's inability to leverage Nasser's support as the Nile Cinema Production Company suffered a series of financial losses under his management.[19] Nasser appointed Sadat president of the Dar al-Tahrir publishing house, the regime's mouthpiece.[20] Undermining Wagih, Dar al-Tahrir published the celebrity magazine *Ahl al-Fann* in 1954, carrying Sadat's name as publisher. The first issue, which came out on April 12, 1954, had Layla Murad's image in color as the front cover and ran an interview with her about the challenges of recording cinematic songs;[21] the back cover carried Anwar Wagdi's image in color. Meanwhile, Wagih wrote a brief column welcoming *Ahl al-Fann* but admitting he was not familiar with the magazine's content.[22]

Choosing between his colleagues mocking his secret affair and denying his paternity, Wagih decided to quit the relationship before the child was born, abandoning Layla and leaving her to wrestle with how to face society with a fatherless child. Denying fatherhood always puts the woman in a critical position, not to mention the legal difficulty of proving the relationship. Egyptian law restricted the right to register the birth of a child to the father; the mother could do so only if she confirmed that a marriage had occurred through a legal contract and witnesses.[23] Layla's position was especially weak on account of media attention and Wagih's political power; she was more vulnerable and intimidated than ever before.

Layla retreated to a rented apartment in Giza, withdrew from the public gaze, and refused to meet journalists, in order to avoid questions about her personal life and to hide her pregnancy. A newspaper reported the story with big headlines, though without naming the parties involved; it said that a famous singer who had recently divorced her actor husband was expecting a child with her new husband. Layla came out of seclusion and told reporters that she had not gotten married.[24] Then one morning she found one of her servants dead in his room, of heart failure due to excessive drinking. She moved to stay with her family, and her emotional distress on account of the servant's death served as a good excuse for hiding from the public eye while fully pregnant. She attended the launch of her film *al-Haya al-Hub* on April 5, 1954, and almost fainted but attributed it to the crowd of fans around her, saying nothing about her pregnancy.

Her Biggest Lie!

Layla gave birth to her first son, Ashraf, that summer; his official birthday is July 13, 1954. The news was not secret: there is anecdotal evidence that her friends communicated the news to her ex-husband, Anwar Wagdi. In the face of Wagih Abaza's refusal to recognize the baby as his legitimate child or give him his family name, Layla was disheartened. Three weeks after she gave birth to Ashraf, and while she was still recovering, Layla publicly denied that she had remarried, was pregnant, or had given birth to a child.[25] She left Cairo for Alexandria, where she spent most of her days alone by the beach; according to a report in September, "Every minute Layla faces questions from children of her neighbors on the beach: Is it true you got married? Why does your groom not come to visit you? Can we see your groom, Mrs. Layla?"[26] According to the same report, Layla answered, "I did not get married and will never do so. . . . I got married only once." She repeated that public denial in November, saying that she considered reports about her marriage and becoming a mother the biggest lies of the year.[27] Layla was too fearful to name Wagih Abaza as her child's father and too ashamed to come out to society as a single mother. One can imagine the pain she suffered after denying having her first baby and the fear that prevented her from acknowledging her new status as a mother.

Three months later, Layla received an invitation from the Department of Public Affairs of the Armed Forces to sing at the first festival of Evacuation Day on October 20, 1954. The department organized the concert in al-Andalus Park in downtown Cairo to celebrate the evacuation agreement between the Free Officers and the British and confirm Nasser's victory over Muhammad Nagib. RCC members Salah Salim, who controlled the minister of national guidance, and Anwar Sadat, president of Dar al-Tahrir for publishing, wished to undermine Wagih's position and invited Layla to sing at the festival against his wishes. Wagih did not attend the festival, while Nasser and several RCC members and cabinet members did; Salim and Sadat were seated next to Nasser. In Nasser's presence, Layla poured out her pain, begging publicly for mercy in two tear-shedding songs, "*Is'al 'Alaya wa Irham 'Inaya*" (Ask about me and grant mercy to my tearful eyes) and "*Utlub 'Inaya*" (If you ask for my eyes).[28] The audience received the songs well and made her repeat them several times. Wagih's comrades interpreted the songs as her begging for mercy and pleading for him to recognize the child. In a subtle reference to Layla's forced or voluntary solitude during pregnancy and her troubles with Wagih, the press reported her appearance at the festival as a comeback after a period of absence.[29]

Layla kept silent about her problems with Wagih but worked tirelessly to persuade him to recognize their child legally. She was not completely powerless: she mobilized her connections and paid money to those who could take her plea to the head of the regime. Some of these intermediaries took advantage of her to collect material gains, while others did the job. The situation was socially awkward and morally burdensome. She was a beloved star with a fatherless child, unable to face society or challenge the father. Denying a child whom everyone knew Wagih had fathered could have led to even more embarrassment for the military regime's leadership. No one wished to pursue the legal option, as the matter would likely have become more scandalous; it would have meant inviting Layla's celebrity acquaintances and Wagih's military comrades to testify about their relationship. Nasser's intelligence personnel had already interrogated Wagih's subordinates in the Nile Company about the relationship, which, according to one of them, "had become a hot topic for social gossip and appeared every week in celebrity magazines."[30] Nasser pressured Wagih to contain the scandal and decided to shut down the financially troubled Nile companies. Wagih resigned from the Department of Public Affairs and withdrew to his home village,[31] wishing to maintain a low-profile presence in Cairo to escape the scandal and the pressure to acknowledge his son with Layla Murad.

Wagih's withdrawal came at a critical time: the military junta needed to mobilize the public around Nasser as the country's sole leader and contain ousted Nagib's popularity. The tension between the president of the RCC,

Muhammad Nagib, and his vice president, Gamal 'Abd al-Nasser, exploded
publicly in February and March of 1954, which became known as the Crisis
of Democracy.[32] Owing to Nagib's popularity, Nasser could not remove him
from his position as RCC president until October 1954. Between March and
October, Nasser purged Nagib's supporters and civilian and military voices
for democracy, dismissing 140 officers loyal to Nagib, and eventually removed
Nagib from the presidency and put him under house arrest. Following an attempt on Nasser's life on October 26, 1954, during a speech in Alexandria, the
regime cracked down on the Muslim Brotherhood and communists. Nasser's
public support among Egypt's population was still limited, increasing his
need for rigorous publicity efforts and plans to rally the street to secure him
in office.[33] To promote himself and his regime's Liberation Rally, he gave
speeches in a cross-country tour, imposed controls over the country's press,
and ordered military censorship of all publications; leading artists performed
songs praising Nasser and produced movies and plays denigrating his rivals.
According to his associates, Nasser orchestrated the campaign himself.[34]
Wagih remained loyal to Nasser, supporting pro-Nasser publicity campaigns
and maintaining his influence in media and politics through his protégés. He
eventually made a victorious comeback, elected to parliament in 1956.

Layla Murad rushed into her marriage to filmmaker Fatin 'Abd al-
Wahab on December 21, 1954, with no engagement period. Her close friends
had taken it upon themselves to help end her depression and solitude, and a
quick marriage seemed a viable solution that would provide her with social
protection, preserve her integrity, and reintegrate her into society as a chaste
wife and a mother, restoring the public image she had enjoyed throughout
her career. Going back to Anwar Wagdi was no longer possible, as he had
announced his engagement to actress Layla Fawzi, thus ending gossip that
he was dating Layla Fawzi while she was still married to another actor; he
paid the ex-husband a large sum of money to divorce Fawzi in May 1954.[35]
Layla's speedy marriage to Fatin was the best solution to the social problem
of having a child without a father. According to her account, Fatin acted
fast; there was no time for courtship or dating. Fatin was a two-time divorcé,
and despite his successful career in filmmaking, almost penniless; Layla possessed substantial wealth. Since her separation from Anwar, she had invested
in real estate and built an apartment building in the upscale neighborhood of

Garden City in downtown Cairo. According to her, the apartment building alone generated enough income for the rest of her life, and so she was financially well off despite her extravagant spending habits.[36]

For many years afterward, Layla continued to offer explanations to justify her rushed marriage to Fatin ʿAbd al-Wahab, maintaining that she hadn't thought to remarry after her divorce from Anwar, wishing only to devote herself to her career. She claimed that she changed her mind only when her friend Saʿid Abu Bakr surprised her by revealing that Fatin ʿAbd al-Wahab was in love with her and wished to marry her.[37] According to Layla, the proposal surprised her, as she had never heard of the filmmaker, but she quickly fell in love with him once they met and agreed to his proposal. Layla's account, however, was at variance with reality, as her production company, al-Kawakib Film Co., had contracted Fatin ʿAbd al-Wahab in 1954 to direct a film starring her brother Munir Murad, with her other brother, Ibrahim, managing the production. Fatin must have known of Layla's critical situation, as he spent the months of 1954 close to Layla, her family, and her production company. In 1959, when Layla gave that account, she was still too scared to speak openly about her previous relationship with Wagih Abaza and the son they had together.

The Gambling Game: The Star and the Masculine State

Layla had little choice but to cave in and resort to silence after falling foul of the heavy hand of the Nasserist state, which developed a web of intimidating power including its security forces and the military-controlled press. On May 17, 1955, the Egyptian daily newspapers published a front-page headline that the vice squad had arrested Layla Murad and others for illegal gambling. They followed up on the incident with daily coverage, labeling it "the gambling den scandal." Even the newspaper *al-Ahram*, which seldom paid attention to sensational or crime news, covered the case daily for two months, until the end of the trial. Layla and many of her fellow artists enjoyed playing cards, and card-playing venues were not a secret. On May 15, 1955, police stormed an upscale villa owned by the daughter of a former pasha and wife of a high-ranking government employee. Police arrested the hostess and her six female guests, including Layla, for illegal gambling activities.

Police released Layla a few hours after the raid, but her arrest gave a high profile to the case and intensified media attention.

The raid and news reports apparently were an attempt to intimidate Layla and damage her public image. Egyptian law criminalized individuals who used their residence for illegal gambling activity but did not criminalize their playing guests, who were treated as witnesses; therefore, the police should not have arrested Layla. News reports claimed that the police had confiscated a large amount of cash used for gambling and that the women had said that the owner of the villa charged them a fee for using her space.[38] According to these reports, Layla and the five other women said that they had not known each other previously but had met each other at the villa. At trial, all the women denied these claims and testified that they were playing cards only for fun in their friend's home when the police arrested them. Layla did not appear in court; her lawyer submitted her testimony together with a medical report that she was too ill to attend in person. The court acquitted Layla and the other women, considering them to be witnesses, and only tried their hostess; then the court acquitted her of the charges of managing a place for illegal gambling and dismissed the entire case.

Although the case was dismissed because the court found no evidence of illegal gambling, the police failed to follow procedure and issue a warrant to raid a private home and arrest those inside. They submitted no evidence to the public prosecutor to justify the raid and arrests, nor could they justify storming a private home in a quiet, upscale neighborhood owned by a respectable couple. No neighbors had complained about noise or abnormal or immoral activities in the house. All of the guests in the villa were women who hailed from wealthy and respectable families of high social status; whether they played card games for money or for fun, they played quietly in a private home and disturbed no one. Aside from involving a star of Layla Murad's stature, the incident was not newsworthy, even including the lack of a warrant.

Considering the regime's control over the media and the tight military censorship over what appeared in the press, the extensive daily press coverage with its sensational headlines would seem to have been intended to warn Layla how delicate and fragile her position was in comparison to that of the military regime's men. Although she never faced criminal charges, the case and its coverage attacked Layla's public image at a critical time. The arrest took place just one week before the release of her film *al-Habib al-Maghul* (*The Unknown Lover*; Hassan al-Sayfi, 1955), which became her last film. Meanwhile, Layla was also pregnant with her second child, her only son with Fatin 'Abd al-Wahab. She fell ill and spent the rest of the year between her summer home in Alexandria and hospitals, away from the public spotlight. She gave birth to her second child through cesarean section in December 1955, the condition of her health in such jeopardy that the daily *al-Akhbar* urged readers to pray for her.

Fortunately, Layla recovered and made a comeback, celebrating her motherhood but implicitly denying her elder son, Ashraf. She appeared on the cover of *al-Kawakib* on March 6, 1956, along with a pictorial interview celebrating Zaki's birth and their moving with her husband Fatin 'Abd al-Wahab to a new villa on the top floor of her apartment building. The cover photo showed her as an elegant homemaker doing needlework.[39] The report celebrated Layla's resuming her career and reintroduced her to the public as a star, mother, wife, and propertied businesswoman. True or not, Layla appeared to be successful, active, and happy. Journalists who interviewed her or visited her home spoke of Zaki as the only child she had, using her nickname, *umm Zaki* (Zaki's mom),[40] which meant that Zaki was her eldest or only child. In the following year, when her autobiography was serialized in *al-Kawakib* starting in March 1957, Layla was silent about her relationship with Wagih Abaza and continued hiding their son, Ashraf, from the public. Her narrative leapt from her final divorce from Anwar Wagdi to her marriage to Fatin 'Abd al-Wahab, with no mention whatever of Abaza or their son. At the conclusion of her autobiography, she said that her happiness with Fatin became complete with the birth of their son Zaki, "who filled my life with happiness."[41] Hiding her three-year-old son Ashraf, Layla wrote:

> I considered Fatin an excellent filmmaker, and I liked his morality, artistic personality, and hard work, but I never thought I'd get married again. After my divorce from Anwar, I decided to devote my life to my art. I attended a party in Sa'id Abu Bakr's house, where I met Fatin for the first time and learned he had discussed his wish to marry me with colleagues. He was practical and announced our engagement during the same party, which lasted until morning. We got ready for marriage and started a life that made me

forget the many troubles I had previously faced. Gracious God completed our happiness with our son Zaki and separated our present happiness from the painful past.[42]

At the end of the 1950s, Layla finally brought Ashraf into the public eye. He participated in and won a competition for the most beautiful child of a celebrity mother. Celebrities including actress Layla Fawzi and radiocaster Galal Mu'awwad served as judges. The press covering the event identified Ashraf as "Layla Murad's son," without mentioning his father's name.[43] Layla began to appear in public as the mother of two boys, Ashraf and Zaki, and many believed that they were full brothers born to her husband, Fatin 'Abd al-Wahab. Wagih gave partial recognition to their son but did not recognize his fatherhood socially: Layla's son carried the Abaza family name but did not become known publicly as Wagih Abaza's son until both parents passed away in 1994 and 1995, respectively. Ashraf had no connection with his biological father: although he gave his family name to Ashraf, Wagih never incorporated him into his nuclear or extended family, never appeared with him in public, and never invited him to a private family gathering. Nonetheless, even after President Sadat (r. 1970–1981) removed Wagih from his last official position as governor of Greater Cairo in 1971, the press gossiped about the former relationship between Layla and Wagih, referring to his last position without explicitly mentioning his name.[44] When Ashraf turned eighteen and graduated from high school, Layla celebrated her son's success by giving him a brand new car, a Nasr 128; the Lebanese celebrity magazine *al-Maw'id* covered the celebration and mentioned Ashraf's family name, Ashraf Abaza.[45] Sources interviewed for this study confirmed that the son and father never met face-to-face until the son had finished high school. The encounter took place unintentionally in a minor road accident, when Wagih got out of his car to make sure the driver of the other car (Ashraf) had not been hurt. The son recognized his father, whose pictures appeared frequently in the press, but sadly enough, the father did not recognize his teenaged son. When Ashraf performed his mandatory military service, he spent his breaks in the house of his maternal uncle, Munir Murad, whenever his mother was not in Cairo--never in his biological father's house.

Wagih excluded Ashraf from his car import business and dealership while his other sons, as well as his wife I'timad, worked in and inherited the large and lucrative business. The obituary for Wagih Abaza, published in 1994,[46] did not include Ashraf among Wagih's children or relatives who survived him; similarly, Layla's obituary did not include any reference to the Abaza family or mention Ashraf's full name. His full name finally appeared in the press a few years after both his parents had passed away, in a piece celebrating Layla's legacy, when at last the Abaza family no longer objected to Ashraf's becoming known as a son of Wagih Abaza and using his full name.

Since then, Ashraf has become widely known as the son of Wagih Abaza and has gone on to develop friendly relationships with his Abaza relatives, although the family still exclude him from their car business and family events. Ashraf may have ignored his legal rights as one of Wagih's beneficiaries out of respect for his mother. His name never appeared in an obituary for any member of the Abaza family, even those of his half-brothers and -nephews who passed away after Wagih's death. To commemorate Wagih Abaza's death and celebrate his legacy, his family commissioned Nasserist journalist 'Abdallah Imam to write a detailed biography of Wagih and provided him with personal documents and photos. The thick celebratory volume (580 pages) appeared a few months following Wagih's death and a few months before Layla's. The biography covers Wagih's life from childhood until the building of his car trade empire, as well as including information about his marriage to I'timad and their children together. Unsurprisingly, the book does not mention Ashraf or his mother, Layla Murad.

Break Time for a Broken Heart: 1956 and After!

Layla was going through her semi-secret struggle to win legal recognition for her eldest son, hiding his existence from society and taking care of two babies, when the events of 1956 swept through Egypt and the Middle East. The Tripartite Aggression / Suez War triggered unprecedented systematic policies against Jews in Egypt. Following Operation Susannah (also known as the Lavon Affair) in 1954 and even more after the Tripartite Aggression, life became increasingly difficult for Egyptian Jews. Operation Susannah was an ill-planned attempt by the Israeli Mossad to destabilize Nasser's Egypt in the early 1950s. In that failed covert operation, Israel mobilized a small

number of young and mostly Egyptian Jews to plant bombs inside Egyptian-
, American-, and British-owned civilian targets, including movie theaters,
libraries, and American educational centers. The attacks were to be blamed
on Egyptian leftists and the Muslim Brotherhood, with the goal of showing that the country had become less orderly under Nasser. The conspiracy
fell apart, and the suspects were rounded up and imprisoned. Two operatives
committed suicide in jail, and the Egyptian authorities tried and executed
another.[47] The Egyptian regime and its supporters were not careful, and in
some cases uninterested in, making a distinction between Jews and Zionists.

After Nasser announced the nationalization of the Suez Canal in the
summer of 1956, Anglo-French-Israeli forces attempted to invade Egypt.
After the invaders were forced to withdraw, the Egyptian regime grew hostile toward foreigners and Jews. The regime detained Jews without Egyptian
citizenship and forced whole families to leave the country. Layla must have
feared a backlash against her immediate family, Jewish relatives, and Jewish
friends as her country came under foreign attacks and the local Jewish community came under domestic assault. The Egyptian Red Crescent (ERC)
singled her out among artists who wore the ERC uniform to show their
patriotism during the Suez War, publicly censuring her for wearing the uniform and warning her not to wear it again because only members of the
organization were allowed to do so. This baffled Layla, as she had contributed
to the organization throughout her career and had readily agreed to star in
their organization's fundraising concerts. She tried to win public sympathy
and tearfully explained to reporters that she wore the ERC uniform because
she didn't want to wear normal clothing while people of her country were
going to war. Layla did no wrong, as the ERC uniform was neither a formal
nor a legally restricted uniform; Egyptian laws banned civilians from wearing military and police uniforms but did not deal with civic organizations'
uniforms. The ERC said nothing against other stars who wore its uniform
before reporters' cameras during the Suez War,[48] which led Layla to believe
that many forces were trying to drive her out of her position as a superstar
diva into that of an undesirable person as part of the regime's systematic
policy to purge Jews following the Israeli aggression against Egypt.

The Egyptian regime rounded up many Jewish males into detention
centers, and many Jewish families had no choice but to leave after being

issued one-way visas to leave the country with no right to return. Layla's two siblings Malak and Murad, who never converted to Islam, and her sister Samiha, who converted and then returned to Judaism, left Egypt for good; her brother Ibrahim, her closest sibling and advisor, also left for France in December 1956. Layla had a complete breakdown: she became afraid of people and suffered from severe anxiety and insomnia. In 1957, she entered a psychiatric clinic in the suburbs of Helwan. Everyone knew about her depression and failing health. Layla needed a break to process what she had gone through emotionally and mentally, and to take care of her health and her two children. She needed to reconsider her personal and professional choices while knowing that the Syrians would not show her movies. With medical help, she managed to regulate her sleeping pattern and resume her life as a mother, wife, and beloved star.

The Myth of Layla's Retirement

The Nasserist regime extended its control over the media and the public sphere. It turned old media, such as radio, and the newly established television into mouthpieces of the regime. The state brought the film industry under its direct control and founded the Egyptian Public Establishment of Cinema (EPEC), which controlled movie production, distribution, and theaters. The state's hegemony coincided with the end of Layla's cinematic career. Did it lead to her disappearance? Did the Nasserist state purge Layla Murad and end her career?

Politics and songs mutually impacted one another in postcolonial Egypt. Nasser's regime directly controlled the entertainment industry, including cinema and music, and used songs to promote its policies; at the same time, producers and artists worked overtly to support the regime's goals, policies, and personnel.[49] Songs promoted Nasser's regime, its accomplishments and leadership. The regime used both well-established stars who had built their careers under the monarchy and rising stars alike. Layla's musical career under Nasser shows that she readily joined the regime's efforts and openly supported the Free Officers, first under Muhammad Nagib's leadership and then under Nasser's. She recorded patriotic songs and anthems for nationalist occasions and when the regime needed her voice to mobilize the public. She invited the press to publicize her image wearing military-like uniforms during the Suez War of 1956 and performed songs for the unification with Syria in 1958 as well as for the Egyptian army and Sinai during the war of attrition after the 1967 defeat. The Nasserist state's radio and television and the press used Layla's voice and image as part of Egyptian popular culture.

Radio's importance as a venue for music increased after 1952 with the expansion of broadcast hours and power. Between the launch of national radio in 1934 and the July Revolution of 1952, the radio broadcast only one Arabic and one European program for inhabitants of Egypt. Between 1952 and 1963, daily broadcasts multiplied eight times, increasing from 15 hours to 18 hours 45 minutes a day. Short- and medium-wave broadcast power also continued to increase.[50] Examining lists of Egyptian radio's daily programs under Nasser confirms that all Egyptian radio stations broadcast at least one of Layla's songs daily; the main one, Cairo Radio, did not differ from short-wave stations, such as Voice of the Arabs and Sudan's Corner. The frequency of broadcasting Layla's songs refutes speculation that Egyptian radio attempted to denigrate Layla when it broadcast one of her songs as performed by another singer. Kamal al-Tawil, who composed the melody, created an awkward situation when he offered the song to Nagat al-Saghira, who was on tour in Syria. Nagat claimed that when she performed the song in Syria and Lebanon with great success, she had not known that Layla had performed it in a film released in 1955 and was negotiating to record the song for radio.[51] The radio censorship bureau had asked Layla to change a few words in the lyrics before airing the song, a request that Layla dismissed.[52] Seeking quick publicity for his melody, al-Tawil insisted that Layla did not have the right to record the song for radio, and he sold it to Nagat the same year. Layla lost the legal case, and so only Nagat's performance was broadcast. Only those who watched Layla's film had a chance to hear her performance of the song, which became associated with Nagat's voice rather than with Layla's.

But that incident aside, the radio kept Layla's name in the category of exceptional artists, above the other three tiers of singers, which for a number of years gave her a financial advantage whenever she recorded a new song for radio and it was broadcast. Years later, when the expenses of buying new lyrics and music composition as well as hiring musicians increased while radio payments stagnated, the deal hurt exceptional artists and discouraged Layla from recording new songs. With a new taxation system, Layla found herself obliged to pay 20 percent of her earnings from radio in the form of taxes while being unable to deduct what she paid for lyrics, music compositions, and musicians.[53] Recording new songs for the radio became so costly that it was no longer worthwhile.

From the time of its inception in 1960, Egyptian television regularly broadcast Layla's films. The Egyptian TV network launched in July 1960 with one channel and 100 broadcast hours a month; it added a second channel the following year and increased its broadcast hours to 699 hours a month in 1963.[54] The number of Egyptians who owned TV sets grew continuously, from 39,000 in 1960 to 200,000 in 1963, after only three years following the launch. The number of those who watched what was broadcast was even larger, since many watched television in coffeehouses, clubs, schools, or friends' and neighbors' homes. According to May 1963 programming, Egyptian television devoted more than forty-eight hours to Egyptian films, about 7.2 percent of its total broadcast time.[55] Thanks to Egyptian television, Layla Murad continued to be a household name among generations of audiences who never heard her live or watched her films in movie theaters. Whenever an old film starring Layla Murad was broadcast, audiences sent a wave of letters to the press asking about her and why she did not appear in new films or *Adwa' al-Madina*)City lights) concerts that radio organized and broadcast every month and were popular among listeners across the Arab world.[56]

In the early 1960s, Layla explained that she had grown more nervous about public performances and deliberately avoided live concerts. She considered that feeling ironic, as she had begun her career performing in live concerts and continued making such appearances for many years.[57] Anxiety over meeting the audience face to face may have resulted from her weight issue: having devoted herself to taking care of her children for several years, she had become overweight. Her body shape triggered some cruel comments such as "Layla Murad added her name to the fat women club,"[58] which made her explode with anger. Layla's memories of Muhammad Karim's severe attitude toward her and all actresses' diet and body shape may have contributed to her self-consciousness about her body. Unaware that age slows the metabolism and at a time when society did not emphasize physical exercise for women, Layla remained defensive about her weight. She acknowledged she loved to eat but said that she could go on a strict diet whenever she needed to. A journalist wrote in 1961:

> Layla lost one of her biggest advantages: her slim body figure. Her weight noticeably increased, and she is about to join the fat women list! However, you should never tell her so; otherwise, she would be angry at you, just as she exploded in my face, saying: false rumors spread by liars. Then she admitted saying: I always gain weight when I don't work, but I manage to lose weight whenever required. I can lose up to 20 kilograms in 15 days."[59]

When the cost of producing a new song went up and paying for lyrics and melodies and hiring musicians cost more than what radio paid, the establishment of radio and TV broadcasts in Arab countries opened new opportunities for income. Layla recorded new songs for Kuwait and Abu Dhabi television, some of which she shared with Egyptian counterparts, but she refused to share what she considered less attractive productions with Egyptian audiences. However, television posed the challenge of replicating cinema's visual aesthetics: TV directors were reluctant to use singers whose body shape did not conform to European standards of slim sex appeal, sidelining middle-aged female singers as being unattractive or overweight. On the other hand, Layla was in a strong position to choose venues for her voice to meet audiences. She refused to record songs for Egyptian television because she thought the musical productions were not sufficiently funded and the quality remained low. She rejected TV offers to produce clips combining her voice with animated images of her, requesting instead to appear in a one-hour TV musical show.[60] Egyptian television was still young and lacked expertise, and so Layla's request sounded unrealistic.

Although she was open to making solo recordings of patriotic songs, Layla refused to appear alongside other Egyptian and non-Egyptian Arab singers in grand patriotic performances. She also chose not to perform in *Adwa' al-Madina* or other public concerts despite the popularity of such broadcast shows.[61] Started in 1953 as a radio program offering excerpts from live concerts, plays, and movie theaters in Cairo, *Adwa' al-Madina* morphed into a series of concerts held in different Egyptian provinces and Arab capitals that the network would broadcast live. Arguably, the series became the most prestigious concert in the Arab world. *Adwa' al-Madina* communicated the voices of well-established singers and newly discovered talent to Arab listeners across the globe on regular and short-wave radio. It is not surprising that stars competed to win an opportunity to perform in these concerts and criticized the organizers whenever they lost.[62] These concerts became the main venue through which to publicize patriotic songs during national celebrations. Rightly or not, Layla chose not to participate in these popular events, but radio did not exclude her.

In sum, Layla Murad's singing career continued as she recorded songs for broadcasts in Egypt and the rest of the Arab world and sang at private parties. Audiences continued to enjoy her songs and movies on the TV screen. Nevertheless, Layla's cinematic career was interrupted, and after 1955 she never appeared in another film. Once she had recovered from her breakdown and after her two children reached school age, she was ready to resume her cinematic career. In 1961, she decided to produce her own films, contradicting her statement made a few years earlier in which she claimed she would not produce films. She explained that she had decided to produce her own films to avoid dealing with producers who had violated their contracts. She actively searched for a good story to transform into a movie script, turning to French literature, and expressed her willingness to buy the Egyptianized version of a French story on which a radio show was based.[63] Her brother Ibrahim likewise searched tirelessly for a suitable film script. At that time, Layla did not hide that she prioritized her family over her career, spending most of her time taking care of her children and sewing clothes for them.[64] The sudden death of Ibrahim in 1963 took a significant toll on her: she spent two years without making any recordings. Then a headline appeared on the cover of *al-Kawakib* magazine in October 1965, confirming that Layla Murad would sing again.[65] To be ready to make a new film, however, she needed more time to go on a diet. According to Layla's narrative, she followed a restrictive diet and lost 18 kilograms (about 40 pounds) in order to appear in films with her usual attractive look.[66] However, critic Kamal al-Najmi dubbed Layla "the singer of cinema" but claimed she did not or could not come back.[67]

Layla was aware of the changes that the film industry had gone through since the early 1960s. In 1963, the state merged confiscated studios and labs into a state-owned production company called the Egyptian Public Establishment of Cinema (EPEC), which became the biggest producer of films, producing about 30 percent of Egyptian films released between 1963 and 1971, when it shut down owing to financial losses and increasing debt. EPEC productions relied heavily on Egyptian literature rather than tapping foreign films and making local versions. Musicals became rare, and there were less than a handful of films featuring singers. The policies of EPEC fluctuated continually between expansion and contraction, between directly producing films and lending money to private production companies. Layla sought a work opportunity in a film produced by EPEC, encouraged by old business with her company and by the friendship her late brother Ibrahim had with ʿAbd al-Hamid Guda al-Sahhar, who became the director of EPEC in 1966. She met with al-Sahhar in his office and suggested a story that he did not like, and so she offered to work on any story of his choice. When she did not hear back from al-Sahhar and EPEC, she went back to him many times and suggested many stories, all of which al-Sahhar rejected. Conforming to EPEC's tendency to tap Egyptian literature, she suggested that she perform in a film based on Ihsan ʿAbd al-Quddus's story "Daʿni li-Waladi" (Leave me for my son), which EPEC had already bought; al-Sahhar claimed that shooting for the film had already begun with the actress Fatin Hamama, which was a lie, as Fatin Hamama had left the country to live abroad. When it became known that Hamama planned not to return to Egypt, Layla offered to replace her, yet al-Sahhar still refused. Countering false reports that EPEC had refused Layla's project because she demanded high fees, Layla offered to partner in the production and contribute to the project's finances; yet again, EPEC refused.[68]

Layla's account that al-Sahhar stood as a barrier between her and the resumption of her cinematic career was confirmed by his own: he did not want Layla to appear in any of EPEC's productions. He admitted that Turkish filmmakers visited Cairo in 1968 and asked to cooperate with EPEC in producing a film starring Layla Murad and Yusuf Wahbi. Al-Sahhar, while welcoming the cooperation, mocked the Turkish suggestion of casting Layla because "the Turkish filmmakers had learned during a previous visit twenty years earlier that Layla Murad and Wahbi were the biggest stars."[69] He told the Turks to give up on Layla and consider the "dozens of Egypt's rising and new stars."[70] He included the story in his memoir as an amusing anecdote, although the cooperation project failed.[71]

In the late 1960s, many stars left the country for Lebanon and Turkey to escape problems with taxation, bureaucratic complications with obtaining travel permits, and the state's security regime. Some studios shut down, and many artists and technicians suffered from unemployment. Egyptian films lost their Arab markets in Syria, Lebanon, and other Arab states to the Indian Bollywood. While al-Sahhar gave Layla Murad the cold shoulder, he took pride in his tireless work to bring artists back from abroad so that studios and unemployed extras could go back to work. He went to Beirut to meet the Egyptian stars and convince them to come back to Cairo, promising to eliminate their problems with taxation and the Duties and Customs Department. He promised to get actresses exemptions from exit visa regulations and secure them permanent travel permits.[72] A few returned, but many others did not; in particular, Fatin Hamama did not return to Cairo for years after Nasser died, and she never made *Leave Me for My Son*.

'Abd al-Hamid Guda al-Sahhar's special connections to Wagih Abaza may explain al-Sahhar's insistence in blocking Layla's return to cinema. In his memoir, *Dhikrayat Sinima'yya* (Cinematic memories), al-Sahhar describes his friendship with Wagih Abaza before and after 1952. It was both a personal and a work relationship, and al-Sahhar was a guest in Wagih's house and office; thus we can understand al-Sahhar's commitment to pay Wagih back by blocking Layla's road. Before July 1952, al-Sahhar worked for the Air Force's magazine, *Silah al-Tayaran*, under Officer Wagih Abaza's editorship. After 1952, al-Sahhar visited Wagih, who had just become one of the most powerful men in the new regime's propaganda machine, in his office in the Nile Company. Wagih commissioned al-Sahhar to write a movie glorying the Egyptian Air Force produced by the Nile Cinema Production Company. Work sessions for the project extended over several dinners in Wagih's home in Heliopolis, during which al-Sahhar enjoyed the Abazas' signature lentil meals. Al-Sahhar commented on the hospitality of these dinners, which frequently lasted through the night until morning without getting any serious work done. Thanks to this special personal patronage, Wagih commissioned al-Sahhar to produce the movie, in addition to scriptwriting, while the Nile Company provided the funds. Wagih meant to provide al-Sahhar with an opportunity to make up for his financial loss in producing *Darb al-Mahabil* (*Fools' Alley*; Tawfiq Salih, 1955).[73] Releasing the film *Shayatin al-Gaw* (*Air*

Devils; Niyazi Mustafa, 1956) in the wake of the Suez War contributed to its success in Egypt and the rest of the Arab countries, particularly in Syria.[74]

Al-Sahhar's anecdote reveals the patron-client relationships formed by Wagih Abaza and other powerful men in the Nasserist state. Scholars have paid close attention to how the Nasserist state expanded and controlled media, including the film industry, to make them a mouthpiece for the regime. They have also studied the state's patronage system with regard to top officials and their relationships to their protégés.[75] Political elites in Egypt after July 1952 never relied on the popular vote, so they did not have to choose their appointees based on experience, qualifications, credentials, or efficiency. The choice of appointees depended on a network of personal loyalties and a web of relationships known as *shilla*.[76] Al-Sahhar's old friendship with and loyalty to Abaza secured him the highest position in the state-owned cinema establishment and to control the film industry. Al-Sahhar himsef had limited cinema production experience; his only film, *Darb al-Mahabil*, registered substantial financial losses, although thanks to the creativity of filmmaker Tawfiq Salih, *Darb al-Mahabil* garnered high praise for its artistry among critics. Abaza's patronage of al-Sahhar began once Abaza became a significant patron capable of using the state's resources to reward his chosen clients. There was no need to calculate the economic risk or fear of any possible financial loss; personal relationships and loyalty to persons went beyond and above any other consideration. Thus, Abaza commissioned al-Sahhar to use state funds to produce *Shayatin al-Gaw* and make up his financial loss in *Darb al-Mahabil*. The relationship between Abaza and al-Sahhar continued even after Abaza lost his position as the regime's liaison with artists and cinema and then made a strong comeback to politics as the governor of al-Buhayra (1960–1968) and al-Gharbiyya (1968–1970). As head of the Egyptian Public Establishment of Cinema, al-Sahhar "contacted my friend Wagih Abaza, the governor of al-Gharbiyya, and agreed to prepare 26 cinema screening units to show movies in the countryside to start operating on May 1."[77]

While al-Sahhar unintentionally revealed his client-patron relationship with Abaza, he also unintentionally revealed that he had blocked Layla Murad's effort to return to the cinema when he was the president of EPEC.

Al-Sahhar became a friend of Ibrahim, Layla's brother, who also managed her production company, al-Kawakib Film. Ibrahim contacted al-Sahhar to cowrite a film with him titled *Risala Ila Allah* (*Message to God*; Kamal 'Ati-yya, 1961) based on Ibrahim's idea. Al-Kawakib Film produced the film, and Ibrahim managed the production that went to theaters in May 1961; there is no evidence that Layla participated directly in the production beyond owning the production company. Releasing the film in the summer turned out to be a financial disaster, since movie theaters were not air-conditioned and theaters attracted moviegoers only in the winter; moreover, Ibrahim ran out of funds and released the film without publicity. The film did not cover its costs, nor did it attract critics' attention, although the female child Zahyya Ayub who starred in the film received praise from the foreign press.[78] Ibrahim had to shut down his office and work for Sawt al-Fann, the company owned by musician Mu-hammad 'Abd al-Wahab, singer 'Abd al-Halim Hafiz, and cameraman Wahid Farid. Ibrahim relied on al-Sahhar to help his production company recover and help his sister Layla star in new films. Thanks to Ibrahim's kind personal-ity and disposition, al-Sahhar grew fond of him and wrote:

> Every time we met, Ibrahim talked about his hope of finding a story that suited his sister Layla and his hope that she would return to movies. We dis-cussed dozens of stories, but we liked none. We were under the influence of Layla's grandly successful films: *Layla Bint al-Fuqara'*, *Layla Bint al-Aghnya'*, and *Ghazal al-Banat*. After several months, I went to him with a new idea, and he happily exclaimed: this suits Layla! I promised him to write down a summary of the story. He died suddenly and left me heartbroken. I mourned him in silence and did not go to offer (his family) condolences. I felt sad and could not grieve.[79]

Al-Sahhar's account shows that he worked with Ibrahim Murad and for Layla Murad's production company in 1961 when al-Sahhar was trying des-perately to attract attention to himself as a writer. Ibrahim must have known about al-Sahhar's close ties to Wagih Abaza, just as al-Sahhar had known about Layla's troubled relationship with him. Al-Sahhar chose not to meet with Layla even at the funeral of Ibrahim, her brother and his friend, lest he upset his powerful patron, Wagih Abaza. The patronage relationship with

Abaza paid off, and in 1966 al-Sahhar became one of the most powerful bureaucrats in the Egyptian film industry. Layla reached out to al-Sahhar, hoping to continue the conversation her late brother had started with him. She visited al-Sahhar in his office several times, and according to her, he always promised to find a promising opportunity for her; but several months would pass between visits without her hearing back, and finally she got the message and gave up.

Thus the Nasserist state's personal patronage networks brought an untimely end to Layla's cinematic career. Shortly after she expressed her frustration about working with the state-owned production company in the late 1960s,[80] Egyptian cinema went through another dramatic restructuring. With Anwar Sadat's rise to power, the state withdrew from production in 1971. In her fifties and after fifteen years away from the camera, Layla stopped trying to appear on the cinema screen. Until her death she held al-Sahhar and EPEC responsible for ending her career, expressing her convictions during the last interview she gave to Egyptian radio in 1978 that al-Sahhar had ignored her repeated requests to work.[81]

A comparison of Layla's trajectory with that of her brother, Munir, illuminates the multiple loads that Layla had to carry as a Jewish Muslim convert, a woman, and a star in a society experiencing rapid changes in public culture and politics. Munir Murad (1922–1981) worked as an assistant director in the company belonging to Anwar Wagdi, his brother-in-law at the time. He launched his career as an actor, composer, and singer in *Ana wa Habibi* (*My Lover and I*; Kamil al-Tilmisani, 1953), produced by his sister's al-Kawakib Film Co. After a few films, he gave up acting and focused on his passion and talent for composing melodies for songs performed by successful singers, including Shadya, 'Abd al-Halim Hafiz, Sabah, and his sister, Layla Murad. As sibling artists, Layla and Munir shared many similarities, but their professional paths differed dramatically during the course of the postcolonial state. They were artists when secular governments during the colonial and postcolonial periods viewed the performing arts as colorful sites for mapping national cultures. Along with other beloved stars, they played central roles in forming national consciousness, unity, and pride.[82] Both of them converted to Islam and married Muslims. Layla, extraordinarily successful under the

monarchy and the early days of the republic, struggled once Nasser consolidated his power, while Munir's musical career flourished; Nasser decorated
him with the Republic Medal during the Science Day celebration in 1966
in recognition of his artistic work in serving the state. Gender disparity is
critical in explaining the striking differences between Layla's and Munir's
trajectories.

With no presumption of a binary relationship between the state and
society, rapid changes in the relationship between the state, as a set of institutional forms through which a ruling class expresses its political nature, and
civil society engendered a public culture in which citizenship and member-
ship in different collectivities were in flux.[83] We should analyze the state
as a multitiered construct constituted by ethnicity, gender, class, affiliation
to dominant or subordinate groups, and urban or rural residence.[84] Munir's Jewish origins did not prevent him from receiving the Science and Art
Badge from Nasser, whereas, despite the protection that Layla received from
Nasser's regime during the rumor crises, owing to her romance with Wagih
Abaza, one of the new ruling elite, that same relationship made her more
vulnerable. Her being a woman rather than a man played a major role in
her being sidelined and suffering marginalization, in contrast to her brother,
who pursued an active and successful music career until his untimely death
of a heart attack in October 1981. Despite the interruption of her cinematic
career, however, she never disappeared from the public gaze, and her career
never stopped entirely. In 1985, she sang at a wedding party while Nagwa
Fu'ad danced, a performance that might have been a gig or a courtesy to the
celebrating family friends but in any case evinced her desire and ability to
perform live in public and her continuing popularity.

Layla fell and broke her leg in late 1989, which led to her final withdrawal
from public life. Her social life became limited to her immediate family plus
phone calls and rare visits from fewer than a handful of friends. In November 1995, her health collapsed, and she was taken to the Misr International
Hospital in Cairo, where she passed away three days later, on November 21,
1995; she was seventy-seven years old. Her body was moved from the hospital to Sayyida Nafisa Mosque for the Islamic ritual prayers and then to
al-Basatin cemetery in southern Cairo for burial. Hushing up rumors that

Layla had received Jewish burial services and was buried in the Jewish cemetery, her children confirmed that she received a Muslim burial, following
their mother's will that stipulated a private religious ceremony in the mosque
that she frequented during her life for prayers and charity donations. Interest
in Layla's life and legacy has grown until the present time, a phenomenon
that the next chapter examines.

CHAPTER 6

THE STARLING OF THE VALLEY
Remembering Layla Murad

Layla Murad did not share any characteristics of the Jewish
girls I had seen. I always became flabbergasted whenever
she was said to be Jewish.

Writer Safi Naz Kazim, 2007

I never noticed her Jewish origins to have any negative
effect on her Egyptian patriotism. She was always critical
of Israel's policies, and she deeply sympathized with the
Palestinian people. She always put her Egyptianness and
Arabism above any other considerations.

MP Mustafa al-Fiqi, 2008

WHEN LAYLA MURAD DIED in November 1995, the headline in the celebrity magazine *al-Kawakib* read, "She lived as a Muslim, died as a Muslim,
and was buried in the Muslim cemetery."[1] The editors no doubt intended the
headline to put to rest rumors that Murad returned to Judaism after she had
converted to Islam in the 1940s. It reveals that questions about Murad's faith,
loyalty to Egypt, and connections with Israel had returned to haunt her in
the last decades of her life, and they have continued to do so after her death.
The intense interest in Layla's life and legacy in the last four decades goes

beyond any interest in a bygone past. Since her definitive withdrawal from public life in the late 1980s, many considered that her life and legacy had become a foreign country whose features were shaped by their predilections.[2] As time and perspective collude to shape her legacy, those who thought and wrote about her for their own reasons generated a semblance of her life.[3] The state, writers, and activists who shaped her life's memory and meaning told their story, not hers. As others retell her life, they make her and her legacy objects for their increasingly elaborate series of reflections and contexts.[4] Her story provides the ruling regime, Arab nationalists, Nasser-antagonists, Islamists, and neoliberals with a protagonist through which they can tell their versions of the dramatic changes Egypt experienced over a century. Layla's legacy demonstrates the power of interpretation in the formation of historical meaning. The tone of Egyptians' writings tells its own tale, a story about popular discourse formation.[5]

The construction and representation of Layla's persona by the state's institutions and writers from across the political spectrum have shaped the memory and meaning of her life to serve their needs. The state and its opposition have constructed Layla's persona and employed her legacy to serve competing agendas concerning relations with Israel, the state's role in the economy, the monarchy and Nasser's legacies, and the ongoing bloody confrontations between the current military regime and Islamists. Layla Murad's story illuminates the evolution of the Egyptian identity as an ethnoreligious and gendered construct. Nonetheless, the ever-changing ways in which Egyptians tell Layla Murad's story illuminate how Egyptians' understanding of their identity has changed over time, partly owing to the prolonged Arab-Israeli conflict, Arab nationalism, and the Islamization of Egyptian society against the backdrop of state security and neoliberal policies.

Dwelling in Gossip

Until the mid-1970s, gossip and celebrity publications continued reporting about Layla Murad's new songs, her aborted attempts to appear in new films, and her social and family life.[6] Meanwhile, the emerging historical writings on Egyptian cinema and music at that time ignored her and her work. Music historian and critic Kamal al-Najmi overlooked her in his first four books published between 1966 and 1972. Although he wrote in detail about the singers who preceded and followed her, al-Najmi failed to include Layla and her musicals in his intensive discussion of musical film.[7] His only acknowledgment: "No female cinematic singer [was noteworthy] after Layla Murad except Shadya and Huda Sultan."[8] Similarly, film critic and instructor at the Cinema Institute Sa'd al-Din Tawfiq made no mention of Layla in his pioneering work on the history of Egyptian cinema, published in 1969, even though five of her movies appeared in his list of the one hundred best Egyptian movies.[9] Celebrating the golden anniversary of Egyptian cinema in 1977, Muhammad al-Sayyid Shusha briefly mentioned Layla in his book on influential figures in the history of Egyptian film, devoting his chapters on musical films to Umm Kulthum, Abd al-Wahab, and Farid al-Atrash.[10] Ironically, it was Shusha who published the first biography of Layla in the 1950s, before her definitive disappearance from the cinema.[11] Layla was still present on the music scene when these publications appeared; she recorded new songs for Egyptian radio, Kuwait television, and the Sawt al-Hub recording label. She recorded more than eight songs composed by both emerging and well-established musicians between 1955 and 1979, many of these songs for nationalist and religious occasions and holidays. While Layla did not appear in any new films after 1955, musical film production declined dramatically, and only a handful of such films were released in the 1960s; moreover, no other singing star made films of a quality comparable to Layla's films from the 1940s and early 1950s. For influential critics to ignore and undermine her position in the history of musical film is unjustifiable. It cannot be explained as a careless error due to Layla's absence or being out of sight; instead, it is the politics of emphasizing or deemphasizing particular artists in the public memory that explains leaving Layla Murad out of those critical writings during that time.

While critics were pushing Layla Murad out of the public memory, she enjoyed a strong presence in the memoirs published by prominent artists in the early 1970s.[12] The main tribute to Layla in her own right during this time was Salih Mursi's serial in *al-Kawakib* magazine in 1975.[13] Mursi ended the biography with Layla's divorce from Anwar Wagdi in 1952 and did not mention her Jewish origins or conversion to Islam; conveniently, this arbitrary ending allowed him to avoid discussing her crisis in late 1952 due to false rumors of her donations to Israel and her relationship to Wagih Abaza. Mursi hastily republished his biography in a book with no additional material one month after Layla's death in 1995, apparently not wanting to lose momentum following her death and mainly because he based his work on his interviews with her in the early 1970s. Perhaps he omitted her troubled years after 1953 from the new edition to honor an agreement with her, or perhaps she refused to share her memories about these years.

Re-staging a Legend

Launching his initiative for peace with Israel, President Sadat visited Jerusalem in 1977. In the following year, with US sponsorship, Egypt and Israel signed a framework for a peaceful solution through negotiations, known as the Camp David Accords, followed by the Egypt-Israel peace treaty in 1979. According to the agreement, Israel withdrew from the Egyptian Sinai in phases that ended in 1984. Both countries had to normalize relationships: exchange ambassadors, regularize airline flights and tourism, and so forth. In compliance with the agreement, the state of Egypt annulled all laws and policies concerning the boycott against Israel in 1980, opening the door for commercial and cultural exchange between people in both countries. Sadat's peace initiative was a turning point in the treatment of Layla Murad in Egypt by the ruling regime and its opposition. In a gesture of the state's commitment to fostering a culture of peace, the Egyptian regime returned Layla to her long-denied central position in popular culture. She received a distinct honor from the Egyptian Association of Film Writers and Critics at the end of 1977; Minister of Culture Yusuf al-Siba'i handed her the award in recognition of her contributions.

Along with several artists of Jewish origin, she also received a medal on the Golden Anniversary of Egyptian cinema in December 1977. Among those who also received a medal were Togo Mizrahi, who had been living in Italy since he left Egypt in the late 1940s. The radio station al-Sharq al-Awsat gave Layla a chance to share with the public the story of her forced disappearance from the cinema in a one-hour interview with Amal al-'Umda. She expressed her unhappiness over the state's EPEC (Egyptian Public Establishment of Cinema), which unjustly frustrated all her attempts to appear in films. She also expressed her longing to return to her career and to receive her due recognition. Officials of Sadat's regime received her plea positively.

She recorded the theme songs for the radio series *Lastu shaytanan wa la mal-
akan* (*I'm Neither Devil nor Angel*; Samir 'Abd al-'Azim, 1979). The airing of
the show twice a day in 1979 and the broadcast of her films on television
magnified the presence of Layla's voice and image in Egyptian homes, cafés,
and streets.

Sadat's regime exploited Layla's popularity to facilitate the peace agreement with the Jewish state and reverse Nasserist policies. More than any
other living star, Layla and her story could serve Sadat's agenda. Repudiat-
ing Nasser's objective of ending the Israeli occupation of Egyptian Sinai by
force, Sadat sought to achieve the same goal through peace. Yet the peace
agreements between Egypt and Israel required normalizing relations between the peoples of both states, which most civil society organizations in
Egypt opposed. Ending discriminatory policies against Egyptian Jews was a
positive move to demonstrate Egypt's seriousness about fostering a culture
of peace and eliminating the legacy of the conflict. The Egyptian state used
popular culture to send messages to its citizens as well as the international
community, communicating to Israel and the West that it had reversed the
anti-Jewish policies inherited from the Nasserist era. Domestically, the regime promoted a culture of peace by reminding Egyptians of their own Jews,
who had been left out of the national memory despite their contributions.
The state highlighted and celebrated Layla's legacy and gave overdue recognition to other Egyptian Jewish artists. In 1978, President Sadat decorated
the retired Jewish actress Nagwa Salim with the State Medal, and Egyptian
radio commemorated the Jewish composer Dawud Husni,[14] whose repertoire the state's Arab Music Troupe performed regularly in public concerts.
Recordings of these concerts were broadcast on state-owned television in a
weekly program devoted to classic Egyptian melodies. The state-controlled
press ran reports on celebrity Egyptian Jews living abroad.[15] Journalists and
film critics, such as Hassan Imam 'Umar and 'Abdallah Ahmad 'Abdallah
(aka Micky Mouse), highlighted the contribution of Jewish artists to Egyptian movies before 1952 on their radio and television programs.

Opening the microphone of the state's radio for Layla Murad confirmed
the end of the exclusion of Egyptians with Jewish origins. Layla's anecdotes
about her forced retirement, as related by her on the radio in 1977 and repeated by others over the following decades, told the story of the Nasserist

state's failure in managing the economy, the film industry in particular. Her account of the injustice that EPEC officials inflicted on her both fleshed out and humanized Sadat's arguments in favor of an open market economy and dissolving the state-owned companiesand contributed to the shift from a state-controlled economy to open market policies. In that regard, the writer and painter Salah Tantawi wrote a book about Layla, published in 1979 through a state-owned publisher. Beautifully written, Tantawi's book, *Rihalat Hub ma'a Layla Murad* (A journey of love with Layla Murad), weaves together Layla's life story with his own evolution from childhood to his coming-of-age and early manhood. Along that trajectory, Layla went from one successful film to another, while the author progressed in his education and social life. Depression and declining health marked the author's adulthood, coinciding with Layla's untimely withdrawal. The book powerfully communicates that a generation of Egyptians blossomed in conjunction with Layla's voice and image, their pain and depression in parallel with her disappearance because of a dysfunctional state's policies and institutions. Tantawi's was the first book to discuss her retirement at length and hold the Nasserist state responsible for wasting such extraordinary talent, as well as for the decline of music and cinema in general. The state-controlled *al-Kawakib* magazine serialized Tantawi's *Rihlat Hub* in 1994.

Countering Normalization

Some Egyptian intellectuals from a range of political continuums explicitly use Layla's Jewish origins and conversion to Islam as a means to claim a victory over Israel and mobilize the public against the normalization of relations with the Israelis. Reconstructing her persona as a sincere Muslim who voluntarily abandoned Judaism, condemned Israel, and stubbornly rejected Israeli temptations provided Egyptians with a role model of an exclusively Muslim Egyptian identity. Others use Layla's Jewish origins as a token to lament the loss of an imagined tolerant past. Tokenizing Egyptian Jews, a community that almost vanished in contemporary Egypt, whitewashes the silence about ongoing discrimination against existing religious minorities, including Egyptian Copts and Baha'is.

To highlight Layla Murad's rejection of Israeli temptations and normalization, opponents of the Peace Treaty reminded the Egyptian public, particularly the younger generations, that the beloved star was Jewish, a fact that had been obscured since the late 1950s. Sayyid Shusha wrote the first biography of Layla Murad, *al-Mughamira al-Hasna'* (The pretty adventuress), in 1956. Publishing the biography in the heyday of Nasser's regime, Shusha did not dare discuss Layla's troubled relationship with Wagih Abaza or mention their child together. In order to harness popular support for Layla after her many troubles, he focused on other sensitive issues, such as rumors of the Israeli donation and her arrest for alleged gambling. The book did not shy away from discussing her conversion and boldly called out some of the anti-Semitism she had faced. At the time of publication, audiences still remembered her Jewish origins, her conversion to Islam, and her struggle to distance herself from the Jewish state. When Layla published her serialized autobiography in *al-Kawakib* the following year, she did not ignore those sensitive issues. Over the following decades, however, mention of her Jewish origins became taboo. All of the biographical works that appeared while she was still alive ignored the question of her religious origins and conversion: biographical accounts by Salih Mursi (1975), Salah Tantawi (1979), and Rafiq al-Sabban (1992) mentioned neither Layla's religion nor the rumors of her alleged connection to Israel. These later biographies capitalized on the weakness of public memory and provided readers with a sanitized narrative of a self-sacrificing and saintly woman. All of them targeted mass readers of middlebrow culture, and Layla played a vital role in choosing how to appear in them.

Nevertheless, the timing of each account was more critical in determining what to include and what to leave out. Shusha published his biography in Lebanon when Layla's career came under attack in the Arab market. Later publications appeared in Egypt decades after Layla's last film. While Shusha intended his account to assure her continuing popularity and stardom, other authors recapped an old glory.

Under President Sadat, thanks to state control over the media and increasing harassment of the opposition press, intellectuals published their dissident political views in the Arabic press outside Egypt.[16] In the expatriate press, opponents of Camp David publicly broached Layla's Jewishness and her rejection of any association with Israel. The Lebanese celebrity magazine *al-Maw'id* published a biographical serial in 1979 that devoted several episodes to her conversion and the crises concerning the spurious donations to Israel.[17] The London-based Arabic magazine *Sayyidati* rushed to center Layla in its campaign against Camp David.[18] To counter any Israeli effort to claim her, the magazine published old pictures of her when she announced her embracement of Islam in 1948. Other Arabic publications in Lebanon and the Persian Gulf followed suit.[19]

The public sphere expanded under the democratic façade of Mubarak's regime (1981–2011). In contrast to Sadat, Mubarak more or less tolerated activists who opposed the normalization of relations with Israel (*tatbi'*). Launching the peace process between Israel and the Palestinians in the early 1990s threatened to undermine the position of anti-*tatbi'*. Layla's story became a tool to mobilize the public against the normalization of relationships between the Arabs, Egyptians in particular, and Israelis. Layla Murad and her faith became a favorite subject of public discussion, shaping her image and legacy within Egypt. From journalists to academics and from musicologists to Islamist preachers, Layla continued to capture public interest.[20] The reconstruction of her story and the utilization of her legacy served competing visions. Many employed her as a role model for a patriotic Egyptian and committed Muslim to serve nationalist and Islamist agendas. In their discussion of Layla's trajectory, politicians and intellectuals from across the political spectrum raised the questions of her religion and Israel, a recurring topic since then.

In May 1990, *al-Hilal* magazine published "The Jewish Artists between Integration and Emigration," the first article in the domestic press to remind readers that Layla Murad was Jewish and had converted to Islam in 1946. The same article erroneously claimed that her brother Munir's conversion was only superficial, to enable him to marry the actress Suhair al-Babli, but that "in reality he was Jewish until his death."[21] In fact, Munir Murad converted to Islam in 1948, long before his marriage to Suhair al-Babli in the 1950s. The author, 'Arafa 'Abdu 'Ali, omitted all language that raised doubts about Munir's conversion when he republished the same article in his subsequent books on the Egyptian Jews.[22] He may have done so for the sake of Munir's ex-wife, Suhair al-Babli, who had just retired and wore the Islamic veil, *hijab*, in the early 1990s, or he may have wished to spare the current generation of Egyptians from the dilemma of how a well-established Egyptian artist, such as Munir Murad, could secretly be Jewish. In any case, 'Ali did not make any explicit effort to correct his misinformation. Others raised doubts about Munir's conversion upon his death in 1981: he did not carry an Egyptian passport, and his son was Jewish and living in the United States. Following news reports about Munir's family holding an Islamic funeral in 'Umar Makram Mosque and the fact that his American Jewish son could not legally inherit from him quickly put to rest any doubts about the sincerity of Munir's embrace of Islam.[23] Munir died only ten days after Sadat's assassination on October 6, 1981, while the country was still holding its breath about the transfer of power to Mubarak. Thus, few paid attention to the controversy over Munir's religious identity; the emphasis shifted to his contributions to Egyptian music, significantly his composition of patriotic songs under Nasser.

'Adil Hasanayn's biography of Layla Murad, *Ya-msafir wa nasy hawak* (You departed and forgot your love), aimed to prove her innocent of donating money to Israel and highlighted the official and popular support she enjoyed to overcome the crisis;[24] it ignored both her Jewish origins and her conversion to Islam. Journalist Hanan Mufid published a biography of Layla Murad in 2003, then reprinted it in 2009 under a slightly different title; it devoted two chapters to Layla's religion and Israel.[25] In the last two decades, several books dealing with various topics--Egyptian feminism, Egyptian cinema, the religious celebrity Sheikh Muhammad Mutawali al-Sha'rawi, the history of Egyptian Jews--have devoted chapters to Layla Murad addressing her conversion to Islam and her stand against Israel.

Layla's conversion to Islam and alleged Israeli attempts to convince her to emigrate have become a favorite topic since her death in the mid-1990s. Authors answer their own questions by emphasizing her Islamic piety and commitment as a faithful Muslim and loyal Egyptian. Two books on televangelist Sheikh Muhammad Mutawali al-Sha'rawi (1911–1998) have allocated chapters to Layla Murad. The state-owned publisher Dar Akhbar al-Yum published a book glorifying Sheikh al-Sha'rawi shortly after his death in 1998that celebrates the success of the conservative preacher in convincing several female artists to wear Islamic *hijab*. The book, authored by one of Akhbar al-Yum's journalists, quotes al-Sha'rawi giving details about his repeated meetings with Layla to answer her religious questions and describing her as "a pious, devoted Muslim woman."[26] The author also claims that Layla wished to act in a historical movie titled "Layla the Muslim." The Muslim Brotherhood activist Mahmud Jami' repeats the story that Layla frequently reached out to al-Sha'rawi for answers to her religious questions.[27] In her version of the same story, Hanan Mufid adds that al-Sha'rawi "taught her [Layla] exegesis, *tajwid* (Qur'an recitation), hadith, rituals, and beliefs to raise her to the rank of the virtuous believers."[28] Mufid ends her book with a picture of herself visiting Layla's mausoleum, decorated with Qur'anic verses elegantly carved in marble. Mufid appears in the picture wearing a *hijab* while reading the Qur'an for Layla's soul. Surprisingly, the young female author, Hanan Mufid, is Christian.

All the accounts about Layla's connection with al-Sha'rawi came after both of them had died. After her death, Layla's son Ashraf was the first to talk to the press about his mother's meetings with al-Sha'rawi.[29] Conservative forces in the Egyptian media have positioned al-Sha'rawi as a saint in the popular culture, an effort in which the regime has participated.[30] Since the mid-1990s, the regime under Mubarak and now under General 'Abd al-Fattah al-Sisi has competed with political Islamist groups over religious propaganda, while the state security forces have violent confrontations with Islamists. While conservative, even reactionary, in his views on a wide range of social and cultural issues, including women, non-Muslim minorities, and music, Shaikh al-Sha'rawi endorsed Mubarak's regime and valued the state's media as a vehicle to register his stardom and popularity. The association of Layla and al-Sha'rawi nicely serves those who wish to make him a saint and those who wish to underline Layla's piety. Both groups emphasize that al-Sha'rawi was trusted by a celebrity Muslim convert to guide her on the Islamic path and that Layla was so pious a Muslim that the religious celebrity devoted his time and energy to her guidance.

After her death, baseless accounts surfaced suggesting that in 1953 she wished to travel to Mecca to perform *hajj* rituals but that Studio Misr objected to her traveling before she finished making *Bint al-Akabir*. Supposedly Layla expressed her longing to fulfill her Islamic duties by including a song for the pilgrims in the film, which became the most famous chant for that Muslim occasion. Thus, according to this account, Studio Misr prevented her from performing the pilgrimage for the rest of her life. But in reality,

Studio Misr had no power over the production processes, as Anwar Wagdi's company produced the film and processed it in its lab; Studio Misr only recorded Layla's songs and could not have decided whether she should leave for Mecca or stay in Cairo. The account that appeared in the press more than a decade after her death has become commonplace, but it contradicts its own purpose,[31] namely, to underscore her sincere Islamic piety. Blaming Studio Misr for preventing her from traveling to Mecca until she died four decades lacks any credibility. Layla never performed *hajj* or *'umra* (visiting Mecca at any time of the year) despite her frequent travels to Lebanon, Europe, and the United States for vacations and visiting family members in the diaspora. Recently, many of her religious songs chanting for Ramadan and other Islamic holidays and rituals have surfaced. She recorded religious songs both before and after her conversion, for example, singing for Saint Sayyida Zeinab, calling her "the granddaughter of our Prophet," in *Layla Bint al-Fuqara* in 1945, as did the non-Muslim female singer Nur al-Huda, who sang for Muslim 'Eid.

Two decades after Layla's death, when her sincere commitment to Islam became a well-established fact, both her conversion and her Islamic beliefs became a form of capital in the Egyptian public sphere. The Muslim Brotherhood attempted to cash in on Layla's conversion. Muslim Brotherhood activist 'Isam Talima credited the founder and leader of the organization, Hassan al-Banna (1906–1949), with bringing about Layla's conversion. In his book published in 2008, Talima quoted veteran Muslim Brother member Mahmud 'Assaf, who said that Hassan al-Banna chatted with Layla's ex-husband Anwar Wagdi when both men coincidentally met in a bank in 1945. Assaf's account, published in 1993, indicates that al-Banna invited Wagdi to visit the Muslim Brotherhood headquarters, though he didn't know whether Wagdi ever visited al-Banna.[32] Talima's book added fabricated details to 'Assaf's account, claiming that Wagdi cried and kissed al-Banna's hands and head.[33] In a recent televised interview, Talima went further, claiming that Wagdi and al-Banna developed a friendship, that Wagdi invited al-Banna to visit his home, and that during his frequent visits, al-Banna convinced Layla to embrace Islam.[34] However, Talima failed to provide any evidence of a relationship between al-Banna and Layla. His fabrication brought mockery against the Muslim Brotherhood from journalists loyal to al-Sisi's regime.[35]

Secularists, Muslim Brotherhood activists, disciples of Sheikh al-Shaʻrawi, and the young Christian journalist Hanan Mufid all wanted to prove that Layla was a Muslim. Dozens of news stories about Layla Murad have appeared since her death, and most of them, including several interviews with her sons, have raised two questions: Islam and Israel. No one has suggested that she was not a true Muslim or that she had a secret connection with Israel or any Zionist group anywhere at any time. The story of her conversion has become interestingly uniform and almost clichéd: she felt an overwhelming desire to embrace Islam upon hearing the call for the *fajr* (dawn) prayer; she woke up her husband, Anwar Wagdi, to share with him her desire to become a Muslim; he responded to her positively using Qur'anic phrases.[36]

The recent stories of her devotion to Islam emphasize her performance of the five daily prayers; her frequent visits to the Sayyida Nafisa Mosque; her daily reading of the Qur'an up to the day of her death, when she left the Holy Book open at the page of Surat Noah; and her last wish: to make the pilgrimage to Mecca.[37] The unvarying stories cite her love for Anwar Wagdi as a factor in her attraction to Islam, assuring that her conversion was voluntary, yet at the same time ignoring the fact that Wagdi never cared to introduce himself to the public as a pious Muslim, instead publicizing stories about his affairs and his leisure time spent drinking alcohol at cabarets.[38]

The recently constructed image of Layla's persona as a pious Muslim does not entirely conform to representations she publicized along with her statement of conversion in 1948. Staged images show her reading the Qur'an, listening to the religious lessons of Sheikh Mahmud Abu al-ʻUyun, and performing prayers after him. Publishing pictures of one's religious practices is, obviously, an attempt to manufacture a public image rather than to portray daily events. In all these images, her gaze is outward, toward the camera, and she wears full makeup along with a sleeveless dress that reveals her bare arms.[39] Any average Muslim with minimal knowledge of rituals would know that women could not perform *wudu'* (ablutions) while wearing lipstick or nail polish, nor could they perform prayers with uncovered arms. In these photos, Layla sought to appear in all her usual secular beauty while publicly staging her piety; although she had announced her conversion a month before publishing these images, people did not believe it, thinking it another publicity campaign for her upcoming movie.[40] Against the backdrop of the Arab-Israeli war, however, these same confirming images of her conversion were used by nationalist publications to evince pride in keeping her from the Israelis.[41]

Layla Murad as a Territorial Victory

Discussions about Layla's devotion to Islam have always focused on her commitment to Egypt and Egyptianness, and her rejection of Israel, raising the possibility of her having accepted invitations to emigrate to and being claimed by Israel. In many interviews, her sons said that their mother always refused to talk to Israeli officials or media and that she always condemned Israeli actions against Palestinians.[42]

Another common trope is how she repeatedly refused to emigrate to or visit Israel despite promises of large amounts of money and various honors.[43] According to these accounts, Layla refused to communicate with Israeli TV personnel, diplomats, or politicians, including the late Israeli prime minister Shimon Peres; her son Zaki stated that she refused generous offers to sing for American Jews.[44] Egyptian commentators understood such offers as Israeli efforts to get Layla into trouble and force her to go to Israel. They claimed that Israel had continually been making such attempts to snatch her from Egypt since 1952. Along with many others, Hanan Mufid used the Arabic word *ightisab*, which translates to both theft and rape, to describe the alleged Israeli attempts to claim Layla Murad.[45] All accounts concerning rejected Israeli offers include language promoting this line: Layla was a truly Egyptian Muslim woman.

In sum, Egyptians have spilled a tremendous amount of ink during the last three decades on two repeated questions. Question: Was Layla Murad Muslim? Answer: Yes. Question: Did she agree to have relations with Israel? Answer: No. It is understandable why her children would want to emphasize that their mother was Muslim and purely Egyptian: they are products of contemporary Egypt's public culture that presumes a contradiction between being Jewish and being Egyptian. On a practical level, if their mother were Jewish, others could have seen them as Jewish too, which would make their lives difficult, if not impossible.

Nevertheless, why have Egyptians from the entire political spectrum, both intellectuals and many others, become preoccupied with Layla's religion? It does not appear to have been a concern for her wider audience, either during her career as a film actress or when she became the sweet voice and image of the black-and-white era on the TV screen. For more than half a century, the Egyptian intelligentsia and media personnel have defined Egyptian national identity in the light of Arab nationalism, Islamism, and the continuing Arab-Israeli conflict. The archetypal Egyptian must be Arab, according to Arab nationalists, and Muslim, according to Islamists. The enemy for both is the Israeli Jew; being both Egyptian and Jewish is unimaginable. The purpose of talking about Layla's religion and Israel is to emphasize a single conclusion: Layla Murad is "ours," not "theirs." She must be Egyptian, meaning she must be Muslim, and she must be Muslim because she was genuinely Egyptian. From the time of the first Arab-Israeli war in 1948, questioning the loyalties of Egyptian Jews to Egypt and the Arab cause became routine.[46] Layla's public announcement of her embrace of Islam during the war was not a co-incidence; she was announcing on which side she wished people to see her.

In the early decades of the twentieth century, a handful of well-educated Egyptian intellectuals formulated discourses of Egyptianness as a territorial secular national identity. This inclusive pluralism gradually faced challenges with the entry of the Muslim Brotherhood and Young Egypt groups into political activism during the interwar period. In the age of mass communication and then the spread of the cyber world, individuals and groups from every order of education, religion, and social conventions enjoyed access to the marketplace of debating national identity, authenticity, and culture. Religion has increasingly become a focal point of national identity, not only as expressed by political Islam or the state but also by politicized and unpoliticized groups and individuals from all walks of life. Religious and exclusive nationalism(s) have contributed to the increased interest in Layla's religion and her potential relations with Israel to emblematize the departure of Egyptians from the former secular territorial Egyptian identity.[47] Religious extremists reject any other religion but Islam, and populist nationalists confuse Judaism with Zionism; all of them have sought to detach Layla from the Israeli enemy.

Mustafa al-Fiqi, an MP representing the ruling National Democratic Party under Mubarak, claimed he had a long relationship with Layla that confirmed that her Jewish origins had no adverse effect on her Egyptian patriotism.[48] Al-Fiqi's essay reveals an intention to treat Layla as an exceptional individual whose Jewish origins did not affect her Arabism and Egyptian-ness, an intention that points up the "natural" contradiction between being Jewish and being Egyptian, as suggested by authors claiming that all Jews, except Layla Murad, had conspired to steal the Arab musical heritage and employed Egyptian cinema to serve Zionism.[49] To embrace Layla in the premises of Egyptianness and Islam, Christian journalist Hanan Mufid suggests that Layla had been a Muslim since childhood and "was never in-fluenced by any other religion, but Islam."[50] Mufid is in agreement with the Islamist writer Safi Naz Kazim, who did not want to believe that Layla was ever Jewish, that she was too lovely. Kazim, who proudly called Layla "the daughter of my neighborhood," wrote:

> They [Jews] did not have cultural weight in my consciousness . . . , but Layla Murad did not share any characteristics of the Jewish girls I had seen. I always became flabbergasted whenever she was said to be "Jewish," which I did not feel about Raqya Ibrahim, another famous [Jewish] star in the forties. *Ulfa*, familiarity, *bashasha*, friendly mien, and *'udhuba*, sweetness, were what the name of Layla Murad meant.[51]

Kazim here "others" Jewish girls as a group of people with a different appear-ance and characteristics from the rest of Egyptian girls, differences that are not positive. Early works of such prominent writers as Nagib Mahfuz and Ihsan 'Abd al-Quddus characterized Jewish girls as free-spirited and inde-pendent; female Muslim protagonists in these works aspired to the elegant appearance and freedom of those working Jewish women.[52] Over time, the image of Jewish women in popular culture became highly sexualized; 'Abd al-Quddus's later works construct Jewish women as materialistic, using their bodies to generate wealth regardless of any moral standards.[53]

With the launch of peace negotiations between Israel and the Palestinians in Madrid in 1991 and their conclusion with the Oslo Accords in early 1993, the fear of breaking the taboo of normalization, *tatbi'*, rose high in Egypt. A handful of Egyptians, Israelis, and Palestinians formed an international coalition for peace in Copenhagen. Egyptian participants in that coalition established the Cairo Peace Society in 1997 to encourage normal relations between Egyptian and Israeli activists. The participation of staunch oppo-nents of Camp David, such as Marxist writer Lutfi al-Khuli (1928–1999), increased anxiety over normalization and eliminating the Jewish "otherness," which might erase the constructed contradictions between Egyptianness and Jewishness. Mubarak's democratic façade gave antinormalization activists from the entire political and intellectual spectrum a noticeable presence and influence inside the political parties, professional syndicates, labor unions, and the press.

Nevertheless, like all the opposition groups, antinormalization activists had almost no effect on the regime's policies concerning Israel and the Palestinian question. These activists celebrated Layla's choosing to be an Egyptian Muslim who rejected and was disgusted by Israel. Her loyalty represented an easy and guaranteed victory against Israel and against Mubarak's regime, which insisted on its peace agreement with the Jewish state. Layla's conversion to Islam and rejection of Israel have been amplified to construct an image of a defeated Israel that "suffers and bleeds from the failure that Layla Murad caused through embracing Islam and being loyal to Egypt."[54] Meanwhile, commentators have treated the conversion of her brother, Munir, with comparative silence; it is the gender and nationalist boundaries that separated the siblings across the borders of Egyptianness.

De-mystifying Layla and Nasser

The rupture in Layla Murad's cinematic career led different political factions in Egypt to speculate about the relationship between Layla's disappearance from the silver screen after her last film in 1955 and the rise of Gamal Abd al-Nasser to the zenith of power in Egypt from 1954 until he died in 1970. Commentators with different pro- and anti-Nasser inclinations have used very weak evidence with and without appropriate context to make arguments about Nasser's role in either shattering or protecting Layla's career. Both Nasserists and Nasser-antagonists recall the 1952 crisis about the false rumors of donating money to Israel, in order to idealize or dehumanize Nasser and his comrades. Nasser-antagonists explicitly accuse the Free Officers of the falsification of that news to hurt Layla Murad, just as they had tried to diminish Umm Kulthum's stature on the basis of her connection with the overthrown royal family.[55] According to the stanch anti-Nasser Wafdist historian Suhair Iskandar, the Free Officers deliberately damaged Layla's reputation by spreading false information about her alleged relations with Israel, attempting to make her vulnerable and susceptible to the regime's pressure, then declaring her innocent and manipulating her. No evidence supports this argument, and it is unlikely that manipulating Layla, or any other female star, was on the agenda of the Free Officers in the second month of their coup. Nevertheless, the young Free Officers did use Layla and her relationship with their own comrade, Officer Wagih Abaza, in their internal struggles, not hesitating to arrest Layla herself in a gambling case.

Writer Samir Gharib, a top executive in the Ministry of Culture under Mubarak, wrote that Layla Murad sent a letter to President Muhammad Nagib on March 21, 1953, complaining that officers had repeatedly arrested her after midnight and detained her each time for hours, and that she had become too depressed and frightened to leave her house.[56] Based on that letter, Gharib and others concluded that the Free Officers had arrested Layla and detained her for no reason other than to destroy or manipulate her.[57] We have no evidence, however, that Layla sent such a letter or that Nagib received it. The alleged letter is in the possession of Kuwaiti collector Ja'far Islah, who included it in a photo album titled *Qabas min ruh Misr*. Islah distributed the album in person among his friends and never registered it for an International Standard Book Number (ISBN) or made it available for sale. The original document, the alleged handwritten letter from Layla to Najib, is neither available to the public nor accessible to researchers who might wish to examine it for authenticity. The image of the letter in Islah's album does not show an official stamp proving that Nagib's office formally received the letter or that the letter went through any formal procedures of bookkeeping or bureaucratic filing. We might think that Layla handed the letter to Nagib, who kept it in his private collection; we know that he kept many documents, including personal and confidential accounts and correspondence, in his private residency after he lost power.[58] Researchers in Egypt also know that many documents have ended up in the hands of collectors, who buy them from random sellers, including trash collectors.[59]

According to the alleged letter, Layla voluntarily went to the RCC headquarters to inform its members about a Zionist attempt to convince her to immigrate to Israel. In that account, this attempt took place abroad while Layla was visiting Greece. The Swedish ambassador invited her to visit a film studio in order to see the up-to-date progress they had achieved. While

she was at the studio, a Jewish man approached her and attempted to entice
her to emigrate from Egypt to Israel. Layla forcefully rejected the offer and
maintained that she was an Egyptian Muslim woman who would rather die
in and for her own country, Egypt. Layla flew back to Egypt the following
day and promptly went to the RCC headquarters to inform Egyptian officials, who thanked her and told her the incident was of no great importance.
And then one month after her meeting with the RCC members, unnamed
officers began arresting her in her home at dawn and detaining her for several hours in solitude.

I do not find the accounts of this alleged letter convincing or even con-
ceivable. Why would the Swedish ambassador invite Layla to tour a film
studio in Greece? Why would Israelis woo an Arab singer to move to their
newly established Ashkenazi state that excluded Arab Jewish culture and
inculcated a hatred for their heritage in Jews from Arab lands?[60] More important, Layla had not left Egypt since her return from Paris with Anwar
Wagdi in October 1952 after Egyptian authorities concluded investigations
that refuted rumors about her alleged donations to Israel. That she would
have left Egypt for Europe in the winter—between her return in November
1952 and drafting the letter in March 1953—is unlikely. She had no work that
required her to travel to Europe. Wealthy Egyptians went to Europe for summer vacations, to escape the heat, but not during the cold European winter.
In September 1953, Layla collected donations in Alexandria for the victims of
an earthquake in Greece, and the Society of Greece's Friends thanked her.[61]
Layla knew that Egyptian authorities had been watching her closely; if the
alleged letter were real, she would not have wanted to contact Greece or the
local Greek community in Egypt.

Someone might have fabricated this letter or pressured Layla to draft
it. If she wrote the letter, she could have written it in March 1954 and mistakenly dated it March 1953, or she might have written it once she returned
from Paris with Anwar Wagdi in October 1952. After the regime verified
the information and exonerated her, perhaps someone among the officers re-
opened the file and blackmailed her--possibly one of Wagih Abaza's protégés
to make her more vulnerable, so that she had no choice but to engage in a
relationship with him on his terms. Another possibility is that one of Abaza's
hostile comrades was behind these hour-long detentions, meant to annoy

him and expose their relationship. In his memoir, Muslim Brother activist Mahmud 'Assaf, who worked with Abaza at the Nile Advertising Company, mentioned that Egyptian intelligence had pressured him to spy on Abaza; to obtain his release, Assaf answered their questions about Abaza's relationship with Layla.[62] Whether Abaza or Abaza's rivals were behind detaining Layla--if such detention ever took place--they had no reason to do so except an interest in fueling their rivalries or to amuse themselves at the expense of a vulnerable woman. Mustafa al-Fiqi, a former diplomat and prominent figure in the former ruling National Democratic Party and the Egyptian parliament under Mubarak, claimed that an official in the Nasserist regime deceived Layla and took her spacious apartment in the upper-class Zamalek neighborhood in exchange for convincing Abaza to recognize their child. According to al-Fiqi, that official never followed through on the mediation; his promise to do so was just a pretext to snatch the apartment.[63]

In his book *al-Watha'iq al-khassa li-Layla Murad*, journalist Ashraf Gharib maintains that Nasser prevented Layla Murad from working in films in retaliation for her open and unconditional support for Muhammad Nagib.[64] Apart from his book, Gharib also disseminated his views through many televised and published interviews in popular media outlets.[65] Anti-Nasserists picked up his conclusion and embedded it in their narratives as if it were an established fact,[66] although Gharib does not provide any concrete evidence that Nasser ordered anyone or any institution to reject Layla for roles in films. He builds his argument on the (false) premise that Nasser managed to retaliate against Layla after winning the first presidential election in 1956; only then did producers and distributors start to exclude her. Nasser became the president and undisputed leader of Egypt in 1954, long before winning the first referendum for the presidency in 1956; the press and officials began calling him President Nasser in October 1954. It is unimaginable that Nasser would care to retaliate against Layla specifically for her support of Nagib, simply because Nagib's leadership was initially supported by all the stars before he was ousted and because Layla and all the other stars publicly supported Nasser once he prevailed over Nagib in 1954. As mentioned previously, the RCC, under the leadership of Nasser, invited Layla to perform in a concert celebrating signing the evacuation agreement with the British in October 1954, a concert attended by Nasser and many RCC members. If Nasser aimed to force Layla out of the film industry, there was no need to wait for two years: Layla was a weak target, and Nasser already wielded and knew how to exercise power. If he intended to purge her, he could have banned her voice from radio and later her voice and image from television as well as from making films. More important, the state's intervention in the film industry did not start until 1958, with the establishment of the Institute of Supporting Cinema (ISC). The film industry's partial state ownership started three years later in 1961, with the nationalization of some privately owned studios, the establishment of the public sector, and the conversion of the ISC into a state-owned production and distribution company.[67] However, the state never monopolized cinema production or nationalized Layla's production company, al-Kawakib Film.

I mention these facts not to exempt the Nasserist regime from responsibility but to underscore that the regime was a complex mesh of individuals and institutions entangled in patronage relationships. Policies and decisions with unintended and contradictory outcomes resulted from dialectical power negotiations between individuals and institutions, not merely from Nasser's top-down instructions. The claim that Nasser banned Layla from making movies ignores Layla's troubling relationship with Free Officer Wagih Abaza, who exercised substantial influence on the local film industry. The anti-Nasserists based their argument on a few incidents in the 1960s in which producers rescinded their offers to Layla, although this overlooks the fact that producers and distributors became reluctant to work with her in the 1950s and 1960s, fearing financial losses resulting from the Syrian ban on Layla's movies. The cancellation of film projects was rarely related to some grand political scheme. For example, Layla's part in the biopic of Anwar Wagdi, *Tariq al-Dumu'* (*The Way of Tears*; Hilmi Halim, 1961), went to singer-actress Sabah. Actor Kamal al-Shinnawi, who wrote, produced, and starred in the film, approached Layla Murad and Layla Fawzi to cast them in the roles they actually played in Wagdi's life.[68] Both women agreed, apparently thinking, as Layla Fawzi's statement later revealed, that the film would have honored Wagdi's legacy. Fawzi initially believed that the film would have corrected the false notion that Anwar was greedy, instead highlighting his generosity regarding poor artists, his talent, and his hard work.[69] Layla rescinded her approval after al-Shinnawi modified the script and rejected her comments. When made, the film came across as a slanderous, dehumanizing rant about Wagdi, the man and the artist, depicting Wagdi as an exploitative and deceptive thief whose greed ended only with his terminal illness and death. According to the film, Wagdi loved only his second wife, Layla Fawzi, and married Layla Murad only to use her as a cash cow. The film shows Wagdi exploiting and monopolizing Layla, who passively watches him accumulating massive wealth by deceiving her. Layla Murad's refusal to participate in the work should not have surprised anyone; the participation of Anwar's widow, Layla Fawzi, should have disappointed many. The film lacked balance in treating Anwar's character and crudely assaulted the deceased artist's legacy and talent. Layla Murad may have feared accusations of taking revenge on her deceased ex-husband, or she may have simply refused to distort reality. To avoid being criticized for attacking a dead colleague and former competitor, al-Shinnawi opened his film with a disclaimer that the film told a fictional story about fictitious characters and that "any similarity between the characters of the film and real individuals were not intentional." However, no one failed to notice that the film meant to depict Anwar Wagdi: indeed, the names of the leading characters rhymed with their actual names: Ashraf Hamdi for Anwar Wagdi and Samya Fu'ad for Layla Murad. Decades later, al-Shinnawi bragged that *Tariq al-Dumu'* was a biopic of Anwar Wagdi that attempted to bring justice to Layla Murad and admitted that he had not wished to press her to play herself.[70]

On the other hand, Nasserists used Layla Murad to idealize Nasser and his comrades. In his two biographies of Wagih Abaza, Nasserist author 'Abdallah Imam ignores the relationship between Abaza and Layla Murad to idealize Abaza as a sincere, patriotic, and faithful family man. Abaza's treatment of Layla would open the door to discussing Abaza's life and career as a reckless womanizer who used his power to have a romantic relationship, then abandoned his child and the vulnerable mother. Imam's position is especially remarkable considering his interest in scrutinizing the personal relationship between Nasser's minister of defense, Field Marshal 'Abd al-Hakim 'Amir and his secret wife, actress Berlanti 'Abd al-Hamid.[71] The Nasserist narrative holds 'Abd al-Hakim 'Amir responsible for the humiliating defeat in the 1967 war rather than acknowledging that Nasser's shortcomings, including his long-standing rivalry with 'Amir, led to the defeat. In addition to highlighting the support of Free Officer Wagih Abaza during the rumors crisis in 1952, Nasserists claim that Nasser intervened to remove the Syrian boycott against her once Egypt and Syria merged in the United Arab Republic in 1958.[72] According to this narrative, the Israeli Mossad was behind the false rumors, intending to use Layla's name in propagating Zionism.[73] Yet no evidence indicates that Nasser pressured the Syrians to lift the boycott; it ended with the unification, as both countries began to follow unified legal codes and policies and there was no reason for the Syrians to exempt the boycott. The quiet lifting of the ban against Layla Murad was an honorable way for the Syrians to avoid explicitly recognizing the need to correct their mistake as the Egyptian press had demanded over the years. More important, both Egyptian and Syrian authorities were able to avoid a serious discussion about the best and most effective way to apply the decisions of the Arab League about the boycott on Israel.

Canonizing Layla Murad

The state lagged in granting Layla Murad deserved recognition during her lifetime. Nasser overlooked her when he decorated many artists, including Layla's youngest brother, Munir Murad, with the Republic Medal during Science Day celebrations in the 1960s. Nevertheless, for more than four decades the state has continued celebrating Layla's legacy in different ways and regularly assuring her position in the canon of modern Egyptian music. Fifteen years after the state decorated her with a medal in 1977 and three years before her death, the state-sponsored Cairo Cinema Festival honored her in 1992. It published *Layla Murad: Awal Cinderella fi al-cinema al-Missriyya* (Layla Murad: The first Cinderella in Egyptian cinema), penned by scriptwriter and film critic Rafiq al-Sabban. The Egyptian Armed Forces sent a representative to her funeral and held a special commemoration for her in November 1995, an honor that performers rarely receive.[74] The participation of a representative of the Armed Forces was remarkable because the family, honoring her wish, had a private, low-key funeral. Four years later, the state issued a postage stamp carrying her picture. Commemorating her death, Dar al-Hilal published Salih Mursi's *Layla Murad*, which *al-Kawakib* had serialized more than two decades earlier.[75] Egyptian radio aired a serialized biography of Layla during Ramadan 1997; and more than ten years later,

Egyptian television produced and aired another biographical series during Ramadan 2009. Airing the shows through the state's radio and television during Ramadan, the annual prime time, offers evidence of the continuing public interest in Layla's life and career, as well as the producers' desire to reach the largest audience.[76]

In 2005, the state-sponsored Arab Music Festival in Cairo also honored her name. Such honors have become more frequent over the past two decades during the annual music and film festivals in Cairo. Even during 2012, the year in which the Muslim Brotherhood was in power, the Cairo Opera House held a concert to honor the life and legacy of Layla Murad, featuring onstage live interviews with her sons and remixes of some of her beloved oldies. The Opera House extended its annual celebrations of Layla's anniversaries outside Cairo and held concerts in her honor in Alexandria and Damanhur in November 2014.[77] The state hosted a series of major national cultural centers in celebration of her centennial birthday in 2018. The National Center of Theater, Music, and Folklore held a celebratory concert at the Al Hanager Art Center inside the Cairo Opera House in early December of that year; a couple of young singers accompanied by the center's house orchestra performed Layla's repertoire.[78] Nothing captures the changes in Egyptian social and popular culture better than a young female singer in *hijab* performing Layla's songs.

Confirming Layla Murad's iconic position in the public memory, the Ministry of Culture marked the building where Layla Murad lived in the Garden City neighborhood of downtown Cairo with a plaque that reads: "Layla Murad Lived Here," which carries a barcode that visitors and passersby can scan with their smartphones to access information about Layla. A newly founded state entity called the National Authority for Civil Coordination initiated the "Lived Here" project to map Egypt's cultural geography by marking the homes of artists, intellectuals, and politicians of modern Egypt.[79] The Egyptian Association of Film Writers and Critics named its annual festival in 2018 in honor of Layla Murad and commissioned journalist Ahmad al-Naggar to write a book about her, which appeared in October 2018. Its title, *Layla Bint Misr* (Layla, a daughter of Egypt), evokes the long legacy of films portraying her as Layla, daughter of the poor, daughter of the rich, and daughter of the nobility; calling her a daughter of Egypt suggests a desire to confirm her Egyptianness or to prevent states other than Egypt from claiming her.

The state of Egypt under President Hosni Mubarak (r. 1981–2011) and now under President ʿAbd al-Fattah al-Sisi, has attempted to install itself as the guardian of Egyptian *turath*, the authentic Egyptian cultural heritage, by celebrating Layla's legacy along with the legacies of other canonical musical figures including Umm Kulthum and Muhammad ʿAbd al-Wahab. The state declared itself a nurturer of good art and good taste by claiming those neoclassical singers and musicians, in a modest attempt to focus attention on achievements in the cultural realm and divert it from the regime's faults, including rampant poverty, unemployment, corruption, and a lack of democracy.[80] The Mubarak and al-Sisi regimes deployed the contributions of high-achieving artists in their battle against conservative Islamists: while jihadists denounced all forms of art and even employed violence against artists and art venues, the state mobilized beloved oldies to counter extremism. Assaults against art became assaults against such household names as Umm Kulthum and Layla Murad, whose voices and images represent Egyptian authenticity.

The Good Old Days Girl

The intense interest of Egyptians in Layla's life and legacy goes beyond an interest in Egyptian *turath* or reviving the past. Layla's films bequeath Egyptians a multilayered text of contending visions.[81] For those who are increasingly nostalgic for the pre-1952 Liberal Era, Layla's repertoire gives them a resplendent image of the Egyptian past, when class and patriarchal boundaries were well defined and respected,[82] traditional values that were expressions of authentic modernity that accompanied modernization and westernization.[83] Layla's performances with Anwar Wagdi in Broadway-type musicals left great pieces of revitalized music coupled with colorful images of a westernized Egypt, beneath whose surface lies a complex construction of references designed to evoke a traditional Egypt that played a part in the formation of nationalism and modernity.[84] On- and off-screen, Layla's image--her extravagant clothing and jewelry, along with her gentrified Cairo neighborhood of Garden City--give contemporary neoliberals and those who are nostalgic for *az-zaman al-gamil*, or the good old days, a vibrant image of the high society they long for.[85] Her Jewish origins evoke a once-glorious pluralism and tolerance antithetical to the present time. A commentary that ran in two different periodicals in January 2005 reads, "Layla's house was in the gentrified Garden City neighborhood in the middle of liberal Cairo, the neighborhood that resembles Layla Murad in many ways. It was in the middle of a civilized tolerant city, not today's Cairo of random slums, crimes, and extremism."[86]

Those who are nostalgic for the pre-Nasser era have constructed Layla as a symbol of the lost glory of pre-1952 Egypt.[87] For them, her disappearance from the cinema screen was a protest against the destruction of that world brought about by the populist regime of Nasser. For them, Layla represents the Egyptian gentry, whose high society of pashas and beys had vanished, replaced by a different world and time to which Layla could not adapt. Such people believe that Layla retired voluntarily because "she was not able to live under the Republic while she used to be the queen of enchantment . . . ; she preferred to distance herself from that revolutionary atmosphere."[88] According to another commentator, "she chose to retire and became the last in a genealogy of *hawanim*, or refined ladies."[89] But these claims are at odds with the fact that she readily chanted anthems and songs to rally public support for the Free Officers' regime. Anti-Nasserists misrepresent Layla's disappearance, claiming that she chose to retire in order to protest the sociocultural changes that came with Nasser's socialist policies. To embrace this manufactured myth, they also ignore the fact that she continued recording new songs for radio and television in Egypt and the rest of Arab countries throughout the Nasserist period and tirelessly sought to star in more films. They even disregard Layla's own words, namely, her admission that she tried multiple times to work for the state-owned film production company.

Images of Layla in the press between the mid-1950s and mid-1980s also put paid to the fabricated myth that she chose to disappear from the public eye so that the public would not see how aging had changed her. For three decades, Layla allowed the publication of photos displaying her actual appearance as she aged: her changing body shape, her up-to-date clothing and hairstyle fashions. She did not hide her attempts to control her weight and maintain her looks, but she never tried present herself as unchanged since the 1940s and early 1950s, when she was young, slim, and romantically desirable.

Even after her death, male journalists, like the filmmaker Muhammad Karim
before them, shamed her for gaining weight and aging,[90] veiling their misogynistic view of women's bodies with an infatuation with the image of the
stunning young Layla. Rather than recognizing and appreciating the physical
changes in her (female) body as a normal part of her ongoing life experience
of parenting and maturing, male journalists ignored the older Layla's presence. They refused to give the new songs she recorded their due attention and
turned a blind eye to her attempts to appear in new films; instead they fostered the myth of her disappearance and retirement as being her own choice.

The Celebratory Turn

Popular writing about the Egyptian Jewish community become a flourishing genre in the 1990s.[91] Authors from all walks of life published books and
articles on the Jews of Egypt. Journalists, cinema critics, and a physician,
from secular leftists to ultra-nationalists and Muslim Brotherhood activists,
provided narratives on these vanished communities. Debates over the contribution of Egyptian Jews resulted from competing agendas of the state,
the political opposition, and proponents and opponents of Camp David. The
increase in Egyptian studies on the Egyptian Jews is part of the escalating
activism against the Camp David Accords and the normalization of relations
with Israel.[92] The growth of historical studies in Egypt, which now tend to
take minorities into account, has also contributed to the flourishing of publications on the Egyptian Jews and other minorities. Publications on Egyptian
Jews that target a wider public readership vary in terms of quality, sources,
and attitude. For instance, the movie critic Ahmad Ra'fat Bahgat displays
strong anti-Jewish sentiments, suggesting that all Jews in the Egyptian film
industry except Layla Murad conspired to employ that medium against
Egypt. Musicologist Farag al-'Antari claims that Egyptian Jewish capital-
ists and their Muslim partners conspired to steal Arab music and transfer
it to Israel in 1932, long before the establishment of the Jewish state.[93] To
promote their Jewish conspiracy theory, those writers intentionally ignore
Layla's father, Zaki Murad, and disparage Jewish artists who enriched Egyptian cinema and music in the first half of the twentieth century.[94] Despite
the apparent irrationality of their theses, both Bahgat's and al-'Antari's books
have received high praise in the Egyptian press,[95] with the notable exception

of a review written by film critic Samir Farid that accuses Bahgat of blatant racism and fascism.[96]

On the other hand, the prominent physician and current leader of the Egyptian Social Democratic Party, Professor Muhammad Abu al-Ghar, has published a book emphasizing the contribution of the Egyptian Jews, including the Murad family, to Egyptian culture and economy, lamenting the departure of Jews from Egypt.[97] Throughout the 1990s, 'Arafa 'Abdu 'Ali was one of the most prolific authors on the topic of Egyptian Jews, publishing three books and numerous articles. His attitude toward the Jews in Egypt varies from one work to another,[98] fluctuating between sympathy for and condemnation of the Egyptian Jewish community. His first two books were an outcry against normalization with Israel and what he calls the "Israelization" of the Egyptian mind.[99]

Throughout the 2000s and in the last decade of Mubarak's regime, TV shows highlighted the integration of Jews into Egyptian society, holding the Muslim Brotherhood responsible for all the problems facing Egypt. The best example is the TV serial based on Layla Murad's biography titled *Qalbi Dalili* (My heart is my guide; Muhammad Zuhair Ragab, 2009).[100] Following the military coup d'état against Muslim Brotherhood President Muhammad Mursi and the massacre of his supporters in the summer of 2013, these historical narratives boomed. They depicted the Brotherhood as the only driving force for intolerance throughout Egypt's modern history; if it weren't for them, Jews would have continued to be an integral part of Egyptian social fabric. The TV soap opera *Harat al-Yahud* (*The Jewish Quarter*; Muhammad Gamal al-'Adl, 2015) gave narrative form to that viewpoint. Aired during Ramadan 2015, the show reconstructed Egypt's sociopolitical history between 1948 and 1954 through a love story set in the Jewish Quarter between a Jewish girl and her Muslim neighbor, an officer in the Egyptian army. Contrary to the historical reality of the Jewish Quarter as a working-class area, the soap opera depicted it as a cosmopolitan middle-class neighborhood of mid-twentieth-century Cairo. The Jewish protagonist, Layla, drew on the screen persona of Layla Murad from movies during that period: delicate, romantic, and loyal to her beloved. Only the Muslim Brotherhood's intolerance toward Jews and Zionist activities disturbed the harmonious fabric of the Quarter's interfaith community.

The show indicates that Jews who emigrated to Israel would be received by Egypt with open arms should they choose to return, which echoed a statement of the member of the Guidance Bureau of the Muslim Brotherhood 'Isam al-'Iryan in 2012. While the Jewish community almost vanished from Egypt, recovering and reviving the Jewish past in Egypt has enabled the state and society to make a case for religious tolerance and pluralism while at the same time avoiding the demands for equal citizenship on the part of existing minorities. Egyptian Baha'is, for example, are silenced and even criminalized even as the state-controlled media continues preaching about tolerance and moderation. Celebrating the Egyptian Jews of the good old days achieves domestic complacency, as well as appealing to Western regimes who wish from time to time to appear as champions of religious freedom and the fight against anti-Semitism. During the last few years and currently under President al-Sisi, the discourse about Layla's Jewish origins has taken on a celebratory tone that disassociates Jewishness and conversion to Islam from the question of Israel and normalization. Jewishness has become evidence of the eternal nature of the Egyptian essence of inclusion, and no one is to blame for the violation of this essence except the Muslim Brotherhood and Islamists. In the contemporary discourse under al-Sisi, as reflected in numerous TV serials, talk shows, and news reports, the Muslim Brotherhood are foreign agents who are responsible for terrorism and violence, as well as the illicit and inhuman trade in drugs and organs.[101] Israel plays no role in contemporary Egyptian problems, and the Jewish state is not the enemy anymore.

Israel has become an ally of the Egyptian regime in its battle against Islamists. It is no secret that Israel cooperates with the Egyptian regime in striking against jihadists in Sinai.[102] The appropriation of Layla Murad has changed accordingly. After 1967 and during the War of Attrition, Layla recorded a song dedicated to the Egyptian army fighting for Sinai; Fathi Qura wrote the lyrics, and Layla's brother Munir composed the music. Layla recorded that song for the radio when Galal Mu'awwad was the head of music and singing for Egyptian radio. After Nasser died in September 1970, Sadat consolidated power in his hands through an internal coup, the Correction Movement, on May 15, 1971. Sadat's regime purged individuals thought to be loyal to Nasser and his legacy, including Mu'awwad, whom the socialist public prosecutor charged with belonging to the Nasser-sponsored secret *al-Tanzim al-Tali'i* (Vanguard Organization). The regime forced Mu'awwad into early retirement in September 1971 at the age of forty. The new leadership of radio and TV programming reviewed all Mu'awwad's productions that had patriotic or political themes, censoring anything thought to honor Nasser and celebrate his legacy. Egyptian radio stopped airing patriotic songs recorded under Nasser, including Layla's. Just as Nasser had banned Layla's anthem "Ala Allah al-Qawi al-I'timad" two decades earlier, Sadat banned her song for Sinai in 1972; it disappeared and was erased from Egyptian radio's memory until it reemerged in October 2013 from a private collection of recordings. The daily *al-Ahram* celebrated the discovery, altering the meaning and context of the song. In a huge twist, *al-Ahram* suggested: "When we listen to it [the song], we realize that it was made for today's events as the Egyptian army strives to uproot terrorists from the desert in Sinai."[103] A few days later, someone named Lola Safwan uploaded the song on YouTube; the pictures that appear with the song are mostly patriotic and militaristic, including pictures of military parades and tanks during the Tahrir Revolution in 2011.[104]

Comparison with the actual song reveals *al-Ahram*'s distortion of the lyrics, the most egregious of which was changing "we will restore Arab Palestine" to "we will destroy the terrorist organization" thereby omitting Palestine and its cause from the song. *Al-Ahram* also inserted the newly coined term *al-Irhabiyya* (the terrorist organization) that the Egyptian regime began using for the Muslim Brotherhood after ousting the President Mursi in June 2013. Layla Murad recorded the song when the Egyptian army was fighting against the Israeli occupation of Sinai; the state-controlled press altered the newly discovered song when the Muslim Brotherhood became the enemy and Israeli forces became an ally against jihadists. During the celebration of Layla's centennial birthday, *al-Akhbar* deployed the same distortion, running a cartoon by 'Amr Fahmi depicting Layla singing the song in front of an Egyptian soldier carrying his weapon and standing on a map of Sinai.[105] The cartoon shows a lengthy quotation from the song that omits the line about liberating Palestine. The Egyptian Ministry of Defense did the same when it incorporated two lines of the song in a remix clip titled "Kokteyl Aghani 'ann Sinai" (Cocktail of songs for Sinai) that the ministry posted on its site on YouTube on April 28, 2018.[106]

Journalist Ahmad al-Naggar reproduced the distorted version of the song in his 2018 book *Layla Bint Misr*.[107] The book itself is no more than a collage of long, cut-and-pasted passages al-Naggar lifted from recently published books and articles about Layla. His plagiarism reached the point that he uncritically reproduced contradictory information about her, for example, giving two different dates for her birth, 1918 on pages 10 and 36 and 1922 on page 39.[108] Nevertheless, the book stands as another example of the discourses using Layla's Islam as the most substantial evidence for her Egyptianness--Layla Murad as a trophy of victory for the regime. The well-known satirical journalist devoted his popular editorial column in the regime-controlled daily *al-Akhbar* to issuing a plea for "Muslim Layla." He expressed his dismay over counting Layla among the Jews of Egypt, because he was sure that her embrace of Islam was sincere and robust. In other words, Ragab stripped Layla of her Jewishness, taking any reference to her Jewish origins as fundamentally contradictory and offensive to her Islamic identity.

The many lives of Layla Murad have served the state and its societal tools in defining and redefining Egyptianness. Recent years have witnessed the entry of younger generations of Egyptians in massive numbers into the alternative public spheres of the social media challenging the grand and dominant narratives, thus showing that the definition and understanding of Egyptianness has been a work in progress. Individuals' sovereignty over their bodies, including sexuality and the acceptance of single motherhood, has come to the fore. Layla Murad's story may serve to show how far Egyptians have moved toward this sovereignty, as well as toward re-forming the religio-gendered construct of Egyptianness.

CAN AN EGYPTIAN BE A
SINGLE MOTHER AND A JEW?

Now the public is sure that the Muslim Layla is innocent
and proud of Islam and Arabs.[1]

al-Fann, November 3, 1952

LAYLA MURAD BUILT FOR HERSELF a unique place in Egyptian popular culture and maintained that position for decades both during and after
her life. Egyptians have embraced her talent and invested in honoring her
unique persona above and beyond the status of a beloved artist and talented
entertainer from the days of good old black-and-white cinema. Both the
state and private media have kept Layla's image and voice alive in Egyptian
public life. Egyptians have turned her into a symbol of their Egyptianness,
of what it means to be truly Egyptian, which challenges the meta-narratives
of being an Arab and a Muslim as requisite for being Egyptian. This notion
of Egyptianness is continues to be reconfigured, as the presence of Layla
Murad's persona in public life and public memory triggers the heretofore
silenced question: Can an Egyptian be a single mother and a Jew?

Since 1952, her being a true Muslim has been the central argument in refuting any connection between Layla and Israel: her loyalty to her homeland, her
patriotism, and her refusal to communicate with an enemy state are explained

by her being a Muslim. Had Layla chosen to continue life as a Jew--a non-Muslim--she could not have been a patriotic Egyptian or loyal to her homeland; being Egyptian means being Arab and Muslim. Those who associated her Egyptianness with her being Muslim and Arab explicitly excluded Jews from the premises of Egyptianness and implicitly excluded all non-Muslims and non-Arabs--e.g., Nubians, Christians, and Baha'is--from the premises of Egyptian identity. Islamizing Egyptian identity has been continued in full force by "secularists" in the "secular media" of state and society under secular reconfiguration throughout the twentieth century and into the twenty-first. The rumors against Layla Murad targeted her Jewish origins, and no Muslim or Christian star encountered similar concerted rumor campaigns. In a practical response, all parties supporting Layla marshaled her conversion to Islam and commitment to Arab identity as evidence to counter the rumors.

The rumors against Layla set the tone and the grounds for the battle: Jewishness or Jewish origins "inherently contradict" Arabness and Egyptianness. From a delicate and defensive position, Layla and her advocates accepted the dichotomy of being either Egyptian or Jewish, meaning that one cannot be both. Since then, any voices that suggest separating Islam from patriotism and loyalty to Arab identity from Egyptian identity have faced marginalization. The rumors and efforts to exonerate Layla made Islam a prerequisite for Egyptian patriotism and Arab loyalty. The impossibility of being both an Arab/Egyptian and a Jew has become a shared paradigm among Zionism, Arab nationalism, and Egyptian patriotism. The questions of Egyptian identity as pluralistic and its crucial separation from religious identity were surprisingly absent from the debates in the early 1950s. At that time, there were still Jews in Egypt who claimed Egyptianness as their citizenship and national identity.

Nevertheless, the fast-changing sociocultural landscape and political uncertainty upon the Free Officers' taking power could explain why Jewish and Christian intellectuals refrained from debating the question. Jews in particular found themselves in a weak position, pinched between Zionist espionage and the state's hostility. Secularist Muslim intellectuals were in no better position to defend Egyptianness as a secular territorial and pluralistic identity. The Free Officers' regime purged many of those who held dissenting views from public life and professions in academia, the judiciary, and the press.

Those who might have defended Egyptian pluralism feared facing purge or imprisonment, and some of them were too dazzled by Nasserist discourse to question the role of religion in the national identity.[2] The memoir of Jewish communist activist Shahata Harun illustrates the pain and confusion of Egyptian Jews who chose to stay in their homeland and embrace both their Jewishness and Egyptianness despite the regime's hostility. Harun argues that they remained clear about their identity despite these rapid domestic and regional changes.[3]

On the eve of the June 5, 1967, defeat, Harun sent a memorandum to President Nasser in February expressing his frustration over the treatment of Jews in Egypt and the rest of Arab countries and urged Nasser to include progressive Jews in efforts to counter the colonialism and racism of Israel.[4] Harun wrote: "Since 1948, the way the Arab regimes treated their Jewish citizens and residents had provided Israel with 60–65 percent of its human power. The rising radical revolutionary regimes in some Arab countries also practice racism that contradicts the principles of socialism."[5] Harun spoke highly of Nasser as a historical and moral revolutionary leader. He also spoke about the troubles he faced as a member of the Jewish community:

> How can I explain and convince fellow Jews with different levels of consciousness of my humanistic and political commitment to the United Arab Republic? How can I explain to them that all Jews, including myself, are deprived of military service and cannot leave the country unless they give up their Egyptian citizenship and residency and never come back? How can I comprehend and explain that all Jews are explicitly blacklisted and deprived of working in public establishments? How can I understand and explain adding Jewish to the nationality in work permits given to foreign Jews and adding "married to a Jew" to their non-Jewish wives, which subjects those wives to all forms of discrimination that authorities might inflict on their husbands?[6]

Harun articulated his rejection of Israeli racism on the part of the Arabs, including Arab Jews, and the discrimination against Jews by Arab regimes, arguing that the former could not justify the latter. He urged Nasser to immediately abolish all instructions, written and unwritten, that enabled the despicable, humiliating, and hurtful discrimination against Egyptian Jews.

Harun was a minority voice among both the minority Jewish and majority Muslim communities who dared to speak up for the rights of Jews to full
and equal citizenship in their Arab countries, a demand that challenged the
dominant paradigms of Zionism and Arab nationalism. His efforts proved
futile, however, as the regime refused to allow the publication of his memorandum or tolerate any public discussion of it. Eventually, on June 5, 1967, the
authorities detained Harun, along with other Egyptian Jews. In fact, Harun
was frequently detained under Nasser's and Sadat's regimes because of his
Jewish faith, his leftist activism, or for both reasons. Police arrested him in
January 1975 during labor demonstrations; he was charged by the general
prosecutor of joining illegal leftist organizations, although the court dropped
the charges and freed him on February 21 of that same year.[7] Following his
release, Harun insisted on embracing both Egyptian and Jewish identities
and his commitment to socialism, saying, "As far as I know, being Egyptian
does not require me to change my religion or political convictions."[8] Harun's
legacy continues in Egypt, as his daughter Magda has served as the head of
the Jewish community since April 2013, working for the acceptance of local
Jewish heritage as being part of Egyptian heritage.[9]

Intellectuals may have overlooked, accidentally or intentionally, the grand
issue of religious pluralism while the state's policies and media imposed a
narrow and exclusive definition of Egyptian identity. Celebrity publications
geared toward the semi-educated public made Islam a condition of Egyptianness and excluded other religious identities, including atheists. Some
Jewish communist activists who made conscious intellectual and political
choices to remain in Egypt as Egyptian citizens despite hostility against
their "Jewishness" converted to Islam and thus were in a weak position to
raise the question of why being Jewish or non-Muslim contravened their
Egyptianness. Saba Mahmood argues that "modern secular governance has
contributed to the exacerbation of religious tensions in postcolonial Egypt,
hardening interfaith boundaries and polarizing religious differences."[10] The
modern state and its political rationality have played a far more decisive role
than Islamic concepts and practices in reproducing inequality and "trans-
forming preexisting religious differences, producing new forms of communal
polarization, and making religion salient to minority and majority identities alike."[11] Mass-mediated popular culture has played a crucial role in

publicizing religious hierarchies, highlighting religious differences, and making religion an essential part of identity.

While the Egyptian Jewish community has almost vanished, Egyptians are becoming at ease with celebrating the Egyptian Jewish heritage as an emblem of the "good old days of diversity." Banking on the Jewish past may be helpful in international relations and attracting foreign tourism without undoing decades of excluding and undermining minorities. Celebrating the past does not challenge the dominant singular narratives that have increasingly expanded Islam's position as the foundation of Egyptianness and undermined, even erased other identities. Celebrating the good old days of diversity does not open the door for existing minorities--for example, Copts and Baha'is--to demand full rights; indeed, since the 1940s the Islamic establishment has gone so far as to force Baha'is to claim Islam as their religion on their state records and IDs.

Single Motherhood and Democratization from Below

Recognizing the rights of single mothers and the rights of children born outside formal marriage would shake the Egyptian patriarchy built on Islamic orthodoxy and its moral ideals that privilege men over women. It would redefine citizenship as being rooted in an inclusive gender equality based on individuals' sovereignty over their bodies and would dismiss the association of rights with gender binaries. As such recognition would preclude the state from weaponizing Islamic orthodoxy, the state has denied women the right to register their newborns in state records; only fathers can do so. Layla Murad's story writes single motherhood into Egyptian history and offers a case in point through which we can come to understand how women have progressed in challenging the legal and social patriarchy, illuminating profound but barely noticeable changes. Women have not always been victorious nor have they always been defeated, and feminist resistance is not always the impulse of their actions.

Women from all classes and social backgrounds have battled the legal system, social stigma, and marginalization to win full rights for themselves and their children and continue to do so. The issue is hardly new: in a recent estimate, Egyptian courts considered fifteen thousand cases in 2014 and twenty thousand cases in 2018.[12] Following her son Ashraf's birth in the summer of

1954, Layla repeatedly denied she had given birth, as the father, Wagih Abaza, refused to recognize the child. She quietly sought to connect with those who could pressure him to acknowledge his parenthood and agree to register the child in the state's birth record formally, making the painful choice not to resort to the court to force Abaza to give his name to their child in fear of the consequences. Layla's situation was almost a replica of the first court case in modern Egypt in which a mother utilized the power of the court to win a man's recognition of her child's fatherhood. In 1927, singer Fatma Sirri sued Muhammad Sha'rawi Bey, son of the feminist leader Huda Hanim Sha'rawi, to compel him to acknowledge their child together through an informal marriage. Three years later, the court granted Sirri her demand but deprived her of her child, judging her unfit to raise the child.[13] How much thought Layla Murad gave to this case is unknowable, but she must have been aware of it because Layla's ex-husband, Anwar Wagdi, and Umm Kulthum co-starred in a film based on the case in 1947.[14] Other celebrity cases in which fathers have refused to recognize their children reveal changes in social attitudes concerning single-motherhood during the past few decades.

Breaking the Taboo and Achieving Democracy from Below

In 2005, a young Egyptian woman, Hind al-Hinnawi, faced a situation similar to Layla's, but she took her case to court. The father of al-Hinnawi's child, the famous actor Ahmad al-Fishawi, hailed from a celebrity family and enjoyed strong media connections; celebrated religious preachers supported the termination of this unwanted pregnancy if al-Fishawi sacrificed a goat. In the face of this, al-Hinnawi's courageous choice gained her the support of feminist activists, a stand that revealed a drastic change in Egyptian society.[15] In the 1920s, ashamed at the prospect of having a performer as a daughter-in-law and the mother of her grandchild, pioneer feminist Huda Sha'rawi had gone against all her feminist pronouncements and mobilized her wealth and connections to block Fatma Sirri's rights; she was eventually able to deprive Sirri of her child forever. But at the turn of the twenty-first century, feminist activists provided Hind al-Hinnawi with moral and legal support, taking advantage of the façade of an open public sphere under Mubarak and establishing several NGOs that focused attention on overdue women's rights, including the right to safety for female bodies. Patriarchal and conservative religious voices have called for depriving children conceived in "illicit" cohabitation of some rights, including carrying their father's name. Remarkably, women activists supported al-Hinnawi's choice not to risk her own health by seeking an abortion. Others criticized her for engaging in *'urfi* (informal) marriage, keeping a pregnancy against the father's will, and subjecting her child to social stigma. Nevertheless, al-Hinnawi did not back down; she won the legal case, and the court forced al-Fishawi to recognize his daughter and provide her with full rights.

The change in the public attitude toward sexuality and women's choice deepened and manifested itself in cases that occurred after the 2011 Revolution in Tahrir Square. Societal debates around the legal case of the actress Zayna against the actor Ahmad 'Izz concerning their twin children demonstrated widespread social support—more for Zayna than for al-Hinnawi--for the full rights of children born outside formal marriage, in contravention of the dictates of conservative religious values and challenging traditional social stigma. The notable change in social attitudes was also evident in recent public campaigns in which many activists participated to pressure artist 'Adel el-Siwi to recognize his child, Dayala, with the young journalist Samah Ibrahim 'Abd al-Salam. Under the hashtag "Haqq Dayala" (Dayala's right), activists rallied with the mother in her legal battle against the denying father. More than three hundred intellectuals and other public figures signed a statement affirming that a father had a moral responsibility to allow his child to carry his name and accused el-Siwi of taking advantage of legal loopholes to avoid the DNA test.[16] The signatures of novelist Ibrahim 'Abd al-Majid and other high-profile intellectuals gave the statement solid credibility.

During these cases, debates focused on women's courage in breaking sexual taboos, challenging the social stigma attached to women in informal marriages, and defending their children's rights to carry their father's name, among other rights. Potentially, such open debates will keep pushing Egyptian society toward a more just gender regime and foment gender democracy from below. But this progress will not be linear or final. Social history teaches us that women are the biggest losers under political dictatorship and the neoliberal economy, both of which represent a vicious war on working people and women in Egypt that is eroding some of the gains women achieved during and following the 2011 revolution. This makes examining democracy from below—that is, investigating ordinary, everyday actions bringing about justice and equity in Egyptian society—as crucial as researching high-profile and collective activism.

Much of my evidence comes from celebrity cases, which may not represent every woman's struggle for legal and social recognition of children born outside formal marriage. Moreover, each case took place in a relatively different context, which likely had some influence on the relationship of power between the mother and father. Nevertheless, the public attention these celebrity cases enjoyed helps scholars study public attitudes about the taboo of having informal marriage and giving birth to children whose fathers deny them. Lawyers and judges adjudicating each lawsuit used the files of previous cases in formulating legal arguments. As publicized in media outlets and social media, legal verdicts and social arguments widely redeployed new notions of gender equity and respectability and have made their discourse readily available for similar cases among ordinary people.

Layla Murad's case demonstrates the importance of using the concept of intersectionality, developed by queer and feminist theorists to discuss the experiences of American minority women, to study women in Egypt and beyond. We cannot explain the consequences of single motherhood that Layla faced only through gender, sexuality, or religious origin but must consider the combinations of these intersecting factors. The experiences of children born in interfaith marriages could also energize the feminist research agenda. The Egyptian legal system privileges Muslims over everyone else and determines the identity of children born in interfaith cohabitations as Islamic. The state also subjects all non-Muslim families to Islamic law should they make use of state courts in questions regarding inheritance and family law. Such a research agenda could address many social issues silenced by the singular hegemonic narrative that equates Islamic identity with Egyptianness. While challenging the singular narrative of Egyptian nationalism to allow the voices of minorities, and minority women in particular, we must be mindful of the process of ethnicization of self and others. Researching Egyptian Jews, Coptic Egyptians, and so on in isolation from the broader, more complex society hardens their isolation as a closed community with a distinctive linear narrative rather than as individuals enmeshed in overlapping and interconnected social webs. Reality is far more complex than being a member of an ethnic community can possibly suggest. Differences coexist and intersect, with similarities between individuals and groups. Ethnicity is not a thing in itself; it is a process through which legal hierarchies and public discourses privilege some and disadvantage others, isolating them behind the invisible walls of "being different." Back in the day, Egyptians who lived in the Jewish Alley recognized their religious differences but did not necessarily explain what a Jew or a Muslim would do merely on the ground of religious differences.

Notes

Introduction: Why Layla Murad?

1. For a comprehensive account of the Free Officers' regime, see Joel Gordon, *Nasser's Blessed Movement: Egypt's Free Officers and the July Revolution* (Oxford: Oxford University Press, 1992).

2. Joel Beinin, *The Dispersion of Egyptian Jewry: Culture, Politics, and the Formation of a Modern Diaspora* (Cairo: American University in Cairo Press, 2005), 75.

3. Barbara Merrill and Linden West, *Using Biographical Methods in Social Research* (London: SAGE, 2009), 1.

4. David Nasaw, "AHR Roundtable Historians and Biography: Introduction," *American Historical Review* 114, no. 3 (June 2009): 573–578, here 573; Peter Ackroyd, *London: The Biography* (London: Chatto & Windus, 2000), 2.

5. Barbara Caine, *Biography and History* (London: Palgrave Macmillan, 2010), 7.

6. Miriam Hansen, "The Mass Production of the Senses: Classical Cinema as Vernacular Modernism," *Modernism/Modernity* 6, no. 2 (1999): 59–77, here 63.

7. Viola Shafik, *Popular Egyptian Cinema: Gender, Class, and Nation* (Cairo: American University in Cairo Press, 2007).

8. Hansen, "Mass Production of the Senses," 62.

9. Walter Armbrust, "The Golden Age before the Golden Age: Commercial Egyptian Cinema before the 1960s," in *Mass Mediations: New Approaches to Popular Culture in the Middle East and Beyond*, ed. Walter Armbrust (Berkeley: University of California Press, 2000), 292–328.

10. Jennifer Coates, *Making Icons: Repetition and the Female Image in Japanese Cinema, 1945–1964* (Hong Kong: Hong Kong University Press, 2016), 33.

11. Virginia Danielson, *The Voice of Egypt: Umm Kulthum, Arabic Song, and Egyptian Society in the Twentieth Century* (Chicago: University of Chicago Press, 1997); Ifdal Elsaket, "The Star of the East: Umm Kulthum and Egyptian Cinema," in *Stars in World Cinema: Screen Icons and Star Systems across Cultures*, ed. Andrea Bandhauer and Michelle Royer (London: I. B. Tauris, 2015), 36–50; Sherifa Zuhur, *Asmahan's Secrets: Woman, War, and Song* (Austin: University of Texas Press, 2000); Christopher Stone, *Popular Culture and Nationalism in Lebanon: The Fairouz and Rahbani Nation* (New York: Routledge, 2008); Mona Ahmad Ghandur, *Sultanat al-Shasha: Ra'idat al-cinema al-Misriyya* (Beirut: Dar Riyad al-Rayes lil-kutub wal-nashr, 2005).

12. Stone, *Popular Culture and Nationalism in Lebanon*, 12.

13. Stone, 12.

14. Danielson, *Voice of Egypt*, 1–2.

15. Walter Armbrust, *Mass Culture and Modernism in Egypt* (Cambridge: Cambridge University Press, 1996), 3, 21.

16. Yingjin Zhang, "From 'Minority Film' to 'Minority Discourse': Questions of Nationhood and Ethnicity in Chinese Cinema," *Cinema Journal* 36, no. 3 (Spring 1997): 73–90, here 3–4.

17. Armbrust, *Mass Culture and Modernism*; Joel Gordon, *Revolutionary Melodrama: Popular Film and Civic Identity in Nasser's Egypt* (Chicago: University of Chicago Press, 2002); Lila Abu-Lughod, *Dramas of Nationhood: The Politics of Television in Egypt* (University of Chicago Press, 2005); Shafik, *Popular Egyptian Cinema*; Dalia Said Mostafa, *The Egyptian Military in Popular Culture: Context and Critique* (London: Palgrave Macmillan, 2016); Keren Zdafee, *Cartooning for a Modern Egypt* (Leiden: Brill, 2019).

18. Roberta L. Dougherty, "Badi'a Masabni, Artiste and Modernist: The Egyptian Print Media's Carnival of National Identity," in Armbrust, *Mass Mediations*, 243–267; Shaun T. Lopez, "The Dangers of Dancing: The Media and Morality in 1930s Egypt," *Comparative Studies of South Asia, Africa, and the Middle East* 24, no. 1 (November 2004): 97–105.

19. Magdy Mounir El-Shammaa, "Shadows of Contemporary Lives: Modernity, Culture, and National Identity in Egyptian Filmmaking" (PhD diss., UCLA, 2007); Heba Saad Arafa Abdelfattah, "Dreams of Alternative Modernities on the Nile" (PhD diss., Georgetown University, 2016).

20. Abu-Lughod, *Dramas of Nationhood*, 7.

21. Stuart Hall, "Coding and Encoding in the Television Discourse," in Stuart Hall et al., eds., *Culture, Media, Language* (London: Hutchinson, 1980), 128–138, here 135.

22. Andrea McDonnell, *Reading Celebrity Gossip Magazines* (Cambridge, UK: Polity Press, 2014), 5–10.

23. Pages of Layla Murad's memoirs are also missing from issues 288, 289, and 290. In sum, out of seven episodes, four episodes are entirely missing, and the second and fifth episodes are partly missing.

24. Yair Mazor, *Somber Lust: The Art of Amos Oz* (Albany: SUNY Press, 2002), 163.

25. Tamar S. Hess, *Self as Nation: Contemporary Hebrew Autobiography* (Waltham, MA: Brandeis University Press, 2016), 213.

26. Merrill and West, *Using Biographical Methods in Social Research*, 1.

27. Merrill and West, 2.

28. For Layla Murad's films on IMDb, see https://www.imdb.com/name/nm0609952/?ref_=fn_al_nm_1.

Chapter 1: The School Girl

1. For more on Ihsan 'Abd al-Quddus and his representation of the Jewish women in al-'Abbasiyya, see Hanan Hammad, "In the Shadows of the Middle East's Wars, Oil, and Peace: The Construction of Female Desires and Lesbianism in Middlebrow Egyptian Literature," *Journal of Arab Literature* 50 (2019): 148–172.

2. Ihsan 'Abd al-Quddus, *Ana Hurra* (Cairo: Maktabit Misr, 1954.

3. Layla Murad, "Mudhakkarat Layla Murad 2: Liqa' mukhtalas ma'a al-angham," *al-Kawakib*, January 23, 1957, 8.

4. Liat Maggid Alon, "The Jewish Bourgeoisie of Egypt in the First Half of the Twentieth Century: Modernity, Socio-cultural Practice and Oral Testimonials," *Jama'a* 24 (2019): 31.

5. Layla Murad, "Mudhakkarat Layla Murad 1," *al-Kawakib*, January 15, 1957.

6. Murad, "Mudhakkarat Layla Murad 2," 8.

7. Murad, 8.

8. Murad, 8.

9. Layla Murad, "Awwal al-Sillim," *al-Kawakib*, July 23, 1957.

10. Ian Nagosik includes Zaki Murad's recording on the second disc of his anthology titled *To What Strange Place: The Music of the Ottoman-American Diaspora 1916–1929*, Tompkins Square Records, TSQ 2608, 2011.

11. Nagosik.

12. Murad, "Mudhakkarat Layla Murad 2," 9.

13. Muhammad al-Sayyid Shusha, *Layla Murad: al-Mughamira al-Hasna'* (Beirut: al-Maktab al-tujari lil-tiba'a wa al-tawzi', 1956), 11; Murad, 9.

14. Layla Murad, "Ana," *al-Kawakib*, April 20, 1954.

15. Shusha, *Layla Murad: al-Mughamira al-Hasna'*, 11–12.

16. Jacob Landau, *Studies in the Arab Theater and Cinema* (Philadelphia: University of Pennsylvania Press, 1958), 74.

17. Landau, 81.

18. Danielson, *The Voice of Egypt*, 45.

19. For more on Bahiga Hafiz, see Mona Ghandur, *Sultanat al-Shahsa: Ra'idat al-cinema al-Missriyya* (Beirut: Dar Riyad al-Rayis lil-kutub wal-nashr, 2005), 195–248.

20. Amira Mitchell, comp., *Women of Egypt 1924–1931: Pioneers of Stardom and Fame*,

Topic World Series TSCD931, 2006; Ann Elise Thomas, review of *Women of Egypt, 1924–1931,*" *Ethnomusicology* 51, no. 3 (Fall 2007): 526–528.

21. Virginia Danielson, review of *Women of Egypt 1924–1931: Pioneers of Stardom and Fame*" *Asian Music* 41, no. 1 (Winter/Spring 2010): 179–181.

22. Layla Murad, "Mudhakkarat Layla Murad 3: Wa saffaqa al-jumhur linawmi," *al-Kawakib*, January 29, 1957, 23.

23. Amal al-'Umda, "Liqa' idha'i ma'a Layla Murad," aired by al-Sharq al-Awsat Egyptian Radio station in 1978; https://www.youtube.com/watch?v=fn74hlt4sW4. Henceforth this source will appear as "Al-'Umda, interview." A partial transcript of the interview is available in Salah Tantawi, *Rihlat hub ma'a Layla Murad* (Cairo: Ruz al-Yusuf, 1979), 343–355, and in Hanan Mufid, *Layla Murad: Sayyidat qitar al-ghina'* (Cairo: al-Hayy'a al-Missriyya al-'amma lil-kitab, 2003), 240-246.

24. *Al-Kawakib*, "Bini wa binak," May 16, 1932.

25. Kamal al-Najmi, *Turath al-ghina' al-'Arabi* (Cairo: al-Hayy'a al-'amma lil-kitab, 1998), 239.

26. *Ruz al-Yusuf*, May 23, 1932, 30.

27. Layla Murad, "Awwal al-Sillim." See also al-Najmi, *Turath al-ghina'*, 232–233.

28. Shusha, *Layla Murad: al-Mughamira al-Hasna'*, 14.

29. Murad, "Mudhakkarat Layla Murad 3," 24.

30. Murad, 24.

31. Murad, 25.

32. Murad, 25.

33. Al-'Umda, interview.

34. Salih Mursi, *Layla Murad* (Cairo: Dar al-Hilal, 1995), 84–87.

35. Murad, "Mudhakkarat Layla Murad 3," 25.

36. Al-'Umda, interview.

37. Lutfi Radwan, ed., *Muhammad 'Abd al-Wahab: Sira dhatiyya* (Cairo: Dar al-Hilal, 1991), 127–132.

38. Al-'Umda, interview.

39. Virginia Danielson, "Layla Murad," *Middle East Studies Association Bulletin* 30, no. 1 (July 1996): 144.

40. Danielson, 144.

41. Murad, "Mudhakkarat Layla Murad 3," 24.

42. Shusha, *al-Mughamira al-Hasna'*, 46.

43. Shusha, 46.

44. Murad, "Mudhakkarat Layla Murad 3," 24.

45. Kamal al-Najmi, *al-Ghina' al-Misri: mutribun wa mustami'un* (Cairo: Dar al-Hilal, [1966] 1993), 9–15.

46. 'Atif al-'Abd, *al-Radio wa al-tilivision fi Misr* (Cairo: Dar al-fikr al-'Arabi, 1987), 293–94.

47. Al-'Abd, 293–94.

48. Khalil Sabat, *Wasa'il al-itisal: Nash'atuha wa tatawuruha*, 4th ed. (Cairo: Al-Anglu al-Missriyya, 1985), 223–329; Magi al-Halawani and 'Atif al-'Abd, *al-Andhima al-idha'iya fi al-duwal al-'Arabiya* (Cairo: Dar al-fikr al-'Arabi, 1987), 303–340.

49. Al-'Abd, *al-Radio wa al-tilivision fi Misr*, 308.

50. Shusha, *al-Mughamira al-Hasna'*, 16.

51. Shusha, 16.

52. "Kayfa ishtaghalna bil-cinema bidafi' al-haja," *al-Ithnein wa al-Kawakib*, December 16, 1946, 20.

53. 'Ali Abu Shadi, *Waqa'i' al-cinema al-Missriyya fi ma'at 'amm 1896–1995* (Cairo: al-Majlis al-a'la lil-thaqafa, 1996), 87; Mahmud 'Ali, *50 sana cinema: Mudhakkarat Muhammad Karim* (Cairo: Kitab al-idha'a wa al-tilivision, 1972), 1:144.

54. For the incident, see Luwis 'Awad, *Awraq al-'umr* (Cairo: Maktabat Madbuli, 1989), 181–207.

55. 'Ali, *50 sana cinema*, 1:154.

56. El-Shammaa, "Shadows of Contemporary Lives," 41.

57. Viola Shafik, "Egyptian Cinema: Hollywood on the Nile," Oxford Islamic Studies Online, http://www.oxfordislamicstudies.com/article/opr/t343/e0209.

58. El-Shammaa, "Shadows of Contemporary Lives," 41–42.

59. Shafik, "Egyptian Cinema."

60. Sa'd Tawfiq, *Qissat al-cinema fi Misr: Dirasa naqdiyya* (Cairo: Dar al-Hilal, 1969), 44.

61. Tantawi, *Rihlat hub*, 18.

62. Tantawi, 18.

63. Mahmud 'Ali, *Dirasat fi tarikh al-cinema al-Missriyya* (Cairo: al-Hayy'a al-'amma li-qusur al-thaqafa, 2012), 166.

64. Murad, "Mudhakkarat Layla Murad 3," 24–25.

65. Murad, 24–25.

66. Murad, 24–25.

67. Tantawi, *Rihlat hub*, 312.

68. Tawfiq, *Qissat al-cinema fi Misr*, 35–37.

69. Tawfiq, 44.

70. Radwan, *Muhammad 'Abd al-Wahab*, 186.

71. Radwan, 186–187.

72. 'Ali, *50 sana cinema*, 1:239, 243–246.

73. 'Ali, 1:235.

74. 'Ali, 1:238.

75. 'Ali, 1:238.

76. Viola Shafik, "Egypt: Cinema and Society," in *African Filmmaking: Five Formations*, ed. Kenneth W. Harrow (East Lansing: Michigan State University Press, 2017), 120.

77. Rebecca Hillauer, *The Encyclopedia of Arab Women Filmmakers*, trans. Nancy Joyce, Deborah Cohen, and Allison Brown (Cairo: American University in Cairo, 2005), 29.

78. 'Ali, *50 sana cinema*, 1:239–240.

79. 'Ali, 1:239.

80. Radwan, *Muhammad 'Abd al-Wahab*, 184.

81. Radwan, 132–133.

82. 'Ali, *50 sana cinema*, 1:244.

83. Layla Murad, "Adwar ahbabtuha," *al-Kawakib*, February 14, 1956.

84. 'Ali, *50 sana cinema*, 1:243.

85. 'Ali, 1:244.

86. For example, see Muhammad Karim, "Musawwir al-cinema" and "al-Mukhrijun wa kayfa ya'malun," *al-Ithnein* (*al-Fukaha was al-Kawakib*), November 15, 1937, 10, 27.

87. 'Ali, *50 sana cinema*, 1:246.

88. 'Ali, 244–245.

89. Murad, "Adwar ahbabtuha."

90. 'Ali, *50 sana cinema*, 1:248.

91. "Al-Qubla al-ha'ra bayna al-riqaba wa al-shaykh Abu al-'Uyun," *al-Kawakib*, July 2, 1957.

92. "Al-Qubla al-ha'ra."

93. "Al-Shaykh al-Baquri yaqul: al-qubla al-tamthiliyya haram," *Ahl al-Fann*, April 12, 1954.

94. Mustafa Darwish, *Dream Makers on the Nile: A Portrait of Egyptian Cinema* (Cairo: American University in Cairo Press, 1998), 12–13.

95. Darwish, 12–13.

96. 'Ali, *50 sana cinema*, 1:242.

97. Zaki Tulaymat, "'Indama qabaltahum: Ahmad Salim," *al-Kawakib*, September 1, 1953, 4, 38.

98. 'Ali, *50 sana cinema*, 1:242, 251–252.

99. 'Ali, 1:247.

100. 'Ali, 1:247.

101. 'Ali, 1:247.

102. 'Ali, 1:250–251.

103. Mursi, *Layla Murad*, 109.

104. Muhammad 'Abd al-Wahab, "Mashru'ati lilmawsim al-jadid," "'Abd al-Wahab fi thalith aflamih al-ghina'iya," and "Yahya al-Hub," *al-Ithnayn* (*al-Fukaha was al-Kawakib*), November 15, 1937, 7, 13, 14–15.

105. Tawfiq, *Qissat al-cinema fi Misr*, 46–47.

106. 'Ali, *50 sana cinema*, 1:252.

107. 'Ali, 1:252.

108. *Al-Sabah*, February 24, 1933, cited in Munir Muhammad Ibrahim, *al-Cinema al-Missriyya fi al-thalathinat: 1930–1939* (Cairo: Sunduq al-tanmiyya al-thaqafiyya, 2002), 168.

109. *Al-Sabah*, May 11, 1932, cited in Ibrahim, 168.

110. *Al-Musawwar*, March 13, 1936, cited in Ibrahim, 169.

111. *Al-Sabah*, February 9, 1934, cited in Ibrahim, 168.

112. *Al-Sabah*, March 23, 1934, cited in Ibrahim, 168.

113. *Al-'Arusa*, March 10, 1937, cited in Ibrahim, 169.

114. *Al-Sabah*, April 7, 1933, cited in Ibrahim, 167.

115. "Barlamaniat," *al-Ithnayn wa al-Dunya*, August 24, 1942, 5.

116. "Barlamaniat," 5.

117. 'Ali, *50 sana cinema*, 1:252.

118. Mursi, *Layla Murad*, 109, 120.

119. "'Eidi . . . ana," *al-Kawakib*, August 25, 1953, 5.

120. Mursi, *Layla Murad*, 124, 125.

121. According to the ticket, the concert was in the evening on Saturday, July 9, 1938.

122. 'Ali, *50 sana cinema*, 1:239.

123. Ibrahim, *al-Cinema al-Missriyya fi al-thalathinat*, 33.

124. Mursi, *Layla Murad*, 109–110.

125. Raga' 'Abdu, "Qissat Hayati," *al-Kawakib*, August 11, 1953, 29–30.

126. 'Abdu.

127. Shusha, *al-Mughamira al-Hasna'*, 17.

128. Murad, "Adwar ahbabtuha."

Chapter 2: The Country Girl

1. The quote appeared in the publicity booklet for the film upon its release. See also Shusha, *al-Mughamira al-Hasna'*, 28–29; and Salah Tantawi, *Rihlat hub ma'a Layla Murad* (Cairo: Ruza al-Yusuf, 1979), 143.

2. The English titles of films are as given in IMDb, even when the translation is not entirely accurate, to make finding the films easier for readers. Keep in mind that "Laila" and "Leila" in the titles are different transliterations of the same Arabic "Layla."

3. Deborah Starr, *Togo Mizrahi and the Making of Egyptian Cinema* (Oakland: University of California Press, 2020), 57.

4. Al-Najmi, *Turath al-ghina'*, 233.

5. Shusha, *al-Mughamira al-Hasna'*, 17.

6. Ibrahim, *al-Cinema al-Missriyya fi al-thalathinat*, 35.

7. Ibrahim, 35.

8. Ilhami Hassan, *Dirasa mukhtasara 'an Tarikh al-cinema al-Missriyya* (Cairo: al-Hayy'a al-'amma lil-kitab, 1976), 144.

9. Tantawi, *Rihlat hub*, 52.

10. Tantawi, 57.

11. "Da'aya awrathatni al-mata'ib," *al-Kawakib*, January 26, 1954, 8–9.

12. Layla Murad, "Mudhakkarat Layla Murad 5: Awwal rajul dakhala qalbi", *al-Kawakib*, February 12, 1957, 23–25.

13. *Al-'Arusa*, March 25, 1932; May 11, 1934; and April 29, 1936; cited in Ibrahim, *al-Cinema al-Missriyya fi al-thalathinat*, 155, 166.

14. *Al-Sabah*, April 7, 1933; cited in Ibrahim, *al-Cinema al-missriyya fi al-thalathinat*, 167.

15. *Al-Sabah*, December 11, 1938; cited in Ibrahim, *al-Cinema al-Missriyya fi al-thalathinat*, 170.

16. Husain 'Uthman, *Hikayat min tarikh al-cinema al-Missriyya: al-Yubil al-dhahabi 1927–1977* (Cairo: Matb'at 'Abdin, 1977), 89–90.

17. For a comprehensive study of Togo Mizrahi's life and career, see Starr, *Togo Mizrahi*.

18. Darwish, *Dream Makers on the Nile*, 16.

19. *Al-Ithnayn* (*al-Fukaha was al-Kawakib*), November 15, 1937, 65.

20. 'Ali, *50 sana cinema*, 1:238.

21. Tantawi, *Rihlat hub*, 85–87.

22. Alon Tam, "Blackface of Egypt: The Theater and Film of Ali al-Kassar," *British Journal of Middle Eastern Studies*, January 2020, DOI: 10.1080/13530194.2020.1714427.

23. Thomas Schatz, *Hollywood Genres: Formulas, Filmmaking, and the Studio System* (New York: Random House, 1981).

24. Deborah Starr, "In Bed Together: Coexistence in Togo Mizrahi's Alexandria Films," in *Post-Ottoman Coexistence: Sharing Space in the Shadow of Conflict*, ed. Rebecca Bryant (New York: Berghahn Books, 2016), 129–156.

25. Starr, 135.

26. Starr, 136.

27. Starr, 136.

28. Shafik, *Popular Egyptian Cinema*, 29–31.

29. Deniz Neriman Duru, "Memory, Conviviality, and Coexistence: Negotiating Class Differences in Burgazadasi, Istanbul," in Bryant, *Post-Ottoman Coexistence*, 157–179.

30. Darwish, *Dream Makers on the Nile*, 24.

31. Tantawi, *Rihlat hub*, 92.

32. "Majd Ruz al-Yusuf 'ala al-massrah wa majd Layla Murad 'ala al-sitar," *al-Ahram*, April 8, 1942; cited in Tantawi, *Rihlat hub*, 91–92.

33. Ahmad al-Sawi Muhammad, "Rusasa fi qalb Tawfiq al-Hakim," *al-Ithnayn*, April 17, 1944; reprinted in 'Ali, *50 sana cinema* 2:84–88, and in Tantawi, *Rihlat hub*, 84, 143–146.

34. Muhammad, "Rusasa fi qalb Tawfiq al-Hakim."

35. 'Ali, *50 sana cinema*, 2:84.

36. Muhammad Karim, "Ta'qib," *al-Ithnayn*, May 29, 1944; cited in 'Ali, *50 sana cinema*, 2:92–94.

37. Murad, "Adwar ahbabtuha."

38. The quote appeared in the publicity booklet of the film upon its release. See also Shusha, *al-Mughamira al-Hasna'*, 28–29; and Tantawi, *Rihlat hub*, 143.

39. "'Indama yasrak al-mumathilun al-kamira," *al-Kawakib*, October 13, 1953, 40–41.

40. Layla Murad, "Mudhakkarat Layla Murad 5."

41. Shusha, *al-Mughamira al-Hasna'*, 20.

42. Nur al-Huda, "Qissat Hayati," *al-Kawakib*, September 15, 1953, 20–21.

43. Walter Armbrust, "Golden Age before the Golden Age," 293.

44. Raymond Durgnat, *Films and Feelings* (Cambridge, MA: MIT Press, 1971).

45. Samir Farid, *Tarikh al-riqaba 'ala al-cinema fi Misr* (Cairo: al-Maktab al-Misri litawzi' al-matbu'at, 2002), 23–24.

46. Farid, 23–24.

47. Wilson Chacko Jacob, *Working Out Egypt: Affendi Masculinity and Subject Formation in Colonial Modernity, 1870–1940* (Durham, NC: Duke University Press, 2011); Lucie Ryzova, *The Age of the Efendiyya: Passages to Modernity in National-Colonial Egypt* (Oxford: Oxford University Press, 2014); Hanan Hammad, *Industrial Sexuality: Gender, Urbanization, and Social Transformation in Egypt* (Austin: University of Texas Press, 2016).

48 Mustafa Lutfi al-Manfaluti, *al-Nazarat* (Cairo: Matba't al-ma'arif, 1910), 1:69, 168, 94.

49. Shafik, *Popular Egyptian Cinema*, 256.

50. Shafik, 256.

51. Beth Baron, *Egypt as a Woman: Nationalism, Gender, and Politics* (Berkeley: University of California Press, 2005), 49.

52. Ali el-Grittly, *The Structure of Modern Industry in Egypt* (Cairo: Government Press, 1948).

53. On the rise of consumerism and the department store, see Mona Russel, *Creating the New Woman: Consumerism, Education and National Identity, 1863–1922* (New York: Palgrave Macmillan, 2004), 29–78; and Nancy Reynolds, *A City Consumed: Urban Commerce, the Cairo Fire, and the Politics of Decolonization in Egypt* (Stanford, CA: Stanford University Press, 2012).

54. Reynolds, 49.

55. Reynolds, 49.

56. Al-Shammaa, "Shadows of Contemporary Lives," 49n71.

57. 'Isam Talima, *Hassan al-Banna wa tajrubat al-fann* (Cairo: Maktabat Whaba, 2008), 41–42. See also Samira al-Maghribi, "al-Ikhwan wa al-Fann," Ikhwan Wiki,

February 11, 2014, https://ikhwanwiki.com/index.php?title=%D8%B3%D9%85%D9%
8A%D8%B1%D8%A9_%D8%A7%D9%84%D9%85%D8%BA%D8%B1%D8%A8%D9
%8A.

58. 'Uthman, *Hikayat min tarikh al-cinema al-Missriyya*, 57.

59. Murad, "Mudhakkarat Layla Murad 5."

60. Tantawi, *Rihlat hub*, 154.

61. Tantawi, 158.

62. Rafiq al-Sabban, *Layla Murad: Awwal Cinderella fi al-cinema al-Missriyya* (Cairo: Matbu'at mihragan al-kahira al-sinima'i al-dawli al-sadis 'ashar, 1992), 11.

63. Murad, "Mudhakkarat Layla Murad 5."

64. Hassan, *Dirasa mukhtasara 'an tarikh al-cinema al-Missriyya*, 89.

65. Yusuf Wahbi, "Anwar Wagdi huwa Yusuf Wahbi al-saghir," *al-Kawakib*, February 9, 1949, 28.

66. "Akhbar faniyya," *al-Kawakib*, November 1949, 63.

67. Anwar Wagdi, "al-Cinema al-Missriyya bi-khayr," *al-Kawakib*, February 1949, 29.

68. Wagdi.

69. For a brief history of the Hasaballah Band, see Ziad Fahmy, *Street Sounds: Listening to Everyday Life in Modern Egypt* (Stanford, CA: Stanford University Press, 2020).

70. I discuss this point further in Chapter 6.

71. Mustafa Amin, "Laylah min alf Layla Murad," *Akhir Sa'a*, May 22, 1946.

72. Tantawi, *Rihlat hub*, 168.

73. Decades later, actress Su'ad Husni (1943–2001) became known as the "Cinderella of Egyptian cinema," but critics continued dubbing Layla Murad the first Cinderella in Egyptian cinema's history.

74. For more on the *zar* rituals, see Hajir Hadidi, *Zar: Spirit Possession, Music, and Healing Rituals in Egypt* (Cairo: American University in Cairo Press, 2016).

75. Tawfiq, *Qissat al-cinema fi Misr*, 83–87.

76. Tawfiq, 87.

Chapter 3: Adam and Eve

1. McDonnell, *Reading Celebrity Gossip Magazines*, 68–69.

2. Sharon Marcus, *The Drama of Celebrity* (Princeton, NJ: Princeton University Press, 2019), 6.

3. For a comprehensive discussion on the scandalous press genre in Egypt, see Muhammad al-Bazz, *Sahafat al-ithara: al-Siyasa wa al-din wa al-jins fi al-suhuf al-Missriyya* (Cairo: Maktabat jazirat al-ward, 2010).

4. Shaun T. Lopez, "Madams, Murders, and the Media: Akhbar al-Hawadith and the Emergence of a Mass Culture in 1920s Egypt," in *Re-envisioning Egypt 1919–1952*,

ed. Arthur Goldschmidt, Jr., Arthur Goldschmidt, and Amy J. Johnson (Cairo: American University in Cairo Press, 2005), 372.

5. "Wa ja'a al-hub," *al-Kawakib*, August 27, 1957.

6. Layla Murad, "Qissa min hayati: Qarar hasim," *al-Kawakib*, April 30, 1957, 38.

7. Murad.

8. Murad.

9. Murad, "Mudhakkarat Layla Murad 5."

10. Mursi, *Layla Murad*, 154–159.

11. Journalist and scriptwriter Bilal Fadl revealed in his TV program *al-Mawhubun fi al-ard* that superstar actress Fatin Hamama shared this information with him, and she confirmed that she never penned any of the articles that appeared in the press carrying her name as author in the 1940s. https://www.youtube.com/watch?v=6MSohtXXt2U.

12. Anwar Wagdi, "Ha'ula' kana lahum sha'n fi hayati," *al-Kawakib*, January 1950, 92–93.

13. "Ha'ula' al-nujum . . . kayfa wa mata bada'a zuhuruhum," *al-Ithnayn wa al-Dunya*, December 16, 1946, 31.

14. Wagdi, "Ha'ula' kana lahumm sha'n fi hayati."

15. Layla Murad, "Risala min Layla Murad," *al-Sabah*, May 18, 1945.

16. "Lamm yatim al-zawaj ba'd," *Musamarat al-Gib*, August 5, 1945, 22.

17. Shusha, *al-Mughamira al-Hasna'*, 39.

18. "Kharaju min dinihim fi sabil al-hub," *Ruz al-Yusuf*, February 7, 1955, 40.

19. Reem A. Meshal, *Sharia and the Making of the Modern Egyptian: Islamic Law and Custom in the Courts of Ottoman Cairo* (Cairo: American University in Cairo Press, 2014), 184.

20. Zubaida Muhammad 'Atta, *Yahud Misr: al-Tarikh al-ijtima'i wa al-iqtisadi* (Cairo: 'Ayn lildirasat wa al-buhuth al-insaniyya wa al-ijtima'iyya, 2011), 113.

21. 'Atta, 113.

22. Both *nedunyah* in Hebrew and *dota* in Ladino (Judeo-Spanish) mean "dowry." Arabic sources use *dota*, quoting the Jewish press in Cairo, rather than the Hebrew term. Egyptian Jews could have used the Ladino word because many of them were Sephardic. I thank Alon Tam, Joel Beinin, Liat Maggid-Alon, and Oded Zinger for explaining this term to me in private correspondence.

23. 'Atta, 119–120.

24. 'Atta, 123.

25. Hanan Kholousy, "Interfaith Unions and Non-Muslim Wives in Early Twentieth-Century Alexandrian Islamic Courts," in *Untold Histories of the Middle East: Recovering Voices from the 19th and 20th Centuries*, ed. Amy Singer, Christoph Neumann, and Selcuk Aksin Somel (New York: Routledge, 2010), 54–70, here 58.

26. Amnon Cohen, *Jewish Life under Islam: Jerusalem in the Sixteenth Century*

(Cambridge, MA: Harvard University Press, 1984), 121; Meshal, *Sharia and the Making of the Modern Egyptian*, 135.

27. Meshal, 121.

28. Meshal, 186. See also Kholousy, "Interfaith Unions and Non-Muslim Wives," 57.

29. Kholousy, 55.

30. Kholousy, 55.

31. Rita James Simon and Howard Altstein, *Global Perspectives on Social Issues: Marriage and Divorce* (Lanham, MD: Lexington Books, 2003), 79.

32. Judith E. Tucker, *In the House of the Law: Gender and Islamic Law in Ottoman Syria and Palestine* (Berkeley: University of California Press, 1998), 180.

33. Kholousy, "Interfaith Unions and Non-Muslim Wives," 61.

34. Kholousy, 62.

35. Jamal J. Nasir, *The Islamic Law of Personal Status* (London: Graham & Trotman, 1990), 54–55.

36. Muhammad 'Azmi al-Bakri, *Mawsu'at al-fiqh wa al-qada' fi al-ahwal al-shakhsiyya* (Cairo: Dar Mahmud lil-nashr wal-tawzi', 2004), 6:102.

37. Sara Salem, "White Innocence as a Feminist Discourse: Intersectionality, Trump, and Performances of 'Shock' in contemporary politics," in *Antagonizing White Feminism: Intersectionality's Critique of Women's Studies and the Academy*, ed. Noelle Chaddock and Beth Hinterliter (New York: Lexington Books, 2019), 47–69.

38. Salem, 51; Helma Lutz, Maria Teresa Herrera Vivar, and Linda Supik, *Framing Intersectionality: Debates on a Multi-faceted Concept in Gender Studies* (Farnham, UK: Ashgate, 2011), 109, 160.

39. Shusha, *al-Mughamira al-Hasna'*, 36.

40. "Kharaju min dinihim fi sabil al-hub."

41. For Mahmud Abu al-'Uyun's biography, see Jamal al-Din Mahmud Abu al- al-'Uyun, "Abi al-Shaykh Abu al-'Uyun," *Majallat al-Azhar*, January 1987, 632–640; February 1987, 778–784.

42. Marc Baer, "Islamic Conversion Narratives of Women: Social Change and Gendered Religious Hierarchy in Early Modern Ottoman Istanbul," *Gender & History* 16, no. 2 (August 2004): 425–458.

43. Beinin, *The Dispersion of Egyptian Jewry*, 233.

44. https://www.youtube.com/watch?v=XSLMJe8e7sI. I thank Eyal Sagui Bizawe for confirming the authenticity of the type.

45. Wasif Jawhariyyeh, *The Storyteller of Jerusalem: The Life and Times of Wasif Jawhariyyeh, 1904–1948*, ed. Salim Tamari and Issam Nassar, trans. Nada Elzeer (Northampton, MA: Olive Branch Press, 2014), 151.

46. Layla Murad, "Mudhakkarat Layla Murad 7: Wa 'arift al-hana liawwal marra", *al-Kawakib*, February 26, 1957, 23–25.

47. Muhammad Badi' Sirbiya, "Layla Murad wa al-dhikrayat sada al-sinin (9):

'Indama ashharat Layla Murad Islamaha," *al-Maw'id*, April 20, 1996, 29; first published in *al-Maw'id* in April 1977.

48. She used the Arabic verb *Ashhartu* ∘, meaning "I publicized"; in the context of religious conversion, it commonly means "I embraced, documented, and publicized" together. While embracing Islam requires no legal action, publicizing and reporting it in the state's records requires that there be at least two male witnesses.

49. Murad, "Mudhakkarat Layla Murad 7."

50. For a broad discussion on the masculinization of citizenship in the Middle Eastern states, see Suad Joseph, "Gendering Citizenship in the Middle East," in *Gender and Citizenship in the Middle East*, ed. Joseph (Syracuse, NY: Syracuse University Press, 2000), 3–30.

51. "Layla al-Muslima," *al-Ithnayn wa al-Dunya*, July 26, 1948, cover and 8–9.

52. Baer, "Islamic Conversion Narratives of Women."

53. "Layla al-Muslima."

54. El-Sayed el-Aswad, "Thaqafat al-satr wa dilalatiha al-ramziyya fi al-haya al-sha'biyya al-'Arabiya," *al-Ma'thurat al-Sha'biyya* 19 (July 2004): 8–27.

55. Israel Gershoni and James Jankowski, *Confronting Fascism in Egypt: Dictatorship versus Democracy in the 1930s* (Stanford, CA: Stanford University Press, 2009); Beinin, *The Dispersion of Egyptian Jewry*; Perri Giovannucci, *Literature and Development in North Africa: The Modernizing Mission* (London: Routledge, 2008).

56. Shusha, *al-Mughamira al-Hasna'*, 46.

57. Shusha, 46.

58. Tharwat Fahmi, "Akhtar hadith sahafi ma'a Layla Murad 'ann al-zawaj wa al-talaq wa al-halal wa al-muhallal wa Anwar Wagdi," *al-Fann*, March 2, 1953, 6. See also Mursi, *Layla Murad*, 210–212.

59. "Hikayat kul yum" *al-Studio*, March 1, 1950, 12.

60. Fahmi, "Akhtar hadith sahafi ma'a Layla Murad."

61. "Hikayat kul yum."

62. "Al-Sulh khayr kaman marra," *al-Studio*, March 8, 1950, 12.

63. Shusha, *al-Mughamira al-Hasna'*, 41.

64. "Al-'Umda, interview."

65. https://www.youtube.com/watch?v=xsqMd7C5osU , min. 1:40.

66. Layla Murad and Anwar Wagdi, "Bayan mushtarak min Layla Murad wa Anwar Wagdi," *al-Studio*, December 1, 1949.

67. Murad and Wagdi, "Bayan mushtarak."

68. "Al-Sulh khayr."

69. "Wa akhiran . . . tamma al-talaq bayna Anwar Wagdi wa Layla Murad," *al-Studio*, March 29, 1950, 13.

70. Salih Gawdat, "Ahl al-fann fi al-mir'ah: Layla Murad," *al-Kawakib*, July 8, 1952, 7.

71. "Anwar wa Layla li-takdhib isha'at al-infisal," *al-Fann*, January 12, 1953, 8.

72. See the promotion in *al-Fann*, February 16, 1953.

73. The promotional advertisement appeared in *al-Musawar* on January 30, 1953, and in *al-Fann*, February 16, 1953, among others.

74. Fahmi, "Akhtar hadith ma'a Layla Murad."

75. "Qissa fi qirtas libb," *al-Kawakib*, December 28, 1954, cover and 20.

76. Shusha, *al-Mughamira al-Hasna'*, 39.

77. Murad, "Mudhakkarat Layla Murad 7."

78. Murad.

79. Murad.

80. "Akhbar al-fann: Layla Murad batalat film 'Abd al-Wahab al-jadid," *al-Fann*, December 29, 1952.

81. Shusha, *al-Mughamira al-Hasna'*, 46–47; 'Adil Hasanayn, *Layla Murad: Ya msafir wa nasi hawak* (Cairo: Amadu, 1993), 53; Hilmi Halim, *Tariq al-Dumu'* (film; 1961).

82. 'Ali, *50 sana cinema*, 2:17–18.

83. Muhammad 'Abd al-Wahab, "Tilmidhati Layla Murad," *al-Kawakib*, February 1, 1949, 28–29.

84. 'Abdallah Ahmad Abdallah, *'Alam Miki Mouse* (Cairo: Dar al-ta'wun lil-tab' wa al-nashr, 1997), 111.

85. Mufid, *Sayyidat al-Qitar al-Ghina'*, 96.

86. Hiba Khurshid, "Hujum min 'a'ilati Layla Murad wa Anwar Wagdi 'ala Qalbi Dalili wa nujum al-musalsal yudafi'un," *Sayyidati*, November 13, 2009, https://www.sayidaty.net/موجو-موجه-ن-م-موجه/ءاوضأو-يتلئاع-يليل-دارم-يليل-رونأو-ودجو-يدي-يلع-يبلق-د-يليل- موجنو-لسلسملا-ديدافعنو#photo/1

87. Mursi, *Layla Murad*, 207–208.

88. Anwar Wagdi, "Kayfa ikhtart zawjati?," *al-Ithnayn wa al-Dunya*, December 16, 1946, 61.

89. "Anwar Wagdi yastajwib Assia Noris," *al-Kawakib*, June 1949, 16–17.

90. "Al-Da'aya fann wa tahwish," *al-Kawakib*, March 1949, 99.

91. Murad, "Mudhakkarat Layla Murad 7."

92. 'Uthman, *Hikayat min tarikh al-cinema al-Missriyya*, 92.

93. 'Uthman, 92.

94. Yusuf Wahbi, "Anwar Wagdi huwa Yusuf Wahbi al-saghir," *al-Kawakib*, February 9, 1949, 28; March 2, 1949, 99.

95. Gawdat, "Ahl al-fann fi al-mir'ah: Layla Murad."

96. Gawdat.

97. Gawdat.

98. According to the sound clip on YouTube, the recording comes from the private collection of journalist Muhammad al-Tab'i (1896–1976); the recorded gathering

took place in Layla's house in the Garden City neighborhood in downtown Cairo on June 13, 1956. Listeners can recognize the voice of singer 'Abd al-Halim Hafiz in addition to those of Layla and her brother Munir. https://www.youtube.com/watch?v=SXM5dgYoOmE.

99. Islamic laws do not allow a thrice-divorced couple to remarry each other unless the woman marries another man and then loses that husband through divorce or death. Arranging a temporary marriage and divorce to meet these conditions is known as a *muhallal*, a more or less accepted arrangement in Egyptian social culture and law. Muslim jurists disagree among themselves about this arrangement. The Hanafi school of law, which Egypt follows, accepts it, although it is considered *makruh* (disfavored). The Egyptian Dar al-Ifta' issued *fatwa*s (religious verdicts), accepting the marriage arrangement based on the ruling of the Hanafi jurists. See al-Bakri, *Mawsu'at al-ahwal al-shakhsiyya*, 6:212–213.

100. "Hayati ma'a Layla Murad kanat ustura," *al-Jil*, April 20, 1953.

101. "Qalb jarih fi hafla sakhiba," *al-Fann*, March 23, 1953, 6–7.

102. "Qalb jarih fi hafla sakhiba."

103. "Qalb jarih fi hafla sakhiba."

104. "Hadatha hadha al-usbu'," *al-Kawakib*, August 4, 1953, 36.

105. Salim al-Lawzi, "I'tirafat fata al-'asr 'ann al-sa'ada wa al-hub wa Layla Murad," *al-Kawakib*, September 15, 1953, 31.

106. Al-Lawzi.

107. Muhammad Badi' Sirbiya, "Hassna' min Faransa sabab talaq Layla min Anwar", *al-Maw'id*, May 1953, 4–5.

108. Mursi, *Layla Murad*, 230–238.

109. Al-Lawzi, "I'tirafat fata al-'asr."

110. Al-Lawzi.

111. Lutfi Radwan, "Ayuha al-qurra' aghithu Anwar Wagdi," *al-Kawakib*, September 22, 1953, 10–11, 31.

112. Radwan.

113. "Hadatha hadha al-usbu'," *al-Kawakib*, September 22, 1953, 36.

114. Radwan, "Ayuha al-qurra' aghithu Anwar Wagdi."

115. Radwan.

116. "Waladi," *al-Kawakib*, March 1951, 49.

117. Radwan, "Ayuha al-qurra' aghithu Anwar Wagdi."

118. Anwar Wagdi, "Min qisass al-nujum: Ghalat fi al-hisab," *al-Kawakib*, January 19, 1954, 28.

119. Lutfi Radwan, "al-Fasl al-akhir fi qissat Anwar Wagdi wa Layla Murad," *al-Kawakib*, October 13, 1953, 10–11.

120. Lopez, "Madams, Murders, and the Media," 389.

Chapter 4: The Blow of Fate

1. Layla Murad, "Kunt fi Paris yum 23 yulyah," *al-Kawakib*, July 22, 1958.

2. Ashraf Gharib, *al-Watha'iq al-khassa li-Layla Murad* (Cairo: Dar al-Shuruq, 2016), 72–73.

3. *Al-Ithnayn wa al-Dunya*, September 1, 1952, 17.

4. Hasanayn, *Ya msafir wa nasi hawak*, 85–86.

5. "Qissat al-50 alf Junayh al-lati tabara'at biha Layla Murad li-Israel," *al-Sabah*, October 10, 1952, 31.

6. "Qissat al-50 alf junayh."

7. "Qissat al-50 alf junayh."

8. "Hadiyya min al-idha'a al-Suriyya," *al-Fann*, September 22, 1952.

9. "Huna al-Qahira: Idha'it aghani Layla Murad," *al-Fann*, October 20, 1952, 22.

10. Hasanayn, *Ya msafir wa nasi hawak*, 87.

11. According to one of her biographers, 'Adil Hasanayn, Layla went to see Anwar Wagdi in Paris, thinking he was behind the rumors as revenge for divorcing him. Hasanayn also speculates that she went to Paris out of love for Wagdi, who had denied the news that they would be back together. Her fans were thus upset that she was so weak and mindlessly followed her heart. Hasanayn, 90.

12. Anwar Wagdi "Qarar wa i'tiraf," *al-Fann*, October 20, 1952.

13. "Al-qiyada al-'amma lil quwwat al-musallaha tubari' Layla Murad min safariha li-Israel wa al-tabaru' biay mablagh wa hadhhi hiya al-watha'iq," *al-Fann*, November 3, 1952, 8–9.

14. "Taqrir ghurfat sina'at al-cinema," *al-Sabah*, July 1, 1948; 'Ali, *Dirasat fi tarikh al-cinema al-Misryya*, 165.

15. W.B., "Nadwat al-mawsim: al-Cinema al-Missriyya bayna tawjihat al-qiyada wa wajib al-fananin," *al-Kawakib*, November 11, 1952, 7.

16. W.B.

17. W.B.

18. "Al-qiyada al-'amma lil quwwat al-musallaha tubari' Layla Murad."

19. Kamal Mansur, "al-Qissa al-haqiqyya li tabaru' Layla Murad li-Israel," *al-Fann*, October 20, 1952, 11–12.

20. "Akhbar al-Fann," *al-Fann*, December 22, 1952, 13.

21. "Mawasim al-isha'at fi Beirut," *al-Kawakib*, February 23, 1954, 14.

22. Murad, "Mudhakkarat Layla Murad 7."

23. "Akhbar al-Fann," *al-Fann*, October 13, 1952, 4.

24. "Layla taqul mazluma wa Anwar yu'akid i'tiraziha bil-Islam," *al-Fann*, October 27, 1952, 3–5.

25. Abu al-Majd al-Hariri, "Layla wa Anwar yuhadiran fi Kulliyat al-Adab Jami'at Fu'ad al-Awwal," *al-Fann*, December 15, 1952, 4–7.

26. "Akhbar al-Fann," *al-Fann*, November 10, 1952, 24.

27. "Anwar Wagdi wa tawzi' aflamih fi Syria," *al-Fann*, December 22, 1952.

28. Anwar Wagdi, "Ila al-Suryun al-abtal," *al-Musawar*, February 27, 1953, 45.

29. Wagdi.

30. "Akhbar min al-Sharq: Mawasim Anwar Wagdi," *al-Fann*, February 23, 1953, 27.

31. "Layla Murad 'ala al-bilaj: Anwar gah yikahalha 'amah," *al-Musawar*, September 24, 1954.

32. "Nujum Misr fi ihda wahadat al-jaysh," *al-Kawakib*, November 18, 1952, 16–17.

33. Actress Madiha Yusri appeared on the *al-Fann* magazine cover on January 26, 1953, wrapped in the flag of the Egyptian monarchy.

34. *Al-Fann*, February 2, 1953, 18–21.

35. "Layla Murad tatabarra' bimablagh 1,000 junayh li mashru' taqwiyat al-jaysh al-Misri", *al-Fann*, December 8, 1952, 14.

36. For more on the film *Mustafa Kamil*, see Joel Gordon, "Film, Fame, and Public Memory: Egyptian Biopics from Mustafa Kamil to Nasser 56," *International Journal of Middle East Studies* 31, no. 1 (1999): 61–79.

37. Midhat 'Asim, "al-Nashid al-ladhi sana'athu al-sudfa," *al-Kawakib*, August 4, 1953, 4.

38. "Kalimati fi khidmat al-thawra," *al-Kawakib*, August 4, 1953, 35.

39. "Kalimati fi khidmat al-thawra."

40. "Tasma'un hadha al-usbu'," *al-Kawakib*, December 23, 1952, 36–37.

41. For the internal power struggle between Nagib and Nasser, see Joel Gordon, *Nasser's Blessed Movement*, chaps. 5 and 6. See also Yoram Meital, *Revolutionary Justice: Special Courts and the Formation of Republican Egypt* (Oxford: Oxford University Press, 2016).

42. Muhammad Idris, "Qitar al-Rahma," *al-Kawakib*, December 23, 1952, 17.

43. "Qitar al-Rahma," *al-Musawar*, January 16, 1953.

44. "Ma'a ahl al-fann fi Qitar al-Rahma," *al-Fann*, December 29, 1952, 4–5.

45. "Ma'a ahl al-fann fi Qitar al-Rahma."

46. I constructed this account of the trip based on the press coverage in several periodicals, including *al-Fann*, December 29, 1952, 4–5, and *al-Musawar*, January 16, 1953.

47. *Al-Musawar*, January 16, 1953, 17–19.

48. 'Adil Hamuda, *al-Watha'iq al-khassa bil-Ra'is Nagib* (Cairo: Ruz al-Yusuf, 1977), 46–47.

49. "Al-Ra'is yashar ma'a al-fann wa al-khayr," *al-Kawakib*, September 15, 1953, 10–11.

50. For the history of bureaucratization and state control over charities pre-1952, see Mine Ener, *Managing Egypt's Poor and the Politics of Benevolence, 1800–1952* (Princeton, NJ: Princeton University Press, 2003).

51. Fu'ad Mikha'il, "al-Thaghr yashar Layla min layali al-'umr," *al-Kawakib*, August 4, 1953, 6.

52. Mikha'il "al-Thaghr yashar," *al-Kawakib*, August 4, 1953, 6.

53. Al-'Umda, interview.

54. Al-'Umda, interview.

55. "Haddiyya: Tadhkarat barid Layla Murad," *al-Kawakib*, January 27, 1953, cover.

56. "Ma'a hadha al-'adad hadiyya: sura bilhajm al-tabi'i lil-najma Layla Murad," *al-Kawakib*, November 20, 1956, cover.

57. "Layla Murad ta'ud ila al-ghina'," *al-Kawakib*, October 12, 1965, cover.

58. El-Shammaa, "Shadows of Contemporary Lives," 29n19. For the impact of these false rumors on Mizrahi's career, see Starr, *Togo Mizrahi*, 45–47.

59. "Al-qiyada al-'amma lil quwwat al-musallaha tubari' Layla Murad."

60. "Awwal hadith ma'a Layla Murad and Anwar Wagdi," *al-Fann*, October 27, 1952.

61. Lutfi Radwan, "*al-Kawakib* fi al-Hijaz," *al-Kawakib*, November 11, 1952, 110–111.

62. Hawa'i, "Kalam fi al-hawa'," *al-Kawakib*, August 25, 1953, 45.

63. "Kalimat al-usbu': Mu'tamar al-idha'a," *al-Kawakib*, August 25, 1953, 3.

64. Muhammad Mahmud Dawwara and Ahmad Mahir Ratib, "Nadwat ahl al-fann: Mushkilat al-fanin al-'Arab tantahi fi *Ahl al-Fann*," *Ahl al-Fann*, April 12, 1954.

65. Dawwara and Ratib.

66. Dawwara and Ratib.

67. "Al-Mutriba Su'ad Muhammad tughadir Misr shakiratan majallat *al-Fann*," *al-Fann*, October 13, 1952, 22.

68. Dawwara and Ratib, "Nadwat ahl al-fann," 14–15.

69. "Su'ad Muhammad: al-Mutriba al-Lubnaniyya allati lam tughani lahnan Lubnanyan wahidan," *al-Fann*, October 6, 1952, 10–11.

70. "Fannanuna yajidun takrim fi biladiha wa yajib ann nukarrim fanannihim wa nurahhib bihim fi biladina," *al-Fann*, September 8, 1952, 7.

71. Layla Murad, "Fi al-mir'ah bayna al-haqiqa wa al-khayal," *al-Kawakib*, August 1951, 8, and "Aflam al-Bakkar tahtafil bi al-ustaz Anwar Wagdi," *al-Fann*, October 1, 1951.

72. "Husni Nagib Bik yaqul: Idha aradna al-nuhud bi al-cinema . . . wajaba ann nansa masalihina al-shakhssiyya," *al-Kawakib*, June 1949, 36–37.

73. "Rabita 'Arabiya fanniyya," *al-Kawakib*, September 1950, 58.

74. Farid al-Atrash, "al-Hay'at al-fanniyya tastati' innqadh al-cinema," *al-Kawakib*, November 1949, 22.

75. "Farid al-Atrash: al-Duwal al-'Arabiya taqdi 'ala al-cinema al-'Arabiya," *al-Shabaka*, October 20, 1969, 22–26.

76. Hassan Ramzi, "al-Sinema fi muftaraq al-turuq," *al-Kawakib*, May 1949, 72.

77. Al-Tahir al-Mahdi bin 'Arifa, *al-Jami'a al-'Arabiya wa al-'amal al-'Arabi al-mushtarak 1945–2000* (Amman: Zahran lil-nashr, 2011(, 226–228.

78. "Dalida 'al al-la'iha al-sawda'," *al-Shabaka*, June 27, 1966, 9.

79. Nasser al-Din al-Nashashibi, *Qissati ma'a al-Sahafa* (n.p., 1983), 363.

80. Yusuf Idris, "Yawmiyat," *al-Jumhuriyya*, February 12, 1962.

81. Yusuf Idris, "Madha naf'al bi-Dalida wa Elizabeth Taylor wa Dany Kaye?," *al-Jumhuriyya*, February 5, 1962.

82. "Raf' al-hadhr 'ann aghani Nagah Sallam fi Dimashq," *al-Shabaka*, March 28, 1966, 8.

83. Al-Nashashibi, *Qissati ma'a al-Sahafa*, 327.

84. "Al-qiyada al-'amma lil quwwat al-musallaha tubari' Layla Murad."

85. "Akhbaruhum 'ala wjuhihm," *Ruz al-Yusuf*, May 30, 1955.

86. Kevin W. Martin, *Syria's Democratic Years: Citizens, Experts, and Media in the 1950s* (Bloomington: Indiana University Press, 2015), 3.

87. Martin, 3.

88. Gharib, *al-Watha'iq al-khassa li-Layla Murad*, 81.

89. Salih Gawdat, "Qabaltu hadha al-usbu'," *al-Kawakib*, August 6, 1957, 19.

90. Ahmad Hamrush, *Qissat thawrat 23 Yulu: Shuhud thawrat Yulu* (Cairo: Maktabat Madbuli, 1984), 449–451.

91. "Hadatha hadha al-usb'," *al-Kawakib*, March 25, 1958, 33.

92. "Bayni wa baynak," *al-Kawakib*, April 8, 1958.

93. "Hadatha hadha al-usbu'," *al-Kawakib*, April 15, 1958, 32.

94. "Anta tasma' wa al-idha'a tadfa'," *al-Kawakib*, August 19, 1958.

95. "Hadatha hadha al-usb': Ta'ud Layla Murad ila al-shasha," *al-Kawakib*, February 18, 1958, 33.

96. Fu'ad Mikha'il, "Akhiran takallamat Layla Murad," *al-Kawakib*, April 22, 1958, 4–5; "Hadatha hadha al-usbu'," *al-Kawakib*, February 18, 1958; "Layla Murad: 'Awda lil-adwa'," *al-Kawakib*, May 12, 1958, cover.

97. Tarazan, "Bayni wa Baynak," *al-Kawakib*, April 1, 1958; June 10, 1958, 44.

98. Tarazan, "Bayni wa Baynak," *al-Kawakib*, April 1, 1958.

99. Shusha, *al-Mughamira al-Hasna'*, 45.

100. Shusha, 45.

101. "Mufawadat bayna Layla Murad wa Farid al-Atrash," *al-Jil*, February 8, 1954.

102. "Layla Murad wa al-sahafa: Layla Murad ghumud la da'i lahu," *al-Kawakib*, November 26, 1957.

103. "Layla Murad wa al-sahafa."

104. Gawdat, "Qabaltu hadha al-usbu'."

105. Gawdat.

Chapter 5: The Unknown Lover

1. Hamrush, *Qissat thawrat 23 Yulu*, 409.

2. Hamrush, 419. See also Joel Gordon, *Nasser's Blessed Movement*, 118–128, 184–185.

3. Tharwat Fahmi, "Bisabab hiwar sahafi ma'a Layla Murad: Muwajaha bil-silah ma'a Anwar Wagdi," *Akhir Sa'a*, December 19, 1995. See also Fahmi, "Akhtar hadith

sahafi ma'a Layla Murad 'ann al-zawaj wa al-talaq wa al-halal wa al-muhallal wa Anwar Wagdi," *al-Fann*, March 2, 1953.

4. "Kalimati fi khidmat al-thawra," *al-Kawakib*, August 4, 1953, 35.

5. Wagih Abaza, "al-Fann la watana lahu," *al-Fann*, April 12, 1954.

6. Shusha, *al-Mughamira al-Hasna'*, 46–48.

7. Tantawi, *Rihlat hub*, 305.

8. Tantawi, 305.

9. *Allahu Ma'ana* (Ahmad Badrakhan, 1955); *Inni Rahila* ('Izz al-Din Dhu al-Faqqar, 1955); *Ard al-Salam* (Kamal al-Shaykh, 1957); *Port Said* ('Izz al-Din Dhu al-Faqqar, 1957); and *Rudda Qalbi*, ('Izz al-Din Dhu al-Faqqar, 1957), to name few examples.

10. Gharib, *al-Watha'iq al-Khassa li-Layla Murad*, 64–68.

11. Fu'ad Mikha'il, "al-Fann 'ala al-kurnish," *al-Kawakib*, September 1, 1953, 32–33.

12. Muhammad Fawzi, "al-Bilaj wa al-hawa wa al-jamal kama ra'aytuh," *al-Kawakib*, September 1, 1953, 10–11.

13. "Layla Murad tajma' rasin fi al-halal," *al-Kawakib*, March 9, 1953, 16.

14. "Hadatha hadha al-usbu'," *al-Kawakib*, September 1, 1953, 40.

15. "Hadatha hadha al-usbu'," 40.

16. 'Abdallah Imam, *Wagih Abaza: Safahat min al-nidal al-watani* (Cairo: 'Arabiya lil-tiba'a wal-nashr, 1995), 566–567.

17. Afaf Lutfi al-Sayyid Marsot, *A Short History of Modern Egypt* (Cambridge: Cambridge University Press, 1985), 118.

18. Imam, *Wagih Abaza: Safahat*, 215–231.

19. Imam, 220–226.

20. Imam, 220–226.

21. Layla Murad, "al-Ughniya al-Sinima'yya tushbih kalimat ahbak," *Ahl al-Fann*, April 12, 1954, 12–13.

22. Wagih Abaza, "Ila *Ahl al-Fann*," *Ahl al-Fann*, April 12, 1954, 3.

23. Muhammad Abu Zahra, *al-Ahwal al-shakhsiyya*, 3rd ed. (Cairo: Dar al-fikr al-'Arabi, 1957), 275–276.

24. "Isha'at al-mawsim," *al-Kawakib*, November 16, 1954, 46–47, 56.

25. Shusha, *al-Mughamira al-Hasna'*, 54.

26. "Layla Murad 'ala al-bilaj."

27. "Isha'at al-mawsim."

28. "Al-Fann yahtafil."

29. "Al-Fann yahtafil bi-laylat al-gala'," *al-Kawakib*, October 26, 1954, 12–17.

30. Mahmud 'Assaf, *Ma'a al-imam al-shahid Hassan al-Banna* (Cairo: Maktabit 'Ayn Shams, 1993), 244.

31. Imam, *Wagih Abaza*, 220–226.

32. See Hazem Kandil, *Soldiers, Spies, and Statesmen: Egypt's Road to Revolt* (London: Verso, 2013), chap. 1.

33. Saïd K. Aburish, *Nasser, the Last Arab: A Biography* (New York: Thomas Dunne Books, 2004) 55–56.

34. Aburish, 56.

35. "Layla Fawzi tutallaq min khalf al-bab," *al-Fann*, May 3, 1954, 4.

36. "Kul Najma wa laha sir! Sabah maksufa wa Layla Murad 'iybuha al-israf," *al-Kawakib*, January 20, 1959, 6.

37. Layla Murad, "Qissatu Hubi," *al-Kawakib*, March 31, 1959, 9–10.

38 For examples of the news coverage, see "al-Qabd 'ala Layla Murad wa al-ifraj 'annha," *al-Akhbar*, May 17, 1955, 1; "Bolis al-Adab hajam 7 sayyidat yal'abna al-qimar wa bayna al-la'ibat mutraba ma'rufa," *al-Ahram*, May 17, 1955, 5; "Qadiyyat nadi qimar al-sayyidat", *al-Akhbar*, May 19, 1955, 3; "Muhakamat hafidat al-basha al-mutahama bi-idarat manzil lil-qimar wa Layla Murad wa baqi al-la'ibat la yahdarn wa al-difa' yatamassak bi-munaqashatihin," *al-Akhbar*, May 20, 1955, 3; and "Layla Murad tahrab min al-sahafa ila al-Iskandariya," *Ruz al-Yusuf*, June 7, 1955.

39. *Al-Kawakib*, March 6, 1956, cover.

40. Shusha, *al-Mughamira al-Hasna'*, 60; Zaki 'Abd al-Tawwab, "Umm Zaki fi villatiha al-jadida," *al-Kawakib*, March 6, 1956, cover and 14–15.

41. Murad, "Qissatu Hubi."

42. Murad, "Mudhakkarat Layla Murad 7."

43. "Ibn Layla Murad ahla min ibn Madiha Yusri," *al-Musawar*, March 28, 1958.

44. Ayman Yamut, "Layla Murad tukhabi' fi sadriha hikayat zawaj sari' wa talaq assra'," *al-Maw'id*, August 1972, 26–29.

45. "Ayam wa Layali," *al-Maw'id*, July 1972.

46. *Al-Ahram*, April 7, 1994, 23.

47. For more on Operation Susannah, see Joel Beinin, "Nazis and Spies: Representations of Jewish Espionage and Terrorism in Egypt," *Jewish Social Studies*, n.s., 2, no. 3 (1996): 54–84.

48. For example, the image of actress Hind Rustum wearing the ERC uniform appeared on the cover of *al-Kawakib*, November 27, 1956.

49. Yasmin Farrag, *al-Ghina' wa al-siyasa fi tarikh Misr* (Cairo: Dar Nahdet Misr lil-nashr, 2014), 47.

50. 'Abd al-Mu'izz 'Abd al-Rahman, *al-Thawra al-thqafiyya fi 11 'aman* (Cairo: Matabi' al-dar al-qawmiyya, 1963), 29.

51. Nagat al-Saghira, "Mudhakkarat Nagat al-Saghira," *al-Kawakib*, March 25, 1958.

52. Nagat al-Saghira, "Saraqat al-nagham," *al-Kawakib*, January 20, 1959.

53. Salih Mursi, "Layla Murad taqul: Ashraf wa Zaki kawanu firqa ismaha al-mala'ika, mushkilty ma'a al-idha'a al-20%, amma mushkiliti ma'a al-cinema is'alu 'annha al-Sahhar", *al-Musawar*, August 7, 1970, 57.

54. 'Abd al-Rahman, *al-Thawra al-thqafiyya fi 11 'aman*, 52.

55. 'Abd al-Rahman, 56–57.

56. Husain 'Uthman, "Layla Murad tuqaddim shrutaha lil-'awda ila al-shasha," *al-Kawakib*, November 7, 1961, 9–10.

57. 'Uthman.

58. 'Uthman.

59. 'Uthman.

60. 'Uthman.

61. 'Uthman.

62. "Sahib Adwa' al-Madina yudafi' 'ann nafsih," *al-Idha'a*, January 17, 1959.

63. 'Uthman, "Layla Murad tuqaddim shrutaha."

64. 'Uthman.

65. *Al-Kawakib*, October 12, 1965, cover.

66. Mursi, "Mushkiliti ma'a al-cinema is'alu 'annha al-Sahhar."

67. Kamal al-Najmi, "al-Mutribun al-'aidun: Kalima sariha," *al-Kawakib*, February 7, 1967, 24–25.

68. Mursi, "Mushkiliti ma'a al-cinema is'alu 'annha al-Sahhar."

69. "Liqa' ma'a 'Abd al-Hamid al-Sahhar," *al-Kawakib*, August 27, 1968.

70. "Liqa' ma'a 'Abd al-Hamid al-Sahhar."

71. 'Abd al-Hamid Guda al-Sahhar, *Dhikrayat sinima'iyya* (Cairo: Maktabit Misr, 1975), 128.

72. "Liqa' ma'a 'Abd al-Hamid al-Sahhar"; al-Sahhar, 134.

73. Al-Sahhar, 70–76.

74. Al-Sahhar, 79.

75. For example, see Laura Ruiz de Elvira, Christoph H. Schwarz, and Irene Weipert-Fenner, eds., *Clientelism and Patronage in the Middle East and North Africa: Networks of Dependency* (New York: Routledge, 2019).

76. Maysa al-Gamal, *al-Nukhba al-Siyasiyya fi Misr: dirasat halat al-nukhba al-wizariyya* (Cairo: Markaz dirasat al-wihda al-'Arabiya, 1998), 25, 135.

77. "Hiwar sarih ma'a ra'is mu'assasat al-cinema," *al-Masa'*, April 21, 1969; al-Sahhar, *Dhikrayat Sinima'iyya*, 148–163.

78. Al-Sahhar, 99.

79. Al-Sahhar, 102.

80. Mursi, "Mushkiliti ma'a al-cinema is'alu 'annha al-Sahhar" ; see also al-'Umda, "interview."

81. Al-'Umda, interview.

82. Christa Salamandra, "Consuming Damascus: Popular Culture and the Construction of Social Identity," in Armbrust, *Mass Mediations*, 182–202.

83. Bertell Ollman, *Dance of the Dialectic: Steps in Marx's Method* (Urbana: University of Illinois Press, 2003), 202.

84. Nira Yuval-Davis, "Women, Citizenship and Difference," *Feminist Review* 57 (Autumn 1997), 4–27.

Chapter 6: The Starling of the Valley

1. *Al-Kawakib*, December 5, 1995. Similar headlines appeared in other publications; for example, see Amina al-Sharif, "Ashraf wa Zaki yakshifan tafasil sanawat 'uzlat um-mihima," *al-Musawar*, November 29, 1995.

2. David Lowenthal, *The Past Is a Foreign Country* (Cambridge: Cambridge University Press, 1985), xvii.

3. D. A. Spellberg, *Politics, Gender, and the Islamic Past: The Legacy of A'isha Bint Abi Bakr* (New York: Columbia University Press, 1994), 1.

4. Ibid. I am using Spellberg's words.

5. Zuhur, *Asmahan's Secret*, 6.

6. For example, see 'Abd al-Shafi al-Qashshashi, *Ashshhar al-nujum wa al-kawakib amama al-adwa' wa khalfa al-kamira* (Cairo: Majalat al-Fann, 1969); al-Nabigha al-Sa'di, *Nujum amam al-qada'* (Cairo: al-Sharika al-Missriyya li-fann al-tiba'a, 1975); "Layla Murad tughani ma'a 'Abd al-Halim Hafiz," *al-Shabaka*, March 2, 1970; Yamut, "Layla Murad tukhabi' fi sadriha hikayat."

7. al-Najmi, *al-Ghina' al-Misri* (Cairo: Dar al-Hilal, 1966); *Aswat wa-alhan 'Arabiya* (Cairo: Dar al-Hilal, 1968); *Mutribun wa-mustami'un* (Cairo: Dar al-Hilal, 1970); *Sihr al-ghina' al-'Arabi* (Cairo: Dar al-Hilal, 1972).

8. Al-Najmi, *Mutribun wa-mustami'un*, 2nd ed. (Cairo: Dar al-Hilal, [1970] 1993), 187.

9. Tawfiq, *Qissat al- cinema fi Misr*.

10. Muhammad al-Sayyid Shusha, *Ruwwad wa Ra'idat al-cinema al-Missriyya* (Cairo: Ruz al-Yusuf, 1978).

11. Shusha, *al-Mughamira al-Hasna'*.

12. For examples of these memoirs, see 'Ali, *50 sana cinema*, vol. 1; and Muhammad Rif'at al-Muhami, *Mudhakirat musiqar al-jil Muhammad 'Abd al-Wahab kama yarwiha binafsih*, 2nd ed. (Beirut: Mu'ssassat 'Izz al-Din lil-Tiba'a wal-Nashr, 1990).

13. Salih Mursi, "Qissat Hayat Layla Murad," *al-Kawakib*, February–May 1975.

14. Ahmad Ra'fat Bahgat, *al-Yahud wa al-cinema fi Misr: Dirasa tahlilya tughati kafat anshitat al-cinema min bidayat al-Qarn al-'Ishrin* (Cairo: Sharitkat al-Qasr lil-Tiba'a wa al-Di'aya, 2005), 113.

15. For example, see "Zaki Munir Murad: 'Azif al-guitar min al-matbakh al-Faransi," *al-Jumhuriyya*, November 6, 1978.

16. Hanan Hammad, "The Iranian Revolution in the Egyptian Press" (MA thesis, University of Texas at Austin, 2004), chap. 1.

17. *Al-Maw'id* republished the biographical series starting on February 8, 1996, a few months after her death. Sirbiya, "Layla Murad wa al-dhikrayat sada al-sinin 9." See

also "Layla Murad wa al-dhikrayat sada al-sinin 12: Wahdaha kanat tusari' al-azamat," *al-Maw'id*, May 11, 1996, 23.

18. Yusuf al-Qa'id, "Hikayatan 'ann Layla Murad," *Nizwa*, October 1, 1996, https://www.nizwa.com/?p=979

19. For example, see "Layla Murad fatahat li bab ayamiha al-sa'ida qabla al-ta'na al-masmuma," *al-Nahar*, December 23, 1985; and 'Abd al-'Alim, "Layla Murad wa al-Mussed."

20. The academic discourse focuses on the artistic and aesthetic aspects of Layla's musicals. See Jihan Ahmad al-Nasser Badr, "Layla Murad wa al-ughniya al-sinima'iyya al-Missriyya" (MA thesis, Academy of Arts: Higher Institute of Arab Music, 2005).

21. 'Arafa 'Abdu 'Ali, "Yahud Misr mina al-indimaj ila al-hijra," *al-Hilal*, May 1990.

22. 'Arafa 'Abdu 'Ali, *Yahud Misr Barunat wa Bu'asa'* (Cairo: Itrak lil-Nashri wa al-Tawzi', 1997).

23. "Wafat al-mulahhin Munir Murad," *al-Akhbar*, October 10, 1981; "Mufaj'at ba'da wafat Munir Murad: la yahmil al-Jinsiyya al-Missriyya wa ibnuh la yarith la'anhu ghayr Muslim," *al-Jumhuriyya*, October 22, 1981.

24. Hasanayn, *Ya msafir wa nasy hawak*.

25. Hanan Mufid, *Sayyidat Qitari al-Ghina': Layla Murad* (Cairo: al-Hayy'a al-Missriyya al-'amma lil-Kitab, 2003), and its more recent version, *Ana Zay Ma Ana wa Inta Bititghayyar: Layla Murad* (Cairo: Afaq lil-Nashr wa al-Tawzi', 2009).

26. Sa'id Abu al-'Aynayn, *al-Sha'rawi wa al-Fannanat: Asrar liqat'at al-hidaya wa hijab al-Milyun dollar* (Cairo: Dar Akhbar al-Yum, 1999), 13–30.

27. Mahmud Jami', *Wa 'araftu al-Sha'rawi* (Cairo: Dar al-Tawzi' wa al-Nashr al-Islamiyya, 2005), 108.

28. Mufid, *Sayyidat Qitari al-Ghina'*, 126–127.

29. Ayman al-Hakim, "Asrar jadida min hayat Layla Murad yakshufuha ibnuha Ashraf Abaza: Umi wa al-Shaykh al-Sha'rawi," *al-Kawakib*, February 7, 1999, 48–49; Zaynab Sulayman, "Hiwar ma'a Ashraf Wagih Abaza," *Nisf al-Dunia*, May 14, 2000.

30. Jacquelene Brinton, *Preaching Islamic Renewal: Religious Authority and Media in Contemporary Egypt* (Oakland: University of California Press, 2016), chap. 8.

31. The account went viral on sites of media outlets, blogs, and social media alike. To cite a few examples, see "Layla Murad . . . haramaha Studio Misr min al-Hajj hatta wafatiha," *Gololy*, May 21, 2013, http://gololy.com/2013/05/21/89982/ليلى-مراد-حرمها-استوديو-مصر-من-الحج-ح.html; Wafa' al-Shami, "Studio Misr yamnda' Layla Murad min ada' faridat al-Hajj," *Sada al-Balad*, September 1, 2017, https://www.elbalad.news/2917739; 'Abir al-Nassrawi, "Ughniyat 'Ya Rayihin lil-Nabi al-Ghali' lil-mutriba al-Missriyya Layla Murad," *Mont Carlo International*, May 16, 2019, https://www.mc-doualiya.com/programs/histoire-chanson-mcd/20190516 أغنية-يا-رايحين-للنبي-الغالي-للمطربة-المصرية-مراد-فيلم-كساك-الحجاج-الرياض-السناباطي

32. 'Assaf, *Ma'a al-imam al-shahid Hassan al-Banna*, 39–41.

33. 'Isam Talima, *Hassan al-Banna wa tajrubat al-fann* (Cairo: Maktabat Wahba, 2008), 38–40.

34. https://www.youtube.com/watch?v=p2kObOJ36eY.

35. https://www.youtube.com/watch?v=QTUPbkme4AI; https://www.youtube.com/watch?v=W41CkvJd1-A.

36. Sirbiya, "Layla Murad wa al-dhikrayat sada al-sinin 9."

37. Khayri Shalabi, "Bortrayh al-masrah," *al-Idha'a wa al-Tiliviziun*, May 4, 1996; al-Hakim, "Asrar jadida"; Sulayman, "Hiwar Ashraf Wagih Abaza"; al-Qa'id, "Hikayatan 'ann Layla Murad."

38. For example, see al-Lawzi, "I'tirafat fata al-'asr"

39. "Layla al-Muslima."

40. "Layla al-Muslima."

41. "A'lanat al-mutriba al-dhahabiyyat al-sawt Layla Murad Islamaha wa qadd kanat hata al-shahr al-madi min banat Israel," *al-'Amal*, July 21, 1948.

42. Al-Hakim, "Asrar Jadida"; Muhammad Sa'd, "Fi al-ihtifal bi-dhikra miladiha: Zaki Fatin 'Abd al-Wahab yakshif asrar Layla Murad," *Moheet*, February 12, 2009, http://www.moheet.com/show_files.aspx?fid=221647; Majdi Jamal, "Zaki Fatin 'Abd al-Wahab: lastu zillan li-Yousuf Chahine," *al-Qahira*, November 11, 2005. See also Mustafa al-Fiqi, "'Ann qurb: Layla Murad," *al-Misri al-Youm*, March 6, 2008.

43. Abu al-'Aynayn, *al-Sha'rawi wa al-Fannanat*, 24; Faraj al-'Antari, *al-Satw al-Suhyuni 'ala al-musiqa al-'Arabiya*, 2nd ed. (Cairo: Dar al-Kalimah, 2000), 105–6; Mufid, *Sayyidat Qitari al-Ghina'*, 128–130; Tawhid Magdi, *Ruz al-Yusuf*, July 21, 1997; al-Hakim, "Asrar Jadida"; Jamal, "Lastu zillan"; al-Qa'id, "Hikayatan 'ann Layla Murad. "

44. Jamal, "Lastu zillan."

45. Al-'Antari, *al-Satw al-Shyuni*, 105; al-Qa'id, "Hikayatan 'ann Layla Murad."

46. For example, in the heyday of what is referred to in modern Egypt's history as the Liberal Era (1923–1952), the founder of the Egyptian Feminist Union, Huda Sha'rawi, voiced this question openly and asked the Egyptian Jews to decide on which side they stood. The Jewish leaders René and Aslan Qattawi responded the following day with a public and robust condemnation of Zionism and declared their commitment to the Egyptian side. See Huda Sha'rawi, "Ila al-Hakham al-Akbar wa yahud Misr," *al-Ahram*, October 13, 1947, 4; Aslan Qattawi and René Qattawi, "Yahud Misr," *al-Ahram*, October 14, 1947, 3.

47. Walid al-Khashshab, "Layla wa Togo: Wahm al-*cinema* al-yahuddiyya," *al-Qahira*, January 1996, 243–44.

48. Al-Fiqi, "'Ann qurb."

49. The best examples are al-'Antari, *al-Satw al-Suhyuni*, and Bahgat, *al-Yahud wa al-cinema fi Misr*.

50. Mufid, *Sayyidat Qitari al-Ghina'*, 127.

51. Safi Naz Kazim, *San'at latafa* (Cairo: Dar al-'Ayn lil-Nashr, 2007), 134–135.

52. Nagib Mahfuz, *Zuqaq al-Maddaq* (Cairo: Maktabit Misr, 1947); Ihsan 'Abd al-Quddus, *Ana Hurra*.

53. Ihsan 'Abd al-Quddus, *La tatrukuni huna wahdi* (Cairo: Ruz al-Yusuf, 1979). See also Hammad, "In the Shadows of the Middle East's Wars, Oil, and Peace."

54. Mufid, *Sayyidat Qitar al-Ghina'*, 130.

55. Suhair Iskandar, "Layla Murad wa Umm Kulthum wa al-Thuwwar al-Ahrar," *al-Wafd*, May 20, 1993.

56. Samir Gharib, "Watha'iq tunshar li-awwal marra 9: Qabas min ruh Misr," *al-Misri al-Youm*, April 24, 2009.

57. Gharib, *al-Watha'iq al-khassa li-Layla Murad*, 92.

58. Hamuda, *al-Watha'iq al-khassa bi-al-ra'is Nagib*, 20–27.

59. In a private communication, Samir Gharib told the author that Ja'far Islah bought Layla Murad's letter and many other documents from Makram Salama, one of the most prominent historical document dealers in Egypt.

60. For a personal account and good discussion on the erasure of Arab-Jewish culture and Jewish identity from Arab lands, see Reuven Snir, *Arab-Jewish Literature: The Birth and Demise of the Arabic Short Story* (Leiden: Brill, 2019), ix–xvi. For a discussion on films and visual media in particular, see Ella Shohat, *Israeli Cinema: East/West and the Politics of Representation* (Austin: University of Texas Press, 1989), and *On the Arab-Jew, Palestine, and Other Displacements: Selected Writings* (London: Pluto Press, 2017). See also Ammiel Alcalay, *After Jews and Arabs: Remaking Levantine Culture* (Minneapolis: University of Minnesota Press, 1993).

61. "Hadatha hadha al-usbu'," *al-Kawakib*, September 1, 1953, 40.

62. 'Assaf, *Ma'a al-imam al-shahid Hassan al-Banna*, 246.

63. Al-Fiqi, "'Ann qurb."

64. Of all the recent biographers of Layla Murad, Gharib is the only author who tried to consult the archives. Despite the limited number of sources Gharib excavated, his work is notably original compared to other authors, who merely plagiarize one another. Aside from Gharib, most authors have uncritically repeated what Mursi published in his *Layla Murad*. Hanan Mufid in particular did so in her book, published twice with slightly different titles and with no clarification that the second book is a reprint of the previous book with a new title.

65. Some of these interviews are available on YouTube. Examples: https://www.youtube.com/watch?v=la-XEZxoNDQ, https://www.youtube.com/watch?v=qD7L3pROyDQ, https://www.youtube.com/watch?v=Qzj5ccpwNrM, https://www.youtube.com/watch?v=HAxMFrn8iqs, https://www.youtube.com/watch?v=I6iKXAkAf2A.

66. For many examples, see 'Abd al-Fattah al-'Ajami, "Layla Murad . . . khanaha Anwar Wagdi wa sadamaha 'Abd al-Wahab wa ajbaraha Nasser 'ala al-i'tizalda," *al-Tahrir*, February 16, 2018.

67. For a comprehensive discussion of the nationalization of the film industry, see Tamara Maatouk, *Understanding the Public Sector in Egyptian Cinema: A State Venture.* Cairo Papers in Social Sciences 35, no. 3 (Cairo: American University in Cairo Press, 2019).

68. "Layla Fawzi: Film Anwar qaddkhaliduh," *al-Kawakib*, May 29, 1995.

69. "Layla Fawzi: Film Anwar qaddkhaliduh."

70. Hanan Mufid, *Sayidat qitar al-ghina'*, 103.

71. 'Abdallah Imam, *'Amir wa Berlanti* (Beirut: Dar al-Jil, 1988).

72. 'Adil 'Abd al-'Alim, "Layla Murad wa al-Mussed: Misr bara'ataha wa al-sha'i'at hakamat 'alayha," *al-Majalla*, November 24, 1987. See also Muhammad al-Shafi'i, "Layla Murad bayna al-malik wa thawrat yulyu," *al-Kawakib*, December 5, 1995, 12–13.

73. 'Abd al-'Alim, "Layla Murad wa al-Mussed"; al-Qa'id, "Hikayatan"; Nabil Sharaf al-Din, "Ya misafir wa nasi hawak: Layla Murad . . . Hudur yatahada al-zayf wa al-'agramah," *Ilaf*, January 19, 2005, http://www.elaph.com/Reports/2005/1/34947.htm.

74. *Al-Kawakib*, December 5, 2005, 4–7.

75. *Al-Ahram* published Hanan Mufid's first book as a supplemental publication with the weekly woman's magazine *Nisf al-Dunia*. The state's al-Hayy'a al-'amma lil-Kitab reproduced Mufid's material in a book in 2003.

76. For the popularity of the televised drama during Ramadan in Egypt, see Abu-Lughod, *Dramas of Nationhood*.

77. Sahar al-Miligi, "al-Opera tuhyy dhikra Layla Murad wa Muhammad Fawzi al-khamis," *al-Misri al-Youm*, November 17, 2014, https://www.almasryalyoum.com/news/details/574246.

78. Ahmad Ibrahim al-Khuli, "Rawa'i' qitharat al-ghina' Layla Murad fi ihtifaliyyat al- qawmi lil-masrah bil-hanagir," Rawafeed News, December 11, 2018, http://www.rawafeed.net/news/5233.html.

79. "'Asha Huna: Mashru' Misri litakhlid rumuz al-thaqafa wa al-siyasa," *al-Jazira*, September 18, 2018, https://www.aljazeera.net/news/cultureandart/2018/9/18/شاع-انه-مشروع-مصري-لتخليد-رومز-اتفاقثلا-والسياسة. See also http://moc.gov.eg/ar/events/التنسيق-الحضاري-ينتهي-من-تركيب-٢٠٠٠-جولة-شاع-ه-قي-الي-على-ضوع-ة-اللة-ةنجلا-ةملعلا-ةيمة/.

80. Laura Lohman, "Preservation and Politicization: Umm Kulthum's National and International Legacy", *Popular Music and Society* 33, no. 1 (2010): 45–60.

81. Armbrust, "The Golden Age before the Golden Age," 292–328.

82. Shafik, *Arab Cinema*, 131–132; Walter Armbrust, "Long Live Patriarchy: Love in the Time of 'Abd al-Wahhab," *History Compass* 7, no. 1 (2009): 251–281.

83. Shafik, *Arab Cinema*, 131–132.

84. Armbrust "The Golden Age before the Golden Age," 292–328.

85. See the interview with the fashion designer Huda al-Naggari in Mufid, *Sayyidatu al-Ghina'*, 227–232.

86. Sharaf al-Din, "Hudur yatahadda al-zayf wa al-'agrama."

87. For discussions of nostalgic representations of the pre-1952 era, see Deborah Starr, *Remembering Cosmopolitan Egypt: Literature, Culture, and Empire* (London: Routledge, 2009); and Mary Youssef, *Minorities in the Contemporary Egyptian Novel* (Edinburgh: Edinburgh University Press, 2019).

88. Hasanayn, *Ya-msafir wa nasy hawak*, 108.

89. Sharaf al-Din, "Hudur yatahadda al-zayf wa al-'agrama."

90. 'Uthman, "Layla Murad tuqaddim shrutaha"; Hilmi Salim, "I'tazalat hatta tazall najma da'iman", *al-Kawakib*, December 5, 1995, 28–29.

91. For a discussion on the Egyptian scholarship on the history of the Jews in Egypt, see Beinin, *The Dispersion of Egyptian Jewry*, 241–251.

92. Beinin, 241–244.

93. Al-'Antari, *al-Satw al-Suhyuni 'ala al-musiqa al-'Arabiya*, 7–12.

94. Ted Swedenburg, "Sa'ida Sultan / Dana International: Transgender Pop and Polysemiotics of Sex, Nation, and Ethnicity on the Israeli-Egyptian Border," in Armbrust, *Mass Mediations*, 88–119.

95. On the praise for Bahgat's book, see Hisham Lashin, "Ahmad Ra'fat Bahgat yahki qissatahum min Shalum ila Raqya Ibrahim," *al-'Aarabi*, May 22, 2005; and Muhammad al-Sisi, "Kitab jadid yafdah istighlal al-yahud lil-cinema al-Missriyya fi iqamat dawlat Israel," *al-Usbu'*, September 5, 2005. On applauding the book of al-'Antari, see 'Abd al-Raziq Fu'ad, "Kitab yasrukh fi wajh al-tatbi' al-musiqi," *al-Qahira*, May 20, 2008, 21.

96. For the debate between Farid and Bahgat, see *al-Qahira*, August 9 and 23, 2005.

97. Muhammad Abu al-Ghar, *Yahud Misr* (Cairo: Dar al-Hilal, 2004).

98. 'Arafa 'Abdu 'Ali, *Malaff al-yahud fi Misr al-haditha* (Cairo: Maktabat Madbuli, 1993); *Yahud Misr: Barunat wa bu'asa'* (Cairo: Itrak lil-Nashri wa al-Tawzi', 1997); and *Yahud Misr nundhu 'Asr al-fara'ina hatta 'amm 2000* (Cairo: al-Hayy'a al-Misriyah al-'amma lil-Kitab, 2000). He has also published five studies in *al-Hilal* magazine, one in the London-based magazine *al-Mijalh*, and a ten-episode series of articles in the Qatari newspaper *al-Sharq*.

99. Arafa 'Abdu 'Ali, *Tahwid 'aql Misr* (Cairo: Sina' lil-Nashr, 1989); *Gitu Isra'ili fi al-Qahirah* (Cairo: Maktabat Madbuli, 1990).

100. The TV serial *Zizinia* (Gamal 'Abd al-Hamid, 1997–2000) is another good example. Nadia Kamel's documentary *Salata Baladi* (2008) provides nuanced social and personal history of the filmmaker's interfaith family. After the fall of Mubarak's regime, Amir Ramsis made a two-part documentary, *'An Yahud Misr* (*On the Jews of Egypt*, 2013, 2014).

101. The best example is the soap opera *'Awalim Khafiyya* (*Hidden World*), which aired on television during Ramadan 2018 and features superstar 'Adil Imam.

102. "Egypt's Sisi acknowledges close coordination with Israel in Sinai," Reuters, January 6, 2019, https://www.reuters.com/article/us-egypt-sisi-usa-idUSKCN1P101X.

103. Ahmad al-Samahi, "Nujum wa funun tuzih al-sitar 'ann ughniya nadira li Layla Murad," *al-Ahram*, October 5, 2013.

104. https://www.youtube.com/watch?v=J9tP22Kz4Rk.

105. 'Amr Fahmi, "Fi dhikra ma'awiyyat milad Layla Murad," *al-Akhbar*, February 21, 2018, 2.

106. https://www.youtube.com/watch?v=W3afWwRoMeE.

107. Ahmad al-Naggar, *Layla Bint Misr* (Cairo: al-Jam'iyya al-Missriyya li-Kuttab wa Nuqqad al-Cinema, 2018), 19.

108. Al-Naggar, 10, 36, 39.

Conclusion: Can an Egyptian Be a Single Mother and a Jew?

1. "Al-qiyada al-'amma lil quwwat al-musallaha tubari' Layla Murad."

2. For the discussion on the relationship between the Nasserist regime and Egyptian intellectuals, see Mustafa 'Abd al-Ghani, *al-Muthaqqafun wa 'Abd al-Nasser* (Cairo: Kutub 'Arabiya, 2007); and Ghali Shukri, *al-Muthaqqafun wa al-sulta fi Misr* (Cairo: Akhbar al-Yum, 1990).

3. Shahata Harun, *Yahudi fi al-Qahira* (Cairo: Dar al-thaqafa al-haditha, 1987).

4. Harun, 10–14.

5. Harun, 11.

6. Harun, 12.

7. Harun, 37–47.

8. Salah Hafiz, "Shihata Harun: Arfud surat al-yahudi al-ta'ih," *Ruz al-Yusuf*, March 2, 1975. See also Harun, 37–47.

9. Ahmad Bilal, "Magda Harun Ra'is al-ta'fa al-yahudyya fi hiwar ma'a al-Masry al-Youm", *al-Masry al-Youm*, August 25, 2016, https://www.almasryalyoum.com/news/details/999437. See also Ahmad Bilal, "Magda Harun Ra'isat al-ta'fa al-yahudyya: Ana bint abuya wa lann usafir ila Israel", *al-Masry al-Youm*, July 15, 2013, https://www.almasryalyoum.com/news/details/236017.

10. Saba Mahmood, *Religious Difference in a Secular Age: A Minority Report* (Princeton, NJ: Princeton University Press, 2015), 1.

11. Mahmood, 2.

12. Samya 'Allam, "Haqq Dayala . . . Missriyyat yukafihna li-ithbat nasab atfalihin," *Rasif 22*, March 21, 2019, https://raseef22.com/article/1072620 حق-الديـة-مصريـات-يكافحـن-لإثبـات-نسـب-أطفالهن

13. For details of the case, see Nihad Suliha, *al-Mar'a bayna al-fann wa al-'ishq wa al-zawaj: Qira'a fi mudhakkarat Fatima Sirri* (Cairo: Dar al-'ayn, 2008), 13–76.

14. *Fatima* (Ahmad Badrakhan, 1947). The founder of *Akhbar al-Yum*, journalist Mustafa Amin, wrote the story for *Fatima*.

15. "Ahmad Fishawi admits to having an illicit affair with Hind Al Hinawi," *albawaba*, March 13, 2005, https://www.albawaba.com/entertainment/

ahmad-fishawi-admits-having-illicit-affair-hind-al-hinawi; "Ihtimam gharbi biqa-
diyyat Ahmad al-Fishawi wa Hind al-Hinnawi," *albawaba*, January 28, 2006, https://
www.albawaba.com/ar/ترفيه/اهتمام-غربي-بقضية-احمد-ألفيشاوي-وهند-الحناوي.

16. "Haqq Diyala . . . al-tafasil al-kamila liqadiyyat ithbat al-nasab bayna ʿAdel el-
Siwi wa sahafiyya shabba," *al-Dostor*, July 10, 2018, https://www.dostor.org/2244298?fb
clid=IwAR0KdYyoEdqLbzo43sWtqMoQ1Cm25CXmmz7IYNOhip4VJ58pDVOCbh
PQ6jo.

Bibliography

Layla Murad's Filmography in Chronological Order

(English titles as given in IMDb where available)

al-Dahaya (*The Victims*; Ibrahim Lama and Bahiga Hafiz, 1935)

Yahya al-Hub (*Long Live Love*; Muhammad Karim, 1938)

Laylah Mumtira (*Stormy Night*; Togo Mizrahi, 1939)

Layla Bint al-Rif (*Leila, the Girl from the Country*; Togo Mizrahi, 1941)

Layla Bint Madaris (*Leila, the Schoolgirl*; Togo Mizrahi, 1941)

Layla (*Laila*; Togo Mizrahi, 1942)

Layla fi al-Zalam (*Laila in the Shadows*; Togo Mizrahi, 1944)

Shuhada' al-Gharam (*Victims of Love*; Kamal Salim, 1944)

Layla Bint al-Fuqara' (*Leila, Daughter of the Poor*; Anwar Wagdi, 1945)

al-Madi al-Maghul (*The Forgotten Past*; Ahmad Salim, 1946)

Layla Bint al-Aghnya' (*Leila the Rich Girl*; Anwar Wagdi, 1946)

Darbat al-Qadar (*The Blow of Fate*; Yusuf Wahbi, 1947)

Khatim Sulaymun (*Solomon's Ring*; Hassan Ramzi, 1947)

Qalbi Dalili (*My Heart Guides Me*; Anwar Wagdi, 1947)

Shadiyat al-Wadi (*The Singer in the Valley*; Yusuf Wahbi, 1947)

al-Hawa wa al-Shabab (*Love and Youth*; Niyazi Mustafa, 1948)

'Anbar (*Anbar*; Anwar Wagdi, 1948)

al-Magnuna (*The Crazy Girl*; Hilmi Rafla, 1949)

Ghazal al-Banat (*The Flirtation of Girls*; Anwar Wagdi, 1949)

Shati' al-Gharam (*The Shores of Love*; Henry Barakat, 1950)

Adam wa Hawwa' (*Adam and Eve*; Husain Sidqi, 1951)

Habib al-Ruh (*Eternal Love*; Anwar Wagdi, 1951)
Ward al-Gharam (*Flowers of Love*; Henry Barakat, 1951)
Min al-Qalb lil-Qalb (*From One Heart to Another*; Henry Barakat, 1952)
Sayyidat al-Qitar (*Lady of the Train*; Yousuf Shahin, 1952)
Bint al-Akabir (*Daughter of the Nobility*; Anwar Wagdi, 1953)
al-Haya al-Hub (*Life Is Love*; Sayf al-Din Shawkat, 1954)
al-Habib al-Maghul (*The Unknown Lover*; Hassan al-Sayfi, 1955)

Films Not Featuring Layla Murad
(in chronological order)

Barsum yabhath 'an wazifa (*Barsum Is Looking for a Job*; Muhammad Bayumi, 1923)
Laila (*Laila*; 'Aziza Amir or Wedad Orfi, 1927)
al-Kukayyin, al-Hawiya (*Cocaine, the Abyss*; Togo Mizrahi, 1930)
Awlad Misr (*Children of Egypt*; Togo Mizrahi, 1930)
Zeinab (*Zeinab*; Muhammad Karim, 1930)
Awlad al-Dhawat (*Sons of Aristocrats*; Muhammad Karim, 1932)
Unshudat al-Fu'ad (*Song of the Heart*; Mario Volpe, 1932)
al-Warda al-Bayda' (*The White Rose*; Muhammad Karim, 1933)
'Uyun Sahira (*Bewitching Eyes*; Ahmad Galal, 1934)
Dumu' al-Hub (*Tears of Love*; Muhammad Karim, 1935)
Chalom al-turgaman (*Chalom the Dragoman*; Leon Angel "Chalom," 1935(
Widad (*Wedad*; Fritz Kramp, 1936)
Zawja bil-Niyaba (*Wife in Waiting*; Ahmad Galal, 1936)
Nashid al-Amal (*The Chant of Hope*; Ahmed Badrakhan, 1937)
Salama fi Kheir (*Salama Is Safe*; Niyazi Mustafa, 1937)
Yum Sa'id (*A Happy Day*; Muhammad Karim, 1940)
Intisar al-Shabab (*Victory of Youth*; Ahmad Badrakhan, 1941)
Mamnu' al-Hub (*Love Is Forbidden*; Muhammad Karim, 1942)
Gawhara (*Gawhara*; Yusuf Wahbi, 1943)
Rusasa fi al-Qalb (*A Bullet in the Heart*; Muhammad Karim, 1944)
Berlanti (*Berlanti*; Yusuf Wahbi, 1944)
al-Qalb luh Wahid (*The Heart Has Its Reasons*; Henry Barakat, 1945)
Lu'bat al-Sitt (*The Lady's Puppet*; Wali al-Din Samih, 1946)
Fatima (*Fatima*; Ahmad Badrakhan, 1947)
al-Batal (*The Champion*; Hilmi Raflah, 1950)
Ana wa Habiby (*My Lover and I*; Kamil al-Tilmisani, 1953)
Al-Zulm Haram (*Injustice Is a Sin*; Hassan al-Sayfi, 1954)
Khataf Mirati (*He Stole My Wife*; Hassan al-Sayfi, 1954)
Allahu ma'ana (*God Is on Our Side*; Ahmad Badrakhan, 1955)

Inni Rahila (*Tragic Departure*; 'Izz al-Din Dhu al-Faqqar, 1955)
Darb al-Mahabil (*Fools' Alley*; Tawfiq Salih, 1955)
Shayatin al-Gaw (*Air Devils*; Niyazi Mustafa, 1956)
Ard al-Salam (Kamal al-Shaykh, 1957)
Port Said ('Izz al-Din Dhu al-Faqqar, 1957)
Rudda Qalb (*My Heart Is Returned*; 'Izz al-Din Dhu al-Faqqar, 1957)
Tariq al-Dumu' (*The Way of Tears*; Hilmi Halim, 1961)
Risala Ila Allah (Kamal 'Atiyya, 1961)
Imra'a 'Ala al-Hamish (*A Woman on the Outside*; Hassan al-Imam, 1963)

Recordings and Audio on YouTube

(all accessed 10/18/21)

Israel tatabaha bi-tasjil nadir jiddan li-Layla Murad; https://www.youtube.com/watch?v=XSLMJe8e7sI

Liqa' nadir ma'a Layla Murad wa Baligh Hamdi wa Samira Said; https://www.youtube.com/watch?v=xsqMd7C5osU

Layla Murad- liqa' idha'i; https://www.youtube.com/watch?v=fn74hlt4sW4

Sanatayn wa ana ahayil fik+ layh khalitni ahibak-'Abd al-Halim wa Layla Murad 1956; https://www.youtube.com/watch?v=SXM5dgYoOmE

Al-Mawhubun fi al-ard ma'a Bilal Fadl/ halqa 3/ Fatin Hamama juz' 1; https://www.youtube.com/watch?v=6MSohtXXt2U

Al-Katib Ashraf Gharib: Layla Murad ujbirat 'ala al-i'tizal wa hadhihi tafasil azmat al-fannan Muhammad Fawzi ma'a 'Abd al-Nasir; https://www.youtube.com/watch?v=qD7L3pROyDQ

Al-Katib al-sahafi Ashraf Gharib . . . radio Sawt al-'Arab . . . Layla Murad ujbirat 'ala al-i'tizal; https://www.youtube.com/watch?v=Qzj5ccpwNrM

Hadha al-sabah: al-katib al-sahafi Ashraf Gharib yahki qissat Islam Layla Murad; https://www.youtube.com/watch?v=HAxMFrn8iqs

al-Naqid al-sinima'i Ashraf Gharib wa sahra khasa fi dhikra al-fannana Layla Murad . . . al-juz' al-thalith . . . al-Kahira al-Yum; https://www.youtube.com/watch?v=I6iKXAkAf2A

'Isam Talima yakshif li-awal marra limadha a'lanat Layla Murad islamaha 'ala yad al-Imam Hassan al-Banna; https://www.youtube.com/watch?v=p2kObOJ36eY

Al-Naqid al-Fanni Ashraf Gharib yanfi Islam "Layla Murad" 'ala yad Hassan al-Banna; https://www.youtube.com/watch?v=QTUPbkme4AI

Al-Musallimani yakshif haqiqat 'alaqit Layla Murad bi- Hassan al-Banna; https://www.youtube.com/watch?v=W41CkvJd1-A

Periodicals

(all based in Egypt unless noted otherwise)

al-Ahad (Lebanon)
Ahl al-Fann
al-Ahram
Akhbar al-Yum
Akhir Sa'a
al-'Amal
al-'Arabi
al-'Arusa
al-Dostor
Dunya al-Kawakib
al-Fann
al-Hilal
al-Idha'a wa al-Tiliviziun
al-Idha'a
al-Ithnayn
Al-Ithnayn: al-Fukaha was al-Kawakib
al-Ithnayn wa al-Dunya
al- Ithnayn wa al-Kawakib
al-Jil
al-Jumhuriyya
al-Kawakib
al-Masa'
al-Maw'id (Beirut)
al-Mijalh (London)
al-Misbah
al-Misri al-Youm
Musamarat al-Gib
al-Musawar
An-Nahar (Beirut)
Nisf al-Dunia
al-Qahira
Ruz al-Yusuf
al-Sabah
Sayyidati (London)
al-Shabaka (Beirut)
al-Sharq (Doha)
al-Studio
al-Tahrir

al-Usbu'
al-Wafd

Published Works

al-'Abd, 'Atif. *al-Radio wa al-tilivision fi Misr*. Cairo: Dar al-fikr al-'Arabi, 1987.

'Abd al-Ghani, Mustafa. *al-Muthaqqafun wa 'Abd al-Nasser*. Cairo: Kutub 'Arabiya, 2007.

'Abdallah, 'Abdallah Ahmad. *'Alam Miki Mouse*. Cairo: Dar al-ta'wun lil-tab' wa al-nashr, 1997.

'Abd al-Quddus, Ihsan. *Ana Hurra*. Cairo: Maktabit Misr, 1954.

———. *La tatrukuni huna wahdi*. Cairo: Ruz al-Yusuf, 1979.

'Abd al-Rahman, 'Abd al-Mu'izz. *al-Thawra al-thqafiyya fi 11 'aman*. Cairo: Matabi' al-dar al-qawmiyya, 1963.

Abdelfattah, Heba Saad Arafa. "Dreams of Alternative Modernities on the Nile." PhD diss., Georgetown University, 2016.

Abu al-'Aynayn, Sa'id. *al-Sha'rawi wa al-Fannanat: Asrar liqat'at al-hidaya wa hijab al-Milyun dollar*. Cairo: Dar Akhbar al-Yum, 1999.

Abu al-Ghar, Muhammad. *Yahud Misr*. Cairo: Dar al-Hilal, 2004.

Abu-Lughod, Lila. *Dramas of Nationhood: The Politics of Television in Egypt*. Chicago: University of Chicago Press, 2005.

Aburish, Saïd K. *Nasser, the Last Arab: A Biography*. New York: Thomas Dunne Books, 2004.

Abu Shadi, 'Ali. *Waqa'i' al-Cinema al-Missriyya fi ma'at 'amm 1896–1995*. Cairo: al-Majlis al-a'la lil-thaqafa, 1996.

Abu Zahra, Muhammad. *al-Ahwal al-shakhsiyya*. 3rd ed. Cairo: Dar al-fikr al-'Arabi, 1957.

Ackroyd, Peter. *London: The Biography*. London: Chatto & Windus, 2000.

Alcalay, Ammiel. *After Jews and Arabs: Remaking Levantine Culture*. Minneapolis: University of Minnesota Press, 1993.

'Ali, 'Arafa 'Abdu. *Gitu Isra'ili fi al-Qahirah*. Cairo: Maktabat Madbuli, 1990.

———. *Malaff al-yahud fi Misr al-haditha*. Cairo: Maktabat Madbuli, 1993.

———. *Tahwid 'aql Misr*. Cairo: Sina' lil-Nashr, 1989.

———. *Yahud Misr Barunat wa Bu'asa'*. Cairo: Itrak lil-Nashri wa al-Tawzi', 1997.

———. "Yahud Misr mina al-indimaj ila al-hijra." *al-Hilal*, May 1990.

———. *Yahud Misr nundhu 'Asr al-fara'ina hatta 'amm 2000*. Cairo: al-Hayy'a al-Misriyah al-'amma lil-Kitab, 2000.

'Ali, Mahmud. *Dirasat fi tarikh al-cinema al-Missriyya*. Cairo: al-Hayy'a al-'amma li-qusur al-thaqafa, 2012.

———. *50 sana cinema: Mudhakkarat Muhammad Karim*. 2 vols. Cairo: Kitab al-Idha'a wa al-Televizion, 1972.

Alon, Liat Maggid. "The Jewish Bourgeoisie of Egypt in the First Half of the Twentieth Century: Modernity, Socio-cultural Practice and Oral Testimonials." *Jama'a* 24 (2019): 31.

al-'Antari, Faraj. *al-Satw al-Suhyuni 'ala al-musiqa al-'Arabiya*. 2nd ed. Cairo: Dar al-Kalimah, 2000.

'Arifa, Al-Tahir al-Mahdi bin. *al-Jami'a al-'Arabiya wa al-'amal al-'Arabi al-mushtarak 1945–2000*. Amman: Zahran lil nashr, 2011.

Armbrust, Walter. "The Golden Age before the Golden Age: Commercial Egyptian Cinema before the 1960s." In Armbrust, *Mass Mediations*, 292–328.

———. "Long Live Patriarchy: Love in the Time of 'Abd al-Wahhab." *History Compass* 7, no. 1 (2009): 251–281.

———. *Mass Culture and Modernism in Egypt*. Cambridge: Cambridge University Press, 1996.

———, ed. *Mass Mediations: New Approaches to Popular Culture in the Middle East and Beyond*. Berkeley: University of California Press, 2000.

'Assaf, Mahmud. *Ma'a al-imam al-shahid Hassan al-Banna*. Cairo: Maktabit 'Ayn Shams, 1993.

el-Aswad, El-Sayed. "Thaqafat al-satr wa dilalatiha al-ramziyya fi al-hayya al-sha'biyya al-'Arabiya." *al-Ma'thurat al-Sha'biyya* 19 (2004): 8–27.

'Atta, Zubaida Muhammad. *Yahud Misr: al-Tarikh al-ijtima'i wa al-iqtisadi*. Cairo: 'Ayn lildirasat wa al-buhuth al-insaniyya wa al-ijtima'iyya, 2011.

'Awad, Luwis. *Awraq al-'umr*. Cairo: Maktabat Madbuli, 1989.

Badr, Jihan Ahmad al-Nasser. "Layla Murad wa al-ughniya al-cinema'iyya al-Missriyya." MA thesis, Academy of Arts, Higher Institute of Arab Music, 2005.

Baer, Marc. "Islamic Conversion Narratives of Women: Social Change and Gendered Religious Hierarchy in Early Modern Ottoman Istanbul." *Gender & History* 16, no. 2 (2004): 425–458.

Bahgat, Ahmad Ra'fat. *al-Yahud wa al-cinema fi Misr: Dirasa tahlilya tughati kafat anshitat al-cinema min bidayat al-Qarn al-'Ishrin*. Cairo: Sharitkat al-Qasr lil-Tiba'a wa al-Di'aya, 2005.

al-Bakri, Muhammad 'Azmi. *Mawsu'at al-fiqh wa al-qada' fi al-ahwal al-shakhsiyya*. Vol. 6. Cairo: Dar Mahmud lil-nashr wal-tawzi', 2004.

Baron, Beth. *Egypt as a Woman: Nationalism, Gender, and Politics*. Berkeley: University of California Press, 2005.

al-Bazz, Muhammad. *Sahafat al-ithara: al-Siyasa wa al-din wa al-jins fi al-suhuf al-Missriyya*. Cairo: Maktabat jazirat al-ward, 2010.

Beinin, Joel. *The Dispersion of Egyptian Jewry: Culture, Politics, and the Formation of a Modern Diaspora*. Berkeley: University of California Press, 1998.

———. "Nazis and Spies: Representations of Jewish Espionage and Terrorism in Egypt." *Jewish Social Studies*, n.s., 2, no. 3 (1996): 54–84.

Bier, Laura. *Revolutionary Womanhood: Feminisms, Modernity, and the State in Nasser's Egypt*. Stanford, CA: Stanford University Press, 2011.

Botman, Selma. *Engendering Citizenship in Egypt*. New York: Columbia University Press, 1999.

Brinton, Jacquelene G. *Preaching Islamic Renewal: Religious Authority and Media in Contemporary Egypt*. Oakland: University of California Press, 2016.

Caine, Barbra. *Biography and History*. London: Palgrave Macmillan, 2010.

Coates, Jennifer. *Making Icons: Repetition and the Female Image in Japanese Cinema, 1945–1964*. Hong Kong: Hong Kong University Press, 2016.

Cohen, Amnon. *Jewish Life under Islam: Jerusalem in the Sixteenth Century*. Cambridge, MA: Harvard University Press, 1984.

Danielson, Virginia. "Layla Murad." *Middle East Studies Association Bulletin* 30, no. 1 (July 1996): 143–145.

———. Review of *Women of Egypt 1924–1931: Pioneers of Stardom and Fame*. Compilation and text by Amira Mitchell, British Library Topic World Series TSCD931, 2006. *Asian Music* 41, no. 1 (2010): 179–181.

———. *The Voice of Egypt: Umm Kulthum, Arabic Song, and Egyptian Society in the Twentieth Century*. Chicago: University of Chicago Press, 1997.

Darwish, Mustafa. *Dream Makers on the Nile: A Portrait of Egyptian Cinema*. Cairo: American University in Cairo Press, 1998.

Dickinson, Kay. "'I Have One Daughter and That Is Egyptian Cinema': 'Aziza Amir amid the Histories and Geographies of National Allegory." *Camera Obscura*, no. 64 (2007).

Dougherty, Roberta L. "Badi'a Masabni, Artiste and Modernist: The Egyptian Print Media's Carnival of National Identity." In Armbrust, *Mass Mediations*, 243–267.

Durgnat, Raymond. *Films and Feelings*. Cambridge, MA: MIT Press, 1971.

Duru, Deniz Neriman. "Memory, Conviviality, and Coexistence: Negotiating Class Differences in Burgazadasi, Istanbul." In *Post-Ottoman Coexistence: Sharing Space in the Shadow of Conflict*, edited by Rebecca Bryant, 157–179. New York: Berghahn Books, 2016.

el-Grittly, Ali. *The Structure of Modern Industry in Egypt*. Cairo: Government Press, 1948.

Elvira, Laura Ruiz de, Christoph H. Schwarz, and Irene Weipert-Fenner, eds. *Clientelism and Patronage in the Middle East and North Africa: Networks of Dependency*. New York: Routledge, 2019.

Elsaket, Ifdal. "The Star of the East: Umm Kulthum and Egyptian Cinema." In *Stars in World Cinema: Screen Icons and Star Systems across Cultures*, edited by Andrea Bandhauer and Michelle Royer, 36–50. London: I. B. Tauris, 2015.

Ener, Mine. *Managing Egypt's Poor and the Politics of Benevolence, 1800–1952*. Princeton, NJ: Princeton University Press, 2003.

Epple, Angelika, and Angelika Schaser. *Gendering Historiography: Beyond National Canons*. Chicago: University of Chicago Press, 2009.

Fahmy, Ziad. *Street Sounds: Listening to Everyday Life in Modern Egypt*. Stanford, CA: Stanford University Press, 2020.

Farid, Samir. *Tarikh al-riqaba 'ala al-cinema fi Misr*. Cairo: al-Maktab al-Misri lit-awzi' al-matbu'at, 2002.

Farrag, Yasmin. *al-Ghina' wal-siyasa fi tarikh Misr*. Cairo: Dar Nahdet Misr lil-nashr, 2014.

al-Gamal, Maysa. *al-Nukhba al-Siyasiyya fi Misr: dirasat halat al-nukhba al-wizariyya*. Cairo: Markaz dirasat al-wihda al-'Arabiya, 1998.

Gershoni, Israel, and James Jankowski. *Confronting Fascism in Egypt: Dictatorship versus Democracy in the 1930s*. Stanford, CA: Stanford University Press, 2009.

Ghandur, Mona. *Sultanat al-Shasha: Ra'idat al-cinema al-Missriyya*. Beirut: Dar Riyad al-Rayis lil-kutub wal-nashr, 2005.

Gharib, Ashraf. *al-Watha'iq al-khassa li-Layla Murad*. Cairo: Dar al-Shuruq, 2016.

Giovannucci, Perri. *Literature and Development in North Africa: The Modernizing Mission*. London: Routledge, 2008.

Gordon, Joel. "Film, Fame, and Public Memory: Egyptian Biopics from Mustafa Kamil to Nasser 56." *International Journal of Middle East Studies* 31, no. 1 (1999): 61–79.

———. *Nasser's Blessed Movement: Egypt's Free Officers and the July Revolution*. Oxford: Oxford University Press, 1992.

———. *Revolutionary Melodrama: Popular Film and Civic Identity in Nasser's Egypt*. Chicago: University of Chicago Press, 2002.

Hadidi, Hajir. *Zar: Spirit Possession, Music, and Healing Rituals in Egypt*. Cairo: American University in Cairo Press, 2016.

al-Halawani, Magi, and 'Atif al-'Abd. *al-Andhima al-idha'iya fi al-duwal al-'Arabiya*. Cairo: Dar al-fikr al-'Arabi, 1987.

Hall, Stuart. "Coding and Encoding in the Television Discourse." In *Culture, Media, Language*, edited by Stuart Hall et al., 128–138. London: Hutchinson, 1980.

Hammad, Hanan. *Industrial Sexuality: Gender, Urbanization, and Social Transformation in Egypt*. Austin: University of Texas Press, 2016.

———. "In the Shadows of the Middle East's Wars, Oil, and Peace: The Construction of Female Desires and Lesbianism in Middlebrow Egyptian Literature." *Journal of Arab Literature* 50 (2019): 148–172.

———. "The Iranian Revolution in the Egyptian Press." MA thesis, University of Texas at Austin, 2004.

Hamrush, Ahmad. *Qissat thawrat 23 Yulu: Shuhud thawrat Yulu*. Cairo: Maktabat Madbuli, 1984.

Hamuda, 'Adil. *al-Watha'iq al-khassa bil-Ra'is Nagib*. Cairo: Ruz al-Yusuf, 1977.

Hansen, Miriam. "The Mass Production of the Senses: Classical Cinema as Vernacular Modernism." *Modernism/Modernity* 6, no. 2 (1999): 59–77.

Harun, Shahata. *Yahudi fi al-Qahira.* Cairo: Dar al-thaqafa al-haditha, 1987.

Hasanayn, 'Adil. *Layla Murad: Ya-msafir wa nasi hawak.* Cairo: Amadu, 1993.

Hassan, Ilhami. *Dirasa mukhtasara 'an Tarikh al-cinema al-Missriyya.* Cairo: al-
Hayy'a al-'amma lil-kitab, 1976.

Hatem, Mervat F. "Economic and Political Liberation in Egypt and the Demise of
State Feminism." *International Journal of Middle East Studies* 24 (1992): 231–251.

Hess, Tamar S. *Self as Nation: Contemporary Hebrew Autobiography.* Waltham, MA:
Brandeis University Press, 2016.

Hillauer, Rebecca. *The Encyclopedia of Arab Women Filmmakers.* Translated by Nancy
Joyce, Deborah Cohen, and Allison Brown. Cairo: American University in
Cairo, 2005.

Ibrahim, Munir Muhammad. *al-Cinema al-Missriyya fi al-thalathinat: 1930–1939.*
Cairo: Sunduq al-tanmiyya al-thaqafiyya, 2002.

Imam, 'Abdallah. *'Amir wa Berlanti.* Beirut: Dar al-Jil, 1988.

———. *Wagih Abaza: Safahat min al-nidal al-watani.* Cairo: 'Arabiya lil-tiba'a wal-
nashr, 1995.

Jacob, Wilson Chacko. *Working Out Egypt: Affendi Masculinity and Subject Formation
in Colonial Modernity, 1870–1940.* Durham, NC: Duke University Press, 2011.

Jami', Mahmud. *Wa 'araftu al-Sha'rawi.* Cairo: Dar al-Tawzi' wa al-Nashr al-
Islamiyya, 2005.

Jawhariyyeh, Wasif. *The Storyteller of Jerusalem: The Life and Times of Wasif Jawhariyyeh, 1904–1948.* Edited and introduced by Salim Tamari and Issam Nassar;
translated by Nada Elzeer. Northampton, MA: Olive Branch Press, 2014.

Joseph, Suad. "Gendering Citizenship in the Middle East." In *Gender and Citizenship in the Middle East,* edited by Joseph, 3–30. Syracuse, NY: Syracuse
University Press, 2000.

Kandil, Hazem. *Soldiers, Spies, and Statesmen: Egypt's Road to Revolt.* London: Verso,
2013.

Kazim, Safi Naz. *San'at latfa.* Cairo: Dar al-'Ayn lil-Nashr, 2007.

Kholousy, Hanan. "Interfaith Unions and Non-Muslim Wives in Early Twentieth-
Century Alexandrian Islamic Courts." In *Untold Histories of the Middle East:
Recovering Voices from the 19th and 20th Centuries,* edited by Amy Singer, Chris-
toph Neumann, and Selcuk Aksin Somel, 54–70. New York: Routledge, 2010.

Landau, Jacob. *Studies in the Arab Theater and Cinema.* Philadelphia: University of
Pennsylvania Press, 1958.

Lohman, Laura. "Preservation and Politicization: Umm Kulthum's National and International Legacy." *Popular Music and Society* 33, no. 1 (2010): 45–60.

Lopez, Shaun T. "Madams, Murders, and the Media: Akhbar al-Hawadith and the Emergence of a Mass Culture in 1920s Egypt." In *Re-envisioning Egypt 1919–1952*, edited by Arthur Goldschmidt, Jr., Arthur Goldschmidt, and Amy J. Johnson, 371–397. Cairo: American University in Cairo Press, 2005.

———. "The Dangers of Dancing: The Media and Morality in 1930s Egypt." *Comparative Studies of South Asia, Africa, and the Middle East*24, no. 1 (2004): 97–105.

Lowenthal, David. *The Past Is a Foreign Country*. Cambridge: Cambridge University Press, 1985.

Lutz, Helma, Maria Teresa Herrera Vivar, and Linda Supik. *Framing Intersectionality: Debates on a Multi-faceted Concept in Gender Studies*. Farnham, UK: Ashgate, 2011.

Maatouk, Tamara. *Understanding the Public Sector in Egyptian Cinema: A State Venture*. Cairo Papers in Social Sciences 35, no. 3. Cairo: American University in Cairo Press, 2019.

Mahfuz, Nagib. *Zuqaq al-Maddaq*. Cairo: Maktabit Misr, 1947.

Mahmood, Saba. *Religious Difference in a Secular Age: A Minority Report*. Princeton, NJ: Princeton University Press, 2015.

al-Manfaluti, Mustafa Lutfi. *Al-Nazarat*. Vol. 1. Cairo: Matba't al-ma'arif, 1910.

Marcus, Sharon. *The Drama of Celebrity*. Princeton, NJ: Princeton University Press, 2019.

Marsot, Afaf Lutfi al-Sayyid. *A Short History of Modern Egypt*. Cambridge: Cambridge University Press, 1985.

Martin, Kevin W. *Syria's Democratic Years: Citizens, Experts, and Media in the 1950s*. Bloomington: Indiana University Press, 2015.

Mazor, Yair. *Somber Lust: The Art of Amos Oz*. Albany: SUNY Press, 2002.

McDonnell, Andrea. *Reading Celebrity Gossip Magazines*. Cambridge, UK: Polity Press, 2014.

Meital, Yoram. *Revolutionary Justice: Special Courts and the Formation of Republican Egypt*. Oxford: Oxford University Press, 2016.

Merrill, Barbara, and Linden West. *Using Biographical Methods in Social Research*. London: SAGE Publications, 2009.

Meshal, Reem A. *Sharia and the Making of the Modern Egyptian: Islamic Law and Custom in the Courts of Ottoman Cairo*. Cairo: American University in Cairo Press, 2014.

Mitchell, Amira. *Women of Egypt 1924–1931: Pioneers of Stardom and Fame*. British Library Topic World Series TSCD931. 2006.

Mostafa, Dalia Said. *The Egyptian Military in Popular Culture: Context and Critique*. London: Palgrave Macmillan, 2016.

Mufid, Hanan. *Ana Zay Ma Ana wa Inta Bititghayyar: Layla Murad*. Cairo: Afaq lil-Nashr wa al-Tawzi', 2009.

———. *Layla Murad: Sayyidat qitar al-ghina'*. Cairo: al-Hayy'a al-Missriyya al-'amma lil-kitab, 2003.

al-Muhami, Muhammad Rif'at. *Mudhakirat musiqar al-jil Muhammad 'Abd al-Wahab kama yarwiha binafsih*. 2nd ed. Beirut: Mu'ssassat 'Izz al-Din lil-Tiba 'at wal-Nashr, 1990.

Mursi, Salih. *Layla Murad*. Cairo: Dar al-Hilal, 1995.

al-Naggar, Ahmad. *Layla Bint Misr*. Cairo: al-Jami'yya al-Missriyya li-Kuttab wa Nuqqad al-Cinema, 2018.

al-Najmi, Kamal. *Aswat wa-alhan 'Arabiya*. Cairo: Dar al-Hilal, 1968.

———. *al-Ghina' al-Misri*. Cairo: Dar al-Hilal, 1966.

———. *Mutribun wa mustami'un*. Cairo: Dar al-Hilal, 1993.

———. *Sihr al-ghina'al-'Arabi*. Cairo: Dar al-Hilal, 1972.

———. *Turath al-ghina' al-'Arabi*. Cairo: al-Hayy'a al-'amma lil-kitab, 1998.

Nasaw, David. "AHR Roundtable Historians and Biography: Introduction." *American Historical Review* 114, no. 3 (2009): 573–578.

al-Nashashibi, Nasser al-Din. *Qissati ma'a al-Sahafa*. (n.p.), 1983.

Nasir, Jamal J. *The Islamic Law of Personal Status*. London: Graham & Trotman, 1990.

Nicholas, Bill. *Introduction to Documentary*. Bloomington: Indiana University Press, 2001.

Ollman, Bertell. *Dance of the Dialectic: Steps in Marx's Method*. Urbana: University of Illinois Press, 2003.

al-Qashshashi, 'Abd al-Shafi. *Ashshhar al-nujum wa al-kawakib amama al-adwa' wa khalfa al- kamira*. Cairo: Majalatu al-Fann, 1969.

Radwan, Lutfi, ed. *Muhammad Abd al-Wahab: Sira dhatiyya*. Cairo: Dar al-Hilal, 1991.

Reynolds, Nancy. *A City Consumed: Urban Commerce, the Cairo Fire, and the Politics of Decolonization in Egypt*. Stanford, CA: Stanford University Press, 2012.

Russel, Mona. *Creating the New Woman: Consumerism, Education and National Identity, 1863–1922*. New York: Palgrave Macmillan, 2004.

Ryzova, Lucie. *The Age of the Effendiyya: Passages to Modernity in National-Colonial Egypt*. Oxford: Oxford University Press, 2014.

Sabat, Khalil. *Wasa'il al-itisal: Nash'atuha wa tatawuruha*. 4th ed. Cairo: Al-Anglu al-Missriyya, 1985.

al-Sabban, Rafiq. *Layla Murad: Awwal Cinderella fi al-cinema al-Missriyya*. Cairo: Matbu'at mihragan al-kahira al-sinima'i al-dawli al-sadis 'ashar, 1992.

al-Sa'di, al-Nabigha. *Nujum amam al-qada'*. Cairo: al-Sharika al-Missriyya li-fann al-tiba'a, 1975.

al-Sahhar, 'Abd al-Hamid Guda. *Dhikrayat sinima'iyya*. Cairo: Maktabit Misr, 1975.

Salamandra, Christa. "Consuming Damascus: Popular Culture and the Construction of Social Identity." In Armbrust, *Mass Mediations*, 182–202.

Salem, Sara. "White Innocence as a Feminist Discourse: Intersectionality, Trump, and Performances of 'Shock' in Contemporary Politics." In *Antagonizing White Feminism: Intersectionality's Critique of Women's Studies and the Academy*, edited by Noelle Chaddock and Beth Hinterliter, 47–69. New York: Lexington Books, 2019.

Schatz, Thomas. *Hollywood Genres: Formulas, Filmmaking, and the Studio System*. New York: Random House, 1981.

Shafik, Viola. *Arab Cinema: History and Cultural Identity*. Cairo: American University in Cairo Press, 1998.

———. "Egypt: Cinema and Society." In *African Filmmaking: Five Formations*, edited by Kenneth Harrow, 117–174. East Lansing: Michigan State University Press, 2017.

———. "Egyptian Cinema: Hollywood on the Nile." Oxford Islamic Studies Online, http://www.oxfordislamicstudies.com/article/opr/t343/e0209.

———. *Popular Egyptian Cinema: Gender, Class, and Nation*. Cairo: American University in Cairo Press, 2007.

El-Shammaa, Magdy Mounir. "Shadows of Contemporary Lives: Modernity, Culture, and National Identity in Egyptian Filmmaking." PhD diss., UCLA, 2007.

Shohat, Ella. *Israeli Cinema: East/West and the Politics of Representation*. Austin: University of Texas Press, 1989.

———. *On the Arab-Jew, Palestine, and Other Displacements: Selected Writings*. London: Pluto Press, 2017.

Shukri, Ghali. *al-Muthaqqafun wa al-sulta fi Misr*. Cairo: Dar Akhbar al-Yum, 1990.

Shusha, Muhammad al-Sayyid. *Layla Murad: al-Mughamira al-Hasna'*. Beirut: al-Maktab al-tujari lil-tiba'a wa al-tawzi', 1956.

———. *Ruwwad wa Ra'idat al-cinema al-Missriyya*. Cairo: Ruz al-Yusuf, 1978.

Simon, Rita James, and Howard Altstein. *Global Perspectives on Social Issues: Marriage and Divorce*. Lanham, MD: Lexington Books, 2003.

Snir, Reuven. *Arab-Jewish Literature: The Birth and Demise of the Arabic Short Story*. Leiden: Brill, 2019.

Spellberg, D. A. *Politics, Gender, and the Islamic Past: The Legacy of 'A'isha Bint Abi Bakr*. New York: Columbia University Press, 1994.

Starr, Deborah. "In Bed Together: Coexistence in Togo Mizrahi's Alexandria Films." In *Post-Ottoman Coexistence: Sharing Space in the Shadow of Conflict*, edited by Rebecca Bryant, 129–156. New York: Berghahn Books, 2016.

———. *Remembering Cosmopolitan Egypt: Literature, Culture, and Empire*. London: Routledge, 2009.

———. *Togo Mizrahi and the Making of Egyptian Cinema*. Oakland: University of California Press, 2020.

Stone, Christopher. *Popular Culture and Nationalism in Lebanon: The Fairouz and Rahbani Nation*. New York: Routledge, 2008.

Suliha, Nihad. *al-Mar'a bayna al-fann wa al-'ishq wa al-zawaj: Qira'a fi mudhakkirat Fatima Sirri*. Cairo: Dar al-'ayn, 2008.

Swedenburg, Ted. "Sa'ida Sultan / Dana International: Transgender Pop and Poly-semiotics of Sex, Nation, and Ethnicity on the Israeli-Egyptian Border." In Armbrust, *Mass Mediations*, 88–119.

Talima, 'Isam. *Hassan al-Banna wa tajrubat al-fann*. Cairo: Maktabat Wahba, 2008.

Tam, Alon. "Blackface of Egypt: The Theater and Film of Ali al-Kassar." *British Journal of Middle Eastern Studies*, DOI: 10.1080/13530194.2020.1714427 (January 2020).

Tantawi, Salah. *Rihlat hub ma'a Layla Murad*. Cairo: Ruz al-Yusuf, 1979.

Tawfiq, Sa'd. *Qissat al-cinema fi Misr: Dirasa naqdiyya*. Cairo: Dar al-Hilal, 1969.

Thomas, Ann Elise. Review of *Women of Egypt, 1924–1931: Pioneers of Stardom and Fame*. Compilation and text by Amira Mitchell, British Library Topic World Series TSCD931, 2006. *Ethnomusicology* 51, no. 3 (2007): 526–528.

Tucker, Judith E. *In the House of the Law: Gender and Islamic Law in Ottoman Syria and Palestine*. Berkeley: University of California Press, 1998.

'Uthman, Husain. *Hikayat min tarikh al-cinema al-Missriyya: al-Yubil al-dhahabi 1927–1977*. Cairo: Matb'at 'Abdin, 1977.

al-'Uyun, Jamal al-Din Mahmud. "Abi al-Shaykh Abu al-'Uyun." *Majallat al-Azhar* (1987): 632–640, 778–784.

Youssef, Mary. *Minorities in the Contemporary Egyptian Novel*. Edinburgh: Edinburgh University Press, 2019.

Yuval-Davis, Nira. "Women, Citizenship and Difference." *Feminist Review*, no. 57 (Autumn 1997): 4–27.

Zdafee, Keren. *Cartooning for a Modern Egypt*. Leiden: Brill, 2019.

Zhang, Yingjin. "From 'Minority Film' to 'Minority Discourse': Questions of Nationhood and Ethnicity in Chinese Cinema." *Cinema Journal* 36, no. 3 (1997): 73–90.

Zuhur, Sherifa. *Asmahan's Secrets: Woman, War, and Song*. Austin: University of Texas Press, 2000.

Index

CPSIA information can be obtained
at www.ICGtesting.com
Printed in the USA
JSHW020043160322
23919JS00003B/3